food

 Other titles in this
series include:

food

A READER *for* WRITERS

Deborah H. Holdstein
Columbia College Chicago

Danielle Aquiline
Oakton Community College

New York   Oxford
Oxford University Press

Oxford University Press publishes works that further Oxford University's
objective of excellence in research, scholarship, and education.

Oxford   New York
Auckland   Cape Town   Dar es Salaam   Hong Kong   Karachi
Kuala Lumpur   Madrid   Melbourne   Mexico City   Nairobi
New Delhi   Shanghai   Taipei   Toronto

With offices in
Argentina   Austria   Brazil   Chile   Czech Republic   France   Greece
Guatemala   Hungary   Italy   Japan   Poland   Portugal   Singapore
South Korea   Switzerland   Thailand   Turkey   Ukraine   Vietnam

For titles covered by Section 112 of the US Higher Education
Opportunity Act, please visit www.oup.com/us/he for the
latest information about pricing and alternate formats.

Published by Oxford University Press
198 Madison Avenue, New York, New York 10016
http://www.oup.com

Cataloging-in-Publication data is on file at the Library of Congress

ISBN 978-0-19-938568-3

Printing number: 9 8 7 6 5 4 3 2 1

Printed in the United States of America
on acid-free paper

brief table of contents

contents

M. F. K. Fisher, **"The Gastronomical Me,"** An Excerpt   2

"That night I not only saw my Father for the first time as a person. I saw the golden hills and the live oaks as clearly as I have ever seen them since; and I saw the dimples in my little sister's fat hands in a way that still moves me because of that first time; and I saw food as something beautiful to be shared with people instead of as a thrice-daily necessity."

Sheila Squillante, **"Four Menus,"** from *Brevity*   6

"Food is love. Samuel Butler said, 'Eating is touch carried to the bitter end.' I understand. I was in Paris with friends. We sat in a park where parents played with their children, bundled in colorful wools for the early March chill. They kicked yellow balls, ran laughing after each other, their hoods flapping behind them. 'I want to eat them!' I exclaimed. I am 32 years old and childless. I am childless and in love with a man who's not sure he wants children. Some days I crave. I am a lean witch cackling hungrily into a bone-cold wind."

Douglas Bauer, **"What Was Served"** from *Fried Walleye and Cherry Pie*   9

"The men's hands and faces scrubbed clean and the dishes on the table, we all took our usual chairs, my grandfather on my right, my mother on my left, my father directly across from me. The farm's two worlds of work coming together; my mother's food and the men's, mostly, field talk."

"With each *paan* they chewed, their jokes grew more risqué, their gossip more personal, and their bodies more horizontal. Soon, the room would be full of red-toothed, shrieking, laughing, swaying women that I hardly recognized as the same harassed housewives who were constantly shooing us children out of the way.

I would rest my head on my grandmother's squishy abdomen and feel her soft flesh rumble as she belly-laughed her way to tears. Although I didn't realize it at the time, this would be the closest I'd ever come to feeling totally at peace."

"You may imagine that my father disapproved of American ways. On the contrary, he immersed himself in the culture of his adopted country. Interstate road trips to amusement parks, Kentucky Fried Chicken, bowling. While he loved being Korean, he was fascinated by cultures other than his own and especially enjoyed commingling them. To this day, I can't picture a bucket of KFC extra-crispy without adjacent bowls of white rice and *kimchi*."

"That's why fine restaurants are wasted on me. I suppose I can appreciate the lighting, or the speed with which my water glass is refilled, but, as far as the food is concerned, if I can't distinguish between a peach and an apricot I really can't tell the difference between an excellent truffle and a mediocre one."

2   Food and Environment   35

"There is, then, a politics of food that, like any politics, involves our freedom. We still (sometimes) remember that we cannot be free if our minds and voices are controlled by someone else. But we have neglected to understand that we cannot be free if our food and its sources are controlled by someone else. The condition of the passive consumer of food is not a democratic condition. One reason to eat responsibly is to live free."

"But this isn't about altruism. It's actually about feeding and paying people— making this truly sustainable. Food activists have to start thinking about this: how to make a living, how to have pensions, how to move subsidies off the industrial and over to the small farms and make it a real job."

Joel Salatin, **"Sowing Dissent"** (Interview with Tracy Frisch)
  Sun Magazine 51

"It comes down to autonomous personhood. If I don't have the freedom to feed my three-trillion-member internal community of microbes in the manner I choose, then the infringement of other rights, such as freedom of the press and freedom of religion, can't be far behind."

Todd Kliman, **"The Meaning of Local"** Washingtonian.com 2013 63

"In the last 30 years, 'local' has evolved from an ideology to a movement to something that looks suspiciously like an ism: more important than any single chef or restaurant—more important, too, than any other philosophy or ideology. It's so ingrained in the world of food today that it's all but impossible to talk meaningfully about food without talking about 'local.'"

Jon Entine and JoAnna Wendel, **"2000+ Reasons Why GMOs Are Safe to Eat and Environmentally Sustainable"** *Forbes* 82

"Every major international science body in the world has reviewed multiple independent studies—in some cases numbering in the hundreds—in coming to the consensus conclusion that GMO crops are as safe or safer than conventional or organic foods. But until now, the magnitude of the research on crop biotechnology has never been cataloged. In response to what they believed was an information gap, a team of Italian scientists summarized 1783 studies about the safety and environmental impacts of GMO foods—a staggering number."

Robin Mather, **"The Threats from Genetically Modified Foods"**
  MotherEarthNews.com 86

"You're eating genetically modified foods almost daily unless you grow all of your food or always buy organic. Federal organic standards passed in 2000 specifically prohibit GM ingredients. Other genetically modified crops— none labeled—now include sweet corn, peppers, squash and zucchini, rice, sugar cane, rapeseed (used to make canola oil), flax, chicory, peas and papaya. About a quarter of the milk in the United States comes from cows injected with a GM hormone, honey comes from bees working GM crops, and some vitamins include GM ingredients. Some sources conservatively estimate that 60 percent or more of processed foods available in the United States contain GM ingredients, because most processed foods contain corn or soy."

"It all boils down to intimacy. Hunting has created an uncommon closeness between the animals I pursue, the meat I eat, and my own sense of self. There is a terrible seriousness to it all that underlies the thrill of the chase, the camaraderie of being with my fellow hunters and deep sense of calm I feel when alone in the wild. I welcome this weight: It fuels my desire to make something magical with the mortal remains of the game I manage to bring home. It is a feeling every hunter who's ever stared into the freezer at that special strip of backstrap, or hard-won bird or beast understands."

"A detail so obvious that most recipes don't even bother to mention it is that each lobster is supposed to be alive when you put it in the kettle. This is part of lobster's modern appeal: It's the freshest food there is. There's no decomposition between harvesting and eating. And not only do lobsters require no cleaning or dressing or plucking (though the mechanics of actually eating them are a different matter), but they're relatively easy for vendors to keep alive. They come up alive in the traps, are placed in containers of seawater, and can, so long as the water's aerated and the animals' claws are pegged or banded to keep them from tearing one another up under the stresses of captivity, survive right up until they're boiled."

"These popular renditions are also remarkably insensitive, and not necessarily just to those who feel themselves to be too fat. Rather, these authors seem unaware of how obesity messages work as admonishment. According to Paul Campos, the people most personally affected by discussions of obesity are those who want to lost ten or fifteen pounds, despite the fact that those who are 'overweight' by current standards have longer life spans that those who are 'thin' or 'normal.'"

"My research into the realm of African American foods was about more than merely locating and identifying them. It was about understanding the connections between the foods and the people who consume them. This went beyond the theory of 'you are what you eat' to 'how does what we eat reflect our cultural identity?' How does our historical, socioeconomic, and political space influence the foods that we consume?"

"We live now in an emerging era of variety and choice, and the revolution in consumption seems to indicate, and in some ways initiate, a revolution in production. As with coffee, so with other food products: the moves toward product diversification often came not from the established and dominant corporations but from independents whose initiatives have undercut and undermined the established practices and market share of those corporations."

"As I thought more about global dietary practices, it occurred to me that the U.S. has perhaps one of the more gender-segregated eating cultures in the world. (Can you imagine a French woman saying she stays away from red meat or a French man saying that chocolate is chick food?)

So while it seems possible that some food preferences could be put down to gender, it's obvious that American culture has a way of exacerbating them."

"But food writing has long specialized in the barefaced inversion of common sense, common language. Restaurant reviews are notorious for touting $100 lunches as great value for money. The doublespeak now comes in more pious tones, especially when foodies feign concern for animals. Crowding around to watch the slaughter of a pig—even getting in its face just before the shot—is described by Bethany Jean Clement (in an article in *Best Food Writing 2009*) as "solemn" and "respectful" behavior."

"Shouldn't we know better than to eat two meals a day in fast-food restaurants? That's one argument. But where, exactly, are consumers—particularly teenagers—supposed to find alternatives? Drive down any thoroughfare in America, and I guarantee you'll see one of our country's more than 13,000 McDonald's restaurants. Now, drive back up the block and try to find someplace to buy a grapefruit."

"One way to think about America's national eating disorder is as the return, with an almost atavistic vengeance, of the omnivore's dilemma. The cornucopia of the American supermarket has thrown us back onto a bewildering food landscape where we once again have to worry that some of those tasty-looking morsels might kill us. At the same time, many of the tools with which people historically managed the omnivore's dilemma have lost their sharpness, or simply failed, in the United States today."

"Howard is one of the 609,034 Chicagoans who live in what's known as a food desert, a concentrated area short on access to fresh meat and produce, but flush with the packaged and fried yield of convenience stores and fast-food outlets. [. . .] The number of Chicagoans living within its boundaries has decreased, albeit slightly; at least one retailer is finding opportunity for growth in the affected areas; the green movement is taking hold, with farmers' markets and backyard gardens blooming; and leaders are recognizing that community education—on eating healthfully, on creating a demand for grocery stores—is critical. And yet, the desert remains."

"The statistical elimination of the term *hunger* does violence to hungry people and to the efforts to end hunger in America. At the same time, the term *food security* should not be dismissed. It is real and important, and it needs to remain as a conceptual category when we talk about inequalities surrounding food."

"This attitude shows up in doctor's offices where overweight and obese patients are often subjected to inquisition-like questioning. Yet they are rarely asked other, arguably more important questions: *What's your experience of your body? How is your quality of life? How do you feel about your weight?*"

"And yet, for all its riches, its vast reach, and its sense of high purpose, the PepsiCo empire is built on shifting sands. Over the course of the past half century, during which PepsiCo's revenues have increased more than a hundredfold, a public-health crisis has been steadily growing along with it. People are getting fatter. In the nineteen-eighties, rates of obesity started to rise sharply in the U.S. and around the world. By the nineteen-nineties, obesity reached epidemic proportions."

"This shift—from too little to too much food—has created a dilemma for the United States Department of Agriculture (USDA), other federal agencies, and many of my fellow nutritionists. Since its inception, the USDA has had two missions: to promote American agricultural products and to advise the public about how best to use those products. The school lunch program derived precisely from the congruence of the two missions. The government could use up surplus food commodities by passing them along to low-income children. As long as dietary advice was to eat more, the advice caused no conflict."

5 Food and American Culture 261

"Elsewhere, they're lining up for lobster rolls at the Lobsta Truck; for artisanal Pittsburgh-style "Sammies" at Steel City Sandwich; for salad, of all things, at the Flatiron Truck: butter lettuce and heirloom carrots sliced mandoline thin, tossed with mustard vinaigrette, and topped with pieces of steak marinated in star anise, cooked *sous vide*, finished on the grill, and sent off with a puff of shiitake-mushroom dust. If there's a muse here, an avatar presiding over all this transmutation of energy to young America's stomach from organs slightly farther south, it's the mud-flap girl emblazoned on the most popular truck in the lot."

"We may not know the date on which the 'first Thanksgiving' took place, but the date on which Americans celebrate Thanksgiving today was originally proclaimed by Abraham Lincoln in 1863 and set as an official federal holiday by a resolution of Congress in 1941.

And, while Americans set aside a single day to give thanks, Native Americans gave thanks at various times throughout the year in different parts of the country. Northwest Coast people, for instance, celebrated the first salmon run of the season by preparing a ceremonial feast of the first salmon caught."

"This article illuminates how women, as primary actors responsible for managing and preparing food in the household and the community, contribute to our understanding of the formation and continuance of food-related cultural practices in Gullah communities. I argue that although food preparation, under pressure of dominant cultural practices, may be viewed as a measure of gender inequality and of women's subordination in the household, it also can promote resistance and strengthen cultural identity in marginalized cultural groups."

"But my nephew warned me that lately there had been a feud. Barbecue had somehow gotten mixed up with issues of race and heritage. Ugly fighting words had been exchanged, leaving a residue of aggrieved feelings. The quarrel had finally touched the third rail of contemporary Carolina anger, the only topic more sensitive than sauce recipes, Strom Thurmond jokes and Charleston genealogy combined: the meaning of the Civil War. And once again, the war had re-enacted its old bitterness, setting brother against brother."

"I believe that good barbecue needs sides the way good blues need rhythm, and that there is only one rule: Serve whatever you like, but whatever you serve, make it fresh. Have someone's mama in the back doing the "taters" and hush puppies and sweet tea, because Mama will know what she's doing—or at least know better than some assembly-line worker bagging up powdered mashed potatoes by the ton."

"Elected officials across the country—including the District's congressional delegate, Eleanor Holmes Norton (D); Newark Mayor Cory Booker (D); and

Colorado Gov. John Hickenlooper (D)—have taken on the 'SNAP/Food Stamp Challenge,' a creation of the nonprofit Food Research and Action Center, as a way of highlighting hunger issues and helping them understand what economically pressed constituents face."

"Over in the *Washington Post* today, they do a flattering article on Montgomery County officials who are spending just $25 on food for the next five days, 'an attempt to simulate the everyday fact of life for residents enrolled in the federal Supplemental Nutrition Assistance Program, once known as food stamps.'"

6 Food, Travel, and Worldviews   321

"Eventually, I put a name to my strange penchant for cooking and eating ethnic foods—most frequently and most notable the foods of third-world cultures. (And yes, that's a term I worry about.) The unflattering name I chose for my activities was 'cultural food colonialism,' which made me your basic colonizer."

"But I don't think any place has taught me what a meal is—not just food and not just fuel—so much as here. 'Get up and eat, else the journey will be long for you!' was the topic of the week's sermon at St. Anthony's church, in the middle of modern Istanbul, when I looked in on it seven months ago."

"Translating took a while, but in the fullness of time I learned that the man was crying because this rice was the best thing he'd ever eaten in his life. The other Karowai nodded in agreement. Never, I believe, has a chef been so complimented."

"It's not much of an exaggeration to say that in Venetian cuisine, everything comes from the sea. In this case, 'sea' means the Mediterranean in general and the Adriatic in particular, but especially the salty expanses of the Venetian lagoon—a vast wetland, one of the largest in the Mediterranean basin, covering about 136,000 acres of mudflats, salt marshes and open water. Several of the islands in this lagoon yield vegetables of extraordinary quality, and its tidal fringes harbor wild ducks and other game birds that are an important part of traditional Venetian cooking."

"So what's our problem with heads? Sure, cheeks are well-known to most urban American diners these days. Tongue has been enjoying something of a comeback. But for as long as I can remember, the appearance of a whole animal head on a plate or in film has rarely been a welcome sight."

"The global marketplace has changed the way people are eating. Societies that are becoming less physically active are also increasing their consumption of energy-dense foods. Even without the academic studies, it's easy to spot—just look around. Many affluent countries are overfed. And unfortunately, it seems that in the developing world, even before people attain a level of affluence that helps ensure their adequate nutrition, they are eating in ways almost guaranteed to make them less healthy."

"I wasn't the first throwback on the block. The pursuit of wild food has become so fashionable a subject in the past few years that one eater.com blogger called this the era of the 'I Foraged with René Redzepi Piece.' Redzepi is the chef of Noma, in Copenhagen (otherwise known as the best restaurant in the world). More to the point, he is the acknowledged master scavenger of the Nordic coast. I'll admit it. I wanted to forage with Redzepi, too."

"Ever since I can remember, my mother has cooked like this, phone tucked under her chin. Of course, back in Brezhnev's Moscow in the seventies when I was a kid, the idea of an 'extravagant czarist dinner' would have provoked sardonic laughter."

rhetorical contents

academic writing

argument

cause and effect

comparison and contrast

definition

description

example and illustration

exposition

journalism

narrative

process analysis

reflection and revelation

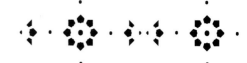

preface

Everyone eats—or should. To say that we are obsessed with food in one way or another in the United States—no matter who we are, where we live, or under what circumstances—is probably a fair statement. Eating has always been a cultural touchstone, and our relationships to the food we eat, the way that food is gathered, and the context in which that food is served have long been not only private, but also public concerns. So has the absence of that food.

Our public interest in food has reached an all-time high, both in popular culture and in our daily lives: think about the rise in television shows about food, interest in popular chefs, blogs, food trucks, specialty coffees, and the like. This, of course, is what might be called a "first-world" preoccupation. *Food: A Reader for Writers* offers readings in some of these first-world areas, but also addresses issues of food absence and related concerns—the food desert, for instance, and the need for food stamps.

Accordingly, there has been increasing attention to food writing as a genre in and of itself. The various readings in this volume come from a wide range of cultures, interests, economic vantage points, and moments in time. The chapter themes in *Food: A Reader for Writers* highlight the complex and multilayered discussions surrounding food and culture: Memory and Identity; Food and Environment; The Politics of Food; Food and Health; Food and American Culture; and Food Travel and Worldviews. A special feature of this book is an Epilogue (Appendix A) showcasing recipes and their cultural and time-specific qualities, revealing the highly context-specific nature of the processes of cooking and eating.

Food: A Reader for Writers is part of a series of brief, single-topic readers from Oxford University Press designed for today's college writing courses. Each reader in this series approaches a topic of contemporary conversation from multiple perspectives:

- **Timeless:** Important selections from various points in time are included.
- **Global:** Readings and voices from around the world are included.
- **Diverse:** Selections come from a range of nontraditional and alternate print and online media, as well as representative mainstream sources.

In addition to the rich array of perspectives on topical issues addressed in the reader, each volume features an abundance of different genres and styles. Useful but nonintrusive pedagogy includes the following:

- **Chapter introductions** that provide a brief overview of the chapter's theme and a sense of how the chapter's selections relate both to the overarching theme and to each other.
- **Headnotes** introduce each reading by providing concise information about its original publication and author.
- **"Analyze" and "Explore" Questions** after each reading scaffold and support student reading for comprehension as well as rhetorical considerations, providing prompts for reflection, classroom discussion, and brief writing assignments.
- **"Forging Connections" and "Looking Further" Prompts** after each chapter encourage critical thinking by asking students to compare perspectives and strategies among readings both within the chapter and with readings in other chapters, suggesting writing assignments (many of which are multimodal) that engage students with larger conversations in the academy, the community, and the media.
- **An Appendix on "Research and Writing about Food"** guides student inquiry and research in a digital environment. Co-authored by a research librarian and a writing program director, this appendix provides real-world, transferable strategies for locating, assessing, synthesizing, and citing sources in support of an argument.

about the authors

Danielle Aquiline is assistant professor of English at Oakton Community College in Des Plaines, Illinois. She holds the MFA in Poetry from Columbia College Chicago.

Deborah H. Holdstein is professor of English at Columbia College Chicago, where she served as dean of the School of Liberal Arts and Sciences from 2007 to 2014. Holdstein has published widely in rhetoric and composition, film, and literature and is a former editor of *College Composition and Communication*.

In December of 2013, Holdstein and Aquiline co-authored *Who Says? The Writer's Research*, published by Oxford University Press.

acknowledgments

We acknowledge the contributors to this volume and their writing, works that we selected from among the many excellent pieces we might have included.

We extend our heartfelt thanks to the following academics who provided valuable feedback on this anthology during its development:

Jody Brooks, Georgia State University; Bill Doyle, University of Tampa; Laura Dubek, Middle Tennessee State University; Bonnie Erwin, Wilmington College; Maricela Garcia, South Texas College; Katherine D. Harris, San Jose State University; Aeron Haynie, University of New Mexico; Tonya Krouse, Northern Kentucky University; Brian Le, California State University–Long Beach; Corey Leis, California State University–Long Beach; Erin Presley, Eastern Kentucky University; Marilee Rust, California State University–Long Beach; Susan Slavicz, Florida State College–Jacksonville; K. T. Shaver, California State University–Long Beach; Joseph Taylor, University of Alabama–Huntsville; Janette Thompson, University of Nebraska at Kearney; Lisa Ottum, Xavier University; Matt Wanat, Ohio University Lancaster; and Sue Whatley, Stephen F. Austin University.

Frederick Speers and Carrie Brandon also deserve our hearty thanks for their interest, support, and enthusiasm for our projects. And, as always, we thank our spouses, Sona Patel and Jay Boersma, for their unwavering support, love, and good food.

food

Food as Memory and Identity

A good entry into the world of writing about food, this chapter on "Food as Memory and Identity" taps into the commonality of experience, whether positive or negative, related to eating, families, and our sense of where we've come from. Whereas the rest of this volume will take on the various social and political aspects related to food, this chapter, in contrast, celebrates and questions issues that are mostly personal.

As you read, it's important to consider the ways in which the individual experiences of these authors inform larger issues of culture, the world, and collective as well as individual histories. This chapter features a wide range of types of writers and writing—from the personal memoir to journalistic writing—and yet although many of the concerns differ, a surprising number of themes, expressed differently, are remarkably similar.

M. F. K. Fisher
"The Gastronomical Me," An Excerpt

One of the pre-eminent food writers in the United States, M. F. K. Fisher (Mary Frances Kennedy Fisher) published *The Gastronomical Me* in 1943. She first began publishing what we might now call "food literature" in the 1930s, and she has had significant influence as one of the first to blend the genres of "food writing" and "memoir." Fisher can be credited with having paved the way for many if not all of the writers you will read in this volume. In this two-chapter excerpt, Fisher evokes the first time she realized the importance of taste and memory; the second section recounts another memory of family and food: her great aunt's ranch. The book itself frames memory and meals against the backdrop of pre–World War II tensions.

This piece is often considered "genre-defining." What might that mean, and why would this essay be so significant to the genre of food writing?

The Measure of My Powers
The first thing I remember tasting and then wanting to taste again is the grayish-pink fuzz my grandmother skimmed from a spitting kettle of strawberry jam. I suppose I was about four.

Women in those days made much more of a ritual of their household duties than they do now. Sometimes it was indistinguishable from a dogged if unconscious martyrdom. There were times for This, and other equally definite times for That. There was one set week a year for "the sewing woman." Of course, there was Spring Cleaning. And there were other periods, almost like festivals in that they disrupted normal life, which were observed no matter what the weather, finances, or health of the family.

Many of them seem odd or even foolish to me now, but probably the whole staid rhythm lent a kind of rich excitement to the housebound flight of time.

With us, for the first years of my life, there was a series, every summer, of short but violently active cannings. Crates and baskets and lug-boxes of fruits bought in their prime and at their cheapest would lie waiting with opulent fragrance on the screened porch, and a whole battery of enameled pots and ladles and wide-mouthed funnels would appear from some dark cupboard.

All I knew then about the actual procedure was that we had delightful picnic meals while Grandmother and Mother and the cook worked with a kind of drugged concentration in our big dark kitchen, and were tired and cross and at the same time oddly triumphant in their race against summer heat and processes of rot.

Now I know that strawberries came first, mostly for jam. Sour red cherries for pies and darker ones for preserves were a little later, and then came the apricots. They were for jam if they were very ripe, and the solid ones were simply "put up." That, in my grandmother's language, meant cooking with little sugar, to eat for breakfast or dessert in the winter which she still thought of in terms of northern Iowa.

She was a grim woman, as if she had decided long ago that she could thus most safely get to Heaven. I have a feeling that my Father might have liked to help with the cannings, just as I longed to. But Grandmother, with that almost joyfully stern bowing to duty typical of religious women, made it clear that helping in the kitchen was a bitter heavy business forbidden certainly to men, and generally to children. Sometimes she let me pull stems off the cherries, and one year when I was almost nine I stirred the pots a little now and then, silent and making myself as small as possible.

But there was no nonsense anyway, no foolish chitchat. Mother was still young and often gay, and the cook too . . . and with Grandmother directing operations they all worked in a harried muteness . . . stir, sweat, hurry. It was a pity. Such a beautifully smelly task should be fun, I thought.

In spite of any Late Victorian asceticism, though, the hot kitchen sent out tantalizing clouds, and the fruit on the porch lay rotting in its crates, or readied for the pots and the wooden spoons, in fair glowing piles upon the juice-stained tables. Grandmother, saving always, stood like a sacrificial priestess in the steam, "skimming" into a thick white saucer, and I, sometimes permitted and more often not, put my finger into the cooling froth and licked it. Warm and sweet and odorous. I loved it, then.

A Thing Shared

10   Now you can drive from Los Angeles to my Great-Aunt Maggie's ranch on the other side of the mountains in a couple of hours or so, but the first time I went there it took most of a day.

Now the roads are worthy of even the All-Year-Round Club's boasts, but twenty-five years ago, in the September before people thought peace had come again, you could hardly call them roads at all. Down near the city they were oiled, all right, but as you went farther into the hills toward the wild desert around Palmdale, they turned into rough dirt. Finally they were two wheel-marks skittering every which way through the Joshua trees.

It was very exciting: the first time my little round brown sister Anne and I had ever been away from home. Father drove us up from home with Mother in the Ford, so that she could help some cousins can fruit.

We carried beer for the parents (it exploded in the heat), and water for the car and Anne and me. We had four blowouts, but that was lucky, Father said as he patched the tires philosophically in the hot sun; he'd expected twice as many on such a long hard trip.

The ranch was wonderful, with wartime crews of old men and loud-voiced boys picking the peaches and early pears all day, and singing and rowing at night in the bunkhouses. We couldn't go near them or near the pen in the middle of a green alfalfa field where a new prize bull, black as thunder, pawed at the pale sand.

15   We spent most of our time in a stream under the cottonwoods, watching her make butter in a great churn between her mountainous knees. She slapped it into pats, and put them down into the stream where it ran hurriedly through the darkness of the butter-house.

She put stone jars of cream there, too, and wire baskets of eggs and lettuces, and when she drew them up, like netted fish, she would shake the cold water onto us and laugh almost as much as we did.

Then Father had to go back to work. It was decided that Mother would stay at the ranch and help put up more fruit, and Anne and I would go home with him. That was exciting as leaving it had been, to be alone with Father for the first time.

He says now that he was scared daft at the thought of it, even though our grandmother was at home as always to watch over us. He says he actually shook as he drove away from the ranch, with us like two suddenly strange small monsters on the hot seat beside him.

Probably he made small talk. I don't remember. And he didn't drink any beer, sensing that it would be improper before two un-chaperoned young ladies.

We were out of the desert and into deep winding canyons before the   20
sun went down. The road was a little smoother, following the dry tawny
hills of that part of California. We came to a shack where there was water
for sale, and a table under the dark wide trees.

Father told me to take Anne down the dry streambed a little way. That
made me feel delightfully grown-up. When we came back we held our
hands under the water faucet and dried them on our panties, which Mother
would never have let us do.

Then we sat on a rough bench at the table, the three of us in the deep
green twilight, and had one of the nicest suppers I have ever eaten.

The strange thing about it is that all three of us have told other people
that same thing, without ever talking of it among ourselves until lately.
Father says that all his nervousness went away, and he saw us for the first time
as two little brown humans who were fun. Anne and I both felt a subtle
excitement at being alone for the first time with the
only man in the world we loved.

(We loved Mother too, completely, but we
were finding out, as Father was too, that it is
good for parents and for children to be alone
now and then with one another . . . the man
alone or the woman, to sound new notes in the
mysterious music of parenthood and childhood.)

> . . . I saw food as something beautiful to be shared with people instead of as a thrice-daily necessity.

That night I not only saw my Father for the first time as a person.   25
I saw the golden hills and the live oaks as clearly as I have ever seen
them since; and I saw the dimples in my little sister's fat hands in a
way that still moves me because of that first time; and I saw food
as something beautiful to be shared with people instead of as a thrice-
daily necessity.

Analyze

1. Fisher's narrative isn't necessarily about eating; in fact, it talks *around*
   the matter of food. What effect does this have on the narrative? How
   might it help to create context for this memoir?

2. "I saw food as something beautiful to be shared with people instead
   of as a thrice-daily necessity." M. F. K. Fisher is seen as one of the
   first food writers in the United States; how does this quote reflect her
   interest in using the subject of food as a gateway to other, even more
   complex inquiries?

3. Consider and analyze the language in these excerpts: words like "thrice," calling one's parents "father and mother," and a decades-old use of the word "gay." Do you notice any other such uses of language? What do they convey about the narrative, and how do particular word choices change the way we respond to a text and the voice of the author?

4. Analyze and comment on the ways in which Fisher uses this narrative to detail the relationship between her father and mother.

Explore

1. Now that you've analyzed Fisher's ways of revealing the roles of her mother and father, use this as a starting point with which to analyze the contrasting roles of two people in your household or living situation.

2. At the end of "The Measure of My Powers," Fisher writes that her grandmother, "saving always, stood like a sacrificial priestess in the steam." In later life, she re-evaluates the scene, noting, "I loved it, then." Reflecting on your own childhood, delineate a domestic process that, like Fisher, you once loved but have rethought.

3. In an essay, detail the process by which Fisher learned to see her father and mother as persons "for the first time." In seeing her parents differently, what did Fisher also learn about herself?

Sheila Squillante
"Four Menus"

Squillante's piece first appeared in *Brevity*, an online journal for short, creative nonfiction. One of the strengths of "Four Menus" is its alternative form, making it quite distinct from the other essays you will read here. Squillante is a poet and essayist, and she serves as associate director of the Low-Residency MFA at Chatham University. She is also editor-in-chief of the *Fourth River Literary Journal*. Squillante here offers a type of metacommentary on the place of food in our lives.

Squillante's essay is more complex than it initially appears. How does each of the four sections have its own, identifiable character? To what effect?

1. We're eating Korean soup tonight. *Yook gae jang*—shredded beef with cellophane noodles, scallions, and some long, fibrous mysterious vegetable. And spice—mouthfuls of red oil that make my nose run and my tongue sing. I am in love with the man across the table whose nose is running too. We glisten and are happy. Happiness is the long tails of soybeans slicked with sesame oil, the strings hanging from our mouths. We sip soup and poke at condiments with our wooden chopsticks—the kind that snap and splinter but who cares? I skewer a piece of jellied fishcake; bring it quivering to his lips. Another new, unexpected texture. When we eat together for the first time, it is before knowledge. Before the waitress knows our spice preferences: his flaming, mine, not meek but milder. Before she has suggested other menu items (*Dol sot bimbim bab* crisping in hot Korean crock-ware) and even steered us clear of some (codfish soup—bland, no depth, not good). All before we know where our tastes will take us. I am a self-proclaimed gourmand, have tried everything offered me at least once, but I have never before this first night eaten the Korean pickled cabbage called kimchi. I know nothing of the way its slight carbonation will incite, the way its crunch will satisfy. It's a revelation, that first bite. I feel extended; I surpass myself. The whole room ferments! Poetry! Kimchi! Philosophy! Later, when we sit kissing on my second-hand couch, he will exclaim, "I love your eyebrows!" and I will touch them and fall.

2. Food is love. Samuel Butler said, "Eating is touch carried to the bitter end." I understand. I was in Paris with friends. We sat in a park where parents played with their children, bundled in colorful wools for the early March chill. They kicked yellow balls, ran laughing after each other, their hoods flapping behind them. "I want to eat them!" I exclaimed. I am 32 years old and childless. I am childless and in love with a man who's not sure he wants children. Some days I crave. I am a lean witch cackling hungrily into a bone-cold wind.

3. In my twenties, I was voted "Most Succulent" among my closest friends. We had just seen a film in which plane crash survivors must resort to cannibalism among the wreckage and the snow. After, it was decided that my ample figure paired with my high energy would make for the tastiest meat. We made a pact: "If we ever crash on top of a snow-topped mountain and I die, you have my blessing to eat me." *Blessing*: an invocation of good fortune. If we crash and I die,

I hope they are blessed with the warmth of a fire and time for slow cooking, for dining with relish and reverence, knowing that my spirit hovers, toasting their survival.

4. For some, food is an inconvenience, something that wastes time. No. Food *extends* time, slows it for us generously. I cook because I believe in a slow life, a life of praise. I cook for my friends because I see them as divine. I cook to make holy moments, to call out and to reflect. I cook complex recipes in atonement. I gave up religion long ago. Now Sundays are for another kind of supper—one that acknowledges the sacrifices of human relationships. Sundays are for mundane tomato sauce stirred through with thyme and oregano and worship for the sensual world. It's a kind of worship that makes it impossible to ignore the implication of the body, the way food changes us, fills us with our own good, hearty love. Food is worship and God, to me, is kimchi, kalamata olives, artichoke hearts and roasted garlic popped hot from its skin and spread warm with butter on bakery bread. God is lamb shanks braised long in orange juice and cabernet; is chopping Spanish onions with a heavy knife; is bittersweet chocolate chunked from dark Swiss bars. Is bittersweet entirely.

Analyze

1. The form of Sheila Squillante's essay differs from what is usually considered a traditional, customary format for the essay. How does it differ? How do the four vignettes contribute to a unified whole? And how would you describe that unified whole?

2. Why does Squillante quote Samuel Butler: "Eating is touch carried to the bitter end"? What might that mean? How is it connected to this essay?

3. This essay clearly tries to develop a manifesto of sorts about what food *means* in a larger, philosophical sense. How would you summarize Squillante's intentions here?

Explore

1. Squillante writes that in her twenties, she was voted "Most Succulent" among her closest friends. How does what turns out to be a fairly benign phrase serve to pique your interest at the start of this section?

2. How does Squillante's sense of self develop alongside her culinary and food awareness? What are the various stages of her life that she invokes, and to what effect?
3. Squillante says that "Food is love." First, define what this might mean. Then, write about the ways food is (or isn't) love for you, referring to Squillante's essay as a touchstone.

Douglas Bauer
"What Was Served"

Douglas Bauer is professor of literature at Bennington College; he is the author of several books of fiction and nonfiction. His work has appeared in *Esquire, Harper's, The Atlantic, Sports Illustrated,* and the *New York Times* magazine. Much of Bauer's work focuses on his family's small farm in central Iowa. "What Was Served," originally in *Fried Walleye and Cherry Pie* (2013), recalls Bauer's childhood and examines connections among food, family, and place.

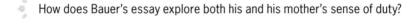

How does Bauer's essay explore both his and his mother's sense of duty?

Our farmhouse sat atop a slight rise in the middle of the acreage. The land, as lawn, sloped away from the foundation and flattened out in all directions until it reached the surrounding corn and soybean fields, then continued extremely into the four distances. A wide, pillared porch wrapped around the north and east sides of the house. As a boy, during the summer months, I sometimes sat for a time on the east porch railing and, if my father and grandfather Bauer happened to be working in the field that was my view, I looked out to watch the two of them on their tractors moving the day's tending implements along the Iowa horizon.

And if the hour were any time from midmorning till noon, I could also look, from that same perch on the porch, just to my right and through the screen door into our kitchen. There my mother was moving about the big floral-patterned-wallpapered room, frequently glancing herself out the windows that gave to that same east field to see where the men were. There was a clock mounted on the wall above the refrigerator, but their location was the way she told the time.

Thinking back, I concoct a daily synchrony: my father and grandfather, out there at their work; my mother just inside, busy at hers. The tractors inching along at an almost imperceptible pace, their sounds made soundless by their distance from the house, and my mother close by in the kitchen, all bustle and noise. The sharp metallic clang of a spoon against a pot, stovetop burners rattling, oven door opening and thudding shut. And woven through it all, the voices from the radio that sat atop the refrigerator. The absentminded mumbles of Arthur Godfrey. "The real-life drama of Helen Trent, who . . . fights bravely, successfully, to prove what so many women long to prove, that because a woman is thirty-five or more, romance in life need not be over." In truth I don't recall if Helen Trent's romantic travails happened in the morning or the afternoon, and I've no idea if my mother, a woman living through her thirties at the time of which I write, brought irony or escape or some sort of identification to her interest as she listened. But she listened.

Surely my memory exaggerates the nature of the dual labors I've described, both the agrarian stateliness of machinery silently progressing and the short-order-cook urgency audible through the screen. Still, this *is* how I remember them and what lingers within it is the impression that of the two, my mother's work was the harder and more manual.

5   The full, hot midday meal she prepared every day but Sunday from the first field work in spring to the end of autumn harvest was called *dinner* (which, obviously enough, made the only slightly less ambitious evening meal *supper*). And what was typically for dinner? Maybe a roast of pork or beef with mashed potatoes and brown gravy. Maybe a baked ham with her signature potato salad—its secret, she claimed, substituting Miracle Whip for mayonnaise; go figure. Maybe beef and homemade egg noodles, or beef stew with carrots and potatoes and onions, the noodle or stew beef simmering in the pressure cooker through the morning.

But for my purposes here I can order anything I want from that summer dinner menu, so I choose my favorite childhood dish—creamed chicken and biscuits. The chicken (until quite recently squawking cluelessly in the henhouse a hundred yards from the kitchen door) was cut into pieces, which were skinned, poached in broth, and removed to cool, then their meat pulled from the bone into loosely shredded strips. Next, cream was slowly stirred into the broth, making a kind of ambrosial prairie velouté.

Finally the strips of chicken were returned to the pot, salt and pepper were added to season, and it was brought to the table to be ladled over baking-powder biscuits and mounds of mashed potatoes.

Can you fathom the gustatory insult of calling such meals—and oh, yes, most every day a baked dessert, often a fruit pie—*lunch*? Neither can I.

I said I sensed my mother's work to be one of mounting manual effort and this impression had a lot to do with her usual mood as she brought the meal together. I can best describe it as a preoccupied brooding of varying strength, sometimes seeming nothing more than her need to hurry, to have everything ready (to make the men wait to eat was to cost them precious field time); often something palpably more layered than that; and always suggesting she was deep in her own world and not all that pleased to be there. I'm confident I can say that she often felt besieged by the terms of her farmwife life and that this feeling steadily intensified, like something heating on the stove, as she cooked through the morning.

I don't believe she felt uniquely put upon. She knew her domestic chores were entirely typical of the place and the times. In fact, she knew that they were fewer than those of many women married to farmers, women who frequently shared the field work with their husbands. And she very much liked being known as a good cook, especially for the things she made especially well. Oatmeal cookies, for one, crisp flat ovals that might better be called the Joy of Butter. And that potato salad for another. No matter where you stand on Miracle Whip, my mother's potato salad was incredibly good, owing, *I* think, as I taste it in my mind, to the indulgent quantity of chopped eggs and the exactly right measurement of chopped onions— just letting you know they're there—blended in.

Instead, I suspect that sense of burden as she moved about the kitchen was brought on in great part by her knowing that the considerable meal she was in the act of making would be followed, after a brief pause, by the need to begin making another one—supper. I suspect much else that frustrated her was neatly symbolized in that.

This sense she had of her days as a farm kitchen version of the *Woman in the Dunes* never really left her, even decades after my father had sold the farm and spent his time puttering and tinkering in the garage and, as often as not, came into the house around noon to make himself a sandwich: *lunch*. I remember her predictably complaining about her three young grandsons, my brother's sons, devouring those addictive oatmeal cookies, which she'd baked for their visit. Peering into the big cookie jar, shaking her head, and making her patented "Tsk!" sound with her tongue against her teeth, she would say, not happily, "I just made these this morning and they're already gone." What she saw in the almost instantly empty jar was not the pleasure her food gave her grandsons but rather that she must now make more of it.

It was noon, maybe fifteen minutes past, when my father and grandfather brought their tractors to a stop. They got down from their seats to unhook the plows or discs or whatever they were pulling, then climbed back up and turned in the direction of the house. It was as if the kitchen's summoning smells had escaped through the open windows into the thick summer heat and moved on like a kind of aromatic weather front until they reached my father and grandfather.

At that age—nine, ten, even eleven—I was beguiled by the world of early television cowboys. (I once asked my fifth-grade teacher to call me by the surname Crockett, after Davy, and she gave me, with her, "No," an appropriately impatient frown.) Watching from our porch, I was a cavalry scout alert for any suspicious movement appearing suddenly out there on the far rim of the world and my father and grandfather were a pair of nasty Apaches on horseback pulling hijacked covered wagons.

Seeing them turning and heading in, I alerted the kitchen. "They're coming."

15   To which my mother replied, "Come set the table," thus ending the fantasy. Cavalry scouts did not set the table.

Inside, I soon began to hear the tractors approaching, their sounds starting faint as rumors and growing as they got closer to the house until they made the loud, raw announcement of their arrival in the barnyard. A minute, two minutes, later, my father, in his blue chambray shirt and darker blue loose-fitting jeans, and my grandfather, in his shirt and pants of matching tan khaki, appeared at the back door, removed their caps, and hung them on hooks. Their protected foreheads looked artificially white, so great was the contrast with the rest of their sun-browned faces. Farmers' tans.

Entering the kitchen, father and son and a life of shared husbandry, they seemed intimately *teamed*. My father was, in his midthirties, a very handsome man. His thick, dark pompadour, of which he was quite proud, was matted down now from his cap and the morning's sweat. He greeted my mother and me and hurried into the small room next to the kitchen to wash up and my grandfather sat down, waiting to go next. His shyness gave him a sweet courtliness, his manner that of a grateful guest. He managed to look fresh no matter how much field dirt powdered his face. It was as if he'd learned from half a century of this work the trick of how to spend hours in the eye of heat and dust without appearing to get any of it on him.

He remarked to my mother that whatever was for dinner smelled awfully good, which was both a compliment and the truth. He was thin, hard-muscled, and walked with a pronounced limp, one hip permanently cocked, from a childhood accident that had made his left leg stiff. It says something about him and how much I loved him that his gait in my memory was a fluidly graceful thing.

Dinner was often the only time I got to see him during the day. He drove in the morning, the sun starting up the sky, from the little house he and my grandmother had built at the edge of the town. I called it "little"—though my child's perspective didn't see it as particularly small—but in fact it was even littler than that; it was as tiny as a cottage in a clearing in a fable. It sat on a large corner lot, so the size of the spot was not the reason for the house's miniature size. Or, as I think about it, probably it was. I suspect the farmer in my grandfather wanted, as much as absolutely possible, to keep the land as land.

The men's hands and faces scrubbed clean and the dishes on the table, we all took our usual chairs, my grandfather on my right, my mother on my left, my father directly across from me. The farm's two worlds of work coming together; my mother's food and the men's, mostly, field talk.   20

While I ate the portions of a Cather hired hand and listened closely to the work conversation, I was part of neither world. I had my place at the table but no place in the life. I certainly had no thought of learning how to cook and helping my mother prepare the meal. Any wish to participate in the kitchen began and ended with the happy acceptance of a spoon to scrape the smears of batter or frosting from a bowl.

But I wanted keenly to be with the men. Some of my classmates who were farmer's sons, fluent in the language of gearboxes and plow size and yields per acre, had, at what seems to me now a very early age, begun their field lives. Like them, I wanted to be integral, to have a daily assignment.

My problem was twofold. My childhood asthma rendered me seriously allergic to any kind of crop dust. This ruled out helping with the harvest. Also, and all too apparent early on, I brought a stunning lack of talent to every facet of the work—how to read a tilled field, for instance, something as simple as distinguishing where the harrow had passed and where it hadn't; or how to smoothly operate a tractor together with the implement it was pulling. Which ruled out pretty much everything else. Now and then I got to drive a tractor somewhere, to take a wagon from one field to another. That was about the extent of what I could do and be trusted to do.

The closest, then, that I could come to being a farmer was to eat like one.

25   More creamed chicken would be great.

And another sliver of pie.

And while you adults drink your coffee, a last biscuit with butter and jam. (A kind of farm kitchen petit four.)

Obviously, I don't mean that I ate to pretend I was a farmer, at least not in any conscious way. I mean that I loved the rhythm and the ritual. To sit across from my father and next to my grandfather and listen to them review the morning and plot the afternoon. How cleanly the soil was turning; where were the spots still too wet from recent rains; how the combine was behaving after its repair. I loved dinner, yes, because my mother's food was damned good. But I loved it more for its culinary power to draw my father and grandfather's privately entwined life in from where they lived it.

Eating these hot, heavy meals, and with no opportunity to work off the calories through an afternoon of sweat and whatever effort might be required, and with *supper* still to come, I was a fat boy. Not till adolescence did I begin to lose the weight. Photos of me from my portly days show a lad smiling bravely into the camera. The fourth-grade class photo particularly haunts my memory. I'm sitting cross-legged on the floor in the first row, dressed in an ill-advised plaid shirt and my husky-section jeans, hunched slightly forward, elbows resting on my thighs, and thus posed, the degree to which my shape is perfectly round is quite remarkable.

30   Finished, we sat digesting all that food while my father and grandfather listened to the radio market report. This went on for what seemed hours, the reader's voice that recognizably midwestern flat, adenoidal twang, droning on and on, quoting the current and futures prices. March soybeans . . . November hogs . . . August wheat. First from the Chicago Mercantile Exchange, then, when you'd thought he was done, from Omaha's, while the farmers at the table listened, sipping coffee, with the silent, rooting concentration I brought to getting the nightly baseball scores. "Um," my father might say. "Huh," my grandfather might add. For all I know there was a scheme proposed and responded to in that.

I understood generally why this market news was vital, which made it no less tedious to listen to. And I think I disliked it not just because it was so deadly boring. I could sense my father and grandfather beginning as they listened to move away from the flavors of the table back into their life.

When at last it was finished, my father looked up at the wall clock. "Well, Dad, what do you say?" And they pushed back their chairs. My grandfather once again thanked my mother and she said, "You're welcome, Dad." I hear her voice in this exchange as undefended and warm and each day freshly pleased, as his thanks was to her. She would tell me years later—when she told me much about the difficult complexities of those years—that she loved him, too, her father-in-law; that she thought he was a kind and lovely man.

I walked with the two of them down the sidewalk, through the gate, and over to their tractors. I helped fill the tanks with gasoline. I placed the crank that started my grandfather's ancient Case in the proper position, below the radiator at the nose of the tractor. Then I stepped away as he stepped in, for I wasn't strong enough to turn it with the necessary force. He assured me the issue wasn't so much strength as getting a feel for the precise leverage. He seemed to take a conjuring moment, then with what I saw as an effortless wrist flick he turned the crank and the tractor woke and belched as if from a huge meal into life.

I watched them mount. My grandfather as always rode sidesaddle, his rod-stiff leg making it impossible for him to sit conventionally. Then the tractors eased away with the rhythmic sashay of horses from the hitching rail. I could imagine them as cowboys and in that way be with them, while the evidence of what they were and I was not was everywhere around me and there was nothing my imagination could do about that.

I waved to them as they headed back out. Picturing it now, I give myself a grand, semaphorical gesture. It's as mawkish a moment in memory's eye as the boy standing in the dusty street waving good-bye to Shane.

Half a century would pass, my father recently having died, when my mother talked to me about those years.

"Your grandfather was the love of your dad's life," she said to me that day she told me, with much else, that she had loved my grandfather, too. "Nobody else, and sure not me, had a chance to get your dad's attention. After Grandpa Bauer died, he retreated more and more into himself. I don't think he ever thought there could be something else to love like he loved his dad. I don't think he ever figured he might want to."

And so, she felt in a vastly different way as much an exile, as excluded from my father and grandfather's world, as I did. My father would have had *his* story, *his* version, of course. But this was hers and it was clear from her tone how completely she believed it. She blamed my grandfather for none of it. Savvy as he was about the work and about the commerce of land, buying and selling a few acres here and there in a lifelong game of farm monopoly, he was as guileless as anyone I've known.

Still, guileless or not, he did, my mother said, strongly urge my father to join him in the life. Yes, I'm sure he loved farming with his son. But that's in part because, unlike his son, he loved farming.

40   Knowing how she felt, it's little wonder my mother's unhappiness built as the hours of morning passed; as she cooked those marvelous meals; as she brought such generosity to the table sometimes so begrudgingly. In a very real sense, she was feeding her competition in a game she couldn't win. But as a boy, I knew nothing, suspected nothing, of whatever else was being wordlessly passed around the table, what portions and flavors were being shared.

Leaving the barnyard and starting back toward the house, the men and their tractors no longer in view, I assign myself the chore of standing at the sink beside her—a short, pretty woman in her early thirties, wearing what was called a house dress of printed cotton and summer sandals—helping her wash the dishes. It seems only right, given everything she served me, and everything she labored not to.

Analyze

1. How is Bauer's essay a farm version of the M. F. K. Fisher narrative? What examples lead you to your response?
2. "She knew her domestic chores were entirely typical of the place and the times." Bauer here describes his mother, the farmwife. Why does Bauer believe this? What instances do you see in the narrative that would convince you?
3. Bauer refers to *Woman in the Dunes*. Look up this reference. How does it work within this narrative? What information might it be intended to support?
4. How does Bauer's essay detail "the rhythm and the ritual" of what it means to live in rural Iowa as a farmer?

Explore

1. What other "rhythms and rituals" have you observed around food and eating, and how do those reveal matters of tradition, culture, work, and social class?
2. Why does Bauer say that the "closest, then, that I could come to being a farmer was to eat like one"? What does this say about his sense of belonging and duty? How might your own observations and your own sense of belonging and duty color the ways in which you feel pressured to be something that you are not?
3. What is the "competition" and "game" that Bauer's mother could not win? Why did it "seem only right" for him to help her with the dishes, "given everything she served me, and everything she labored not to?" What are the larger implications of this memoir, especially given these quotes?

Shoba Narayan
"The God of Small Feasts"

Shoba Narayan writes about food and travel, and her work has appeared in such publications as *Conde Nast Traveler, The National, Gourmet, Time,* and the *New York Times.* A former commentator for NPR's "All Things Considered," Narayan writes a weekly column for the Indian business daily, *Mint Lounge.* "The God of Small Feasts," first published in *Gourmet* magazine, won the James Beard Foundation's M. F. K. Fisher Award for Distinguished Food Writing. The essay eventually became her first book, *Monsoon Diary* (2003), which was a finalist for the James Beard Award.

In what way does the author's "destiny" begin "in the kitchen?"

"**H**ere," said my mother, pressing a dark-brown slab of one of her mysterious cooking ingredients into my hands. "Smell this."

I was nine. I obeyed.

"It smells stinky," I said, wrinkling my nose as I turned over the hard, pockmarked resin in my palm. "Like a . . . ," I giggled, unable to say the rude word.

My mother smiled, as if I had understood some fundamental cooking concept. "It's asafetida," she said. "You sprinkle it on foods like beans and lentils so they won't give you gas."

5   We were standing in our cavernous kitchen, the mosaic-tiled floor cool against my bare feet, my mother in her starched cotton sari and me in my pigtails and skirt, ready to flee. On the raw cement walls, smoke from the wood-burning stove left stains in Rorschach-like blotches. My mother was making yet another attempt to reveal to me the mysteries of South Indian cooking. I was more interested in fighting with the boys over cricket balls.

Cooking—and eating—in India is a communal activity governed by a complex system of rules, rituals, and beliefs. My mother recited examples to me whenever she got the chance. Cumin and cardamom arouse, so eat them only after you get married, she instructed. Fenugreek tea makes your hair lustrous and increases breast milk, so drink copious amounts when you have babies. Coriander seeds cool the body during summer; mustard and sesame seeds lend heat during winter. Cardamom aids digestion, cinnamon soothes, and lentils build muscles. Every feast should have the three P's: *pappadams, pachadi,* and *payasam* (lentil wafers, yogurt salad, and sweet pudding). Any new bride should be able to make a decent *rasam* (*dal*-and-tomato soup). If you cannot make *rasam,* do not call yourself the lady of the house. And so it went.

At nine, I had little interest in such matters. The kitchen was merely a place I might dart into between aiming catapults at sleepy chameleons and playing under the banyan tree in our overgrown garden. And, in a household headed by my grandmother and teeming with 14 cousins, four pairs of aunts and uncles, numerous servants, and any number of visiting relatives, there were always plenty of others to do the cooking.

The only time we youngsters were conscripted into helping out in the kitchen was during the annual *shraadam,* a daylong ceremony, celebrated on the anniversary of my grandfather's death, when the entire clan gathered to pay obeisance to our ancestors. The servants were given the day off, and the women cooked an elaborate 24-course feast—enough food to feed not just the family but 12 Brahman priests, our two cows, and all the crows in the neighborhood. The women would lay down banana leaves in the grass, arranging food as carefully for the birds as they did for the guests indoors. Crows are believed to carry the souls of forebears. The more crows we fed, the better it would be for our lineage.

On *shraadam* day, the whole household awoke before dawn. My grandmother stood in the middle of the kitchen, bellowing orders like an army general. There were strict rules. Everything had to be fresh and prepared according to a menu that had been decided on generations ago. Dairy and grains couldn't mix and were placed at opposite ends of the kitchen. Later, hands had to be washed after touching leftovers.

Blurred figures rushed about within the smoky mists, boiling water, stirring the ghee, grinding coconut, roasting spices. Coal embers glowed like beacons under heavy bronze cauldrons filled with rice. My cousins and I scampered between pantry and kitchen, ferrying ingredients back and forth. My mother and aunts chopped vegetables at a furious pace as my grandmother presided over the stove.

There were many such feasts in our household. After a meal's end, the curtains were drawn in the living room. As the ceiling fan swirled lazily overhead, the women sat cross-legged on bamboo mats, a brass betel tray in the center. In it were stacks of betel leaves, chewed as digestives, surrounded by crushed betel nuts, tobacco paste, and an assortment of fragrant spices—sugar-coated fennel, nutmeg, and cardamom wrapped in pieces of silver foil.

The women brushed the tender betel leaves with tobacco paste, filled them with the nuts and spices, then folded the leaves into triangles called *paan*. They popped these into their mouths, chewing gently until their tongues and teeth were stained red from the opiate combination.

With each *paan* they chewed, their jokes grew more risqué, their gossip more personal, and their bodies more horizontal. Soon, the room would be full of red-toothed, shrieking, laughing, swaying women that I hardly recognized as the same harassed housewives who were constantly shooing us children out of the way.

I would rest my head on my grandmother's squishy abdomen and feel her soft flesh rumble as she belly-laughed her way to tears. Although I didn't realize it at the time, this would be the closest I'd ever come to feeling totally at peace.

Inevitably, however, the conversation would turn toward errant offspring and how young girls ought to learn cooking as preparation for later life. I would sneak a betel leaf and scurry away. I had no intention of being court-martialed by a bevy of relatives trying to entice, entreat, or threaten me into the kitchen.

I continued to spurn cooking into my adolescence. When I reached 14, by some mysterious alchemy—was it genes? destiny?—a passion for the sensuality of food slowly, slowly began to take root. Ever the rebel, I kept it a secret.

Madras, India, 1986. At 18, I have just been accepted into Mount Holyoke College, in South Hadley, Massachusetts, but the consensus in my family is that I shouldn't go. America is full of muggers and all kinds of criminals, my teenage pest of a brother proclaims. No unmarried girl should venture into such a promiscuous society, my septuagenarian grandmother adds. Why go abroad to study when there are world-class Indian institutions to choose from here? An uncle asks. Get married first, my mother says with finality—then go to Timbuktu if you want.

After days of pleading, the elders relent a bit. I am to cook them a vegetarian feast with the perfect balance of spices and flavors. It is a test, one they are sure I will fail. And in it lies my destiny. If my meal is a success, I can go to the United States.

The elders pick a Friday, considered an auspicious day by many Hindus, for my debut as a cook. Though they've given me this advantage, they try to hide their smirks as they inform me that I need not stretch myself. They are not looking for complex *masalas* or complicated curries, merely good food.

I begin with tender green beans, forgiving and flexible, which I cut into small pieces and sauté in oil with mustard seeds and *urad dal*. I sprinkle the beans with desiccated coconut, watching as the thin strips flutter downward: falling tea leaves foretelling my future.

I chop cucumbers, tomatoes, and red onions for the *pachadi* and douse them in thick yogurt, over which I arrange fresh green cilantro in concentric swirls. Under the yogurt-white landscape the red onions appear like bluish veins. Red tomatoes, white yogurt, and blue onions. Red, white, and blue. Is it an omen, or just my imagination?

I tease some spinach over a low flame until it blossoms into a green as deep and bright as the eye of the ocean—and smile with secret satisfaction. The spinach is for *palak paneer*, the one dish in my menu that is not from South India and that will stand out as a misfit. Renegade food made by a rebel; the thought pleases me. I purée the spinach and stir in asafetida, tomatoes, pearl onions, and cubes of creamy fried *paneer*—fresh cheese with the texture of warm tofu—suppressing a bubble of laughter.

Tomatoes brew in tamarind water with turmeric and salt as I cook red lentils. I blend them in, garnishing the *rasam* with cilantro, mustard seeds, and roasted cumin. The scent of cilantro perfumes the air and soothes my soul. Tomato *rasam* is the vegetarian's equivalent of chicken soup. It's the only comfort food I know. When the monsoons ravaged the red earth of my homeland, my grandmother would puræe the *rasam* with sticky rice and add a spoonful of warm *ghee*. We would watch the swaying trees arch under the sheets of rain, contentedly spooning the *rasam*–rice mixture from silver bowls.

I hover over virgin rice, cooking it until each grain is softened but   25
doesn't stick. I stir in turmeric soaked in lemon juice, then ginger, peanuts, and curry leaves I've fried in oil. The rice looks like a painter's palette. Cadmium yellow speckled with burnt sienna.

As sweet butter turns into golden *ghee*, the food of gods, the litany I learned at my mother's knee echoes in my head: *Ghee* promotes growth, ginger soothes, garlic rejuvenates. My grandfather eluded the cholesterol police by drinking a tumblerful daily and living till 104.

Dessert is a simple *payasam*, rice pudding, with roasted pistachios, plump raisins, and strands of saffron strewn on top. The feast ends with aromatic South Indian coffee, a mixture of ground plantation and peaberry beans with a dash of chicory. I filter the coffee powder through a muslin cloth, then mix it with boiling cow's milk that froths on top and, following my mother's prescription, just enough sugar to take out the bitterness but add nothing to the taste.

The elders arrive, resplendent as peacocks in their silk saris and gleaming white dhotis made from spun Madras cotton. Even my teenage cousins are dressed to kill. They survey the ancient rosewood table that totters under the weight of the stainless-steel containers I have filled. I arrange banana leaves on the floor and invite everyone to sit down on the bamboo mats.

My guests pick and sample, judiciously at first. They don't want to eat, but they can't stop themselves. They fight over the last piece of *paneer*, taste overtaking caution. Grandma leans back and belches unapologetically.

I can go to America.   30

Analyze

1. Narayan's essay spends a good deal of time on ritual, while implying almost immediately the relationship between mother and child.

Later on, Narayan describes the relationship with her grandmother. How do these rituals and relationships intertwine? To what effect?

2. In what ways does the lens of adulthood change Narayan's reflections and memories of childhood and family?

3. Analyze the language of the essay. Whereas M. F. K. Fisher might use a word such as "thrice," Narayan's language tends to be far more earthy. What effect do these language choices have on your analysis of the essay?

Explore

1. Explore the ways in which Narayan's essay ends with a beginning— and with a revelation. Why do you think she chooses to end it this way? What does it mean?

2. Narayan's evolving expertise is seen as a metaphor for her evolving maturity and sense of accomplishment. Discuss the parallel between the two.

3. There seem to be implied similes between cooking and nature. Find these examples in the essay and discuss their effect. For instance, what is the purpose of watching "swaying trees arch under the sheets of rain" with a direct connection to "contently spooning the *rasam*–rice mixture from silver bowls"?

Roy Ahn
"Home Run: My Journey Back to Korean Food"

"Home Run: My Journey Back to Korean Food" first appeared in *Gastronomica* (2009) and explores Ahn's parents' immigration from South Korea to the United States in the mid-1970s. Ahn recounts his experience with a reintroduction to the food of his family.

What does this essay tell us about the importance of preserving cultural heritage while being a full participant in one's own country?

Last winter, I dined with my then-pregnant wife, Amy, at a Korean restaurant in a suburban strip mall, where all good Korean food establishments seem to be. This hole-in-the-wall, located on a stretch of highway outside Boston flanked by retail plazas and ranch houses, was filled with Koreans like myself, plus a Caucasian or two, Amy being one. The proprietor sat us in a spot away from the section with barbecue-grill tabletops, but the smell of seared beef mixed with garlic, soy sauce, and brown sugar still permeated our clothing. (Pop quiz: How long does the smell of beef *bulgogi* linger in a pair of blue jeans? Answer: Until it gets thrown into a washing machine.)

The waitresses spun like dervishes from table to kitchen to table, bringing out vegetable and fish *banchan* dishes in one pass and clearing them away in another, with little respite between customers to wipe their beads of sweat. I took particular notice of the diners' white bowls, which reminded me of outsized pieces from Go, my late father's favorite board game.

After a cup of tea and our own *banchan*, we awaited the main courses. Mine would be *galbi-chim*—braised short ribs—served with rice. I imagined pulling the meat off the bone and the flecks of burnt sesame seeds staining the white rice a deep brown, so I was understandably shocked when the waitress placed before me a bowl of oxtail soup. Had she misunderstood? No, I quickly realized. I had ordered the wrong dish.

On the surface, confusing *galbitang* with *galbi-chim* would seem an innocuous lapse. Both are beef dishes whose names share the same Korean-language prefix. But the two couldn't be more different. Imagine a Bavarian confusing knockwurst with bratwurst! As I lowered pieces of *kimchi* into the beef broth to give it a spice kick, and as Amy sipped her way through her bowl of bean-curd-and-vegetable stew, I wondered whether my slipup was an omen: could I be losing my ethnic bearings? If so, there could hardly be a worse time.

I was harboring all sorts of yuppie anxieties about first-time fatherhood— the unit cost of diapers and 529 College Savings Plans chief among them. But as a Korean-American, I was also worrying about our son's cultural identity. I especially looked forward to introducing him to my culinary heritage. That task would be solely up to me—Amy is from a multiple-generation Wisconsin family with European roots, and our culinary union is best described as Land of Rice meets Land of Cheese. Consider some of the foods you might see in her parents' house near Madison: pepper jack, 5 *butterkasse*, and Limberger cheeses, along with sauerkraut, pickled Brussels sprouts, and wursts of all kinds.

As for my parents, they won't be around to introduce my son to their native foods, teach him how to bow properly to his elders, sing Korean nursery rhymes, or explain to him that the number four represents bad luck for Koreans. Both of them died in a car accident when I was twenty-four.

I was born in Seoul in 1972. My parents, a physician and an elementary school teacher, were concerned about raising children in South Korea at a time when military conflict with North Korea seemed imminent, so they immigrated to the United States with my older sister and me when I was four. My official, stamped Korean passport noted that I was "90 cm" tall and weighed "11 kg"—about the equivalent of a twenty-five-pound bag of rice. But soon enough I began to grow, my chubbiness a testament to my successful American acculturation.

As a kid living in suburban Detroit, I loved two things above all else: Baskin-Robbins and the Detroit Tigers. (I still think the ice-cream-inside-miniature-batting-helmet remains one of the industry's greatest inventions.) Inside our apartment I would mark out my own baseball diamond, sprinkle the floor with talcum powder, and, using my father's thick medical textbooks as bases, slide my way across the room as though I were Lou Brock. Like many American boys, I dreamed of becoming a professional baseball player but lacked the athleticism to play beyond high school. My dream of pro ball quashed, I once told my mother that I wanted to become president of a Fortune 500 company. She laughed. A Caucasian businessman would never allow a Korean to have that job, she said, steering me into the sciences instead.

My childhood love of ice cream notwithstanding, my favorite Korean dish was a bowl of rice drizzled with soy sauce and topped with a raw egg. I learned to crack the egg over the rice while it was still piping hot, so the egg would cook a little. Sometimes my mother would add some sliced *daikon* to this silky porridge that glided so easily down my throat. Over time, I began to add my own flourishes—a handful of cooked ground beef and a pinch of dried red-pepper flakes.

10   During my teenage years, after we moved to Los Angeles, I chose to downplay my ethnic roots. I was a Ralph Lauren–clad American teenager living in "The Valley," and my Korean heritage was an inconvenience. This applied to my culinary traditions, too. When I went out, I ate all the things my friends did—pizza, hot dogs, enchiladas, and fries with greasy

chili that turned the paper wrapper orange. It's worth noting that two Korean-American boys were among my circle, but we rarely went out for food from the homeland. Whatever the reason, they were much more comfortable than I was with being Korean-American. Still, when my circle of guy friends went out, we'd usually opt for fried zucchini with ranch dressing at Carl's Jr., chicken burritos at a Mexican food chain on Ventura Boulevard, or pasta at the Cheesecake Factory in Beverly Hills, all the while rocking out in our cars to the Beastie Boys and Run-DMC.

When I got home, I chased down all that American food with Korean fare. My mother, who spoke to me almost exclusively in her native tongue, cooked it herself or stocked up on prepared foods from our local Korean supermarkets. Variations of *kimchi* abounded: red-pepper-flecked radish cubes, cucumber slices, bellflower root, and cabbage. Occasionally, too, there was yellow daikon, which paired well with ground beef, spinach, and rice. Or she would make ginseng chicken stew and *japchae*, a stir-fry of glass noodles, sliced carrot and onion, slivers of beef, and pink-and-white fishcake in a soy and sesame-oil sauce. Food to fuel the brain for studying deep into the night: a mother's loving manifesto for her son. I never had the heart to tell her that the food had the opposite effect—the sugar crash put me to sleep atop my school papers.

I should mention that our house in California had two refrigerators: one in the kitchen for American food, and one in the garage for the Korean food. I'm not sure why my mother was willing to go dual-fridge. I imagine she'd had enough bellyaching from me about the garlicky stench of "Mom and Dad's food" and complaints of how embarrassing it would be if my friends ever got a whiff of the real stuff we ate. She must have decided it wasn't worth the aggravation.

My father, for his part, took my resistance to Korean food poorly. He'd wanted me to be proud of his homeland. "Italian food smells, too," he once told me. But Korean dishes flavored with garlic smell different than Italian ones, and I imagined the odor exuding from my every pore. Leftover Korean food was even worse, announcing itself like a flatulent guest at a wedding. Never mind that a diet of smelly fermented vegetables, stews, noodles, and meats has nourished Koreans for generations.

You may imagine that my father disapproved of American ways. On the contrary, he immersed himself in the culture of his adopted country. Interstate road trips to amusement parks, Kentucky Fried Chicken, bowling. While he loved being Korean, he was fascinated by cultures other than his own and especially enjoyed commingling them. To this day, I can't picture a bucket of KFC extra-crispy without adjacent bowls of white rice and *kimchi*. My father's stacks of Japanese novels were piled right alongside Westerns by Louis L'Amour, and he listened to instructional language tapes on Spanish and Mandarin in his spare time. He often serenaded us on road trips with his rendition of "Tears on My Pillow," a number he'd learned from the soundtrack of *Grease*. Once, I watched him eat a bowl of white rice with ketchup, straight up. Another time, he used chopsticks to pluck Vienna sausages out of their tin. He was so pleased with his concoctions, so original in his wackiness, that I believe I inherited my own willingness to improvise from him.

15   My mother, by contrast, was never comfortable in the States. She struggled to pick up English and didn't make many friends outside her Korean church. A short woman with permed black hair, large brown eyes, and caramel-colored skin, darker than that of most Korean women I knew, she watched a lot of Korean soap operas on the VCR and seemed content to have a vicarious American experience through her children.

Little Korean boys do not take formal cooking lessons from their mothers; the kitchen is considered a woman's domain. Nonetheless, I made excuses to spend time with her there. Cooking Korean dishes means a lot of sautéing, boiling, grilling, and frying. She rarely baked. I considered my mother a great cook, although she always told me she was only so-so, modestly claiming there were other women at church who possessed skills far superior to her own.

I don't recall that we did a lot of talking while I watched her cook. She did not share with me the latest in church gossip, nor did she try to impart wisdom in the form of hackneyed analogies about food and life. Such things are better left for movies involving white people and karate. Instead, I recall marveling at the way she so deftly used a paring knife to peel fruit, her thumb applying pressure until the skin unfurled in a continuous ribbon. She had good hands for peeling, with strong fingers, neither long nor stubby. I watched her make simple dishes that, later on, when my parents both went to work, became my latchkey-kid staples.

There was one American experience my entire family did enjoy: eating steamed crabs at the Redondo Beach Pier. The dining experience was far from formal. We'd place our order, lay several pages of the *Los Angeles Times* atop one of the many communal tables, and wait for the crabs to steam. I remember how excited I was to buy lemons (for cleaning our hands afterward) and rent crab mallets. I'd crack my crab with authority, as though I were a judge lowering a gavel. Using my hands to eat, I tried my best to avoid touching the mustard-colored crab guts. Afterward, I played Skee-Ball until I drained my parents of ones and fives. As a family, we walked off our meals along the beach, sometimes until the sun set. My parents seemed so contented there. My mother was at ease at the beach, less concerned about fitting in, and she laughed a lot.

For a few years after my parents' deaths, I lived in a weird fog, unable to focus on my future or reconcile my past. I lost interest in all things Korean, including food. When my mother was alive, she would ask me questions in Korean and I would respond in English. After she was gone, my grip on the language loosened.

I began to work summers as a cook at an artists' colony café in a resort   20 town in the Rocky Mountains. There, under the best of all possible circumstances—cooking for, and being inspired by, the master printmakers, woodworkers, painters, and ceramic artists who came through the colony—I learned to make crème brûlée, venison stroganoff, and other European dishes. In that nurturing atmosphere, as my confidence in cooking grew, so did my expressiveness through food. (Within limits, of course: my idea for a "healthful" sugar cookie made with lemon Ricola cough drops never made it onto diners' plates.) But something even more unexpected occurred: latent Korean influences began to insinuate themselves into the food I prepared. I fried rectangles of tofu in vegetable oil. I tenderized flank steak in garlicky *kalbi* marinades. I slipped scallions into whatever dishes I could. Sesame oil found its way into my sauces.

I can't say that I channeled my parents by cooking Korean food, or that food reinvigorated my innate sense of Korean-ness. I'm not at all certain about the synapses that get fired when human beings experience emotions from cooking and eating the foods of their childhoods. All I can say for sure is that something sublime happened in that mecca of Korean cuisine—the Rockies—where I rediscovered my native food heritage. My mother left behind no recipe cards. Instead, I created dishes based on my recollections of watching her cook, imagining her in that café kitchen with me, telling me to add a few more red-pepper flakes or dial down the sesame oil.

I still harbor mixed feelings about my parents' move to the United States. Would they still be alive today if we had stayed in Korea? It is, of course, a fool's errand to speculate about something like that. What I do know is that, because of their sacrifice, I have had terrific experiences and opportunities, and that our son, Charlie, will inevitably have the same. One day, if he so chooses, he may even become a corporate CEO—a Fortune 500 one at that. Or a professional baseball player, if I have any say in the matter.

As I write this, Charlie is just three months old. He has my mother's skin tone and big eyes, but otherwise no physical features that specifically remind me of either of my parents. He has my faint black eyebrows and Amy's broad smile. And because he does not cry when I play songs—well, not as much as usual, anyway—I've come to believe that Charlie likes music, especially party music, as much I do. Just last week, he and I danced in our living room to the Commodores' "Brick House."

Meanwhile, food remains a primary conduit through which I hope to instill in him the lessons of one half of his ethnic roots. I'm sad that my parents aren't around to help indoctrinate him into their culture. Even though it might be naive to think that by teaching him to eat and cook Korean he'll also learn about who they were, my gut tells me this is so.

25   Amy and I live near a Korean supermarket that sells a lot of foods from my youth: perfectly circular Shingo pears, each one cradled in its own Styrofoam nest, and too-sweet candies made from sweet bean, jelly, and agar-agar. I think how cool it will be to have these foods at Charlie's first birthday party. For that celebration I can imagine cooking dishes that capitalize on my knowledge of Korean and non-Korean cuisines. I will sauté fiddleheads with leeks and reserve the leek fronds for garnish. I will make potstickers, doing my best, just as my mother did, to get that even seal on the wrappers, which is so critical to keeping the ground pork and vegetable filling moist. I will put creative spins on Korean classics. I will wrap *bibimbap* ingredients—sliced beef, spinach, carrot slivers, bean sprouts, fried egg, rice—in *nori* straightjackets, drizzle them with wasabi aioli, and present these oversized, funnel-shaped hand rolls in metal Belgian *frites* stands. For dessert, I will experiment by baking sweet red beans *en croûte*.

Of course, I am getting ahead of myself. At the moment, Charlie's diet is limited to two options—fresh breast milk, or thawed-and-warmed breast milk.

Another way Charlie will learn is through language. At the peak of one of his nighttime crying fits last week, I found myself soothing him with calming words—"It's okay, it's okay"—but in Korean, the way my mother might have. Amy is learning the language, too. She has taken classes in

Korean through an adult-education center. In fact, she can read and write Korean far better than I can. I intend to join her in these classes, or at least sit in front of a laptop with Charlie and complete our Rosetta Stone exercises together. I mean, who wouldn't benefit from learning the Korean word for elephant (*koo-kee-ree*)? Perhaps this way I will register even farther east on the Korea-meter.

Recently, we had a family dinner at a Korean restaurant in Cambridge. It was a more formal, or, at any rate, more urbane place than the one where I had made my ordering mistake. The host put us in a private room where we had to take our shoes off. During dinner, as Amy nursed Charlie beneath a cotton shawl, I dissected the ingredients in the *banchan* I ate, the proper method of constructing our *ssam* (lettuce wraps), using rice and meat and red *kochujang* paste. I pronounced aloud the Korean names of as many dishes as I could. And this time I remembered most of them accurately.

Amy fears that our son won't get a sufficient dose of Korean culture. It's 30 a familiar refrain. But I will make sure to offer Charlie Korean food and, as my parents did with me, exercise patience if he doesn't want any. We will stick to one fridge in our house.

Analyze

1. You'll notice that Ahn frames his essay: that is, he begins and ends with a narrative about a meal with his wife. Why might Ahn choose to frame the essay this way? To what effect?

2. Similarly, it could be said that Ahn's narrative rambles to some extent. Analyze why this might be deliberate on Ahn's part and what it might say about an overall point to the essay.

3. How would you describe the characterization of Ahn's parents? How do the specific details of these characterizations point toward Ahn's own evolution?

Explore

1. Ahn writes, "I can't say that I channeled my parents by cooking Korean food, or that food reinvigorated my innate sense of Korean-ness." He continues to indicate that he "rediscovered" his "native food heritage" in the Rockies. How does food help one reinvigorate one's heritage?

What are aspects of your own experience that reflect this type of "native food heritage" that you might have "rediscovered?" How?

2. This is as much a narrative about assimilating into the larger culture as it is about food. How does food serve as a symbol of cultural perpetuation and tradition as well as assimilation?

3. Ahn notes that when he was a teenager, he "chose to downplay my ethnic roots." How do you see this in your friends? How do you see this in yourself? Explain, referring to Ahn's narrative to elaborate your points.

David Sedaris
"Tasteless"

A leading, popular voice in nonfiction, David Sedaris is an award-nominated humorist, essayist, and radio personality. He first came to public attention in 1992 through "The Santa Land Diaries," broadcast on National Public Radio. Sedaris is also a playwright—writing with his sister, humorist Amy Sedaris—and has written nine books. "Tasteless" comes from *The New Yorker* magazine, a piece that celebrates Sedaris's inability to discern flavor.

How do humor and seriousness intertwine in this essay? And to what effect?

One of the things they promise when you quit smoking is that food will regain its flavor. Taste buds paved beneath decades of tar will spring back to life, and an entire sense will be restored. I thought it would be like putting on a pair of glasses—something dramatic that makes you say, "Whoa!"—but it's been six months now, and I have yet to notice any significant change.

Part of the problem might be me. I've always been in touch with my stomach, but my mouth and I don't really speak. Oh, it chews all right. It helps me form words and holds stuff when my hands are full, but it doesn't do any of these things very well. It's third-rate at best—fifth if you take my teeth into consideration.

Even before I started smoking, I was not a remarkably attentive eater. "Great fried fish," I'd say to my mother, only to discover that I was eating a chicken breast or, just as likely, a veal cutlet. She might as well have done away with names and identified our meals by color: "Golden brown." "Red." "Beige with some pink in it."

I am a shoveller, a quantity man, and I like to keep going until I feel sick. It's how a prisoner might eat, one arm maneuvering the fork and the other encircling the plate like a fence: head lowered close to my food, eyes darting this way and that; even if I don't particularly like it, it's *mine*, God damn it.

Some of this has to do with coming from a large family. Always afraid 5
that I wouldn't get enough, I'd start worrying about more long before I finished what was in front of me. We'd be at the dinner table, and, convict-like, out of one side of my mouth, I'd whisper to my sister Amy.

"What'll you take for that chicken leg?"

"You mean my barbecued rib?"

"Call it what you like, just give me your asking price."

"Oh gosh," she'd say. "A quarter?"

"Twenty-five cents! What do you think this is—a restaurant?"   10

She'd raise the baton of meat to her face and examine it for flaws. "A dime."

"A nickel," I'd say, and before she could argue I'd have snatched it away.

I should have been enormous, the size of a panda, but I think that the fear of going without—the anxiety that this produced—acted like a kind of furnace, and burned off the calories before I could gain weight. Even after learning how to make my own meals, I remained, if not skinny, then at least average. My older sister Lisa and I were in elementary school when our mother bought us our first cookbook. The recipes were fairly simple—lots of Jell-O-based desserts and a wheel-shaped meat loaf cooked in an angel-food-cake pan. This last one was miraculous to me. "A meat loaf—with a hole in it!" I kept saying. I guess I thought that as it baked the cavity would fill itself with rubies or butterscotch pudding. How else to explain my disappointment the first dozen times I made it?

In high school, I started cooking pizzas—"from scratch," I liked to say, "the ol' fashioned way." On Saturday afternoons, I'd make my dough, place it in a cloth-covered bowl, and set it in the linen closet to rise. We'd have our dinner at seven or so, and four hours later, just as "Shock Theater," our local horror-movie program, came on, I'd put my pizzas in the oven. It might have been all right if this were just *part* of my evening, but it was everything: all I knew about being young had canned Parmesan cheese on it. While my classmates were taking acid and having sex in their cars, I was arranging sausage buttons and sliced peppers into smiley faces.

15   "The next one should look mad," my younger brother would say. And, as proof of my versatility, I would create a frown.

To make it all that much sadder, things never got any better than this. Never again would I take so many chances or feel such giddy confidence in my abilities. This is not to say that I stopped cooking, just that I stopped trying.

Between the year that I left my parents' house and the year that I met Hugh, I made myself dinner just about every night. I generally alternated between three or four simple meals, but if forced to name my signature dish I'd probably have gone with my Chicken and Linguine with Grease on It. I don't know that I ever had an actual recipe; rather, like my Steak and Linguine with Blood on It, I just sort of played it by ear. The good thing about those meals was that they had only two ingredients. Anything more than that and I'm like Hugh's mother buying Christmas presents. "I look at the list, I go to the store, and then I just freeze," she says.

I suggest that it's nothing to get worked up about, and see in her eyes the look I give when someone says, "It's only a dinner party," or "Can we have something *with* the Chicken and Linguine with Grease on It?"

I cook for myself when I'm alone; otherwise, Hugh takes care of it, and happily, too. People tell me that he's a real chef, and something about the way they say it, a tone of respect and envy, leads me to believe them. I know that the dinners he prepares are correct. If something is supposed to be hot, it is. If it looks rust-colored in pictures, it looks rust-colored on the plate. I'm always happy to eat Hugh's cooking, but when it comes to truly tasting, to discerning the subtleties I hear others talking about, it's as if my tongue were wearing a mitten.

20   That's why fine restaurants are wasted on me. I suppose I can appreciate the lighting, or the speed with which my water glass is refilled, but, as far as the food is concerned, if I can't distinguish between a peach and an apricot I really can't tell the difference between an excellent truffle and a mediocre one. Then, too, the more you pay the less they generally give you to eat. French friends visiting the United States are floored by the size of the portions. "Plates the size of hubcaps!" they cry. "No wonder the Americans are so fat."

"I know," I say. "Isn't it awful?" Then I think of Claim Jumper, a California-based chain that serves a massive hamburger called the Widow

Maker. I ordered a side of creamed spinach there, and it came in what looked like a mixing bowl. It was like being miniaturized, shrunk to the height of a leprechaun or a doll and dropped in the dining room of regular-sized people. Even the salt and pepper shakers seemed enormous. I ate at Claim Jumper only once, and it was the first time in years that I didn't corral my plate. For starters, my arm wasn't long enough, but even if it had been I wouldn't have felt the need. There was plenty to go around, some of it brown, some of it green, and some a color I've come to think of, almost dreamily, as enough.

Analyze

1. As you read "Tasteless," what are the indications that you are in the presence of a humorous work? Be specific.
2. What do we learn about the author as we read this essay? How does his use of language reveal not only humor, but also the author's persona? How would you describe it?
3. Sedaris "slides" between narrative vignettes. How do these various scenes work together to create a cohesive narrative? What would you say the overall thrust of the piece might be?

Explore

1. As we have read, food can reveal culture and identity. What does Sedaris reveal to his readers when his first cookbook features recipes such as "Jell-O-based desserts and a wheel-shaped meat loaf cooked in an angel-food-cake pan?"
2. How does Sedaris present himself as the "anti-foodie," saying that "fine restaurants are wasted on him?"
3. Despite the humor of the essay, what are the more serious points raised by Sedaris? How is the use of humor effective in raising these serious implications? Does humor enhance or diminish their importance? Why?

Forging Connections

1. How does the genre of memoir—autobiographical food writing— transcend the time in which it was written? For instance, what are

the common assumptions or concerns that reveal themselves in, say, M. F. K. Fisher's essay and another essay in this chapter? How are the central concerns different? What do you conclude about these similarities and differences?

2. How do our eating habits (or "foodways," as they might now be called) become emblematic of culture in essays by Ahn, Narayan, and Sedaris? And how might these emblems speak to the ways in which we conceive of our own identities? Be specific in your responses, not only as you refer to these essays but also as you refer to your own experience.

Looking Further

1. Research, find, and read another memoir about food. Create a presentation for your class or lead a discussion in which you compare it regarding theme, language, and overall point to one of the essays from this chapter. How is each of these essays effective? Although you will focus on one essay from this chapter and one you will find on your own, let your perspective be informed by the other memoirs you've read here. Be specific in your comparisons.

2. As revealed by several of the essays in this chapter, our eating customs are often born of our own perceptions of our individual roles in the family and our roles out in the world. These customs also shape our respective identities. Using the essays in this chapter as starting points, find sources (written and visual) to create an argument illustrating the ways in which these roles are reinforced by the culture(s) that surround us.

Food and Environment

2

One cannot spend an evening watching television—cable or otherwise—without seeing an advertisement for something that is "sustainable," "geo- this or that," "organic," or "environmentally friendly." Clearly, what we eat and our "environmental footprint" (something else we're always hearing about) are significant topics in our world.

Although we are inundated by these concepts as colonized by advertisers, they are, nonetheless, important concerns. As the readings in this chapter argue, it is important that we critically examine the nexus or intersection of our eating habits and the environments in which we live. The essays here are not to any extent meant to be the final words on any aspect of these very complex issues. We hope you will use them as starting points for your further explorations as a concerned citizen.

Wendell Berry
"The Pleasures of Eating"

Wendell Berry is not only a prolific novelist and essayist, but also an environmental activist and cultural critic. Berry is among the first to turn the public's attention to industrialized farming and the ethical and environmental problems of our system of producing food. "The Pleasures of Eating" is part of *What Are People For?* (1990), and it examines the politics and ethics of the foods we eat, asking readers to remember that "eating is an agricultural act."

*How is eating an "agricultural act?"

Many times, after I have finished a lecture on the decline of American farming and rural life, someone in the audience has asked, "What can city people do?"

"Eat responsibly," I have usually answered. Of course, I have tried to explain what I mean by that, but afterwards I have invariably felt there was more to be said than I had been able to say. Now I would like to attempt a better explanation.

> I begin with the proposition that eating is an agricultural act.

I begin with the proposition that eating is an agricultural act. Eating ends the annual drama of the food economy that begins with planting and birth. Most eaters, however, are no longer aware that this is true. They think of food as an agricultural product, perhaps, but they do not think of themselves as participants in agriculture. They think of themselves as "consumers." If they think beyond that, they recognize that they are passive consumers. They buy what they want—or what they have been persuaded to want—within the limits of what they can get. They pay, mostly without protest, what they are charged. And they mostly ignore certain critical questions about the quality and the cost of what they are sold: How fresh is it? How pure or clean is it, how free of dangerous chemicals? How far was it transported, and what did transportation add to the cost? How much did manufacturing or packaging or advertising add to the cost? When the food product has been manufactured or "processed" or "precooked," how has that affected its quality or price or nutritional value?

Most urban shoppers would tell you that food is produced on farms. But most of them do not know what farms, or what kinds of farms, or where the farms are, or what knowledge of skills are involved in farming. They apparently have little doubt that farms will continue to produce, but they do not know how or over what obstacles. For them, then, food is pretty much an abstract idea—something they do not know or imagine—until it appears on the grocery shelf or on the table.

The specialization of production induces specialization of consumption.   5 Patrons of the entertainment industry, for example, entertain themselves less and less and have become more and more passively dependent on commercial suppliers. This is certainly true also of patrons of the food industry, who have tended more and more to be mere consumers—passive, uncritical, and dependent. Indeed, this sort of consumption may be said to be one of the chief goals of industrial production. The food industrialists have by now persuaded millions of consumers to prefer food that is already prepared. They will grow, deliver, and cook your food for you and (just like your mother) beg you to eat it. That they do not yet offer to insert it, prechewed, into our mouth is only because they have found no profitable way to do so. We may rest assured that they would be glad to find such a way. The ideal industrial food consumer would be strapped to a table with a tube running from the food factory directly into his or her stomach.

Perhaps I exaggerate, but not by much. The industrial eater is, in fact, one who does not know that eating is an agricultural act, who no longer knows or imagines the connections between eating and the land, and who is therefore necessarily passive and uncritical—in short, a victim. When food, in the minds of eaters, is no longer associated with farming and with the land, then the eaters are suffering a kind of cultural amnesia that is misleading and dangerous. The current version of the "dream home" of the future involves "effortless" shopping from a list of available goods on a television monitor and heating precooked food by remote control. Of course, this implies and depends on a perfect ignorance of the history of the food that is consumed. It requires that the citizenry should give up their hereditary and sensible aversion to buying a pig in a poke. It wishes to make the selling of pigs in pokes an honorable and glamorous activity. The dreams in this dream home will perforce know nothing about the kind or quality of this food, or where it came from, or how it was produced and prepared, or what ingredients, additives, and residues it contains—unless, that is, the dreamer undertakes a close and constant study of the food industry, in which case he or she might as well wake up and play an active and responsible part in the economy of food.

There is, then, a politics of food that, like any politics, involves our freedom. We still (sometimes) remember that we cannot be free if our minds and voices are controlled by someone else. But we have neglected to understand that we cannot be free if our food and its sources are controlled by someone else. The condition of the passive consumer of food is not a democratic condition. One reason to eat responsibly is to live free.

But if there is a food politics, there are also a food esthetics and a food ethics, neither of which is dissociated from politics. Like industrial sex, industrial eating has become a degraded, poor, and paltry thing. Our kitchens and other eating places more and more resemble filling stations, as our homes more and more resemble motels. "Life is not very interesting," we seem to have decided. "Let its satisfactions be minimal, perfunctory, and fast." We hurry through our meals to go to work and hurry through our work in order to "recreate" ourselves in the evenings and on weekends and vacations. And then we hurry, with the greatest possible speed and noise and violence, through our recreation—for what? To eat the billionth hamburger at some fast-food joint hellbent on increasing the "quality" of our life? And all this is carried out in a remarkable obliviousness to the causes and effects, the possibilities and the purposes, of the life of the body in this world.

One will find this obliviousness represented in virgin purity in the advertisements of the food industry, in which food wears as much makeup as the actors. If one gained one's whole knowledge of food from these advertisements (as some presumably do), one would not know that the various edibles were ever living creatures, or that they all come from the soil, or that they were produced by work. The passive American consumer, sitting down to a meal of pre-prepared or fast food, confronts a platter covered with inert, anonymous substances that have been processed, dyed, breaded, sauced, gravied, ground, pulped, strained, blended, prettified, and sanitized beyond resemblance to any part of any creature that ever lived. The products of nature and agriculture have been made, to all appearances, the products of industry. Both eater and eaten are thus in exile from biological reality. And the result is a kind of solitude, unprecedented in human experience, in which the eater may think of eating as, first, a purely commercial transaction between him and a supplier and then as a purely appetitive transaction between him and his food.

And this peculiar specialization of the act of eating is, again, of obvious   10
benefit to the food industry, which has good reasons to obscure the connection between food and farming. It would not do for the consumer to know
that the hamburger she is eating came from a steer who spent much of his
life standing deep in his own excrement in a feedlot, helping to pollute the
local streams, or that the calf that yielded the veal cutlet on her plate spent
its life in a box in which it did not have room to turn around. And, though
her sympathy for the slaw might be less tender, she should not be encouraged to meditate on the hygienic and biological implications of mile-square
fields of cabbage, for vegetables grown in huge monocultures are dependent
on toxic chemicals—just as animals in close confinements are dependent
on antibiotics and other drugs.

The consumer, that is to say, must be kept from discovering that, in the
food industry—as in any other industry—the overriding concerns are not
quality and health, but volume and price. For decades now the entire industrial food economy, from the large farms and feedlots to the chains of supermarkets and fast-food restaurants, has been obsessed with volume. It has
relentlessly increased scale in order to increase volume in order (probably) to
reduce costs. But as scale increases, diversity declines; as diversity declines,
so does health; as health declines, the dependence on drugs and chemicals
necessarily increases. As capital replaces labor, it does so by substituting machines, drugs, and chemicals for human workers and for the natural health
and fertility of the soil. The food is produced by any means or any shortcuts
that will increase profits. And the business of the cosmeticians of advertising is to persuade the consumer that food so produced is good, tasty, healthful, and a guarantee of marital fidelity and long life.

It is possible, then, to be liberated from the husbandry and wifery of the
old household food economy. But one can be thus liberated only by entering
a trap (unless one sees ignorance and helplessness as the signs of privilege, as
many people apparently do). The trap is the ideal of industrialism: a walled
city surrounded by valves that let merchandise in but no consciousness out.
How does one escape this trap? Only voluntarily, the same way that one
went in: by restoring one's consciousness of what is involved in eating; by
reclaiming responsibility for one's own part in the food economy. One
might begin with the illuminating principle of Sir Albert Howard's, that
we should understand "the whole problem of health in soil, plant, animal,
and man as one great subject." Eaters, that is, must understand that eating

takes place inescapably in the world, that it is inescapably an agricultural act, and how we eat determines, to a considerable extent, how the world is used. This is a simple way of describing a relationship that is inexpressibly complex. To eat responsibly is to understand and enact, so far as we can, this complex relationship. What can one do? Here is a list, probably not definitive:

1. Participate in food production to the extent that you can. If you have a yard or even just a porch box or a pot in a sunny window, grow something to eat in it. Make a little compost of your kitchen scraps and use it for fertilizer. Only by growing some food for yourself can you become acquainted with the beautiful energy cycle that revolves from soil to seed to flower to fruit to food to offal to decay, and around again. You will be fully responsible for any food that you grow for yourself, and you will know all about it. You will appreciate it fully, having known it all its life.

2. Prepare your own food. This means reviving in your own mind and life the arts of kitchen and household. This should enable you to eat more cheaply, and it will give you a measure of "quality control": you will have some reliable knowledge of what has been added to the food you eat.

3. Learn the origins of the food you buy, and buy the food that is produced closest to your home. The idea that every locality should be, as much as possible, the source of its own food makes several kinds of sense. The locally produced food supply is the most secure, freshest, and the easiest for local consumers to know about and to influence.

4. Whenever possible, deal directly with a local farmer, gardener, or orchardist. All the reasons listed for the previous suggestion apply here. In addition, by such dealing you eliminate the whole pack of merchants, transporters, processors, packagers, and advertisers who thrive at the expense of both producers and consumers.

5. Learn, in self-defense, as much as you can of the economy and technology of industrial food production. What is added to the food that is not food, and what do you pay for those additions?

6. Learn what is involved in the best farming and gardening.

7. Learn as much as you can, by direct observation and experience if possible, of the life histories of the food species.

The last suggestion seems particularly important to me. Many people are now as much estranged from the lives of domestic plants and animals (except for flowers and dogs and cats) as they are from the lives of the wild ones. This is regrettable, for these domestic creatures are in diverse ways attractive; there is such pleasure in knowing them. And farming, animal husbandry, horticulture, and gardening, at their best, are complex and comely arts; there is much pleasure in knowing them, too.

It follows that there is great displeasure in knowing about a food economy that degrades and abuses those arts and those plants and animals and the soil from which they come. For anyone who does know something of the modern history of food, eating away from home can be a chore. My own inclination is to eat seafood instead of red meat or poultry when I am traveling. Though I am by no means a vegetarian, I dislike the thought that some animal has been made miserable in order to feed me. If I am going to eat meat, I want it to be from an animal that has lived a pleasant, uncrowded life outdoors, on bountiful pasture, with good water nearby and trees for shade. And I am getting almost as fussy about food plants. I like to eat vegetables and fruits that I know have lived happily and healthily in good soil, not the products of the huge, bechemicaled factory-fields that I have seen, for example, in the Central Valley of California. The industrial farm is said to have been patterned on the factory production line. In practice, it looks more like a concentration camp.

The pleasure of eating should be an extensive pleasure, not that of the mere gourmet. People who know the garden in which their vegetables have grown and know that the garden is healthy and remember the beauty of the growing plants, perhaps in the dewy first light of morning when gardens are at their best. Such a memory involves itself with the food and is one of the pleasures of eating. The knowledge of the good health of the garden relieves and frees and comforts the eater. The same goes for eating meat. The thought of the good pasture and of the calf contentedly grazing flavors the steak. Some, I know, will think of it as bloodthirsty or worse to eat a fellow creature you have known all its life. On the contrary, I think it means that you eat with understanding and with gratitude. A significant part of the pleasure of eating is in one's accurate consciousness of the lives and the world from which food comes. The pleasure of eating, then, may be the best available standard of our health. And this pleasure, I think, is pretty fully available to the urban consumer who will make the necessary effort.

I mentioned earlier the politics, esthetics, and ethics of food. But to speak of the pleasure of eating is to go beyond those categories. Eating with the fullest pleasure—pleasure, that is, that does not depend on ignorance—is

15

perhaps the profoundest enactment of our connection with the world. In this pleasure we experience and celebrate our dependence and our gratitude, for we are living from mystery, from creatures we did not make and powers we cannot comprehend. When I think of the meaning of food, I always re-member these lines by the poet William Carlos Williams, which seem to me merely honest:

> There is nothing to eat,
> seek it where you will,
> but the body of the Lord.
> The blessed plants
> and the sea, yield it
> to the imagination intact.
> *1989*

Analyze

1. Consider how one might eat responsibly. What would Wendell Berry think is the most appropriate way to do this?
2. How might one "be liberated" of the "husbandry and wifery of the old household food economy?" What does this mean?
3. How does Berry describe the disconnect between the consumers of food and where that food comes from? To what effect?

Explore

1. Berry offers a list of seven definitive steps that one can take to become a more responsible eater. How might this apply to your life? To that of your family or friends?
2. Berry argues that the "overriding concerns" of the food industry are volume and price and not quality and health. How does he make this argument? Does he do so effectively? How might this also apply to your own experience with food?
3. The author implicates readers for not knowing where the food we eat comes from. Research the components of a meal that you find you eat fairly often, and try to find where the food came from, how it got to your table (or restaurant), and the like. What do you find?

Peter Meehan
"Seafarming at the End of the World"

Peter Meehan is currently co-editor of the quarterly journal, *Lucky Peach*. He has authored or co-authored numerous cookbooks, and he formerly wrote about restaurants for the *New York Times*. In a 2012 article in the *Wall Street Journal*, Meehan is described as having a "dark worldview" that he shares with co-author David Chang. "Seafarming at the End of the World" appeared in *Lucky Peach* in 2013, and it is an ethnographic approach to understanding "aquaculture," as Meehan calls it, a reaction to industrialized fishing.

Based on this article, is conservation really so twentieth century?

Things are not looking good in our oceans and seas, our bays and waterways, our rivers and streams. Not for the things that live in them and, increasingly, not for the people who live along them.

The International Programme on the Ocean, a group of oceanographers and other aquatically minded scientists, gathered at Oxford University in 2011 and published the findings of their symposium, which they summarized rather tidily: "The combination of stressors on the ocean is creating the conditions associated with every previous major extinction of species in Earth's history."

This scenario doesn't seem to dim Bren Smith's enthusiasm for raising imperiled sea creatures. Bren, who originally sent me the report, cheerily shouted to me, "WE'RE IN THE MIDDLE OF ONE OF THE LARGEST EXTINCTIONS IN THE OCEAN EVER!" as his oyster boat threaded its way through the Thimble Islands off the coast of Connecticut.

I visited him on the upper side of the Long Island Sound, where he works, a few weeks after flooding from a storm had muddied the waters— muddy waters suffocate oysters, not to mention his business—and it would be only a matter of weeks before Sandy would come and deliver to him and his oysters another ruinous walloping. "I've been wiped out three times out of the last ten years—I mean completely wiped out," Bren says, "including last year, the entire crop . . ."

Bren's operation is notable because its model is newish: a "3-D sea farm," 5 he calls it. He raises mussels and scallops near the top of the water, and clams and oysters along the Sound's floor. Kelp, which grows during the winter, connects the two. The acreage his operation covers is minimal compared to its output—at least when the New Weather isn't busy killing what he raises.

I went out with him to slurp some oysters and talk about sea-farming at the end of the world.

Where Are We?

We were in the Thimble Islands, a little-known East Coast archipelago of privately owned islands—some small enough for just one dwelling, and a few large enough to hold several houses.

All the homes are private. You know what's crazy? They've found some old Model Ts on one of the islands; back when the winters were colder the water would freeze solid enough that you could commute to work over the ice. Now it's mostly summer places. Six of them are owned by this woman who's a magnate from a party store who got obsessed with collecting these islands and bought one for every one of her kids and grandkids. Rich people's business.

Some are rented—not quite timeshares, exactly. Some of the older families, sort of the Connecticut Yankees who are land rich and cash poor pay off their taxes by renting them out for a week. There's actually one sort of advertised hotel out there, where you can rent the whole building, but it's mainly a really tight-knit community. The kids just keep coming back; even the working class people here go back generations. It's that classic sort of island thing where people love it and won't leave and all hate each other.

10   There's a quarry on Bear Island where this famous pink granite comes from. The Statue of Liberty, the Brooklyn Bridge, Congress—they're all made out of the pink granite from that island and a quarry nearby on the mainland. And—this is a little in dispute but I know it for sure—when Howard Roark stands on the quarry's edge in Ayn Rand's *The Fountainhead* that's on Bear Island over there.

How Did You Get Here?

I grew up in Newfoundland in a little fishing village with nine houses. I dropped out of high school when I was fourteen and moved to Gloucester. Somebody told me I was a child laborer, but I was like, "All Newfies drop out of school." At fourteen, I even felt like I was like a little late to do so! Then I went to Alaska for about five years from when I was about sixteen. I went back and forth—I was on crab boats, cod boats, trawling, longlining, and so on. So the first half of my fishing career was like the worst form of food production. I was a complete raper and pillager up in Alaska. We didn't know better, or I didn't. I used to fish for McDonald's and they'd take all the sea lice—ridden, wormy fish—just the worst stuff.

I'm actually the worst oysterman ever, because I get seasick. Up in the Bering Sea, we'd be out for three months at a time. It's just brutal in the belly of the boat. I'd puke for the first two weeks, and after that I'd be fine. No one ever works through seasickness, you know? A lot of us used to get seasick the first two weeks.

I still work all the time. I haven't taken a vacation in six years, not even a weekend. And I love this—every second of it. Though I do eat terribly. I just don't have the time or money to do better. I'm an expert at putting together a gas-station dinner. We don't cook; my wife is an artist. When we moved here we lived in an old Airstream trailer for seven years while we built our house so we didn't have heat, a bathroom, or any way to cook. We'd just eat out every night. We didn't shop, and are still stuck in that rut.

What Is Seafarming?

I got turned off by industrial fishing in part because the fish just started to disappear. I was starting to get some level of slow consciousness there, and I started to explore aquaculture. Of course, aquaculture was just beginning to get industrialized as land culture was getting deindustrialized, so my first exposure to it was terrible. I worked at some salmon farms, and they were awful. Very awful. I finally got interested in more of a self-directed life. Owning my own life—not so much owning my own company but owning my own experiments and failures. I decided I wanted to take my life and be sustainable. I was sick of working for people, mainly. That's when I stumbled onto the idea of oystering.

Of course, oyster grounds are hard to get. The shellfishing grounds in   15 this area are mainly owned by five families. But in 2006, the powers that be released grounds here for the first time in 150 years to attract people under forty back into fishery. A bunch of us tried and got in. I'm the last one standing. Everyone else bought boats, went into debt, things like that. They were all fishermen, but this is not fishing—this is farming. Fishing is when you're chasing things, trying to hit the fish; it's like a lottery. But out here it's about touching every oyster and clam, every five weeks, keeping 'em free of anything unwanted, shaping them. (*Bren rubs off the brittle front edge of the oyster shells as they are growing, giving it a deeper, more cupped shape.*) It's really more like farming.

I've got sixty acres, but I do most of my production in just twenty of it. Beautiful thing is that I have this really small footprint. It's vertical farming. On top, on the long lines, I grow kelp and Gracilaria, a red seaweed. Below them, mussels are hanging in socks and scallops in lantern cages, and below that are oysters and clams. This is the first multi-species vertical ocean farm in the country. I'm the first one ever to get permitted for surface gear on Long Island Sound. It took me two years and an incredible amount of money to get the permits. The reason is the aesthetics. A lot of these very wealthy people don't wanna see anything on the water even though they're foodies and environmentalists.

These species that I raise here filter out carbon, nitrogen, even heavy metals. (Thank God we don't have that problem here in the Thimble Islands, but it is a reason to grow oysters in other places—not for eating, but to help clean up polluted waterways.) Besides what the shellfish do on their own, their cages function as artificial reefs—everything is attracted to 'em; we've counted 150 different species in these waters, way beyond what you'd normally expect to see these days.

We're getting a lot of creatures from down south. I just found a seahorse. No one's ever seen so many tropical fish around here. This year's been incredible. Four or five times already this summer, fishermen have been catching these crazy fish—tropical fish—that are coming because of the water-temperature changes.

The other reason no one's doing this 3D seafarming thing is that it's so experimental: I'll run it at a loss for quite a while because the kelp market already exists, it's mainly foreign, and there's a lot of local competition. We have to figure out how to Americanize it. I've got to get up to some economy of scale. Next year two more long lines will go in. I'll see how it goes as it grows. But I think you can only do local farming at my small scale and make a living by having some soft subsidy model where I'm growing food for local communities, doing a lot of education work, working with kids, nonprofits, legislators, and scientists.

What Was and Will Be

There used to be oyster reefs so big here—like six feet high—that you'd   20
actually have to navigate your boats around them. Oysters are a founda-
tional species: they're the base of the ecosystem, which attracts everything,
just like a coral reef. Take the Chesapeake Bay: the entire bay used to be
filtered out once a week by the oysters. There were hundreds of millions of
them! Oysters pull all the algae out of the water. When there's nothing to
do that, you get huge algae blooms, which suck up all the oxygen and lead
to higher nitrogen levels in the water. When the algae dies, it falls to the
bottom and smothers what's down there, and you end up with these huge
dead zones. Oysters were the natural buffer against that problem, but we
killed them off so thoroughly that they can't come back on their own.
Wild oysters are effectively gone.

Some scientists think oysters are going to be the first ocean species to be
driven extinct by climate change. They're a very delicate crop, and thrive at
very particular temperatures. The acidification of the oceans weakens their
shells. Disease spreads as the water temperatures rise. And when a hurricane storm surges and loosens up all the silt and dirt that's in our waterways
now, the oysters drown in mud. Irene was the biggest storm surge since
1938. It was a big deal, and three feet of mud came in, which was bad. But
the real bad news was that it loosened up the bottom here, so now smaller
storms are bringing in more mud and having an outsized impact.

Oysters are used to filtering 30 to 50 gallons of water a day. If they're
coated in mud, they just die. A clam can squish up and move. Same thing
with scallops. Oysters are stuck wherever they are. That's why, with the BP
spill in the Gulf, they did most of their testing on oysters. Oysters can't flee,
regardless of how they feel about the water conditions.

There's a debate in the scientific community. I don't want to stand here
and tell you oysters are gonna go away. There are hopeful people who believe in adaptation. The question is just the speed. Oysters showed up something like 300 million years before dinosaurs. Before any fish. They've done
well. The question is just how much and how fast they can change, and how
they deal with the pressure we're putting on them. We're helping to extend
their life through farming but we're having incredible die-offs on the West
Coast, where they're losing hundreds of millions of oysters. They think it's
because of the acidification that comes with rising temperatures.

So it's actually the twin evils of greenhouse gases: climate change and ocean acidification. They're very linked because the ocean soaks up a third of the carbon in the world and we've maxed it out as a carbon sink. It pulls out way more carbon than land-based plants like tropical forests. And all of that leads to water temperatures rising and a changed pH that affects the shells of crustaceans. They're finding all these other odd things as well, like that fish are getting much smaller, not just because of overfishing but because of the changing temperatures. I just read this thing where they got forty of the top oceanographers in the world and they said we're in the middle of one of the largest extinctions in the ocean ever. Like, the top three or something, and we're not at the beginning of it: we're in the middle of it. This is happening. So the news is bad.

25   So you can stop overfishing, you can create huge marine parks, and everything's gonna die anyway. My argument is that it's not about conservation any more, it's about development. It's not "How do we save the oceans?" but "How do the oceans save us?" Let's move beyond depletion—even beyond restoration—to a place where we're actually improving the environment and fixing all these other social problems from jobs to climate change. This is where I always get in fights with conservationists and environmentalists. I think we need an industrial policy to create local food, create fuel, pull nitrogen and carbon out of the system, and to do it by creating good jobs on the water. I mean, I am a deeply self-interested party, who may be prone to exaggeration and lying, but I think kelp farming and this sort of integrated aquaculture we're doing here really could be an answer.

I mean, the kelp alone! My seaweed pulls five times the amount of carbon as a tree out of the water. Because kelp grows so fucking fast and it doesn't take much area. My first mate Ron and I can create thousands and thousands and thousands of pounds of seaweed. And you could dot the coastline with these kinds of farms. With agriculture, what do we normally compete for? Land and fresh water. I don't use any of that.

I'm addicted to kelp. It's an ocean farmer's dream: fastest growing plant in the world, and it's a winter crop, which is invaluable for me. I'll plant next month, by March we'll have six to twelve feet—just stunning. It's our East Coast native sugar kelp and it can be used in cooking just like Japanese kombu. There are some slight differences, but not in terms of taste. It's got more protein than soybeans, more vitamin C than citrus fruits, more calcium than milk. There are all these other uses, too. I'm working with a biofuel company here in Connecticut. You take a one-acre area and you get 2,000 gallons of ethanol per year.

The process for turning kelp into fuel is much faster than land-based fuel—two or three times as fast to process it. They basically just liquefy it. We could use the high-quality stuff grown in clean water for food, and I could grow kelp in very polluted areas like Bridgeport Harbor, which is chock full of heavy metals, and use it for fertilizer, for fish food, and plenty of other things, too.

And we can scale up. I can't even believe them, but the numbers coming out of the scientific literature—you take 3 percent of the oceans and dedicate them to seaweed and you can actually feed the world. If you take an area half the size of Maine you can replace all the oil in the United States.

There's a counterargument to what I'm talking about that says this is about   30 financializing or exploiting the environment in the name of saving it. There's some truth to that, but I think we're past the point where we can pretend like sitting around and not touching anything will save us. Things are too far gone. I'm not some industrialist. I am deeply, deeply of this new generation of green fishermen, protecting the environment, both for life and livelihood. God, I sound mad, don't I? "Forty acres and a mule! Life and livelihood!"

But this isn't about altruism. It's actually about feeding and paying people—making this truly sustainable. Food activists have to start thinking about this: how to make a living, how to have pensions, how to move subsidies off the industrial and over to the small farms and make it a real job. Not just poor farmers or workers, but actually a working class of equal dignified professionals.

If you're actually modeling this out and can get a lot of people to do it, it will create jobs and food, and it will be good for the water.

It drives me nuts when I hear about people who want to go back to agrarian culture. They haven't thought it through. We can't walk away from this coast and come back in twenty years and expect it to be covered in oysters. That's not going to happen. As an oysterman, how can I address climate change? I can't go to Kentucky to stop coal plants. I can grow kelp. That's how I can help.

Regardless of what happens, it's a wonderful time to be alive. History's moving so fast and we're doomed and I'm Irish and the great thing about life is that it's short. This is how I want my hours spent, out here, doing this as long as I can. It's hard work. It's not profitable and it destroys your body. I crawl out of bed like a crab every morning. My back's gone, my shoulders are going, and most of the time my hands are so rough my wife makes me have sex like a lobster.

35   I hope we can turn the tide back a bit—create more jobs and better food along our coasts—but hope isn't my thing. Work is. And I'll keep working these waters until the storms and the banks shut me down. What I usually say is this: just as I remade myself a green fisherman, I'm going to be part of the first generation of green fishermen put out of work.

But I think the answer with oysters and shellfish is an adaptation strategy. Can we work hard now so another generation of fishermen, with new techniques and technologies, can earn a living out here? Long term, it doesn't look good. But you never know.

Analyze

1. Meehan takes an ethnographic approach to his subject. What does that mean? What are the implications and effects for you as a reader of this approach?

2. How does Meehan support his argument that the oyster population in New England is being depleted, and quickly? Is this support effective? Why or why not?

3. What are "food activists?" How do the sea farmers described by Meehan fit this category? What are their characteristics?

Explore

1. Broaden Meehan's heading, "What Was and Will Be," applying it to a larger inquiry about overfishing. What resources do you find? What are the implications of global fishing, for instance, for the American economy and its fishing industries?

2. According to Meehan, how is "this" no longer about conservation? What do you think it *is* about? In your view, are Meehan's conclusions realistic? Why or why not? Explain.

3. Meehan's article grapples with larger questions about conservation and food sustainability. But overfishing isn't the only threat to ecologies of food. Explore another issue related to the topic of food sustainability and create a presentation for your class that presents an argument and examples in a fashion similar to Meehan.

Joel Salatin
"Sowing Dissent"
(Interview with Tracy Frisch)

A controversial and often polarizing American farmer-turned-activist, Salatin describes himself as a "Christian, libertarian, environmentalist, capitalist, lunatic farmer." Be that as it may, Salatin is (in almost contradictory fashion) a respected voice in the crusade against factory farming and in favor of holistic and chemical-free ways of raising livestock. In this interview, which first appeared in *The Sun* magazine, Joel Salatin explores with interviewer Tracy Frisch his philosophy behind and operation of Polyface Farm in Virginia.

 How is this interview a form of dissent?

Thanks to his appearances in documentaries like *Food, Inc.* and Michael Pollan's 2006 best-selling book about our food choices, *The Omnivore's Dilemma*, Joel Salatin may be one of the most well-known farmers in the United States today. Yet his successful, innovative, dirt-under-the-fingernails agricultural practices are far from the norm in this country. A prolific author and charismatic speaker, Salatin has been preaching his unique brand of agrarian gospel for more than two decades, and his scathing criticism of factory farming ruffles more than a few feathers. Describing himself as a "Christian, libertarian, environmentalist, capitalist, lunatic farmer," he calls for revolutionary change in how we produce and distribute food, how we relate to nature, and, in some regards, how we organize society. He even questions our current understanding of what constitutes food.

Born in the U.S. in 1957, Salatin moved to Venezuela with his family when he was six weeks old. He is a third-generation farmer; his grandfather was an early adherent of J. I. Rodale, the founder of the modern organic-farming movement in the U.S. In 1961, after losing their farm in Venezuela, Salatin's parents moved to the U.S. and acquired a 550-acre tract of run-down land in the Shenandoah Valley of Virginia. To heal the severely eroded land, his father planted trees. The family raised beef cattle, and his parents also worked away from the farm, his father as an accountant and his mother as a high-school physical-education teacher.

While he was still in high school, Salatin started selling rabbits, chickens, eggs, and butter from the farm. After graduating from Bob Jones University, where he majored in English, he worked at the local newspaper as a feature writer. At the age of twenty-five he returned to farming full time on the family property, which he later named Polyface Farm.

Salatin's innovative practices include frequently moving his animals from one pasture to another (rather than feeding them in a central location) and selling his farm products directly to consumers and restaurants. He was offering pastured poultry and grass-fed beef long before these concepts gained popularity in the marketplace. His example continues to catch the attention of new and struggling farmers seeking something more promising than high-tech methods that deplete their land's fertility, demand high costs, and offer diminishing financial returns.

5   Polyface Farm also trains apprentices in eco-farming methods. Through its farm store and metropolitan buying clubs, it supplies five thousand families, and it delivers its products to fifty restaurants and ten retail outlets. On principle the farm limits sales to a radius of 250 miles. In recent years it has made $1 million in annual gross sales.

Salatin began self-publishing his books in 1993. His early works—including *Pastured Poultry Profits* and *You Can Farm*—serve as how-to manuals for developing a successful ecological farming business. Over time Salatin has directed his writing to a more general audience in order to foster awareness about the threats to—and the benefits of—healthy, natural food, publishing such books as *Everything I Want to Do Is Illegal* and *The Sheer Ecstasy of Being a Lunatic Farmer*. His latest volume, *Folks, This Ain't Normal: A Farmer's Advice for Happier Hens, Healthier People, and a Better World*, was released last October by the Hachette Book Group and is the first of his books that Salatin did not publish himself.

For this interview Salatin and I sat at the dining-room table in the house where he grew up. Earlier that day I had taken part in one of his "Lunatic Farmer" tours, held several times a month during the growing season. Among the seventy-five participants, a few had driven from as far away as Ohio and Connecticut to see their mentor's farm and methods with their own eyes.

FRISCH: What makes working on your farm so appealing?

SALATIN: We raise fifty beef cattle, three hundred hogs, fifteen thousand broiler chickens, one thousand turkeys, and one thousand rabbits on our farm, and I get to make all these animals happy every day. There's also a real satisfaction in seeing the land heal. Every year it gets better. And I feel a tremendous joy in working with young people to help them become successful farmers, to give them a springboard from which they can launch their own land-healing enterprise.

We're not just interested in healing the land. Producing good food 10 makes healthy, happy customers too. It's wonderful when a patron tells us, "I had this physical problem, and I changed what I eat, and now I'm not allergic to chicken anymore." Or they have more energy, or their cholesterol is down. We feel responsible for the health of our customers, and we don't take that lightly. As farmers we should be in the healing business: healing our soil, healing our water, and healing our patrons—not growing food that is nutrient deficient or pathogenic.

Have you ever tried to make monosodium glutamate? Have you ever tried to make high-fructose corn syrup? Food that you can't pronounce or make in your kitchen is like a foreign invader to the community of three trillion microbes inside your body that are going to digest it. When I talk about healing, I'm referring to this entire spectrum, from our intestinal bacteria to the whole farm.

FRISCH: In the context of agricultural production, aesthetics is rarely, if ever, mentioned. In fact, there's a saying that the stink of manure "smells like money." In contrast, you write in *The Sheer Ecstasy of Being a Lunatic Farmer* that if it smells bad or is not beautiful, it is not good farming.

SALATIN: A farm should be aesthetically, aromatically, and sensuously appealing. It should be a place that is attractive, not repugnant, to the senses. This is food production. A farm shouldn't be producing ugly things. It should be producing beautiful things. We're going to eat them.

One of the surest ways to know if a wound is infected is if it is unsightly and smells bad. When it starts to heal, it gets a pretty sheen and doesn't smell anymore. Farms that are not beautiful and that stink are like big wounds on the landscape.

Farms have become so repugnant that they have been relegated to the 15 edges of society. And anytime you isolate an economic sector to society's periphery, that sector will start taking economic, societal, and ecological shortcuts, because no one is there to see what comes in or goes out the back door. When the butcher, baker, and candlestick maker are working in the village, the inherent transparency facilitates accountability, which is the essence of integrity. That comes from embeddedness in the community.

FRISCH: What do we teach our children when we call soil "dirty"?

SALATIN: We're teaching them to disconnect their ecological umbilical cord. In our culture today a profound number of people don't have a link to the land. We live in a fantasy world.

That's the reason I advocate exposing children to home gardening. In the world of video games if you wreck your car, the game gives you a new car. But if you're gardening and your tomato wilts, that's final. It's gone. If your chicken dies because you didn't take care of it, it's truly dead. This fantasy culture we are creating is incredibly dangerous: people think we can extricate ourselves from our ecological niche.

FRISCH: I suspect that you find a lot of things to emulate and celebrate about the farms and agrarian culture of bygone days.

20   SALATIN: Farms used to be diversified, symbiotic operations. They were seen as the centerpiece of the economy. So many of the things that have been moved off the farm—baking, weaving, leather tanning, shoemaking—used to be embedded in farm life. All of these home industries were done near the resource. The processing of the farm products, which added to their value, was seen as an integral part of work on the farm, not a separate business.

Today we view the farm as a production unit, responsible only for sending raw materials across the globe for processing, often to be disseminated back to within a few miles of the farm. I call it "economic apartheid." It's colonialism. As the processing has moved off the farms, the farms have become the new colonies.

FRISCH: People work hard on Polyface Farm. You're out tending animals before dawn. This type of farming is more physically demanding than mainstream agriculture with huge equipment, where people are simply pushing buttons on machinery or even sitting in an office.

SALATIN: If land stewardship is to be done well, it's going to take more loving stewards on the land. It can't be done well when we have driverless tractors run by GPs. Where's the appreciation of the landscape in that?

The ultimate outsourcing is the outsourcing of decision making. Right now the average piece of farmland is being governed by people who will never set foot on it or see the ramifications of their decisions. They don't ever have to see it, smell it, or live with it.

If you raise chickens for Tyson Foods, you're consulted by their field man,   25
who is credentialed and has learned all there is to know about chickens in the
laboratory. The chickens you're raising are *his* chickens. You, as the farmer, get
the privilege of having the mortgage and removing the dead chickens. This
greatly affects the way you are going to farm—for instance, by encouraging you
to use genetically modified grains that are pushed by subsidy programs.

The Food Safety Modernization Act, signed into law by President
Obama last year, uses the phrase "science-based" eleven times as a regulatory term to ascertain whether a farm is using proper procedures. But
whose science is the government referring to? The science of the compost
pile, of the earthworm, of Aunt Matilda's pickles? Or the science of genetic
engineering and irradiation?

FRISCH: So you distrust the regulating agencies' view of "sound science"?

SALATIN: Yes. Take the example of outdoor poultry processing, which is
currently illegal. The government says that if you don't have an enclosed
slaughterhouse, then the air is unsanitary. That's the official science. The
official protocol to sanitize the chicken is to put it through a chlorine-
bleach bath and expose it to UV light before taking it to market. These
government regulators live in a world of gloomy, confined processing facilities that are running 24/7 year-round.

We have an open-air facility at Polyface. Our farm runs seasonally, we
don't process every day, and our chickens are raised in a field with fresh air and
sunshine. But the official protocols say you have to have chlorine and an enclosed building to have clean chickens. So we had a culture taken from our
chickens and one taken from chickens from the supermarket that had been
through the chlorine baths, and we had them analyzed in a neutral lab off-site.
The chickens from the supermarket averaged 3,600 colony-forming units of
bacteria per milliliter. The chickens from our farm averaged 133 units.

When the head of the Virginia meat-and-poultry inspection program   30
and his federal superior sat in my living room, trying to shut down our
farm, I showed them that report. Wouldn't you think they'd turn cart-
wheels and say, "Here's chicken that is more than twenty-five times
cleaner than chicken produced by the usual methods!" and consider
changing their protocol? Instead they asked how many bathrooms we
have, how many light bulbs in the ceiling, how many changing lockers for
employees.

So are they after clean chicken or not? If we can gut a chicken in the kitchen sink and have it meet the regulators' empirical standard, who cares where it was done? And yet the government isn't willing even to study outdoor poultry processing, because it's so far outside the paradigm. It's similar to when they closed the goat-milk operation of a friend of mine. If they had pulled a sample from a bucket of his goats' milk and it was cleaner than what's in a grade-A bulk tank, it wouldn't have mattered to them, because their scientific protocol requires that the sample be pulled from an enclosed environment. The poor farmer with only two goats is shut down because he can't afford a ten-thousand-dollar bulk tank.

I have met a lot of these bureaucrats, and they absolutely believe that if farmers like me were turned loose on the marketplace, the hospitals would soon overflow with sick people. Their motivation is sincere and their intentions noble, but they are misguided and ignorant about the true antidotes to nutrient deficiency and food pathogenicity.

FRISCH: The philosopher and animal-rights advocate Peter Singer believes that requiring farmers to send animals to licensed slaughterhouses makes it more difficult to have a humane farm. What are your thoughts on this?

SALATIN: This is one time when Peter Singer and I are in complete agreement. Farms like mine are required to take an animal conceived, birthed, and reared on our property and then, on its last day of life, commit the ignominy of putting it on a trailer and hauling it up the road to a place where it is commingled with unfamiliar animals and slaughtered by people who never cared for it. That's outrageous. In fact, I would go a step further and say that nobody should be compelled to slaughter animals every day of his or her life. Even the priestly Levites of the Bible drew straws to rotate the sacrificial responsibilities in the Temple. If we integrate the slaughtering with other farm work, nobody has to do it every day, and the animals never have to leave their familiar surroundings. It changes the emotional ramifications of the activity.

35   But our culture never asks what makes pigs happy. It looks upon them as if they were merely piles of protoplasmic structure to be manipulated. A culture that views life in that fashion will view its citizens and other cultures the same way.

FRISCH: You've written that if the Founding Fathers could have seen into the future, food sovereignty would have been guaranteed in the Constitution. What makes this a priority issue for you?

SALATIN: It comes down to autonomous personhood. If I don't have the freedom to feed my three-trillion-member internal community of microbes in the manner I choose, then the infringement of other rights, such as freedom of the press and freedom of religion, can't be far behind.

It is important that small farmers be able to reach people who want to practice personal autonomy, because the regulatory climate is marginalizing, demonizing, and criminalizing much of this heritage-based, indigenous type of food production.

FRISCH: I've been listening to news of food-borne-illness outbreaks during the last several months: cantaloupe in Colorado, chopped romaine lettuce in California, ground beef in multiple states. This used to be a concern only when traveling to a third-world country. Why is there so much food contamination in the U.S.?

SALATIN: The problem is that scientists are confusing sterility with safety. Massachusetts Institute of Technology recently released a video that says we're only 15 percent human. We're 85 percent nonhuman. When you measure our bacteria, our cells, the cloud of stuff we have around us, like the *Peanuts* character Pigpen, we live in a bacterial–fungal bath. Sterility has its place—in surgery, for example—but life is not sterile. What we need to do is create circumstances where the good bugs beat out the bad bugs. 40

In the cantaloupe, the romaine lettuce, and the ground beef we have bypassed the immunities that are supposed to act as a barrier that's too high for the pathogens to jump over. Those hurdles are everything from biologically active soil to farm diversity and crop rotation, where you don't grow the same crop in the same field every year.

Certainly the *E. coli* outbreak in lettuce in California in 2010 was the result of dust-borne bacteria carried on the wind from a large, high-density cattle feedlot, where *E. coli* can thrive. In fact, there are feedlots in which the livestock are drugged so heavily that their manure isn't compostable. It's too sterile.

If I wanted to build a farm full of pathogens, here's what I'd do: I'd diminish the diversity and rear only one kind of animal, so as not to confuse the pathogens. I'd crowd the animals close together, so the pathogens would have easy access to hosts. Sunshine is the number-one sanitizer in nature, so I would lock the animals indoors. I'd make sure they didn't get any exercise, so they would have poor muscle structure. I'd make sure the animals breathed in a fecal particulate that would make lesions in their respiratory membranes, bypass their immunological barriers, and go straight into their bloodstream to cause infections. I'd routinely give them drugs to suppress their natural immune systems. And I'd feed them an extremely nutrient-deficient diet of chemically fertilized feedstuffs.

What have I just described? Science-based American farming!

Joel Arthur Barker's book *Paradigms* popularized the word *paradigm*. One of his principles is that every paradigm at its apparent point of perfection is on the verge of collapse. Many think our culture is approaching the zenith of food production through genetic modification, chemical fertilization, and factory farming, when these things are actually the beginning of the collapse.

It took five hundred years for metallurgy and socio-political events to create the ultimate warrior, a knight in a suit of armor, mounted on a horse. This was the perfect impregnable war machine. Within twenty years it was obsolete due to the invention of gunpowder, which was the ultimate democratization of power.

45   Nature tends to move toward the democratization of power when there is too much domination from the top. Right now there is three times as much centralization in the U.S. food industry as there was in 1906, before the Food Safety and Inspection Service was established. Seven outfits controlled 60 percent of the nation's beef in 1906; today three companies control 80 percent. That's a significantly greater concentration of power.

But nature bats last. Nature begins looking for the chinks in that armor. Nature acts like gunpowder, if you will, to democratize the power structure.

That's exactly what I think is happening in our food system, and it's borne out by the health problems we're seeing on a massive scale, including our epidemics of obesity and type 2 diabetes. The U.S. leads the world in per capita rates of the five most prevalent chronic diseases: cancer, heart disease, diabetes, high blood pressure, and lung conditions like asthma.

FRISCH: Let's talk about the animals on the farm. In your article "Let the Animals Do the Work," you put forth the idea that farm animals are naturally disposed to particular activities that can contribute to a farm's ecology.

SALATIN: Farmers are choreographing a biological ballet of plants and animals. That's a profoundly different way of looking at a farm than the industrial approach, which emphasizes force and dominance and a mechanistic framework. On my farm we ask, "What is the essence of the pig? What is the 'chickenness' of the chicken?" The only question our culture asks is how we can grow it faster, bigger, cheaper. That isn't noble. That isn't sacred. And it certainly isn't healing.

We want to create a habitat that allows the animal to fully express its 50 distinctiveness. If we can figure out a way to use that plow that is the end of a pig's head to our benefit, the pig is happier, and we get more work done.

We use pigs to make our compost. We sprinkle corn into layers of hay, straw, and manure in the winter. In the spring the pigs seek out the fermented corn, and in so doing they stir up the mixture and turn it into fluffy compost. No machine or petroleum is involved. We don't even have to steer the pigs. And they don't need spare parts or an oil change. It's like buying machinery that appreciates in value.

When we get our work done with things that don't rust, break down, or depreciate, then we don't have to work in large volumes to cover all the infrastructure costs. If you are going to use a twenty-thousand-dollar compost turner and employ an operator to run it, you'd better be making a lot of compost to pay for the machine and the operator. But if you are doing it with a pig that runs on corn, that doesn't require an operator, and that you can sell for more than you bought it for, you can be just as profitable per cubic yard of compost with two cubic yards as with five thousand cubic yards.

By integrating the animals into the work of the farm, we save money on operating costs, and the animals become co-laborers and team players, rather than just bacon or hamburgers. Their lives become part of our dance.

FRISCH: How do you answer critics who might say, "So you use pigs for work, and then you kill them for food. How is that respecting the animal?"

SALATIN: Everything is eating and being eaten. If you don't believe me, go 55 lie naked in your flower bed for three days and see what gets eaten. All life springs from the sacrifice of something living. The death–decay–life cycle is the most fundamental and important ecological principle in the world. We give life to others as we sacrifice ourselves.

With this in mind, the practical question is "How do we sanctify the animal's death?" By honoring the "pigness" of the pig and offering it meaningful work as a co-laborer and healer of the land, we respect the life that nurtures us and make its death more sacred.

FRISCH: People for the Ethical Treatment of Animals [PETA] is offering a million-dollar prize for the commercialization of chicken meat produced in a lab from animal stem cells.

SALATIN: PETA's problem is that they are trying to get life without sacrifice. We revere life *because* it requires sacrifice. To break—or even aspire to break—the cycle of life and death, decomposition and regeneration, has profound emotional and spiritual ramifications.

FRISCH: But humans don't need to eat meat to survive, so is it a necessary sacrifice? Some might say the animal gives up its life simply for our pleasure. Wouldn't *not* eating meat be a minor sacrifice on our part, as opposed to the animal's major sacrifice: its life?

SALATIN: Why think animals are more special than carrots? Just because a life-form appears more closely related to humans doesn't mean it's more important than one that doesn't, such as a bacterium. That said, animals do fulfill important functions. They are the only way nature has to defy the gravitational pull of fertility. Due to downward movement valleys gradually become more fertile while slopes and hilltops become infertile. But herbivores eat the plants in the valleys and defecate on the slopes and hilltops, where they're safer from predation.

Animals, especially herbivores—such as goats, sheep, cows, yaks, and water buffaloes—convert soil-building perennials into nutrient-dense foods. Were we to eliminate farm animals, we would run out of soil due to the inefficient carbon cycle of a plant-only tillage-based system. Omnivores—poultry and pigs—recycle scrapped and spoiled produce into food for humans. These days our culture thinks it's environmentally healthy to put kitchen scraps into a bin to be sent to a composting facility via diesel truck, to be bagged and sold as compost. Historically humans, plants, and animals could not be segregated like this; they were intricately integrated.

The notion that we could have a functional planet if people did not eat animals indicates a profound ignorance of ecology. Animals would soon overpopulate the earth. Oh, you say predators would increase? I'm sure people would love to live next to large predators. Plant destruction would lead to population collapse. Erosion and soil destruction would follow. Even urban areas now have deer-hunting seasons, because if the deer population isn't controlled, they'll destroy all the vegetation. With little vegetation, temperatures increase, the rain stops, and the earth is destroyed.

One of the basic mandates of humans is to stimulate the creation of more healthy soil, plant, and animal matter than would otherwise occur in a static state. Today we have marvelous technologies like electric fencing, plastic piping, microchip energizers, and shade cloth that allow humans to do this better than ever before. The productivity of well-managed livestock systems is far higher than static wild systems. Unfortunately most farms are not operating this way, but that is an indictment against humans, not animals.

I would certainly hope that anyone placing animals on such a high pedestal would not spend more on his or her dog or cat than on making sure hungry children in Africa got fed. This is a litmus test of priorities. Americans spend more on vet care for their dogs and cats than the entire continent of Africa spends on healthcare. As a culture we have Bambified ourselves into foolishness, and it's reflected in our values and our day-to-day activities.

Eating grass-fed beef or food-scrap-fed chicken is actually one of the most healing things you can do for the planet. This is not ultimately about pleasure; it is about fulfilling our role in nature. Humans are arguably the most important species on the planet; therefore, we must be thoughtful about how we fill our niche.

FRISCH: You don't rely solely on human and animal power at Polyface. What technological innovations allow your farm to perform better in terms of productivity, labor requirements, and environmental impact?

SALATIN: I cannot overstate the importance of electric fencing. It enables us to move huge numbers of animals from one part of the property to another, which duplicates the wild system of nature. With electrified netting we can run chickens onto a different pasture every day. We can encircle three to five acres of forest on which to run hogs. This is no Iowa hog mudhole.

In addition to the pigs, we also have amazing machinery that allows us to efficiently turn manure and plant matter into compost. We use the animals as much as possible at Polyface, but pigs don't haul fertilizer into the field. Manure spreaders that draw power from the tractor's engine were the big breakthrough. Before that kind of machinery, manure was spread by farmhands who had to manually load it with a primitive pitchfork onto a cart pulled by mules and then shovel it and fling it on the ground. It makes me tired just thinking about it. So it wasn't frequently done, and soil fertility decreased.

In the U.S. we should have been using petroleum and modern technology to build healthy soil. Instead petroleum is put into chemical fertilizer, which further deteriorates the soil. We have squandered our mother lode of fossil fuels. Americans haul off 70 percent of all the urban compostable waste and dump it into landfills. It's unconscionable.

70   This is the number-one thing that has to change in modern agriculture. We cannot afford to continue floating our food on oil. Farmers need to grow the carbon and fertilizer on-site, not bring it in from elsewhere. They need to move toward compost generation with light carbon footprints and away from factory-farming methods with heavy footprints.

FRISCH: How does your farm's energy use compare to that of a conventional farm?

SALATIN: We did an audit here two years ago, when fuel prices spiked, because we'd read that 50 percent of the average farm's expenses is energy. The audit concluded that energy was only 5 percent of our expenses. That includes the cost of delivering our products to our customers, an expense that the average farm doesn't have. The price of diesel fuel could go as high as almost ten dollars a gallon, and our farm would still be able to absorb the cost, because our energy expenses are currently so low. I should note that, for the purpose of that audit, we did not include the energy use associated with the feed we buy for the pigs and poultry.

Analyze

1. This contribution to *Food: A Reader for Writers* is an interview rather than an article or essay. How is reading an interview and its form different from reading an essay or article?
2. Given the interview format, how does Salatin's argument develop? What is Salatin's argument?
3. What does Salatin mean by "land stewardship?"

Explore

1. Salatin calls our food processing and production system a form of "economic apartheid." He goes on to say, "It's colonialism. As the processing has moved off the farm, the farms have become the new colonies." What does Salatin mean? Discuss the ways in which Salatin explains these concepts.
2. Salatin is the leading voice for "radical progressive farmers." What parts of Salatin's argument represented in the interview might seem especially radical? Be sure to define your sense of what "radical" means as you explore the possibilities.

3. "Farmers are choreographing a biological ballet of plants and animals. That's a profoundly different way of looking at a farm . . . than the industrial approach." Bringing in additional research that you will have discovered, examine the ways in which Salatin's way of farming is different from what is now considered the norm.

Todd Kliman
"The Meaning of Local"

Todd Kliman is the dining editor of *The Washingtonian*, and he is a James Beard award–winning food critic and online presence. In addition to his noted work as a critic, Kliman taught for ten years, at both American University and Howard University in Washington, DC. In 2005, he won a James Beard award for the Best Newspaper Column on food. His writing has appeared in *The New Yorker, The Washington Post, Harper's,* and *National Geographic Traveler.* At Howard University, Kliman was the editorial advisor to Chris Rock's humor magazine, *The Illtop Journal,* fashioned after the *Harvard Lampoon.* As you might suspect, Kliman's essay explores the value of "eating locally."

How does this article conceptualize the notion of "local eating?"

Several years ago, I was at dinner with a friend, a fellow food lover, a man for whom dining out is preferable to virtually every other form of human interaction. The meal was no joy for either of us. It was mediocre and expensive, and I said so with a sigh when the check came.

"It was honest," my friend said, leaping to defend what had seemed to me indefensible.

The chef was known for sourcing locally and from small farmers. He had cultivated these purveyors, had worked with them to come up with products he wanted, and he aimed to present them as cleanly as possible, without engaging in kitchen tricks that might mask the purity of his raw materials. He was honest—in other words, he didn't go in for cheap, processed products and try to pass them off on the dining public. He valued the small farmers who worked so hard to put out high-quality goods. He did things "the right way."

My friend was therefore willing to extend to the chef the benefit of the doubt.

5   Me, I was peeved that he had squandered ingredients that a chef at a family-run Ethiopian or Vietnamese restaurant, tasked with turning frozen poultry and veggies into tasty dishes, would have regarded as a special treat. Peeved that, not for the first time, a chef seemed to have labored under the notion that credit was given for good intentions.

I've since had countless meals like this and countless conversations with true believers who worry that I'm not grasping the urgency of their message.

In the last 30 years, "local" has evolved from an ideology to a movement to something that looks suspiciously like an ism: more important than any single chef or restaurant—more important, too, than any other philosophy or ideology. It's so ingrained in the world of food today that it's all but impossible to talk meaningfully about food without talking about "local."

And yet what do we talk about when we talk about "local"?

Not nearly enough, it turns out.

A Brief History of Local

10   In 1971, Alice Waters opened Chez Panisse, the restaurant that would forever alter the direction of food in America. From her kitchen in Berkeley, California, she sought the freshest possible ingredients, often from within a few miles of the restaurant.

Her focus on sourcing locally was, quite literally, a radical statement at a time when factory farming, agribusiness, and chain restaurants had recently cemented their dominance of the food supply. In the world of fine dining, Waters's shunning of luxury ingredients flown in from Europe, white tablecloths, bowing waiters, and snooty maître d's had the same bracing effect that punk rock, bubbling up in the culture at that time, had on popular music.

What Waters was to the West Coast, Nora Pouillon was to the East. In 1979, Pouillon opened Restaurant Nora, on a quiet, leafy block north of DC's Dupont Circle. Twenty years later, it would become the first certified organic restaurant in the country.

The designation requires strict adherence: Ninety-five percent of all products in the kitchen must be organic. Restaurant Nora has been eclipsed in the last decade or so by a slew of places spreading her message with greater urgency and excitement, but it's impossible to deny Pouillon's influence. Ann Cashion, who went on to create the model for the small locally minded bistro at Cashion's Eat Place and later at the original Johnny's Half Shell, got her start under Pouillon, and Ann Yonkers, now codirector of the FreshFarm Markets, worked for her as a recipe tester and cookbook editor.

Pouillon says her motivation was simply to "find a more natural way to do things." As a young and idealistic chef, she was troubled to learn that farmers could be allowed to "contaminate the soil and jeopardize families," so she began driving to farms in Virginia, Maryland, and Pennsylvania, quizzing farmers about their practices.

Jean-Louis Palladin was on a similar quest at the Watergate, determined to unearth the products unique not only to America but also to his chosen patch of the world. Palladin was concerned mainly with distinctiveness, not purity, but he and Pouillon frequently found themselves in the same company.

Pouillon eventually settled on a group of purveyors who were as committed and passionate as she was. She also began organizing bus tours, taking chefs to Pennsylvania to introduce them to the farmers important to her. From these trips emerged Tuscarora Organic Growers, a collective of Pennsylvania farmers that many area restaurants today turn to for their meats and produce.

It wasn't enough, Waters and Pouillon and others argued, for food to taste good. It had to be good. A chef might be armed with a battery of techniques to transform his or her raw materials, but if those materials weren't superlative to begin with, Waters wasn't interested. Shopping counted as much as cooking.

It Depends What Your Definition of "Contiguous" Is

Of the three dozen food-world personalities I interviewed for this article, none could point to an agreed-upon definition of local.

From as far north as Pennsylvania to as far south as Virginia was as close to a consensus as I could find. One chef defined local as his ability to "reasonably" drive to and from a farm in a day, a definition that seemed to provide wiggle room for four or even five hours. Another offered the drive-in-a-day yardstick, without the modifier "reasonably," and I imagined him gunning it deep into the woods of North Carolina for some fresh-killed quail, then turning around and speeding up I-95 in hopes of making it back to his kitchen before his midnight deadline.

20   Whole Foods defines local differently for each region of the country. DC belongs to the Mid-Atlantic, which includes New Jersey, Ohio, Kentucky, Maryland, Virginia, and Pennsylvania. Until recently, if you shopped at a Whole Foods in this area, where your meat and produce came from was a matter of "contiguity"—anywhere in a neighboring state was considered local.

That meant, for example, that tomatoes from North Carolina were considered local in Arlington stores—because North Carolina and Virginia share a border—while those that traveled a shorter distance from New Jersey were not.

This summer, Whole Foods is changing to a new definition, under which foods grown within about 100 miles or in the same state as the store will be considered local.

But if there's no agreed-upon definition of what local is, that means it can be anything at all, and it's simply how a chef or restaurant or farmer or business chooses to define it. It means the term is essentially meaningless, a point Emily Sprissler drove home rather decisively when I rang her up at Mayfair & Pine, a British gastropub in DC's Glover Park that has since closed.

"America," Sprissler declared, "is my local."

25   Was she saying local is a limitation?

"I don't find it limiting. I just don't pay attention to it."

A comparison between France and America followed, along with a discussion of economies of scale. "Look, France is the size of Texas," she said. "It's easy to get anything you want there, and quickly, and it's all great. If I'm only going to get products within a hundred miles or whatever, [the definition] is limiting."

Here Sprissler stopped herself, perhaps realizing she'd come dangerously close to branding herself a heretic in the church of local. She began again, choosing her words more carefully: "I'm trying as hard as I can, from toilet paper to tenderloin, to put American products in my restaurant. I'm giving my money to another American so that they can keep their job and put food on their table. I do a miso chicken—there's a company in Massachusetts that makes its own miso, and it's amazing. There's a lot of amazing products out there, and I don't care if they're from Michigan or Wyoming."

She was proud. Proud and defiant and convinced of the rightness of her approach. And she ought to be, both because it was hers and because it seemed a chance to expose her diners to the best artisanally made products from around the country.

But what did it say that she seemed so determined to align herself with   30
the local movement, even as she rejected its core tenets?

Inherently Better?

Let's look at the foundations of the local movement—the arguments that are most often advanced to make the case not merely for its worth but for its necessity:

Local reduces our "carbon footprint."

The phrase is eco-shorthand for the fuel expenditures an ingredient generates before it lands on the table. It's less simple than it sounds, a romantic notion only sometimes supported by the data.

Eggs that have been trucked in from 50 miles away or less are no great environmental stressor, but when the definition of local is as loose as it is, 50 miles is seldom to be counted on.

And not all methods of delivery are equal. One restaurateur told me he's   35
constantly wrestling with questions such as "Is a large 18-wheeler coming from 80 miles away better than 50 pickup trucks bringing the same ingredients from 50 miles away?"

I told him that sounded like an SAT question.

Right, he said. And with no correct answer.

Local is good for the local economy.

This would appear to be true. As it would be true for giving your money to any small, independently owned business in your neighborhood.

The problem is the notion that this money is a driver of the local econ-   40
omy. You're supporting a person who presumably spends that money locally. But of course, how many of us do? We live in a global, interconnected world where Amazon and others have displaced the neighborhood store, making shopping cheaper, faster, and more efficient.

One thing we can be sure of is that supporting a local producer helps keep that producer in business, and that is indeed a very good thing.

Local equals changing the system.

Local and organic foods currently make up 3 percent of food consumption in America, so it's highly unlikely that those of us who contribute to this small percentage with our purchases are, as political pundits like to say, moving the needle.

You may feel good about your personal actions in a large and indifferent universe. You may salve your conscience in avoiding companies that you consider to be adding to the growing social ills that beset us as a nation. But this isn't the same as altering the status quo.

45   Local is fresher and better.

Local is not inherently fresher, nor is it inherently better. And it isn't even always the case that when it's fresher, it's better.

I love Rappahannock oysters, and if a restaurant can truck them up from Virginia's Northern Neck just hours after dredging them from the water, I consider that a treat. But I prefer British Columbia oysters, which, though presumably not as fresh—the air time alone is double that of a trip from the Northern Neck—are richer, sweeter, firmer, and more delicate.

Now, local potatoes? Fantastic. They taste like an altogether different species from the trucked-in variety most of us grew up with. Local corn? Ditto. Local tomatoes? Sometimes. I haven't had many local tomatoes that compare to the juicy sweetness of a Jersey beefsteak. Local chickens? From a free-range, hormone-free source like Polyface, absolutely (and if it's a special occasion and I'm not inclined to linger over the pinch of forking over $20 for a roaster, all the more so). From a giant factory farm on the equally local Delmarva Peninsula? Not if I can help it. Local cheese? Rarely.

We ought to be talking about "perishability," says Eric Ziebold, the chef at CityZen, a gastronome's paradise in DC's Mandarin Oriental hotel.

50   For every piece of produce, Ziebold says, there's a "window" of freshness. The window for a ripened peach, for instance, is within the first six hours after being picked. Here he waxes poetic, describing that first bite after pulling one straight from a tree—the texture exquisitely poised between soft and firm, a sweetness that's almost floral, the juice exploding in your mouth and running down your arm. Over the next six hours, the peach begins to degrade. For his purposes, Ziebold says, a peach delivered to the restaurant within 18 hours of being picked is still usable—it might work in a purée or a sauce—though it will have already lost its purity. After 24 hours, it's "pretty much a different piece of fruit entirely."

Ziebold is perhaps pickier than most farmers-market shoppers, and initially I'm tempted to dismiss his words as the obsessive talk of a man who's fanatical about purity and quality. But it occurs to me that that mania to experience a piece of fruit at its ripe and beautiful peak is the reason so many food-loving urbanites flock to farmers markets in season—indeed, that promise is woven deep within the "local" pitch. Better, fresher. If you drop big money on a peach, isn't it fair to expect that the peach—which presumably hasn't had to be trucked great distances and has been harvested not by a mass-production outfit but by the more attentive and loving hands of the small farmer—would be exceptional?

And yet how many farmers-market peaches have you tasted in this area that were worthy of that adjective? I've had many good ones, but I can't remember the last time I had the ecstatic encounter Ziebold describes.

There's a good explanation for that, he says: "If you're a farmer selling in DC, you don't necessarily want to sell a peach that's going to get used that instant. They know that you're going to go back to the office, and they want to give you a little better window. So it's not a tree-ripened peach you're getting."

Closer to the source, he says, it's likely to be a different story: "If you visit that farm and pick up a peach and you don't use it in six hours, it's crap. But if you do use it in six hours, it's the best peach you've eaten in your life."

It never occurred to me that the quality of produce at the urban farmers   55
market isn't the same as the quality of produce at a rural farmers market.

That's one lesson. The other, deeper lesson involves stretching Ziebold's point to its logical conclusion. If perishability is paramount, if tasting things at their freshest is what matters most, then visiting a farmers market isn't the only way to ensure that outcome. In some instances, it might not even be the best way.

"I could get something FedExed that's potentially fresher than a farmers market," Ziebold says.

So can we all. The Internet has opened up sourcing possibilities previously available only to insiders—oysters from Brittany, salmon from Alaska, caviar from Russia.

Of course, the carbon footprint is likely to be considerably higher. More to the point: The romance is clearly missing.

The Literal Fruit of Our Privilege

And romance is not nothing. It's very definitely a something. Local   60
couldn't exist without it.

The wish to connect local food to something larger, to fetishize it as an object of desire, underpins the farmers-market experience and enables its supporters to justify dropping 80 bucks on a single bag of groceries.

Listen to Robb Duncan, who owns Dolcezza—the excellent gelato shops in Georgetown, Dupont Circle, Fairfax, and Bethesda—explain the appeal of going to the farmers market: "You eat this food and it's delicious, and it makes you feel happy to meet this farmer named Zachariah, and he doesn't put any pesticides in his produce, and you walk around as part of this beautiful, beautiful community of people."

This is the farmers market as embodiment of a surviving hippie aesthetic, and for many it's a powerful inducement to spend, whether they came of age in the '60s or, like Duncan, merely wish they did.

There's also the market experience as ratifier of status, in which the notion of simplifying our lives is held out to the busy, scattered urbanite as a glimpse of a new good life and a $4 tomato becomes the literal fruit of our privilege.

65   I ask Ann Yonkers—who, with Bernadine Prince, has run the area's FreshFarm Markets since 1997—what, beyond the makings of a meal, she thinks her customers come to the markets to buy.

Yonkers is as committed to the cause as anyone in Washington. When FreshFarm began in 1997, there were only about four farmers markets in the area; today there are ten FreshFarms alone. The nonprofit is among the finest purveyors of its kind in the country, with goods coming from 118 farmers and producers.

Yonkers is justifiably proud of this growth and speaks with the tones of an evangelist who believes she has found a path to, if not enlightenment, then happiness. Again and again I'm struck, as we speak, by the way she invests a material good—a cheese, a leg of lamb, a squash—with the aura of the spiritual.

Her customers, she says, aren't just dropping their disposable income on what some might see as luxury items; they're "participating in change." In other words, shopping at a farmers market isn't an upper-middle-class indulgence—or not just. It's also a political act.

70   I ask if she might share with me some of the ways people can participate in change.

"You can participate in change just by what you eat and buy and who you give your money to," she says. "People come to our markets and they feel empowered."

There's also the matter, she says, of "change for yourself."

Change for yourself?

"Discovering flavor. Just by virtue of how fresh [the products] are." Not new flavors, Yonkers is quick to emphasize—the flavor of familiar things, like melons and potatoes. That these things actually have flavor and aren't the bland, colorless specimens that generations of agribusiness have taught us to accept. "Eating all these different varieties"—like the many different kinds of tomatoes.

75   Sampling tomato varieties equates with participating in change?

"That's a huge level of change," she says. "The markets have brought back biodiversity, a lot of which was lost in the '50s. We've seen the whole return to grass-fed—and all these reforms as a result of that. Farmers are raising heritage breeds and heirlooms."

I tell her that this particular change, while important agriculturally, seems to me something less than the spiritual change she spoke of when we began talking. I tell her that mostly what I'm hearing from her and others is the opportunity for personal discovery in tasting new foods and cooking differently, and how that personal discovery—valid and worthy in itself— is being framed as a profound social and political act, and thus marketed as something more than it is.

Yonkers acknowledges that a strong sense of the spiritual "runs through the whole movement," then makes an analogy to Catholicism, with its ritualistic consumption of the body of Christ via the Communion wafer. She stops short of saying that taking Communion is akin to shopping at a farmers market, but I gather that for her, and perhaps for her many customers, the experiences are aligned.

"Food," she says, "is holy."

There's Truth, and Then There's Truth

You sit down at a restaurant and open the menu. There's a note at the top: 80 "Proud to support our farmers." Near the bar, you find a chalkboard with the names of all the farms whose products presumably contributed to your meal. The waiter announces the day's specials, noting not only every ingredient for every dish but also the source for that ingredient, as if you just spent the weekend at Path Valley or Toigo Orchards or any of the other farms that are standbys of the restaurant scene. As if you're on intimate terms with the workers who till the soil and plow the fields.

You're not simply supporting the restaurant, you're made to feel; you're supporting a community, an economy, a way of life. You're feeling good: about dinner, about the restaurant, about yourself—hell, maybe even about the world and your place in it.

And why wouldn't you?

Hearing and reading these paeans to local farmers, you'd assume that most of the raw materials that come through those kitchen doors are local, wouldn't you? Perhaps not everything—salt and pepper, for instance, aren't local. But a lot. Three-quarters of all the products, say. Or more than half.

You're assuming too much.

85   For most restaurants, the answer is around 30 percent. That figure tends to be higher in the warmer months and lower in the colder ones. "In the summertime, 40 to 50 percent maybe," Tom Meyer of Clyde's Restaurant Group says.

Maybe.

Touting a connection to the land and saluting "our" farmers seems a dubious practice when only a third of all the products are from local purveyors. I don't doubt that, from the restaurant's perspective, the 30 percent is more meaningful than the other 70 percent because it took time and effort to procure. All products aren't equal. But if local is something to support, something that matters, shouldn't it matter for the other 70 percent?

One restaurateur says that neither he nor any of his peers is buying items like onions and carrots and celery from local sources. They're making their investment, he says, in "corn and tomatoes—things that make a difference."

A cynic might say: things that get noticed.

90   Another restaurateur, a man deeply committed to local, confesses that while he sources regularly from more than a dozen purveyors, the milk and cream in his area restaurants aren't local.

Milk and cream? Shouldn't those be the least we can assume comes from nearby farms?

He'd much rather serve locally produced milk and cream in his restaurants, he says, but can't find a consistent source to meet the volume he needs—a problem many restaurateurs also allude to. One local dairy delivery company adheres to such a strict radius that it won't permit its trucks to go a few extra miles to make a drop-off at one of his restaurants.

The channels of distribution for local farmers aren't well developed, in marked contrast to the enormously efficient networks that bring food to supermarkets and chain restaurants. Products that might meet a particular need, at a volume that makes them attractive to chefs, aren't always getting to the restaurants that want them.

These are real concerns and ought not to be minimized. Local requires more work, more thought, and more investment.

95   At the same time, when you've embraced an ideology that revolves around notions of purity and piety, no one wants to hear about the obstacles that prevent you from being more holy. Excuses will be construed as weakness. You open yourself to charges of hypocrisy if you're anything less than completely faithful in your adherence.

Or, at the very least, to charges of hype.

The fact that distribution is lacking is real. So is the fact that it's possible to source minimally from local farmers and still fly the flag of local.

Lying with Local

Elaine Boland possesses the flinty skepticism of many small farmers accustomed to selling their hard-earned products to urbanites. To talk to her for any length of time is to hear a woman who has grown weary of interactions with people who don't grasp the rhythms of the seasons and the exigencies of life lived close to the land.

She says she "rededicated" her company, Fields of Athenry, in Purcellville, to these older, elemental values after her daughter was diagnosed with Cushing's syndrome, which results from exposure to high levels of the hormone cortisol. Two holistic doctors suggested she try a nutrient-rich diet. The diet helped, and Boland was moved to rethink her operation. If eating high-quality, humanely kept animals could save her daughter, it might save many other lives by preventing those ailments from occurring in the first place. Boland asks if I've ever eaten her meats. I say I have, twice—a lamb shoulder at Vermilion, in Old Town, and a lamb sausage at Haute Dogs & Fries, in Purcellville.

"'Cause I won't sell to most chefs," she says.

Why is that?

Boland goes silent and tells me she fears she'd get in trouble if she spoke her mind. Then, having resolved her inner contradiction, she sighs and says, "A lot of 'em, they buy just enough to use your name on their menu. I don't want somebody ordering two or three chickens off of me and a couple of chuck roasts and putting my name on their menu. When they're probably running 300, 400 dinners a week? You have to be supplementing it with someone else."

I ask how she decides whom she'll sell to and whom she won't.

She laughs ruefully. "I had to learn. I had to learn who was honest and dedicated to this. I learned the hard way."

Today, if a chef expresses interest in featuring her meats, she invites him or her out to the farm along with the kitchen staff. What would appear to be an innocuous meet-and-greet is, in fact, a rigorous screening process, a way for Boland to assess a chef's "level of engagement in talking about whole animal, head to hoof, their love of organ meats, their interest in

100

105

buying whole animals. There are very few chefs who do that, buy the whole animal. Very few can make the off-product sell, because they really can cook. They'll say to me, 'We don't have to stick to a set menu. We'll figure out how to use the product—don't worry.'"

The screening helps her figure out who is interested in a legitimate relationship, with its give-and-take and dependency, and who is merely interested in taking on a new supplier—or worse, acquiring a bit of fashionable window dressing.

"I don't want to be used," she says, sounding like a twice-jilted lover.

Deep Throat Speaks

A trusted source within the industry, a man I've come to refer to as Deep Throat for the reliable gossip he feeds me, said the practice that Elaine Boland describes is "more common than you think," adding: "Truth in advertising is one of the biggest issues with this."

Every one of the insiders I spoke with talked about local as doing the right thing, citing its importance for our bodies, our land, our communities, our economies, our farmers. But over the months, I came to distinguish among them as I listened.

110   Here, for instance, are my notes from a conversation with a young, locally minded restaurateur with a small chain of restaurants:

"It's always been a big part of our mission and strategy, and it's really exciting to see it start to become a standard in the food space.

"Putting the farmers' names on that board like we do. It's all about transparency.

"We shouldn't get so obsessed with the stricter definitions. That's not the über thing.

"That's what it's all about for us—emotional connection. When our customers see a picture of a farmer and they learn that story. It's about making people feel good about their decision at every touch point."

115   Now listen to Spike Gjerde, chef and owner of Woodberry Kitchen in Baltimore.

Asked to define "local," he says the word is the basis "for asking some very important questions." Namely: "What are the farmer's practices and what are the impacts on the environment of those practices?"

Gjerde often laments the years he missed in the cause. "I'm 20 years late to this," he says. I hear something of Alice Waters's ethos in his words, particularly when he says that it's not enough to "serve something good."

The "aim of all this," he says, "should be to connect the diner to something larger"—in his case, an appreciation of the Chesapeake, "our Yellowstone, our national treasure." But more broadly, an understanding of where our food is grown and by whom, and a curiosity about how our choices—our dollars—affect the system. "At Woodberry," he says, "we use the restaurant to sell the local products. Conversely, a lot of restaurants are using local to sell the restaurant."

It's not Gjerde's fidelity to a high-church standard of purity that impresses me. It's his understanding of the idea that dinner at a restaurant is a complex interplay of many people, only one of whom is the chef. And that a restaurant has a responsibility to the larger culture.

Perhaps this is why Gjerde doesn't exult over what he has accomplished but   120
continues to torture himself with how he should be doing so much more.

I tell him this sounds like a definition for neuroticism.

Gjerde laughs. "I don't see how you can be engaged in this thing and not be like that."

The Purist's Dilemma

Local has achieved a status unthinkable to many of its earliest adherents, a fact that causes some of them, such as civil-rights warriors or women's-rights advocates, to wax nostalgic over their progress even as they lament that local doesn't mean as much as it once did.

When she opened Cashion's Eat Place in 1995, Ann Cashion says, she took her cues in the kitchen from what her purveyors had on hand, buying whole animals and butchering them herself. The off-cuts were troubling to diners; they wanted the chops. They were dismayed at paying top dollar for something they considered scraps, and they couldn't understand her capriciousness—why she kept yanking the chops from the menu.

Cashion is a supporter of Bev Eggleston, who has so often been described   125
as patron saint of the local-food movement that he himself invokes the term, albeit mockingly, in conversation. Eggleston was featured in Michael Pollan's book *The Omnivore's Dilemma*, and there are seemingly as many mentions of his name on menus in Washington as there are beet-and-goat-cheese salads. As recently as five years ago, EcoFriendly Foods, Eggleston's company, sold only whole animals to chefs, but because of growing demand,

he recently made parts available to his 50 or so clients from Virginia to New York, having decided "we can't live by our ideals as this point."

He explains: "I'm not as eco-friendly as I would like to be. I wouldn't even call us sustainable—I'd call us resourceful." He uses the analogy of a relationship, citing the compromises necessary to keep a connection going, and says compromise is a reality for many of his clients, too.

Many chefs want to "do the right thing," Eggleston says, but they're under pressure from their bosses who "want to fly the flag of local," yet they bristle at the increase in food costs. Under those conditions, it's easier to "just buy the parts and never even consider the whole animal and what it can do for you."

Cashion suggests this is simply the new reality. The new local. And though it represents progress on the one hand—more high-quality products are on menus than ever before, and that, she says, "improves life for everyone"—on the other hand she thinks something is definitely missing.

What is that?

130   She pauses for a long moment, then launches into an elegant and impassioned statement of the local ideal, of the give-and-take between chef and farmer, the sense of mutual dependence, the idea that a chef might allow herself to be inspired by the products that arrive at the back door each day, that what hits the table later that night is inconceivable without the input and inspiration of the farmer. Patrick O'Connell, chef at the Inn at Little Washington, a sumptuous respite in the Virginia hinterlands, is even more pointed in lamenting what has been lost.

He attributes the popularity of local to our almost insatiable hunger, in this plastic, commodified culture, for something real and authentic, uncorrupted by corporations. It is, he says, a sad sign of what the past few decades have wrought. The job of the restaurant is to recognize this spiritual hunger. To feed souls as well as stomachs.

"First it was give me something good to eat," he says. "Then it was give me something good to eat and entertain me. Then it was give me something good to eat and take me somewhere I've never been. Now it's prove to me that there is some hope left in the world. Give me a respite from the misery of this world. Let this meal be a sanctuary."

I tell him that sounds like an awful lot to ask of anything, let alone a restaurant.

It is a lot to ask, he says, but isn't this very notion of going beyond embedded in the promise of local, the idea of connecting diners to something larger than themselves? Situating them in time and place? Delivering them to the spiritual?

It seems to pain him, I say, that more chefs and restaurateurs don't regard   135
local with his level of existential seriousness.

"The kind of buzzy stuff that's going on now, I find it kind of tedious and kind of depressing, to be quite honest," he says. "It's contributing to the loss of a sense of place rather than accentuating a sense of place if every restaurant in Washington, DC, has lamb from the Shenandoah."

There follows a lengthy disquisition about chefs who mistake putting out high-quality ingredients on a plate for cooking—"the elevation of those ingredients, through learned technique, into something superlative."

He interrupts himself to say he isn't arguing that the current iteration of local isn't "a good idea for the entire culture and deserving of support."

No?

He sighs. "No. But part of the tragedy of American culture is that we   140
cheapen everything."

A Glimpse of the Future, Part One

The man who, perhaps more than any other, makes me want to believe in the potential of local is Michael Babin. As founder of the Neighborhood Restaurant Group, Babin presides over ten restaurants including Evening Star Cafe, Vermilion, Birch & Barley, ChurchKey, and the new Bluejacket.

The most prominent name in Babin's growing stable is Tony Chittum, the former chef at Vermilion (he's now at the soon-to-reopen Iron Gate Inn, in Dupont Circle) whom many regard as the most passionate, committed supporter of local in our area.

Prior to Chittum's arrival in 2007, Vermilion was a middling restaurant with no discernible focus. Chittum gave it an identity, establishing it as a showcase of the best products from the Chesapeake and the Shenandoah. And while local and artisanal might have become trendy, Chittum's simple, soulful dishes were most assuredly not.

Whether Chittum's arrival spurred Babin to embrace local to the extent he eventually did or Babin would have drifted in that direction anyway is hard to know. But few restaurateurs are more involved in local than he is, and Babin often cites Chittum as inspiration.

One morning last summer, I drove out with Babin to tour a pet project   145
of his, the Arcadia Center for Sustainable Food & Agriculture, a nonprofit

operation that manages a small farm near Mount Vernon. It hadn't rained in two weeks, and the crops looked desiccated in the triple-digit heat. Something called "farm camp" was in session; grade-schoolers were learning about crop rotation and—in what sounded like a parody of an urbanite's idea of camp—making pesto.

Arcadia isn't a new idea. Clyde's Restaurant Group runs a farm in Loudoun County. EatWell operates one in La Plata, Maryland. But Arcadia is different, if only because Babin envisions it as something more than a steady source of fresh, local ingredients for his restaurants.

"The farm isn't here to feed the restaurants," he told me. "The restaurants exist to support the farm." Babin is boyish and intense and has the manner of a perpetual grad student, curious and alert to new ideas. A big-city restaurant owner with his own farm on a historic piece of property is a ready-made storyline for a TV show or magazine spread, but it was clear to me that Farm as Symbol held little interest for him.

Thinking he might aid the cause of local by making it more accessible, Babin bought a school bus last year, refitted it with coolers, and had it painted green. The Mobile Market rolled out in May. The bus is loaded up every morning with vegetables and fruits from Arcadia and makes stops five days a week in nine neighborhoods in DC, Maryland, and Virginia that are considered food deserts, lacking the grocery stores and markets of more affluent neighborhoods. Babin called it a "crying need."

What was preoccupying him when I met him was the idea of a large "food hub," a distribution center that would enable more farmers to get their products to more restaurants, and to do so more efficiently. There are more than a dozen of these hubs in Virginia and a few in Maryland. Babin has begun thinking of creating a vast network out of them.

150   The more forward-thinking members of the movement regard this next-step networking as essential to making good on the enormous promise of local.

Bev Eggleston hopes they'll work toward what he calls "a parallel food system."

"We don't think we can take down Big Agriculture," Eggleston says. "We used to be that naive; we used to think that was possible. But an alternative transportation system—you can use the analogy of the Beltway. We want to take the pressure off the Beltway, all that traffic. So you have mass transit, you have rail, you have bikes. When farmers are really organized and collaborate, that's what you want. It's not about local; it's about regional and logistical ability. Local isn't moving fast enough for where we need to go. We're moving toward the idea of systems that work versus where things came from."

A food hub, Babin told me, would go some way toward fulfilling that hope. It might even, he said, help bring local out of the realm of the privileged few.

We were standing on a sloping patch of grass that overlooked one end of the property; he gazed beyond a ridge of trees toward a 130-acre stretch of land that he hoped at some point to buy and convert to farmland. I said he didn't sound like a restaurateur or a businessman; he sounded like a social worker who, having achieved a breakthrough with one client, takes on an entire neighborhood.

"People think local is the answer," he said. "It's really the beginning of   155
the answer."

A Glimpse of the Future, Part Two

Mention the word "local" and the image that most often leaps to mind is a farmers market stocked with ripe produce. Or a chef stomping through a farm to pick his own vegetables and herbs for that night's dinner. It most assuredly isn't a diner, especially not a diner with 15 locations—a chain, the seeming antithesis of the movement toward artisanal, fresh, and organic.

A decade ago, I never imagined I'd one day tout the virtues of Silver Diner, let alone hold it up as a symbol of Doing the Right Thing. But times have changed. More to the point: Silver Diner has changed.

From June to July last year, I visited the Greenbelt location of Silver Diner four times for dinner. Among the ten-plus meals I eat out every week, these didn't stand out as particularly memorable—they weren't Culinary Experiences—but I was struck by how much better they were than they needed to be. They were certainly better than what I remembered of the chain some years back, before cofounder Ype Von Hengst overhauled the operation in 2010.

He began sourcing eggs and milk from Amish country—Lancaster, Pennsylvania. He switched to grass-fed, hormone-free beef and nitrate-free sausage and even added local, dry-aged bison from Monkton, Maryland. Local wines aren't fixtures on menus at many three- and four-star restaurants, yet Silver Diner carries four. There are local beers, too. The last of my four meals included two soft-shell crabs from Crisfield, Maryland, that had been battered and fried and served with a chunky tomato-and-basil salad.

160   Why make such sweeping changes when no one expects a diner to be anything but a diner? Why attempt such an about-face when there's no necessity?

Von Hengst disagrees. He's vehement. There is a necessity. An urgent necessity.

"I want us to be in business for another 25 years," Von Hengst says. "This is not a fad, this local. Everyone's going to have to get with the program. This is how we're all eating now."

In the first year of his revamp, when he eliminated 35 percent of his old menu, Silver Diner spent an extra million dollars on food, and Von Hengst worried that it might take a few years to attract the customers he needed to sustain the new model. He has since raised prices slightly to cover the higher costs, and his customer base has grown. Local accounted for 10 percent of the menu two years ago but today makes up 30 percent. That might not sound like much, but it's right around average for restaurants that advertise their commitment to local. Von Hengst believes he can bring that up to 40 or 50 percent in five years.

He hopes to work directly with more small farms, to get their products trucked to a central location—an idea not so different from Babin's notion of a food hub. The farmers spend so much of their time farming that they often don't have enough time to spend selling, Von Hengst says. Better that than the other way around, but if there's a centralized source for them and if more restaurants and communities could be exposed to their products....

165   Here he stops and shares what he hopes is a not-so-crazy dream.

"Bear with me a moment, okay?" All we need to do is connect and organize, he says, and we can turn the local dream into a broader reality. The greatest lesson his work with regional purveyors has taught him is that he wields a power he didn't realize he possessed—a single purchasing decision from Silver Diner, with its volume, can have an enormous effect on the market. Now, suppose other chains—Applebee's, Chili's, T.G.I. Friday's— were to take his example and replicate it on a national scale.

"The Inn at Little Washington and other restaurants that get their good stuff brought to them at the back door every day—that's great," Von Hengst says. "But fine dining is only a small segment of our world—a special class of restaurant that can only be reached by a few. Now, imagine the chains getting in on this with all the people they reach every day and all the volume they do in their buying. Can you imagine the impact?"

The triumph of an idea in this country, Patrick O'Connell says, is the mass adoption of that idea—and its inevitable dilution as it's reinterpreted and bastardized. The corporatization that Von Hengst invites me to ponder is the extension of this principle to the extreme. In a sense, the idea of Silver Diner multiplied by tens and even hundreds stands for the nullification of local as many in the movement like to see it, as a celebration of the authentic, the artisanal, the uncorrupted.

I'm not surprised to discover that Silver Diner itself counts few fans among the movement, though I thought some might be more supportive. Tom Meyer of Clyde's Restaurant Group, who is far from a purist, likens Silver Diner's version of local to "putting Tiffany lamps on the salad bar." It makes the salad bar look nicer, but it forever ruins your image of Tiffany lamps.

That crack is more revealing of the movement's advocates than it is of   170 Silver Diner.

You can say the local movement is about distinctions. You can also say it's about us versus them. You can say it's about spiritual connection. You can also say it's about signifiers of status. You can say it's about doing the right thing. You can say it's about business as usual. You can say there have been great gains in four decades. You can say there remain deep divisions in the food world— divisions the local movement and its advocates were supposed to have paved over. Have and have-not. Foodie and food philistine. Vibrant neighborhoods full of resources and food deserts with precious few outlets for even fresh food.

There's no romance about what Von Hengst is doing. There is realism, however imperfect or impure. A sense—perhaps nascent at this point, but real—of the truly transformative. A glimpse of a future in which local makes good, at last, on its immense latent promise.

If I am to believe—and I want to believe, I do—it will be in this imperfect realism, grounded in the problems of our world and not in a romantic quest for perfection and purity.

Analyze

1. How is "honest" food not necessarily the same as "good" food? Why would Kliman's friend seem to suggest that "honest" is more ethical than "good"?

2. This article might be seen as a critique of the movement called "local food." What are the flaws that Kliman finds with this movement? Is he persuasive in his critique? How so or how not?

3. How do you analyze and describe Kliman's language? For instance, he uses such terms as "true believers," "Looks suspiciously like an 'ism," and other evocative words and phrases. What effect do these have? How would you characterize Kliman's tone as a result?

Explore

1. Explore the ways in which Kliman's points suggest the importance of nuance. What is nuance? How does it pertain to Kliman's list of refutations about "eating local"?
2. Kliman believes that for the local food movement to be sustainable and effective, it must be "grounded in the problems of our world and not in a romantic quest for perfection and purity." Drawing on additional resources, what are some of the "problems" of our world as they pertain to food and our expectations of it?
3. Find an article that argues in favor of "local eating." Compare and contrast it with Kliman's piece. Which article makes its arguments most effectively? Why?

Jon Entine and JoAnna Wendel
"2000+ Reasons Why GMOs Are Safe to Eat and Environmentally Sustainable"

JoAnna Wendel is a self-described "science nerd" and science writer, who, with Jon Entine, a colleague at the Genetic Literacy Project and a Senior Research Fellow at George Mason University, finds no credible evidence showing risks to human health or the environment with the consumption of genetically engineered foods. Both conduct ongoing research into the safety of genetically modified organisms (GMOs), and their interim, if controversial, results were published (2013) in the article you will read here.

How does this article contribute to an understanding of genetically modified organisms?

A popular weapon used by those critical of agricultural biotechnology is to claim that there has been little to no evaluation of the safety of GM crops and there is no scientific consensus on this issue. Those claims are simply not true.

> "The science just hasn't been done."
> —*Charles Benbrook, organic researcher, Washington State University*

> "There is no credible evidence that GMO foods are safe to eat."
> —*David Schubert, Salk Institute of Biological Studies*

> "[The] research [on GMOs] is scant. . . . Whether they're killing us slowly—contributing to long-term, chronic maladies—remains anyone's guess."
> —*Tom Philpott, Mother Jones*

> "Genetically modified (GM) foods should be a concern for those who   5
> suffer from food allergies because they are not tested. . . ."
> —*Organic Consumers Association*

The claim that genetically engineered crops are "understudied"—the meme represented in the quotes highlighted above—has become a staple of opponents of crop biotechnology, especially activist journalists. Anti-GMO campaigners, including many organic supporters, assert time and again that genetically modified crops have not been safety tested or that the research done to date on the health or environmental impact of GMOs has "all" been done by the companies that produce the seeds. Therefore, they claim, consumers are taking a "leap of faith" in concluding that they face no harm from consuming foods made with genetically modified ingredients.

That is false.

Every major international science body in the world has reviewed multiple independent studies—in some cases numbering in the hundreds—in coming to the consensus conclusion that GMO crops are as safe or safer than conventional or organic foods. But until now, the magnitude of the research on crop biotechnology has never been cataloged. In response to what they believed was an information gap, a team of Italian scientists summarized 1783 studies about the safety and environmental impacts of GMO foods—a staggering number.

The researchers couldn't find a single credible example demonstrating that GM foods pose any harm to humans or animals. "The scientific research conducted so far has not detected any significant hazards directly connected with the use of genetically engineered crops," the scientists concluded.

10   The research review, published in *Critical Reviews in Biotechnology* in September, spanned only the last decade—from 2002 to 2012—which represents only about a third of the lifetime of GM technology.

"Our goal was to create a single document where interested people of all levels of expertise can get an overview on what has been done by scientists regarding GE crop safety," lead researcher Alessandro Nicolia, applied biologist at the University of Perugia, told Real Clear Science. "We tried to give a balanced view informing about what has been debated, the conclusions reached so far, and emerging issues."

The conclusions are also striking because European governments, Italy in particular, have not been as embracing of genetically modified crops as has North and South America, although the consensus of European scientists has been generally positive.

The Italian review not only compiled independent research on GMOs over the last ten years but also summarizes findings in the different categories of GM research: general literature, environmental impact, safety of consumption and traceability.

The "general literature" category of studies largely reveals the differences between the US, EU and other countries when it comes to regulating GM crops. Due to lack of uniform regulatory practices and the rise of non-scientific rhetoric, Nicolia and his colleagues report, concern about GMOs has been greatly exaggerated.

15   Environmental impact studies are predominant in the body of GM research, making up 68% of the 1,783 studies. These studies investigated environmental impact on the crop-level, farm-level and landscape-level. Nicolia and his team found "little to no evidence" that GM crops have a negative environmental impact on their surroundings.

One of the fastest growing areas of research is in gene flow, the potential for genes from GM crops to be found—"contaminate" in the parlance of activists—in non-GM crops in neighboring fields. Nicolia and his colleagues report that this has been observed, and scientists have been studying ways to reduce this risk with different strategies such as isolation distances and post-harvest practices. The review notes that gene flow is not unique to GM technology and is commonly seen in wild plants and non-GM crops. While gene flow could certainly benefit from more research, Nicolia and his colleagues suggest, the public's aversion to field trials discourages many scientists, especially in the EU.

In the food and feeding category, the team found no evidence that approved GMOs introduce any unique allergens or toxins into the food supply. All GM crops are tested against a database of all known allergens before commercialization and any crop found containing new allergens is not approved or marketed.

The researchers also address the safety of transcribed RNA from transgenic DNA. Are scientists fiddling with the "natural order" of life? In fact, humans consume between 0.1 and 1 gram of DNA per day, from both GM and non-GM ingredients. This DNA is generally degraded by food processing, and any surviving DNA is then subsequently degraded in the digestive system. No evidence was found that DNA absorbed through the GI tract could be integrated into human cells—a popular anti-GMO criticism.

These 1783 studies are expected to be merged into the public database known as GENERA (Genetic Engineering Risk Atlas) being built by Biofortified, an independent non-profit website. Officially launched in 2012, GENERA includes peer-reviewed journal articles from different aspects of GM research, including basic genetics, feeding studies, environmental impact and nutritional impact. GENERA has more than 650 studies listed so far, many of which also show up in the new database. When merged, there should be well over 2000 GMO related studies, a sizable percentage—as many as 1000—that have been independently executed by independent scientists.

In short, genetically modified foods are among the most extensively   20
studied scientific subjects in history. This year celebrates the 30th anniversary of GM technology, and the paper's conclusion is unequivocal: there is no credible evidence that GMOs pose any unique threat to the environment or the public's health. The reason for the public's distrust of GMOs lies in psychology, politics and false debates.

Analyze

1. The article begins by quoting three "reputable" sources regarding genetically modified organisms. How do the authors go on to quickly refute these claims? Be specific.

2. What is gene flow? Why is it significant to the authors' argument? Similarly, what are "transcribed RNA and transgenic DNA"? What effect does it have on your reading to understand these terms (or not)?
3. Examine the integration of scientific research with journalistic-style reporting. What effect does this have on the style of the essay? What might the authors have explained more carefully, if anything? What might enhance the effectiveness of this article?

Explore

1. The authors refer to a highly technical article entitled "An Overview of the Last 10 Years of Genetically Engineered Crop Safety Research," published in *Critical Reviews in Biotechnology* (available easily if you are online). What does this scientific article accomplish that the more popular article does not? Why?
2. Judging by the nature of the authors' argument, discuss the intended or target audience for this particular article. How does it differ from other articles you find on the same or similar topic?
3. The last line of the article says, "The reason for the public's distrust of GMO's lies in the psychology, politics, and false debates." What does this mean? What might be examples that would fall under each of these three categories—psychology, politics, and false debates?

Robin Mather
"The Threats from Genetically Modified Foods"

Someone who lives what she writes, Robin Mather is a journalist whose passion is not only food but also its sourcing. She is a senior associate editor at *Mother Earth News*, and she has written for publications that include the *Chicago Tribune*, the *Detroit News*, *Cooking Light*, and *Relish*. Her 1995 book, *A Garden of Unearthly Delights: Bioengineering and the Future of Food,* explores the controversies of bioengineering in the food industry. The selection below echoes the concerns of Mather's book and argues that the interests of Big Agriculture outweigh those of the greater good.

How does this essay offer a different perspective—from the one preceding it—regarding GMOs?

Glyphosate, Roundup's active ingredient, has been linked to birth defects in birds and amphibians, as well as to cancer, endocrine disruption, damage to DNA, and reproductive and developmental damage in mammals. Roundup-Ready crops are genetically modified to withstand drenching with this weedkiller.

Eighteen years after the first genetically modified food, the Flavr Savr tomato, came to market, the controversy about genetically modified foods rages. The call to label GM foods continues to build, yet the federal government has not responded. GM foods now illegal in many developed countries have been part of the American diet for nearly two decades. As GMOs have come to dominate major agribusiness sectors, a handful of chemical/biotech companies now control not only genetically modified seeds but virtually our entire seed supply.

(You may see genetically modified plants and animals referred to as GMOs, for "genetically modified organisms," or GE, for "genetically engineered." The terms are essentially interchangeable. We use GMO as a noun and GM as an adjective. —MOTHER EARTH NEWS)

"Genetic modification" refers to the manipulation of DNA by humans to change the essential makeup of plants and animals. The technology inserts genetic material from one species into another to give a crop or animal a new quality, such as the ability to produce a pesticide. These DNA transfers could never occur in nature and are not as precise as proponents make them sound.

Some genetically modified crops have been engineered to include genetic   5 material from Bt *(Bacillus thuringiensis),* a natural bacterium found in soil. Inserting the Bt genes makes the plant itself produce bacterial toxins, thereby killing the insects that could destroy it. The first GM crop carrying Bt genes, potatoes, were approved in the United States in 1995. Today there are Bt versions of corn, potatoes and cotton.

Roundup-Ready crops—soybeans, corn, canola, sugar beets, cotton, alfalfa and Kentucky bluegrass—have been manipulated to be resistant to glyphosate, the active ingredient in Monsanto's broadleaf weedkiller Roundup.

These two GM traits—herbicide resistance and pesticide production—are now pervasive in American agriculture. The Department of Agriculture's National Agricultural Statistics Service says that, in 2010, as much as 86 percent of corn, up to 90 percent of all soybeans and nearly 93 percent of cotton were GM varieties.

You're eating genetically modified foods almost daily unless you grow all of your food or always buy organic. Federal organic standards passed in 2000 specifically prohibit GM ingredients. Other genetically modified crops—none labeled—now include sweet corn, peppers, squash and zucchini, rice, sugar cane, rapeseed (used to make canola oil), flax, chicory, peas and papaya. About a quarter of the milk in the United States comes from cows injected with a GM hormone, honey comes from bees working GM crops, and some vitamins include GM ingredients. Some sources conservatively estimate that 60 percent or more of processed foods available in the United States contain GM ingredients, because most processed foods contain corn or soy.

GM foods are not labeled in the United States because the biotech industry has convinced the Food and Drug Administration (FDA) that GM crops are "not substantially different" from conventional varieties. The FDA, however, does no independent testing for human or animal safety and relies strictly on the research conducted by the manufacturers of the products. The main GM producer, Monsanto, makes it nearly impossible for independent scientists to obtain GM seeds to study. Meanwhile, many countries require labeling (the European Union, Australia), and some have even banned all GM foods (Japan, Ireland, Egypt).

10   Genetic modification technology does have extraordinary potential. In the practice known as "pharming," animals are genetically modified to give milk, meat or blood from which medicines are manufactured, as when GM goats produce milk containing a blood-thinning drug called ATryn. Research laboratories use GM mice to seek cures for diseases. As much as 90 percent of the cheese manufactured in the United States is made with GM rennet. Yet with current minimal levels of oversight on the crops and livestock produced, many people have serious worries about GMO technology. Many of us simply want the *right to know* what is in our food.

Bt Crops: Boon or Bane?

Monsanto has led the invasion of Bt crops, starting with corn, cotton and potatoes. Syngenta has developed Bt corn as well, as have Bayer, Dupont and others. Such crops are marketed to growers as pest-resistant.

Some researchers have concerns about the effect of Bt crops on human health. Professor emeritus Joe Cummins of the University of Western Ontario told the U.S. Environmental Protection Agency that "there is evidence that [Bt] will impact directly on human health through damage to the ileum [the final portion of the small intestine, which joins it to the large intestine] . . . [which] can produce chronic illnesses such as fecal incontinence and/or flu-like upsets of the digestive system."

In 2000, an Aventis brand Bt-corn variety, "Starlink," which the EPA had approved for animal feed but not for human consumption, was found in supermarket taco shells. Uproar ensued, and a number of countries adopted new laws refusing to import GM corn from the United States, which disrupted corn exports, as the *Choices* magazine article documents.

Widespread testing and introduction of genetically modified crops coupled with absence of independent oversight make it inevitable that such slips will continue to occur.

Corn borer resistance to Bt is already seen as a problem in GM corn.   15 "Protecting against the development of corn borer resistance is the responsibility of all producers using Bt corn," wrote Ric Bessin, an Extension entomologist at the University of Kentucky's College of Agriculture. Bessin cautioned growers that they must provide "refuge plantings" of non-GM corn to battle resistance. The same requirement is true for other Bt hybrids.

Since GM crops are often grown from "stacked hybrids," or varieties that have been manipulated to express several GM effects at once, pests may be developing resistance to many different GM traits. These "super bugs" may make all types of Bt ineffective at pest control.

Bt may also harm beneficial insects such as green lacewings and lady beetles.

Terminator Technology

With virtually all GM seed, farmers may soon be unable to save seed from their crops.

GM seed stock can be bred to include "terminator technology," which prevents the seeds from producing viable second-generation seed for saving. (Most genetically modified crops are hybrids, which wouldn't breed true anyway. But farmers forced to buy GM seed, as has happened in India and other countries, have lost the food security that centuries of seed-saving brought.)

20   Although this technology, sometimes called Genetic Use Restriction Technology (GURT), has not been implemented, the USDA has stated its support of it. The USDA said in 2001 that it is "committed to making terminator technology as widely available as possible, so that its benefits will accrue to all segments of society. ARS [the USDA's Agricultural Research Service] intends to do research on other applications of this unique gene control discovery. When new applications are at the appropriate states of development, this technology will also be transferred to the private sector for commercial application."

In 2007, Monsanto purchased Delta & Pine, which owned three of the first United States patents on terminator technology as well as patents in Canada and Europe. Monsanto has said that it will not adopt sterile seed technology, but has also said it "does not rule out the potential development and use of these technologies in the future." Syngenta, said to hold more patents on terminator technology than any other company, has won additional patents related to this technology in Australia, Russia, Europe, Brazil, Canada, China, Egypt and Poland.

GM varieties can pollute neighboring crops in "pollen trespass." GM corn has polluted traditional varieties in Mexico, threatening traditional culture and genetic diversity. "Native seeds are for us a very important element of our culture," said Oaxacan farmer Aldo Gonzlez. "The [Mayan] pyramids could be destroyed, but a fistful of corn is the legacy that we can pass on to our children and grandchildren, and today we are being denied that possibility."

Saving GM seed can land you in court and even bankrupt you. Monsanto has sued nearly 150 farmers for "patent infringement," alleging that farmers stole the company's patent-protected seeds, whether by wind-blown pollen, spilled seed on the farmer's property, "volunteer plants from a neighbor's property, or in other ways." Monsanto maintains a staff of 75 attorneys, with an annual budget of $10 million, specifically to prosecute these cases, which have resulted in judgments in favor of Monsanto totaling more than $15.2 million. The company requires farmers to sign "technology agreements" before planting its GM seed, authorizing property investigations, but farmers whose property has suffered trespass from neighbors are not protected.

Biotechnology companies can prosecute these cases as patent infringement because they own all rights to the seed. Their ability to patent seeds rises from the 1983 U.S. Supreme Court ruling in *Diamond v. Chakrabarty* that Ananda Chakrabarty's GM oil-eating bacteria could be patented even though it was a life form, and therefore could be protected under patent law. The landmark ruling opened the door to all GM patents today.

Roundup: Risky Business?

Roundup is one of Monsanto's powerful broadleaf weedkillers. Since   25
Roundup's patent expired in 2000, a number of companies have begun to manufacture products using Roundup's active ingredient, glyphosate. The Environmental Protection Agency says that glyphosate is among the most widely used pesticides in the U.S.

Glyphosate is not made using genetic modification. Instead, crops labeled Roundup-Ready are genetically modified to withstand drenching with this weedkiller.

In a 2011 report called *Roundup and Birth Defects: Is the Public Being Kept in the Dark?*, eight international scientists cited study after study linking glyphosate to birth defects in birds and amphibians, as well as to cancer, endocrine disruption, damage to DNA, and reproductive and developmental damage in mammals, even at very low doses. Moreover, the report said, Monsanto and the rest of the herbicide industry had known since the 1980s that glyphosate causes malformations in animals, and that EU governments ignored these studies. Here in the United States, the EPA continues to assert that Roundup is safe.

Another concern is environmental damage. Roundup ends up in wetlands due to runoff and inadvertent spraying. In one study, the recommended application of Roundup sold to homeowners and gardeners killed up to 86 percent of frogs in one day, according to University of Pittsburgh assistant professor Rick Relyea. Even at a third of the recommended strength, Relyea found, Roundup killed 98 percent of all tadpoles. Amphibians, living in water and on land, are considered bellwether environmental species.

Roundup also damages soil. Two Purdue scientists, professor emeritus Don Huber and G. S. Johal, said in a paper published in 2009 that "the widespread use of glyphosate . . . can significantly increase the severity of various plant diseases, impair plant defense to pathogens and disease and immobilize soil and plant nutrients rendering them unavailable for plant use." The pair warned that "ignoring potential non-target side effects . . . may have dire consequences for agriculture such as rendering soils infertile, crops nonproductive and plants less nutritious."

30   Huber is point-blank about glyphosate's dangers. "Glyphosate is the single most important agronomic factor predisposing some plants to both disease and toxins," he said in the interview with *The Organic and Non-GMO Report*. "These toxins can produce a serious impact on the health of animals and humans. The toxin levels in straw can be high enough to make cattle and pigs infertile," Huber said.

The Importance of Independent Review

As the system now stands, biotech companies bring their own research to the government body overseeing their proposed products. The agency may be the US Dept. of Agriculture, the federal Food and Drug Administration or the Environmental Protection Agency.

These government bodies do no independent studies on the safety and efficacy of the proposed products. Instead, they rely strictly on the research conducted by the companies.

"We don't have the whole picture. That's no accident. Multibillion-dollar agricultural corporations, including Monsanto and Syngenta, have restricted independent research on their genetically-engineered crops," wrote Doug Gurion-Sherman of the Union of Concerned Scientists in a February 2011 *Los Angeles Times* op-ed piece. "They have often refused to provide independent scientists with seeds, or they've set restrictive conditions that severely limit research options."

Concern about lack of independent review extends to university-level research, which is often partly funded and/or controlled by the agrochemical companies, and often gives agrochemical companies exclusive rights to academic discoveries—even though the universities are taxpayer-funded.

35   Researchers at the University of Nebraska developed a new GM soybean with resistance to an herbicide called dicamba. Their research was partially funded by Monsanto, which gained the company exclusive use of the new

soybean through a licensing agreement with the university signed in 2005. Monsanto will "stack" the dicamba resistance gene with a Roundup-Ready genetic change (in other words, creating crops that are resistant to two herbicides, forcing growers to use both).

It seems unlikely that scientists whose research is designed and paid for by agrochemical companies would choose to conduct studies that may reduce or remove that funding, even if they could obtain the seeds they needed to do truly independent research.

Moreover, the agrochemical companies refuse to release their own research, citing concern that "proprietary information" could be disclosed.

Scientific American called on biotech companies to end restrictions on outside research in a 2009 editorial. "Food safety and environmental protection depend on making plant products available to regular scientific scrutiny," the magazine's editors wrote. "Agricultural technology companies should therefore immediately remove the restriction on research from their end-user agreements. Going forward, the EPA should also require, as a condition of approving the sale of new seeds, that independent researchers have unfettered access to all products currently on the market."

When scientists have obtained agrochemical companies' research data, usually through freedom-of-information requests, they have found entirely different conclusions than the company did. Three French scientists analyzed the raw data from three Monsanto rat studies in 2009 and found that three GM corn varieties caused liver and kidney toxicity and other kinds of organ damage. The European Food Safety Authority, at the request of the European Commission, reviewed the French report and said that it "does not raise any new safety concerns," although other scientists continue to insist the French report is correct.

All three corn varieties are now in the human food chain in the United States.   40

rBST: Genetically Modified Milk

BST (for "bovine somatotropin") is produced in cows' pituitary glands. It's also sometimes called BGH (for "bovine growth hormone"). It occurs naturally and, since the 1920s, has been known to increase milk production. It is a peptide, not a steroidal, hormone.

rBST stands for "recombinant bovine somatotropin," and is a GM version of this naturally occurring hormone. Injecting the GM hormone causes cows to produce about 10 percent more milk. This report shows the reduction in milk production when rBST injections stop. In 1985, the FDA ruled that meat and milk from rBST-injected cows were safe, and consumers in several states unknowingly ate and drank both while Monsanto, Upjohn and others ran tests on their GM hormone.

The FDA approved the GM hormone in late 1993, saying there was "no significant difference" in milk from injected and uninjected cows. Its ruling meant that dairies could not label their milk as coming from uninjected cows, because doing so, the FDA said, suggested that there is a difference and the FDA said there was no difference.

There *is* a difference. rBST injections in cows raise levels of the naturally occurring IGF-1 (insulin-like growth factor 1), a protein that stimulates cell growth. The IGF-1 in milk from injected cows is easily absorbed in the small intestine. Dr. Samuel Epstein, a professor at the School of Public Health, University of Illinois Medical Center in Chicago, has warned for more than 20 years that high levels of IGF-1 raise the risk of cancer, especially breast, colon and prostate cancer. He has said that rBST milk is "super-charged with high levels of abnormally potent IGF-1, up to 10 times the levels in natural milk and over 10 times more potent."

45   Injecting cows in the same places over and over increases the chance of infection at injection sites, plus rBST-injected cows frequently suffer from chronic mastitis, an infection of the udder. Mastitis is uncomfortable for the cow, causing its udder to swell and making it painful for her to lie down or be milked. Milk from cows with mastitis is lower in the calcium and solids that cheese makers need and often has a "ropy," unattractive appearance. Both injection site and mastitis infections must be treated with antibiotics.

Monsanto began selling rBST in 1994. In 2003, the FDA charged several dairies with "misbranding," and Monsanto sued Oakhurst Dairy in Maine for labeling its milk from cows *injected with GM hormone!*

As the public reacted to rBST by reaching for organic milk instead, American retailers began to pledge not to sell rBST milk. rBST is illegal in Japan, Australia, New Zealand and Canada, and the European Union banned it permanently in 1999.

In 2008, a group of rBST-using farmers formed a group called American Farmers for the Advancement and Conservation of Technology, or AFACT, with help from Monsanto. AFACT tried to ban no-rBST labeling claims in many states, but dropped those efforts in most states—except Ohio, where the ban effort ended in a lawsuit. An Ohio circuit court found in 2010 that there *was* a compositional difference between rBST milk and milk from untreated cows, and that the FDA's position was *"inherently misleading."* The court found higher levels of a cancer-causing compound, lower-quality milk because of higher fat and lower protein, and higher white cell counts, which means the milk sours more quickly.

Packaging for injectable rBST lists a number of other side effects for cows, including abscesses, ulcers on udders, reduced pregnancy rates, visibly abnormal milk and hoof disorders.

Despite Monsanto and other biotech companies' claims that rBST   50 would be a boon for farmers, the University of California at Davis reported that its use in California between 1994 and 1996 "probably resulted in an increase in milk production of less than 1 percent per year."

Can GMOs Feed the World?

Fans of GMOs assert that genetically modified crops and livestock can help end hunger. They also claim that GMOs can help stop climate change, reduce pesticide use and increase crop yields.

Are these claims true? We conclude no.

The international report *The GMO Emperor Has No Clothes* outlined the evidence in detail gleaned from many sources.

Genetically modified crops do not produce more food or use fewer pesticides, the report said. As resistant weeds and bugs develop, farmers have to apply ever more herbicides and insecticides. "The biotech industry is taking us into a more pesticide-dependent agriculture, and we need to be going in the opposite direction," says Bill Freese of the Center for Food Safety in Washington, D.C.

If GM crops don't increase yield, don't reduce pesticide use and show   55 no significant promise for feeding the world, why should government and industry promote them?

If GMOs fail, shareholders in Monsanto, Bayer and Syngenta will see their investments plummet. And who are those shareholders? Very possibly, you. According to Yahoo! Finance, more than 80 percent of Monsanto's stock is held by institutional holders and mutual funds such as Vanguard, Davis, Fidelity and Harbor Capital.

If GMOs don't benefit the farmers who pay more to buy GM seed, and if they don't benefit the customers who eat them unknowingly, who gains from GMOs?

Stockbrokers. And you, if you have investments that own stock in Monsanto or other biotech companies.

Seed Company Monopolies

Monsanto now controls so much of the world's seed stock that the U.S. Justice Department launched an "unprecedented series of public meetings" into the company's business practices as part of a formal antitrust investigation in March 2010. "The price of a bag of soybean seed, for example, has roughly quadrupled since Monsanto began licensing genes," the *Wall Street Journal* reported in that article.

60   The Seed Industry Structure chart demonstrates how tightly and startlingly consolidated the seed industry has become. That's one reason why Monsanto's name comes up again and again in any conversation about GMOs: The company is far and away the largest involved in GM patented seed.

(*The GMO Emperor Has No Clothes* also includes an appendix detailing Monsanto's long corporate history of misleading research, cover-ups, bribes, and convictions in lawsuits covering a range of issues, from Agent Orange to toxic waste discharge to GM soybeans.)

GMO Food Labeling: The Right to Know

The FDA and GMO supporters say that labeling genetically modified foods would be cumbersome and costly, ultimately raising food prices.

Labeling proponents point to the European Union, Russia, Brazil, Japan, China, Thailand, Taiwan, South Korea, Australia and New Zealand, all of which require labels for GM foods, and report costs are far lower than the industry and the FDA claim.

Survey after survey and poll after poll have shown that consumers overwhelmingly favor labeling.

65   In October 2011, the Center for Food Safety, a Washington, D.C.-based nonprofit, filed a petition demanding the FDA require labeling on all food produced using genetic engineering. The center filed the petition on behalf of the Just Label It! campaign, a coalition of more than 350 organizations and individuals concerned about food safety and consumer rights. The FDA's governing rules require it to open a public docket where citizens can comment on the petition.

That doesn't mean the FDA will listen to those comments, however. The agency received nearly 6,500 comments on its proposed 1992 policy, and more than 80 percent demanded mandatory labeling of genetically modified foods. Despite that outpouring, the FDA did not respond to those comments and decided against labeling.

Part of the reason for the FDA's lack of responsiveness may be the revolving door between government and the industries they regulate.

Just one example is Michael R. Taylor, now Deputy Commissioner for Foods at the FDA. Taylor is an attorney who started his career at the FDA in 1976. In 1981, he moved to the law firm of King & Spaulding, representing Monsanto, and developed the firm's food and drug law arm. While there, he worked to get Monsanto's GM bovine growth hormone, rBST, approved.

In 1991, Taylor left King & Spaulding to return to the FDA as the newly created Deputy Commissioner for Policy. One of his first acts was to draft and implement language that prevented dairy farmers and milk producers from labeling their milk as coming from cows not injected with rBST. The FDA approved rBST two years later, in 1993.

Taylor moved to the US Dept. of Agriculture the following year, where 70 he became Administrator of the Food Safety & Inspection Service. During his two-year tenure, Taylor oversaw the adoption of the National Organic Standards Act, including its original proposal to have GM crops labeled as organic. The organic industry launched an all-out effort to protect its standards, and the GM proposal was dropped (as was a proposal to allow crops fertilized with raw sewage sludge to bear the organic label).

Taylor next returned to King & Spaulding for a short time, but then joined Monsanto as its vice-president for public policy. He was there until 2009, when he was appointed senior advisor to the FDA commissioner, and was named to his current position at the FDA in 2010.

Among other former Monsanto employees now or formerly holding posts in the agencies which oversee the company's practices: Supreme Court Justice Clarence Thomas; Dr. Michael A. Friedman, a former FDA deputy commissioner who subsequently joined Monsanto as a senior vice-president; and Linda J. Fisher, an assistant administrator at the EPA before joining Monsanto as a vice-president and then returned to the EPA as deputy administrator.

FDA officials have openly criticized efforts to label GM crops and food. When Oregon voters considered Measure 27, a mandatory GMO labeling law, in 2002, FDA Deputy Commissioner Lester Crawford said in a letter to the governor of Oregon that mandatory labeling could "impermissibly interfere" with the food industry's ability to sell its products, and could violate interstate commerce laws.

The Oregon initiative was soundly defeated, and money was the reason why. "In campaign financial disclosure reports . . . Monsanto took the financial lead against Measure 27, with contributions totaling $1,480,000. Next was Dupont, with $634,000. Other large contributions came from biotech companies Syngenta, Dow Agro Sciences, BASF and Bayer Crop Science. Grocery Manufacturers of America [a trade organization], PepsiCo, General Mills and Nestle USA contributed a total of $900,000 by the reporting date," said Cameron Woodworth in *Biotech Family Secrets*, a report for the Council for Responsible Genetics.

75   Other high-ranking federal officials have lobbied against labeling. "If you label something, there's an implication there's something wrong with it," said Jose Fernandez, the U.S. State Department's assistant secretary for economic, energy and business affairs. He was speaking on an October 2011 panel organized by CropLife International, a trade organization representing the biotech industry.

The assertion that labeling somehow implies inferior quality is transparently specious. Fruits and vegetables labeled "organic" made up the highest growth in sales of all organics in 2010, according to the Organic Trade Association, up 11.8 percent from 2009 sales. Total U.S. organic sales were nearly $28.7 billion in 2010, up 9.7 percent from 2009.

What You Can Do about GMOs

- If you think GM foods should be labeled, you can sign on to the Just Label It! campaign and send letters to the FDA and your congressional representatives to urge them to require labeling of GM foods. You'll find sample language and a petition at the Just Label It! website.
- If you grow your own food, buy your seed from companies that have signed the GMO-free pledge. See the Safe Seed list, maintained by the Council for Responsible Genetics.
- Buy organic whenever possible and look for foods labeled "Non-GMO verified." The Non-GMO Project is an independent nonprofit that requires independent, third-party verification before awarding its label.
- Help combat seed industry monopolies and build local food security by supporting local growers who refuse to use genetically modified seeds and GM drugs on their livestock, and work to pass food sovereignty laws in your community. Food sovereignty laws can prohibit

GM foods in your community. Learn more from food sovereignty expert Dr. Vandana Shiva's blog.

- Finally, if you have investments, consider moving out of funds that invest in biotech stock. If you are unable to do so, write letters to your fund's managers to tell them of your objection to this investment policy.

Analyze

1. How do Mather's position and her arguments differ from those of Entine and Wendel? Be specific.
2. Analyze Mather's writing style—that is, her word choice, her tone. What would you say about it? How do these enhance her arguments (or not)?
3. "If GMO's don't benefit the farmers who pay more to buy GM seed, and if they don't benefit the customers who eat them unknowingly, who gains from GMO's?" Do the risks, then, outweigh the rewards, according to Mather? How effective is her argument, based on your analysis of the essay?

Explore

1. "It seems unlikely that scientists whose research is designed and paid for by agro-chemical companies would choose to conduct studies that may reduce or remove that funding, even if they could obtain the seeds they needed to do truly independent research." Looking at sources apart from this essay, what are the ethical issues that Mather invokes? How do they contribute to your understanding of this essay?
2. Mather offers a call to action at the end of this essay, giving five pieces of advice for what we can do about GMO's. Investigate further these particular suggestions to determine their feasibility. What do you find?
3. Integrate the Mather piece with the article before it by Entine and Wendel. Compare and contrast the articles, focusing on the ways in which each develops its argument, their different styles, and their different perspectives. As you explore and analyze, which, in your view, is the more effective argument? Be sure to explain your point of view with details from the articles themselves.

Hank Shaw
"On Killing"

Truly an Internet presence, whose blog about honest food, "Hunter, Angler, Gardener, Cook," features recipes and articles that advocate for hunting, foraging, and fishing, Hank Shaw describes himself as someone who spends his "days thinking about new ways to cook and eat anything that walks, flies, swims, crawls, skillets, jumps, or grows." Writes Shaw, "I am the omnivore who has solved his dilemma." "On Killing" comes from the website, but the article has been widely circulated and published in *Best American Food Writing*, 2011.

How does this article contribute to an understanding of the culture of hunting?

I have been dealing a lot of death lately. I've hunted five of the past eight days, and have killed birds on each trip. My larder is filling, and Holly and I are eating well. Lots of duck, some pheasant and even a little of the venison I have left over from the 2010 season. That is the good side of all this, the side of hunting that most people can embrace. I hunt for a lot of reasons, but for me the endgame is always the table.

It is the journey to that table that can sometimes give people pause. What I do to put meat in my freezer is alien to most, anathema to some. In the past seven years, I can count on one hand the times I've had to buy meat for the home. This fact alone makes me an outlier, an anomaly. And that I am unashamed—proud, really—of this seems to cause a lot of folks I meet to look at me funny: I am a killer in their midst.

Not too long ago, I was at a book signing event for *Hunt, Gather, Cook* when a young woman approached me. She was very excited about foraging, and she had loved that section of my book. Then her face darkened. She told me she'd also read my section on hunting. "How can you enjoy killing so much? I just don't understand it. You seem like such a nice person, too." It took a few minutes for me to explain myself to her, and I am grateful that she listened. She left, I think, with a different opinion.

A few weeks later, I was at the University of Oregon talking about wild food to some students. When I mentioned hunting, I could feel the temperature in the room drop. It occurred to me that no one there was a hunter, nor were they close to any hunters. I called for a show of hands. One guy raised his. I asked him briefly about his hunting experience, and it was obvious that it had been traumatic for the poor kid. I let the topic slide and moved on to mushrooms.

When I was in Cambridge, Massachusetts, I spoke with more than 100 ⁵ diners during my book dinner at Craigie on Main. Only four were hunters, although a few more wanted to start. Over the course of the night, I fielded weird question after weird question from diner after diner. *Have I ever shot someone? Did I actually eat what I shot? Wasn't I afraid of diseases?* It was a stark show of ignorance. Not stupidity, mind you, just an utter lack of knowledge of what hunting is all about.

To be sure, these encounters were in college towns among a certain set of people. I had some book events, notably those in Montana, Pittsburgh and Austin, where most everyone who attended either hunted or was at least familiar with it. And in most places I could be assured of a healthy smattering of fellow hook-and-bullet types or farmers, who are equally familiar with the death of animals.

But the fact remains: Most people reading this have never killed anything larger than an insect, and among those who have it's usually been a fish, or an accident—like running over someone's dog. Most people have no idea what it's like to take the life of another creature, let alone why someone would actively seek to do so. Let me try to explain to you the way I did to my young foraging friend on book tour. Let me tell you what it means to kill, at least for me.

To deal death is to experience your world exploding. It is an avalanche of emotion and thought and action.

Armed with a shotgun, it is often done without thought, on instinct alone. A flushing grouse gives you no more than a few seconds to pull the trigger before it disappears into the alders. A rabbit can leap back into the brambles in even less time. Unless you are perfect in that split second, the animal wins. And being human, we are far from perfect. Even with ducks, where you often have plenty of time to prepare for the shot, their speed and agility are more than adequate defenses. We hunters fail more than we succeed.

This is why we will often whoop it up when we finally bring a bird down: ¹⁰ We are not being callous, rejoicing in the animal's death. It is a hard-wired reaction to succeeding at something you have been working for days, months, even years to achieve. In some corner of your brain, it means you will eat today. This reaction can look repulsive from the outside.

Should you arm yourself with a rifle, you then must wrestle your conscious mind. Buck fever is real. A huge set of antlers will hypnotize the best of us, man and woman alike. Even if the animal lacks antlers, as mine often do, you have to contend with The Twin Voices: On one shoulder sits a voice shouting, *Shoot! Shoot! You might not get another chance!* On the other shoulder sits another voice, grave and calm: *Be careful. You must not put that bullet in a place where the animal will suffer. Better to pass a shot than wound an animal.* A wise hunter does not kill lightly.

In that moment when the game shows itself and you ready yourself to shoot, all that matters is that you do your job correctly. And that job is to kill cleanly and quickly. The animal deserves it; we would want no less were the tables turned. And make no mistake: A great many hunters, myself included, do this mental table-turning with some frequency. Seeing animals die so often makes us think of our own death, and I can assure you most of us would rather die with a well-placed shot than wither in a hospital.

We also know all too well that we are fallible creatures. When we fail to kill cleanly, when we wound the animals we seek, it is our duty to end their suffering ourselves. If there is a moment in this whole process that breaks my heart, it is this one. Everything wants to live, and will try anything it can to escape you. We see ourselves in this struggle, feel tremendous empathy for the struggling bird, the fleeing deer. It is a soul-searing moment where part of you marvels at the animal's drive to live—*to escape!*—at the same time the rest of you is consumed with capturing it as fast as possible so you can end this miserable business. This internal conflict is, to me, what being human is all about. A coyote or a hawk has no remorse. We do.

I am not ashamed to tell you that I have shed a tear more than once when I've had to deliver the coup de grace to a duck. I'm not sure what it is about ducks, but they affect me more than other animals. I always apologize to it, knowing full well that this is a weak gesture designed mostly to help me feel better. But it does help me feel better. At least a little. So I keep doing it.

15   As the moment of killing fades, death rides home with you in the back of the truck. Once home, you must transmogrify the animal you killed into meat. The transformation is a mystical one, and every time I "dress" game—such a pleasant euphemism, that—I marvel at how fast my mind toggles from hunter to butcher to cook.

It is a necessary process, and one that is vital to why I have chosen this life, why I am a hunter.

I look down at my keyboard and see death under my fingernails. I smell the fat and gore and meat of dead ducks upon me; it's been a good week of hunting. And because I eat everything on a duck but the quack, I have become intimate with the insides of waterfowl. Over the years, I've gutted and taken apart so many animals that I know the roadmap blindfolded. And that road leads to meals long remembered. I reach into a deer's guts without thought: I want those kidneys, and that liver. I turn my arm upwards and wrap my fingers around its stopped heart, slick and firm. It will become heart cutlets, or jaeger schnitzel.

Once plucked and gutted, I can take apart a duck in 90 seconds. Maybe less. My fingers intuitively know which way and how hard to pluck each feather from a pheasant's carcass. I know just where to put my boning knife, sharp as lightning, to slice the tendons that hold a hog's tongue into its head. I use the same knife to caress its hind legs, separating the natural muscle groups apart along each seam. Some will become roasts, others salami. Animal becomes food. The pop of a goose's thigh bone disjointing from its body no longer sickens me; all it means is that I need to slip my knife under that bone and around the coveted "oyster," the best bite on any bird.

Wasting meat is the sin I cannot forgive. When I kill an animal, its death is on my hands, and those animals to whom I've had to deliver the coup de grace are especially close to me. There is a bond between us that requires that I do my part to ensure they did not die for nothing. This is why I spend so much time creating recipes for every part of the animal. Nature wastes nothing, and neither should I. It pains me to know that some hunters do not share this feeling, that they care only for backstraps or breasts—and while I know that coyotes and buzzards will eat what we do not, I do not hunt to feed those creatures.

You might ask me that with all this, why bother eating meat at all? Why 20 deal with all the moral and emotional implications? In the face of such constant death, is it not better to be a vegetarian?

For me, no. It is a cold fact that no matter what your dietary choice, animals die so you can eat. Just because you choose not to eat the flesh of animals does not mean that their homes did not fall to the plow to become acres of vegetables and soybeans, wheat and corn. Habitat, more than any-thing, determines the health of a species. The passenger pigeon may have been snuffed out by hunting, but it was the massive destruction of virgin forest—forest cleared to grow crops—that brought the pigeon to the brink.

I have nothing against vegetarians, and the vast majority I've met understand what I do and respect it. But to those few who do not, I say this: We all have blood on our hands, only I can see mine.

It all boils down to intimacy. Hunting has created an uncommon closeness between the animals I pursue, the meat I eat, and my own sense of self. There is a terrible seriousness to it all that underlies the thrill of the chase, the camaraderie of being with my fellow hunters and deep sense of calm I feel when alone in the wild. I welcome this weight: It fuels my desire to make something magical with the mortal remains of the game I manage to bring home. It is a feeling every hunter who's ever stared into the freezer at that special strip of backstrap, or hard-won bird or beast understands.

Meat should be special. It has been for most of human existence. And no modern human understands this more than a hunter. I am at peace with killing my own meat because for me, every duck breast, every boar tongue, every deer heart is a story, not of conquest, but of communion.

Analyze

1. Contrary to other narratives, Shaw offers a defense of hunting. How does he do so? To what effect?
2. Shaw begins his article by stating, "I have been dealing a lot of death lately." What does this opener make you think the article will be about? Does the rest of the article meet your expectations? Why?
3. "To deal death is to experience your world exploding. It is an avalanche of emotion and thought and action. Armed with a shotgun, it is often done without thought, on instinct alone." How is Shaw's view of hunting (as exemplified by this quote) anything but monolithic? What in the article backs up your response to this question?

Explore

1. Shaw was moved to write this piece after encountering audience members full of "non-hunters," and he acknowledges that "most people reading this have never killed anything larger than an insect. . . . Most people have no idea what it's like to take the life of another creature, let alone why someone would actively seek to do so." How do you fit into Shaw's audience? How does your position inform your reading of this particular piece and his sense of his complex audiences?

2. While Shaw's argument is often conflicted-seeming and complex, how would an audience of non-eaters of meat respond? Why?

3. Examine the ways in which Shaw's article looks at the contested and often intimate relationship between humans and their environments. Use Shaw's lens as a way to similarly explore your own relationship to your environment.

Forging Connections

1. The authors in this chapter each in some way grapple with the intersections of human beings and their environments. Create a presentation or lead a discussion (and, if your instructor wishes, crate an accompanying document) in which you introduce the complex and multilayered relationship between our food source as humans and our surroundings (or environments). Argue a point of view, using no fewer than three essays from this chapter to back up your points.

2. Use several articles from this chapter to create a debate, one in which you argue both sides. For instance, Shaw writes about the culture of hunting; find resources to argue against Shaw. If you prefer, use the two essays about GMOs (Entine and Wendell and Mather) and, finding additional sources, continue the argument, taking a position. Use this exercise as a gateway to a discussion about greater accountability on the part of authors in building and supporting their arguments.

Looking Further

1. Consider the various topics in this chapter—including GMOs, hunting, the local food movement, overfishing, and organic farming—and research and read blogs and other voices on the Internet concerned with these subjects. Select two and analyze each for its use of research, appeal to the audience, choice of language, and the authors' overall credibility. Create a presentation or write a report with your findings. Which source is superior? Why?

2. Identify a popular marketing campaign from a food manufacturer or restaurant, and analyze the campaign from two perspectives: as a consumer (noting its effectiveness, for instance) and as an environmentally concerned citizen. What might the differences be in these two perspectives, and why?

The Politics
3
of Food

The entries in this chapter might seem to take on a somewhat "snarky" turn. That is, each in its own way is a critique of what we eat, of who eats what, of the stereotypes surrounding food, and issues related to food and privilege.

Each of the authors, in his or her way, articulates these various critiques with very different approaches, whether academic and dry, humorous, or spirited—and sometimes all of these. Your skills as a reader will be called upon to analyze and explore the ways in which each makes an argument and whether the evidence called upon is appropriate or excessive.

David Foster Wallace
"Consider the Lobster"

Novelist, essayist, and short-story writer David Foster Wallace was called "influential" and "innovative" by Los Angeles *Times* book editor David Ulin. This essay, which first appeared in *Gourmet* magazine in 2004, later became the title essay in a collection by the same name published in 2007 by Back Bay Books. In this piece, inspired by a trip to the Maine Lobster festival, David Foster Wallace dips into the animal rights debate by asking whether it is indulgent to cook a live lobster for the sake of human pleasure.

As you read, consider this: what are ways in which one must reconcile human desire and wants with what seems best for the greater good—or in this case, for what David Foster Wallace argues is essentially a "giant sea insect"?

For 56 years, the Maine Lobster Festival has been drawing crowds with the promise of sun, fun, and fine food. One visitor would argue that the celebration involves a whole lot more.

The enormous, pungent, and extremely well marketed Maine Lobster Festival is held every late July in the state's midcoast region, meaning the western side of Penobscot Bay, the nerve stem of Maine's lobster industry. What's called the midcoast runs from Owl's Head and Thomaston in the south to Belfast in the north. (Actually, it might extend all the way up to Bucksport, but we were never able to get farther north than Belfast on Route 1, whose summer traffic is, as you can imagine, unimaginable.) The region's two main communities are Camden, with its very old money and yachty harbor and five-star restaurants and phenomenal B&Bs, and Rockland, a serious old fishing town that hosts the Festival every summer in historic Harbor Park, right along the water.[1]

Tourism and lobster are the midcoast region's two main industries, and they're both warm-weather enterprises, and the Maine Lobster Festival represents less an intersection of the industries than a deliberate collision, joyful and lucrative and loud. The assigned subject of this article is the 56th Annual MLF, July 30 to August 3, 2003, whose official theme was "Lighthouses, Laughter, and Lobster." Total paid attendance was over 80,000, due partly to a national CNN spot in June during which a Senior Editor of a certain other epicurean magazine hailed the MLF as one of the best food-themed festivals in the world. 2003 Festival highlights: concerts by Lee Ann Womack and Orleans, annual Maine Sea Goddess beauty pageant, Saturday's big parade, Sunday's William G. Atwood Memorial Crate Race, annual Amateur Cooking Competition, carnival rides and midway attractions and food booths, and the MLF's Main Eating Tent, where something over 25,000 pounds of fresh-caught Maine lobster is consumed after preparation in the World's Largest Lobster Cooker near the grounds' north entrance. Also available are lobster rolls, lobster turnovers, lobster sauté, Down East lobster salad, lobster bisque, lobster ravioli, and deep-fried lobster dumplings. Lobster Thermidor is obtainable at a sit-down restaurant called The Black Pearl on Harbor Park's northwest wharf. A large all-pine booth sponsored by the Maine Lobster Promotion Council has free pamphlets with recipes, eating tips, and Lobster Fun Facts. The winner of Friday's Amateur Cooking Competition prepares Saffron Lobster Ramekins, the recipe for which is available for public downloading at www.mainelobsterfestival.com. There are lobster T-shirts and lobster bobblehead dolls and inflatable lobster pool toys and clamp-on lobster hats with big scarlet claws that wobble on springs. Your assigned correspondent saw it all, accompanied by one girlfriend and both his own parents—one of which parents was actually born and raised in Maine, albeit in the extreme northern inland part, which is potato country and a world away from the touristic midcoast.[2]

For practical purposes, everyone knows what a lobster is. As usual, though, there's much more to know than most of us care about—it's all a matter of what your interests are. Taxonomically speaking, a lobster is a marine crustacean of the family Homaridae, characterized by five pairs of jointed legs, the first pair terminating in large pincerish claws used for subduing prey. Like many other species of benthic carnivore, lobsters are both hunters and scavengers. They have stalked eyes, gills on their legs, and antennae. There are dozens of different kinds worldwide, of which the relevant species here is the Maine lobster, *Homarus americanus*. The name "lobster" comes from the Old English *loppestre*, which is thought to be a corrupt form of the Latin word for locust combined with the Old English *loppe*, which meant spider.

Moreover, a crustacean is an aquatic arthropod of the class Crustacea, 5 which comprises crabs, shrimp, barnacles, lobsters, and freshwater crayfish. All this is right there in the encyclopedia. And an arthropod is an invertebrate member of the phylum Arthropoda, which phylum covers insects, spiders, crustaceans, and centipedes/millipedes, all of whose main commonality, besides the absence of a centralized brain–spine assembly, is a chitinous exoskeleton composed of segments, to which appendages are articulated in pairs.

The point is that lobsters are basically giant sea-insects.[3] Like most arthropods, they date from the Jurassic period, biologically so much older than mammalia that they might as well be from another planet. And they are—particularly in their natural brown–green state, brandishing their claws like weapons and with thick antennae awhip—not nice to look at. And it's true that they are garbagemen of the sea, eaters of dead stuff,[4] although they'll also eat some live shellfish, certain kinds of injured fish, and sometimes each other.

But they are themselves good eating. Or so we think now. Up until sometime in the 1800s, though, lobster was literally low-class food, eaten only by the poor and institutionalized. Even in the harsh penal environment of early America, some colonies had laws against feeding lobsters to inmates more than once a week because it was thought to be cruel and unusual, like making people eat rats. One reason for their low status was how plentiful lobsters were in old New England. "Unbelievable abundance" is how one source describes the situation, including accounts of Plymouth pilgrims wading out and capturing all they wanted by hand, and of early Boston's seashore being littered with lobsters after hard storms—these latter were treated as a smelly nuisance and ground up for fertilizer. There is also the fact that premodern lobster was often cooked dead and then preserved, usually packed in salt or crude hermetic containers. Maine's earliest lobster industry was based around a dozen such seaside canneries in the 1840s, from which lobster was shipped as far away as California, in demand only because it was cheap and high in protein, basically chewable fuel.

Now, of course, lobster is posh, a delicacy, only a step or two down from caviar. The meat is richer and more substantial than most fish, its taste subtle compared to the marine-gaminess of mussels and clams. In the U.S. pop-food imagination, lobster is now the seafood analog to steak, with which it's so often twinned as Surf 'n' Turf on the really expensive part of the chain steak house menu.

In fact, one obvious project of the MLF, and of its omnipresently sponsorial Maine Lobster Promotion Council, is to counter the idea that lobster is unusually luxe or rich or unhealthy or expensive, suitable only for effete palates or the occasional blow-the-diet treat. It is emphasized over and over in presentations and pamphlets at the Festival that Maine lobster meat has fewer calories, less cholesterol, and less saturated fat than chicken.[5] And in the Main Eating Tent, you can get a "quarter" (industry shorthand for a 1‰-pound lobster), a 4-ounce cup of melted butter, a bag of chips, and a soft roll w/ butter-pat for around $12.00, which is only slightly more expensive than supper at McDonald's.

Be apprised, though, that the Main Eating Tent's suppers come in   10 Styrofoam trays, and the soft drinks are iceless and flat, and the coffee is convenience-store coffee in yet more Styrofoam, and the utensils are plastic (there are none of the special long skinny forks for pushing out the tail meat, though a few savvy diners bring their own). Nor do they give you near enough napkins, considering how messy lobster is to eat, especially when you're squeezed onto benches alongside children of various ages and vastly different levels of fine-motor development—not to mention the people who've somehow smuggled in their own beer in enormous aisle-blocking coolers, or who all of a sudden produce their own plastic tablecloths and try to spread them over large portions of tables to try to reserve them (the tables) for their little groups. And so on. Any one example is no more than a petty inconvenience, of course, but the MLF turns out to be full of irksome little downers like this—see for instance the Main Stage's headliner shows, where it turns out that you have to pay $20 extra for a folding chair if you want to sit down; or the North Tent's mad scramble for the NyQuil-cup-size samples of finalists' entries handed out after the Cooking Competition; or the much-touted Maine Sea Goddess pageant finals, which turn out to be excruciatingly long and to consist mainly of endless thanks and tributes to local sponsors. What the Maine Lobster Festival really is is a midlevel county fair with a culinary hook, and in this respect it's not unlike Tidewater crab festivals, Midwest corn festivals, Texas chili festivals, etc., and shares with these venues the core paradox of all teeming commercial demotic events: It's not for everyone.[6] Nothing against the aforementioned euphoric Senior Editor, but I'd be surprised if she'd spent much time here in Harbor Park, watching people slap canal-zone mosquitoes as they eat deep-fried Twinkies and watch Professor Paddywhack, on six-foot stilts in a raincoat with plastic lobsters protruding from all directions on springs, terrify their children.

Lobster is essentially a summer food. This is because we now prefer our lobsters fresh, which means they have to be recently caught, which for both tactical and economic reasons takes place at depths of less than 25 fathoms.

Lobsters tend to be hungriest and most active (i.e., most trappable) at summer water temperatures of 45–50°F. In the autumn, some Maine lobsters migrate out into deeper water, either for warmth or to avoid the heavy waves that pound New England's coast all winter. Some burrow into the bottom. They might hibernate; nobody's sure. Summer is also lobsters' molting season—specifically early- to mid-July. Chitinous arthropods grow by molting, rather the way people have to buy bigger clothes as they age and gain weight. Since lobsters can live to be over 100, they can also get to be quite large, as in 20 pounds or more—though truly senior lobsters are rare now, because New England's waters are so heavily trapped.[7] Anyway, hence the culinary distinction between hard- and soft-shell lobsters, the latter sometimes a.k.a. shedders. A soft-shell lobster is one that has recently molted. In midcoast restaurants, the summer menu often offers both kinds, with shedders being slightly cheaper even though they're easier to dismantle and the meat is allegedly sweeter. The reason for the discount is that a molting lobster uses a layer of seawater for insulation while its new shell is hardening, so there's slightly less actual meat when you crack open a shedder, plus a redolent gout of water that gets all over everything and can sometimes jet out lemonlike and catch a tablemate right in the eye. If it's winter or you're buying lobster someplace far from New England, on the other hand, you can almost bet that the lobster is a hard-shell, which for obvious reasons travel better.

As an à la carte entrée, lobster can be baked, broiled, steamed, grilled, sautéed, stir-fried, or microwaved. The most common method, though, is boiling. If you're someone who enjoys having lobster at home, this is probably the way you do it, since boiling is so easy. You need a large kettle w/ cover, which you fill about half full with water (the standard advice is that you want 2.5 quarts of water per lobster). Seawater is optimal, or you can add two tbsp salt per quart from the tap. It also helps to know how much your lobsters weigh. You get the water boiling, put in the lobsters one at a time, cover the kettle, and bring it back up to a boil. Then you bank the heat and let the kettle simmer—ten minutes for the first pound of lobster, then three minutes for each pound after that. (This is assuming you've got hard-shell lobsters, which, again, if you don't live between Boston and Halifax, is probably what you've got. For shedders, you're supposed to subtract three minutes from the total.) The reason the kettle's lobsters turn scarlet is that boiling somehow suppresses every pigment in their chitin but one. If you want an easy test of whether the lobsters are done, you try pulling on one of their antennae—if it comes out of the head with minimal effort, you're ready to eat.

A detail so obvious that most recipes don't even bother to mention it is that each lobster is supposed to be alive when you put it in the kettle. This is part of lobster's modern appeal: It's the freshest food there is. There's no decomposition between harvesting and eating. And not only do lobsters require no cleaning or dressing or plucking (though the mechanics of actually eating them are a different matter), but they're relatively easy for vendors to keep alive. They come up alive in the traps, are placed in containers of seawater, and can, so long as the water's aerated and the animals' claws are pegged or banded to keep them from tearing one another up under the stresses of captivity,[8] survive right up until they're boiled. Most of us have been in supermarkets or restaurants that feature tanks of live lobster, from which you can pick out your supper while it watches you point. And part of the overall spectacle of the Maine Lobster Festival is that you can see actual lobstermen's vessels docking at the wharves along the northeast grounds and unloading freshly caught product, which is transferred by hand or cart 100 yards to the great clear tanks stacked up around the Festival's cooker—which is, as mentioned, billed as the World's Largest Lobster Cooker and can process over 100 lobsters at a time for the Main Eating Tent.

So then here is a question that's all but unavoidable at the World's Largest Lobster Cooker, and may arise in kitchens across the U.S.: Is it all right to boil a sentient creature alive just for our gustatory pleasure? A related set of concerns: Is the previous question irksomely PC or sentimental? What does "all right" even mean in this context? Is it all just a matter of individual choice?

As you may or may not know, a certain well-known group called People for the Ethical Treatment of Animals thinks that the morality of lobster-boiling is not just a matter of individual conscience. In fact, one of the very first things we hear about the MLF . . . well, to set the scene: We're coming in by cab from the almost indescribably odd and rustic Knox County Airport[9] very late on the night before the Festival opens, sharing the cab with a wealthy political consultant who lives on Vinalhaven Island in the bay half the year (he's headed for the island ferry in Rockland). The consultant and cabdriver are responding to informal journalistic probes about how people who live in the midcoast region actually view the MLF, as in is the Festival just a big-dollar tourist thing or is it something local residents look forward to attending, take genuine civic pride in, etc. The cabdriver—who's in his seventies, one of apparently a whole platoon of re-tirees the cab company puts on to help with the summer rush, and wears a U.S.-flag lapel pin, and drives in what can only be called a very deliberate way—assures us that locals do endorse and enjoy the MLF, although he himself hasn't gone in years, and now come to think of it no one he and his wife know has, either. However, the demilocal consultant's been to recent Festivals a couple times (one gets the impression it was at his wife's behest), of which his most vivid impression was that "you have to line up for an ungodly long time to get your lobsters, and meanwhile there are all these ex–flower children coming up and down along the line handing out pam-phlets that say the lobsters die in terrible pain and you shouldn't eat them."

And it turns out that the post-hippies of the consultant's recollection were activists from PETA. There were no PETA people in obvious view at the 2003 MLF,[10] but they've been conspicuous at many of the recent Festivals. Since at least the mid-1990s, articles in everything from *The Camden Herald* to *The New York Times* have described PETA urging boy-cotts of the MLF, often deploying celebrity spokespeople like Mary Tyler Moore for open letters and ads saying stuff like "Lobsters are extraordi-narily sensitive" and "To me, eating a lobster is out of the question." More concrete is the oral testimony of Dick, our florid and extremely gregarious rental-car guy, to the effect that PETA's been around so much in recent years that a kind of brittlely tolerant homeostasis now obtains between the activists and the Festival's locals, e.g.: "We had some incidents a couple years ago. One lady took most of her clothes off and painted herself like a lobster, almost got herself arrested. But for the most part they're let alone. [Rapid series of small ambiguous laughs, which with Dick happens a lot.] They do their thing and we do our thing."

This whole interchange takes place on Route 1, 30 July, during a four-mile, 50-minute ride from the airport[11] to the dealership to sign car-rental papers. Several irreproducible segues down the road from the PETA anec-dotes, Dick—whose son-in-law happens to be a professional lobsterman and one of the Main Eating Tent's regular suppliers—articulates what he and his family feel is the crucial mitigating factor in the whole morality-of-boiling-lobsters-alive issue: "There's a part of the brain in people and animals that lets us feel pain, and lobsters' brains don't have this part."

Besides the fact that it's incorrect in about 11 different ways, the main reason Dick's statement is interesting is that its thesis is more or less echoed by the Festival's own pronouncement on lobsters and pain, which is part of

a Test Your Lobster IQ quiz that appears in the 2003 MLF program courtesy of the Maine Lobster Promotion Council: "The nervous system of
a lobster is very simple, and is in fact most similar to the nervous system
of the grasshopper. It is decentralized with no brain. There is no cerebral
cortex, which in humans is the area of the brain that gives the experience
of pain."

Though it sounds more sophisticated, a lot of the neurology in this
latter claim is still either false or fuzzy. The human cerebral cortex is the
brain-part that deals with higher faculties like reason, metaphysical self-
awareness, language, etc. Pain reception is known to be part of a much older
and more primitive system of nociceptors and prostaglandins that are
managed by the brain stem and thalamus.[12] On the other hand, it is true
that the cerebral cortex is involved in what's variously called suffering,
distress, or the emotional experience of pain—i.e., experiencing painful
stimuli as unpleasant, very unpleasant, unbearable, and so on.

Before we go any further, let's acknowledge that the questions of whether   20
and how different kinds of animals feel pain, and of whether and why it
might be justifiable to inflict pain on them in order to eat them, turn out to
be extremely complex and difficult. And comparative neuroanatomy is only
part of the problem. Since pain is a totally subjective mental experience, we
do not have direct access to anyone or anything's pain but our own; and even
just the principles by which we can infer that others experience pain and
have a legitimate interest in not feeling pain involve hard-core philosophy—
metaphysics, epistemology, value theory, ethics. The fact that even the most
highly evolved nonhuman mammals can't use language to communicate
with us about their subjective mental experience is only the first layer of
additional complication in trying to extend our reasoning about pain and
morality to animals. And everything gets progressively more abstract and
convoluted as we move farther and farther out from the higher-type mammals
into cattle and swine and dogs and cats and rodents, and then birds and
fish, and finally invertebrates like lobsters.

The more important point here, though, is that
the whole animal-cruelty-and-eating issue is not
just complex, it's also uncomfortable. It is, at
any rate, uncomfortable for me, and for just
about everyone I know who enjoys a variety of
foods and yet does not want to see herself as
cruel or unfeeling. As far as I can tell, my own

> . . . the whole animal-
> cruelty-and-eating
> issue is not just
> complex, it's also
> uncomfortable.

main way of dealing with this conflict has been to avoid thinking about the whole unpleasant thing. I should add that it appears to me unlikely that many readers of *Gourmet* wish to think hard about it, either, or to be queried about the morality of their eating habits in the pages of a culinary monthly. Since, however, the assigned subject of this article is what it was like to attend the 2003 MLF, and thus to spend several days in the midst of a great mass of Americans all eating lobster, and thus to be more or less impelled to think hard about lobster and the experience of buying and eating lobster, it turns out that there is no honest way to avoid certain moral questions.

There are several reasons for this. For one thing, it's not just that lobsters get boiled alive, it's that you do it yourself—or at least it's done specifically for you, on-site.[13] As mentioned, the World's Largest Lobster Cooker, which is highlighted as an attraction in the Festival's program, is right out there on the MLF's north grounds for everyone to see. Try to imagine a Nebraska Beef Festival[14] at which part of the festivities is watching trucks pull up and the live cattle get driven down the ramp and slaughtered right there on the World's Largest Killing Floor or something—there's no way.

The intimacy of the whole thing is maximized at home, which of course is where most lobster gets prepared and eaten (although note already the semiconscious euphemism "prepared," which in the case of lobsters really means killing them right there in our kitchens). The basic scenario is that we come in from the store and make our little preparations like getting the kettle filled and boiling, and then we lift the lobsters out of the bag or whatever retail container they came home in . . . whereupon some uncomfortable things start to happen. However stuporous the lobster is from the trip home, for instance, it tends to come alarmingly to life when placed in boiling water. If you're tilting it from a container into the steaming kettle, the lobster will sometimes try to cling to the container's sides or even to hook its claws over the kettle's rim like a person trying to keep from going over the edge of a roof. And worse is when the lobster's fully immersed. Even if you cover the kettle and turn away, you can usually hear the cover rattling and clanking as the lobster tries to push it off. Or the creature's claws scraping the sides of the kettle as it thrashes around. The lobster, in other words, behaves very much as you or I would behave if we were plunged into boiling water (with the obvious exception of screaming).[15] A blunter way to say this is that the lobster acts as if it's in terrible pain, causing some cooks to leave the kitchen altogether and to take one of those little lightweight plastic oven timers with them into another room and wait until the whole process is over.

There happen to be two main criteria that most ethicists agree on for determining whether a living creature has the capacity to suffer and so has genuine interests that it may or may not be our moral duty to consider.[16] One is how much of the neurological hardware required for pain-experience the animal comes equipped with—nociceptors, prostaglandins, neuronal opioid receptors, etc. The other criterion is whether the animal demonstrates behavior associated with pain. And it takes a lot of intellectual gymnastics and behaviorist hairsplitting not to see struggling, thrashing, and lid-clattering as just such pain-behavior. According to marine zoologists, it usually takes lobsters between 35 and 45 seconds to die in boiling water. (No source I could find talked about how long it takes them to die in superheated steam; one rather hopes it's faster.)

There are, of course, other fairly common ways to kill your lobster on-site and so achieve maximum freshness. Some cooks' practice is to drive a sharp heavy knife point-first into a spot just above the midpoint between the lobster's eyestalks (more or less where the Third Eye is in human foreheads). This is alleged either to kill the lobster instantly or to render it insensate—and is said at least to eliminate the cowardice involved in throwing a creature into boiling water and then fleeing the room. As far as I can tell from talking to proponents of the knife-in-the-head method, the idea is that it's more violent but ultimately more merciful, plus that a willingness to exert personal agency and accept responsibility for stabbing the lobster's head honors the lobster somehow and entitles one to eat it. (There's often a vague sort of Native American spirituality-of-the-hunt flavor to pro-knife arguments.) But the problem with the knife method is basic biology: Lobsters' nervous systems operate off not one but several ganglia, a.k.a. nerve bundles, which are sort of wired in series and distributed all along the lobster's underside, from stem to stern. And disabling only the frontal ganglion does not normally result in quick death or unconsciousness. Another alternative is to put the lobster in cold salt water and then very slowly bring it up to a full boil. Cooks who advocate this method are going mostly on the analogy to a frog, which can supposedly be kept from jumping out of a boiling pot by heating the water incrementally. In order to save a lot of research-summarizing, I'll simply assure you that the analogy between frogs and lobsters turns out not to hold.

25

Ultimately, the only certain virtues of the home-lobotomy and slow-heating methods are comparative, because there are even worse/crueler ways people prepare lobster. Time-thrifty cooks sometimes microwave them alive (usually after poking several extra vent holes in the carapace, which is a precaution most shellfish-microwavers learn about the hard way). Live dismemberment, on the other hand, is big in Europe: Some chefs cut the lobster in half before cooking; others like to tear off the claws and tail and toss only these parts in the pot.

And there's more unhappy news respecting suffering-criterion number one. Lobsters don't have much in the way of eyesight or hearing, but they do have an exquisite tactile sense, one facilitated by hundreds of thousands of tiny hairs that protrude through their carapace. "Thus," in the words of T. M. Prudden's industry classic *About Lobster*, "it is that although encased in what seems a solid, impenetrable armor, the lobster can receive stimuli and impressions from without as readily as if it possessed a soft and delicate skin." And lobsters do have nociceptors,[17] as well as invertebrate versions of the prostaglandins and major neurotransmitters via which our own brains register pain.

Lobsters do not, on the other hand, appear to have the equipment for making or absorbing natural opioids like endorphins and enkephalins, which are what more advanced nervous systems use to try to handle intense pain. From this fact, though, one could conclude either that lobsters are maybe even *more* vulnerable to pain, since they lack mammalian nervous systems' built-in analgesia, or, instead, that the absence of natural opioids implies an absence of the really intense pain-sensations that natural opioids are designed to mitigate. I for one can detect a marked upswing in mood as I contemplate this latter possibility: It could be that their lack of endorphin/enkephalin hardware means that lobsters' raw subjective experience of pain is so radically different from mammals' that it may not even deserve the term *pain*. Perhaps lobsters are more like those frontal-lobotomy patients one reads about who report experiencing pain in a totally different way than you and I. These patients evidently do feel physical pain, neurologically speaking, but don't dislike it—though neither do they like it; it's more that they feel it but don't feel anything *about* it—the point being that the pain is not distressing to them or something they want to get away from. Maybe lobsters, who are also without frontal lobes, are detached from the neurological-registration-of-injury-or-hazard we call pain in just the same way. There is, after all, a difference between (1) pain as a purely neurological event, and (2) actual suffering, which seems crucially to involve an emotional component, an awareness of pain as unpleasant, as something to fear/dislike/want to avoid.

Still, after all the abstract intellection, there remain the facts of the frantically clanking lid, the pathetic clinging to the edge of the pot. Standing at the stove, it is hard to deny in any meaningful way that this is a living creature experiencing pain and wishing to avoid/escape the painful experience. To my lay mind, the lobster's behavior in the kettle appears to be the expression of a *preference*; and it may well be that an ability to form preferences is the decisive criterion for real suffering.[18] The logic of this (preference p suffering) relation may be easiest to see in the negative case. If you cut certain kinds of worms in half, the halves will often keep crawling around and going about their vermiform business as if nothing had happened. When we assert, based on their post-op behavior, that these worms appear not to be suffering, what we're really saying is that there's no sign that the worms know anything bad has happened or would *prefer* not to have gotten cut in half.

Lobsters, however, are known to exhibit preferences. Experiments have shown that they can detect changes of only a degree or two in water temperature; one reason for their complex migratory cycles (which can often cover 100-plus miles a year) is to pursue the temperatures they like best.[19] And, as mentioned, they're bottom-dwellers and do not like bright light: If a tank of food lobsters is out in the sunlight or a store's fluorescence, the lobsters will always congregate in whatever part is darkest. Fairly solitary in the ocean, they also clearly dislike the crowding that's part of their captivity in tanks, since (as also mentioned) one reason why lobsters' claws are banded on capture is to keep them from attacking one another under the stress of close-quarter storage.

In any event, at the Festival, standing by the bubbling tanks outside the World's Largest Lobster Cooker, watching the fresh-caught lobsters pile over one another, wave their hobbled claws impotently, huddle in the rear corners, or scrabble frantically back from the glass as you approach, it is difficult not to sense that they're unhappy, or frightened, even if it's some rudimentary version of these feelings . . . and, again, why does rudimentariness even enter into it? Why is a primitive, inarticulate form of suffering less urgent or uncomfortable for the person who's helping to inflict it by paying for the food it results in? I'm not trying to give you a PETA-like screed here—at least I don't think so. I'm trying, rather, to work out and articulate some of the troubling questions that arise amid all the laughter and saltation and community pride of the Maine Lobster Festival. The truth

30

is that if you, the Festival attendee, permit yourself to think that lobsters can suffer and would rather not, the MLF can begin to take on aspects of something like a Roman circus or medieval torture-fest.

Does that comparison seem a bit much? If so, exactly why? Or what about this one: Is it not possible that future generations will regard our own present agribusiness and eating practices in much the same way we now view Nero's entertainments or Aztec sacrifices? My own immediate reaction is that such a comparison is hysterical, extreme—and yet the reason it seems extreme to me appears to be that I believe animals are less morally important than human beings;[20] and when it comes to defending such a belief, even to myself, I have to acknowledge that (a) I have an obvious selfish interest in this belief, since I like to eat certain kinds of animals and want to be able to keep doing it, and (b) I have not succeeded in working out any sort of personal ethical system in which the belief is truly defensible instead of just selfishly convenient.

Given this article's venue and my own lack of culinary sophistication, I'm curious about whether the reader can identify with any of these reactions and acknowledgments and discomforts. I am also concerned not to come off as shrill or preachy when what I really am is confused. Given the (possible) moral status and (very possible) physical suffering of the animals involved, what ethical convictions do gourmets evolve that allow them not just to eat but to savor and enjoy flesh-based viands (since of course refined *enjoyment*, rather than just ingestion, is the whole point of gastronomy)? And for those gourmets who'll have no truck with convictions or rationales and who regard stuff like the previous paragraph as just so much pointless navel-gazing, what makes it feel okay, inside, to dismiss the whole issue out of hand? That is, is their refusal to think about any of this the product of actual thought, or is it just that they don't want to think about it? Do they ever think about their reluctance to think about it? After all, isn't being extra aware and attentive and thoughtful about one's food and its overall context part of what distinguishes a real gourmet? Or is all the gourmet's extra attention and sensibility just supposed to be aesthetic, gustatory?

These last couple queries, though, while sincere, obviously involve much larger and more abstract questions about the connections (if any) between aesthetics and morality, and these questions lead straightaway into such deep and treacherous waters that it's probably best to stop the public discussion right here. There are limits to what even interested persons can ask of each other.

Endnotes

1. There's a comprehensive native apothegm: "Camden by the sea, Rockland by the smell."
2. N.B. All personally connected parties have made it clear from the start that they do not want to be talked about in this article.
3. Midcoasters' native term for a lobster is, in fact, "bug," as in "Come around on Sunday and we'll cook up some bugs."
4. Factoid: Lobster traps are usually baited with dead herring.
5. Of course, the common practice of dipping the lobster meat in melted butter torpedoes all these happy fat-specs, which none of the Council's promotional stuff ever mentions, any more than potato-industry PR talks about sour cream and bacon bits.
6. In truth, there's a great deal to be said about the differences between working-class Rockland and the heavily populist flavor of its Festival versus comfortable and elitist Camden with its expensive view and shops given entirely over to $200 sweaters and great rows of Victorian homes converted to upscale B&Bs. And about these differences as two sides of the great coin that is U.S. tourism. Very little of which will be said here, except to amplify the above-mentioned paradox and to reveal your assigned correspondent's own preferences. I confess that I have never understood why so many people's idea of a fun vacation is to don flip-flops and sunglasses and crawl through maddening traffic to loud hot crowded tourist venues in order to sample a "local flavor" that is by definition ruined by the presence of tourists. This may (as my Festival companions keep pointing out) all be a matter of personality and hard-wired taste: The fact that I just do not like tourist venues means that I'll never understand their appeal and so am probably not the one to talk about it (the supposed appeal). But, since this note will almost surely not survive magazine-editing anyway, here goes:
   As I see it, it probably really is good for the soul to be a tourist, even if it's only once in a while. Not good for the soul in a refreshing or enlivening way, though, but rather in a grim, steely-eyed, let's-look-honestly-at-the-facts-and-find-some-way-to-deal-with-them way. My personal experience has not been that traveling around the country is broadening or relaxing, or that radical changes in place and context have a salutary effect, but rather that intranational tourism is radically constricting, and humbling in the hardest way—hostile to my fantasy of being a real individual, of living somehow outside and above it all.

(Coming up is the part that my companions find especially unhappy and repellent, a sure way to spoil the fun of vacation travel:) To be a mass tourist, for me, is to become a pure late-date American: alien, ignorant, greedy for something you cannot ever have, disappointed in a way you can never admit. It is to spoil, by way of sheer ontology, the very unspoiledness you are there to experience. It is to impose yourself on places that in all noneconomic ways would be better, realer, without you. It is, in lines and gridlock and transaction after transaction, to confront a dimension of yourself that is as inescapable as it is painful: As a tourist, you become economically significant but existentially loathsome, an insect on a dead thing.

7. Datum: In a good year, the U.S. industry produces around 80 million pounds of lobster, and Maine accounts for more than half that total.

8. N.B. Similar reasoning underlies the practice of what's termed "debeaking" broiler chickens and brood hens in modern factory farms. Maximum commercial efficiency requires that enormous poultry populations be confined in unnaturally close quarters, under which conditions many birds go crazy and peck one another to death. As a purely observational side-note, be apprised that debeaking is usually an automated process and that the chickens receive no anesthetic. It's not clear to me whether most gourmet readers know about debeaking, or about related practices like dehorning cattle in commercial feedlots, cropping swine's tails in factory hog farms to keep psychotically bored neighbors from chewing them off, and so forth. It so happens that your assigned correspondent knew almost nothing about standard meat-industry operations before starting work on this article.

9. The terminal used to be somebody's house, for example, and the lost-luggage-reporting room was clearly once a pantry.

10. It turned out that one Mr. William R. Rivas-Rivas, a high-ranking PETA official out of the group's Virginia headquarters, was indeed there this year, albeit solo, working the Festival's main and side entrances on Saturday, August 2, handing out pamphlets and adhesive stickers emblazoned with "Being Boiled Hurts," which is the tagline in most of PETA's published material about lobster. I learned that he'd been there only later, when speaking with Mr. Rivas-Rivas on the phone. I'm not sure how we missed seeing him *in situ* at the Festival, and I can't see much to do except apologize for the oversight— although it's also true that Saturday was the day of the big MLF parade

through Rockland, which basic journalistic responsibility seemed to require going to (and which, with all due respect, meant that Saturday was maybe not the best day for PETA to work the Harbor Park grounds, especially if it was going to be just one person for one day, since a lot of diehard MLF partisans were off-site watching the parade (which, again with no offense intended, was in truth kind of cheesy and boring, consisting mostly of slow homemade floats and various midcoast people waving at one another, and with an extremely annoying man dressed as Blackbeard ranging up and down the length of the crowd saying "Arrr" over and over and brandishing a plastic sword at people, etc.; plus it rained)).

11. The short version regarding why we were back at the airport after already arriving the previous night involves lost luggage and a miscommunication about where and what the local National Car Rental franchise was—Dick came out personally to the airport and got us, out of no evident motive but kindness. (He also talked nonstop the entire way, with a very distinctive speaking style that can be described only as manically laconic; the truth is that I now know more about this man than I do about some members of my own family.)

12. To elaborate by way of example: The common experience of accidentally touching a hot stove and yanking your hand back before you're even aware that anything's going on is explained by the fact that many of the processes by which we detect and avoid painful stimuli do not involve the cortex. In the case of the hand and stove, the brain is bypassed altogether; all the important neurochemical action takes place in the spine.

13. Morality-wise, let's concede that this cuts both ways. Lobster-eating is at least not abetted by the system of corporate factory farms that produces most beef, pork, and chicken. Because, if nothing else, of the way they're marketed and packaged for sale, we eat these latter meats without having to consider that they were once conscious, sentient creatures to whom horrible things were done. (N.B. PETA distributes a certain video—the title of which is being omitted as part of the elaborate editorial compromise by which this note appears at all—in which you can see just about everything meat-related you don't want to see or think about. (N.B.[2] Not that PETA's any sort of font of unspun truth. Like many partisans in complex moral disputes, the PETA people are fanatics, and a lot of their rhetoric seems simplistic and self-righteous.

Personally, though, I have to say that I found this unnamed video both credible and deeply upsetting.))

14. Is it significant that "lobster," "fish," and "chicken" are our culture's words for both the animal and the meat, whereas most mammals seem to require euphemisms like "beef" and "pork" that help us separate the meat we eat from the living creature the meat once was? Is this evidence that some kind of deep unease about eating higher animals is endemic enough to show up in English usage, but that the unease diminishes as we move out of the mammalian order? (And is "lamb"/"lamb" the counterexample that sinks the whole theory, or are there special, biblico-historical reasons for that equivalence?)

15. There's a relevant populist myth about the high-pitched whistling sound that sometimes issues from a pot of boiling lobster. The sound is really vented steam from the layer of seawater between the lobster's flesh and its carapace (this is why shedders whistle more than hard-shells), but the pop version has it that the sound is the lobster's rabbitlike death scream. Lobsters communicate via pheromones in their urine and don't have anything close to the vocal equipment for screaming, but the myth's very persistent—which might, once again, point to a low-level cultural unease about the boiling thing.

16. "Interests" basically means strong and legitimate preferences, which obviously require some degree of consciousness, responsiveness to stimuli, etc. See, for instance, the utilitarian philosopher Peter Singer, whose 1974 *Animal Liberation* is more or less the bible of the modern animal-rights movement: "It would be nonsense to say that it was not in the interests of a stone to be kicked along the road by a schoolboy. A stone does not have interests because it cannot suffer. Nothing that we can do to it could possibly make any difference to its welfare. A mouse, on the other hand, does have an interest in not being kicked along the road, because it will suffer if it is."

17. This is the neurological term for special pain receptors that are (according to Jane A. Smith and Kenneth M. Boyd's *Lives in the Balance*) "sensitive to potentially damaging extremes of temperature, to mechanical forces, and to chemical substances which are released when body tissues are damaged."

18. "Preference" is maybe roughly synonymous with "interest," but it is a better term for our purposes because it's less abstractly philosophical— "preference" seems more personal, and it's the whole idea of a living creature's personal experience that's at issue.

19. Of course, the most common sort of counterargument here would begin by objecting that "like best" is really just a metaphor, and a misleadingly anthropomorphic one at that. The counterarguer would posit that the lobster seeks to maintain a certain optimal ambient temperature out of nothing but unconscious instinct (with a similar explanation for the low-light affinities about to be mentioned in the main text). The thrust of such a counterargument will be that the lobster's thrashings and clankings in the kettle express not unpreferred pain but involuntary reflexes, like your leg shooting out when the doctor hits your knee. Be advised that there are professional scientists, including many researchers who use animals in experiments, who hold to the view that nonhuman creatures have no real feelings at all, only "behaviors." Be further advised that this view has a long history that goes all the way back to Descartes, although its modern support comes mostly from behaviorist psychology.

    To these what-look-like-pain-are-really-only-reflexes counterarguments, however, there happen to be all sorts of scientific and pro-animal-rights countercounterarguments. And then further attempted rebuttals and redirects, and so on. Suffice to say that both the scientific and the philosophical arguments on either side of the animal-suffering issue are involved, abstruse, technical, often informed by self-interest or ideology, and in the end so totally inconclusive that as a practical matter, in the kitchen or restaurant, it all still seems to come down to individual conscience, going with (no pun) your gut.

20. Meaning a *lot* less important, apparently, since the moral comparison here is not the value of one human's life vs. the value of one animal's life, but rather the value of one animal's life vs. the value of one human's taste for a particular kind of protein. Even the most diehard carniphile will acknowledge that it's possible to live and eat well without consuming animals.

Analyze

1. Look at the title of this article. Whom is Wallace asking to consider the lobster? In whose consideration is he the most interested? Why?
2. Analyze the ways in which Wallace attempts to invite the reader's sympathies. For instance, analyze the effect of images such as "The lobster will sometimes cling to the container's sides, or even hook its claws over the kettle's rim like a person trying to keep from going over the edge of a roof." What others do you find, and what effect do they have?
3. Trace and describe Wallace's discussion of the history of lobster-eating. How does he use the history and current contexts for eating lobster to support his overall point? And how would you articulate Wallace's point?

Explore

1. Use Wallace's critique of lobster eating as a framework by which you approach another type of behavior you observe regarding food. How would you describe this behavior? How does this behavior possibly cause you to question the ethics of eating that particular food? Why or why not?
2. Wallace refers to pro-animal rights arguments and counterarguments. Do some research. What are these arguments, for and against eating animals as part of the human diet? What are the most convincing arguments on either side? Why?
3. At the end of the article, after the litany of rhetorical questions, Wallace acknowledges the "ethical" considerations that arise between "aesthetics and morality." Wallace seems to say that "foodies" (or gourmets, as he calls them) are more interested in aesthetics than morality. Find other articles that treat either the ethics or the beauty of food. Using these in discussion groups, explore the notions of "aesthetics" and "morality" as they relate to the culture of foodie-ism at large.

Julie Guthman
"Can't Stomach It: How Michael Pollan et al. Made Me Want to Eat Cheetos"

Julie Guthman is a *New York Times* blogger and professor at the University of California, Santa Cruz. Her forthcoming book, *Weighing In: Obesity, Food Justice, and the Limits of Capitalism*, questions myths surrounding food and our obsession with it. In this piece, Guthman challenges the contemporary rhetoric used to define the "obesity crisis." Specifically, she takes on such noted writers as Michael Pollan, whom she sees as self-righteous and too privileged to understand the deeper contexts of the "obesity crisis."

What seems to be Guthman's perspective on the reasons for obesity? How would you characterize her approach to the problem?

It has become common to speak of an "epidemic of obesity." Serious news sources routinely feature articles on obesity; some even suggest that the obesity epidemic is one of the greatest public health threats of our times, perhaps rivaling AIDS or avian flu. Obesity is commonly linked to other social problems, as well. It has been named as a cost to businesses in terms of worker productivity, a cause for poor pupil performance, a weight-load problem for the airlines due to increased fuel costs, and even a security threat in terms of military preparedness. Proposed and implemented social solutions have included snack taxes, corporate-sponsored exercise breaks, stronger food labeling laws, and, most troublingly, state-mandated student weigh-ins at public schools, with results included on report cards (as if fat kids and their parents need to be reminded).

Obesity further serves as a bonanza for social reformers who deploy the rhetoric of fat in support of their various projects, from farm-to-school programs to mixed-use housing and transportation centers; and for puritans who wish to use fatness as an example of the moral decrepitude to which we must just say no. Finally, the obesity epidemic, and its tendency to dignify obsessions that equate thinness and beauty, is hugely profitable, contributing, by some estimates, to a one-hundred-billion-dollar-per-year weight-loss industry that distributes specialized products and services apart from the money made on bariatric and cosmetic surgery. Television shows like *The Biggest Loser*, sponsored by purveyors of diet foods, fitness centers, and pharmaceuticals, contribute to the false idea that diets work, thereby increasing the market for such goods and services. And if the daily e-mail spam I receive for Anatrim serves as any indication, the underground market in pharmaceuticals is cashing in, too.

Taken together, the above set of observations suggests that obesity has achieved the status of an infectious disease. Although obesity has not been deemed infectious—at least yet—the criteria employed by researcher Nancy Tomes to establish the existence of a germ panic equate obesity in degree, if not kind, to the problem of tuberculosis in the early twentieth century: a) the "disease" is deemed newsworthy; b) its incidence reflects other societal problems, giving activists and reformers an angle for addressing their specific concerns; and c) it has commercial potential to sell products or services, so that public concern is heightened by economic interests.[1] Tomes' study also discusses the central role that popular culture, in the form of news coverage, entertainment media, and popular nonfiction, plays in contributing to the hysteria that constitutes such a panic. These factors are all true of obesity. In particular, a rash of popular books has appeared on the so-called obesity epidemic. While these books take a variety of positions on the topic, virtually all claim to "expose the lies" and/or tell the "real" story about the epidemic and/or who is gaining by it. For example, J. Eric Oliver's *Fat Politics: The Real Story Behind America's Obesity Epidemic*, while voicing skepticism of the ways in which obesity has been framed, contributes to the frenzy through its tone.[2]

Lately, another group of writers has gotten in on the act. A more refined and measured group, their books turn on the theme of "what to eat"—the specific title of Marion Nestle's most recent volume.[3] Other books in this group include Peter Singer's *The Way We Eat: Why Our Food Choices Matter*, Anna Lappé's *Grub: Ideas for an Urban Organic Kitchen*, and Jane Goodall's *Harvest for Hope: A Guide to Mindful Eating*.[4] Of all these books, the sine qua non is Michael Pollan's *The Omnivore's Dilemma: A Natural History of Four Meals*.[5] It is like no other because not only does Pollan know his stuff, he can write his way out of a paper bag, and his book sales show it. Virtually all of these authors extol the virtues of the organic and the local while arguing for a commonsense, ecumenical approach to diet choices (no food faddism here). That makes them refreshing in relation to the usual weight loss books and painfully restrictive messages of latter-day health foodism. Or does it?

Many of these authors share a common rhetorical strategy. They refer 5
to the statistics of rising obesity rates among Americans, the surfeit of
calories taken in relative to those expended, and the inexorable road
toward illness with concomitant rising healthcare costs (never tabulated
against the healthcare costs of weight loss attempts). They then go on to
discuss the ubiquity of fast, junky food (what Kelly Brownell calls the
"toxic environment") in order to make their points about what constitutes
"real" food.[6] But whereas most of the popular writers on fat attribute
growing obesity to a variety of culprits—television viewing, long drive-to-
work times, supermarket product placement, working mothers, clothing
designers (allowing baggy clothes), marketing to children, poverty, affluence, and modernity (i.e., everything under the sun)—Pollan is much
more pointed in his analysis. As he puts it, "All these explanations are true,
as far as they go. But it pays to go a little further, to search for the cause
behind the causes. Which, very simply, is this: When food is abundant
and cheap, people will eat more of it and get fat."[7] Pollan then points to an
even more specific culprit: corn.

Pollan's excellent writing makes for a compelling story about how corn
has become the foundation of the national diet. He traces this first to
the transport of *Zea mays* from regions now known as central Mexico to
points north, where it easily took hold in a variety of microclimatic conditions and outdid wheat in terms of its yield and ease of cultivation. But
corn's strength turned to its weakness; it was prone to systematic overproduction in US agriculture, so that even historically, surpluses ended up to
no good. Corn liquor, of course, was the beverage of choice (and necessity)
in pre-Prohibition drinking binges. Since the 1970s, the overproduction of
corn has been buttressed by a farm policy that subsidizes corn production,
in part to appease the farm lobby and in part for geopolitical ends, with
erstwhile Secretary of Agriculture Earl Butz having first encouraged planting "from fencerow to fencerow." Pollan reminds us that corn is omnipres-
ent in a fast-food meal: the high fructose corn syrup that sweetens the soda;
the feed of the steer that goes into the hamburger beef; often the oil that
fries the potatoes; and as one of the many micro-ingredients that stabilizes
the bun. Corn byproducts, it turns out, are even used in the packaging and
serving utensils. Processed food, Pollan argues, makes us "walking corn,"
and the "Alcohol Republic" has now given way to "the Republic of Fat."[8]

Pollan's critique of the cost-cutting measures of the fast-food giants,
the nutritional impoverishment of processed food, and an agricultural

subsidy system that encourages ecologically problematic monocropping, horrendous animal husbandry practices, and food-dumping in the name of "aid" (often at the expense of farmers in the global South) is spot on. In fact, I could think of no clearer path to a more ecological and socially just food system than the removal of those subsidies. Yet, in evoking obesity, Pollan turns our gaze, perhaps inadvertently, from an ethically suspect farm policy to the fat body. One of the questions I want to raise in this essay is whether it is necessary for fat people to bear the weight of this argument.

There is much to criticize in the public conversation about obesity. The evidentiary basis of an "epidemic" is fairly weak, as it relies on changes in average Body Mass Index (BMI), itself a contested, albeit convenient way to measure obesity. For example, as a weight to height ratio, BMI cannot differentiate between fat and lean body mass.[9] For that matter, discussions of an epidemic provide very little specificity as to dimensions of the growth in girth. To draw out two extremes of the problem statement, it is unclear whether a relatively small number of people have become extremely fat, or whether many people have put on a few pounds. Given the way the BMI is normalized and categorized, a small average weight gain among a large population can shift enormous numbers of people from one category into the next, say from "overweight" to "obese," and thereby deepen the impression of an epidemic.[10] Moreover, the relationship between food intake, exercise, and growing obesity is poorly understood. Michael Gard and Jan Wright's exhaustive review of obesity research shows that the mechanical notion that weight gain results from a surplus of calories in to calories out has not been borne out in the research; at best, caloric metabolism appears to explain less than half of individual variation in body size, with much of the residual remaining "black boxed."[11] Finally, claims that obesity is a primary cause of disease (or a disease itself) are filled with logical flaws, chief among them that obesity may be symptomatic of diseases of concern, such as Type II diabetes.[12] For all of these reasons, Gard and Wright argue that obesity research itself has become so entangled with moral discourses and aesthetic values that the "science of obesity" can no longer speak for itself.[13]

These popular renditions are also remarkably insensitive, and not necessarily just to those who feel themselves to be too fat.[14] Rather, these authors seem unaware of how obesity messages work as admonishment. According to Paul Campos, the people most personally affected by discussions of obesity are those who want to lose ten or fifteen pounds, despite the fact that those who are "overweight" by current standards have longer life spans than those who are "thin" or "normal."[15] In a course I taught, called the Politics of Obesity, I was not particularly surprised by the number of students who wrote in their journals (a required element of the class) of their hidden "fatness" or eating disorders. However, the number of entries that stated how the course itself had produced body anxiety and intensified concern over diet and exercise was shocking, given that a good deal of the material took a critical stance toward obesity talk. The philosopher Michel Foucault might have called this the "productive" power of obesity talk—that in naming a behavior as a problem, it intensifies anxiety around that problem.[16] In that way, swipes at obesity, especially coming from those who themselves have never been subject to such scrutiny or objectification, or the pain and frustration of weight loss, strikes me as naive. Yet, entirely absent from the pages of the recent popular books is any authorial reflection on how obesity talk further stigmatizes those who are fat, or on how this social scolding might actually work at cross-purposes to health and well being.

But there is something even more disturbing about these books and the claims they reproduce. To repeat Pollan's claim: "When food is abundant and cheap, people will eat more of it and get fat."[17] People eat corn because it's there. They are dupes. Jane Goodall makes a similar leap when she writes, "There is no mechanism that turns off the desire—instinct, really—to eat food when it is available."[18] Even Marion Nestle's concern with supermarket aisles suggests that people mechanically react to product placement. This raises an important question: why are Pollan, Goodall, and Nestle not fat? If junk food is so ubiquitous that it cannot be resisted, how is it that some people remain (or become) thin?

It appears, unfortunately, that these authors see themselves as morally superior to fat people in the sense that they characterize fat people as being short of subjectivity. Goodall makes the above assertion having just written of "sad," "overweight," "over-indulged" cats and dogs being "killed by kindness," seeming to equate fat people with family pets.[19] In the "documentary" *SuperSize Me*, virtually all shots of fat people are headless and certainly speechless, and usually the camera captures backsides only. Some might argue that having no personal identifiers protects fat people in the camera's eye, but headlessness also invokes mindlessness. Moreover, such protection assumes that fat people are ashamed of their bodies and eating habits. Since thin people *are* consistently pictured with heads, it logically

10

follows that they are not so ashamed. This presumption is precisely the problem that Kathleen LeBesco captures in *Revolting Bodies*, including her critique of the fat acceptance movement itself.[20] At best, fat people are seen as victims of food, bad genetic codes, or bad metabolism; at worst, they are slovenly, stupid, or without resolve. Perhaps, she argues, fat people exercise agency in their fatness. Meanwhile, she notes, many thin people can indulge in all manners of unhealthy behaviors without being called to account for their body size. What LeBesco makes clear, in other words, is that fat people are imbued with little subjectivity no matter what they do, while thin people are imbued with heightened subjectivity no matter what *they* do.

That, then, is the most pernicious aspect of the Pollan et al. analysis. If junk food is everywhere and people are all naturally drawn to it, those who resist it must have heightened powers. In the reality television show *The Biggest Loser*, where fat people compete to lose the most weight (about which much could be said), the contestants are treated paternalistically; the hard-body trainers are treated as super-subjects who readily and regularly bestow life wisdom on their charges. So when Pollan waxes poetic about his own rarefied, distinctive eating practices, he makes a similar move. The messianic quality and self-satisfaction is not accidental. In describing his ability to overcome King Corn, to conceive, procure, prepare, and (perhaps) serve his version of the perfect meal, Pollan affirms himself as a super-subject while relegating others to objects of education, intervention, or just plain scorn.

Even if it were true that obesity is the public-health threat it is purported to be, even if it could be proven that it results from fast-food consumption in a clear and identifiable way, and even if we didn't care about the stigmatization of obesity or treating fat people as objects, is Pollan's way the way out? At the end of a book whose biggest strength is a section that lays out the environmental history and political economy of corn, his answer, albeit oblique, is to eat like he does. The meal that he helped forage and hunt and cooked all by himself, as he puts it, "gave me the opportunity, so rare in modern life, to eat in full consciousness of everything involved in feeding myself: for once, I was able to pay the full karmic price of a meal."[21] Notwithstanding Pollan's arguably narrow understanding of a "full karmic price" (how, for example, does this rectify the exploitation of farm laborers?), my question is: To what kind of politics does this lead? Despite his early focus on corn subsidies, Pollan does not urge his readers to write to their congressional representative about the folly of such subsidies, to comment to the FDA about food additives, or even, for that matter, to sabotage fields where genetically engineered corn is grown.[22]

Indeed, no suggestion is made that we ought to alter the structural features of the food system, so that all might come to eat better. Pollan betrays himself in his admiration of Joel Salatin, a beyond-organic farmer who is hard-lined in his denunciation of state regulation, seeing it as an impediment to building a viable local food chain. Unfortunately, this antiregulatory approach to food politics has really taken hold, especially in my part of the country. I have read countless undergraduate papers at my university that begin with the premise that the global food system is anomic, and that "if people only knew where their food came from," food provisioning would somehow evolve to be more ecological, humane, and just. Many of my students have strong convictions that they should and can teach people how and what to eat, as if you could "change the world one meal at a time" without attention to policy.[23]

I worry that Michael Pollan reinforces this highly privileged and apolitical idea and reinforces the belief that some people—in this case thin people—clearly must have seen the light that the rest are blind to. Pollan is a damn good writer and a smart man, which makes *The Omnivore's Dilemma* a compelling read. But I can't stomach where it leads. In a funny way, it makes me crave some corn-based Cheetos.

15

Endnotes

1. Nancy Tomes, "The Making of a Germ Panic, Then and Now," *American Journal of Public Health* 90, no.2 (2000): 191.
2. J. Eric Oliver, *Fat Politics: The Real Story Behind America's Obesity Epidemic* (New York: Oxford University, 2006).
3. Marion Nestle, *What to Eat* (New York: North Point Press, 2006).
4. Jane Goodall, Gary McAvoy, and Gail Hudson, *Harvest for Hope: A Guide to Mindful Eating* (New York: Warner Books, 2005); Anna Lappé and Bryant Terry, *Grub: Ideas for an Urban Organic Kitchen* (New York: Tarcher, 2006); Peter Singer and Jim Mason, *The Way We Eat: Why Our Food Choices Matter* (Emmaus, PA: Rodale Press, 2006). The coauthors' names were omitted from the main text because these books are clearly being sold on the relative fame of their primary authors.

5. Michael Pollan, *The Omnivore's Dilemma: A Natural History of Four Meals* (New York: Penguin, 2006).

6. Kelly D. Brownell, *Food Fight: The Inside Story of the Food Industry, America's Obesity Crisis, and What We Can Do About It* (New York: McGraw–Hill, 2004).

7. Pollan, *Omnivore's Dilemma*, 102.

8. Ibid., 101.

9. Glenn Gaesser, *Big Fat Lies: The Truth about Your Weight and Your Health* (New York: Burze Books, 2002), Paul Campos et al., "The Epidemiology of Overweight and Obesity: Public Health Crisis or Moral Panic?" *International Journal of Epidemiology* 35, no.1 (2006).

10. Bruce Ross, "Fat or Fiction? Weighing the Obesity Epidemic," in *The Obesity Epidemic: Science, Morality, and Ideology*, ed. Michael Gard and Jan Wright (London: Routledge, 2005).

11. Michael Gard and Jan Wright, *The Obesity Epidemic: Science, Morality, and Ideology* (London: Routledge, 2005). This point was deduced from a discussion on pp.47–50, where the authors note that some researchers have claimed that genetic factors account for 50 to 90 percent of individual variation. Gard and Wright make the point that genetic factors are acting as a "black box" to defend the calories in–calories out model.

12. Oliver, *Fat Politics*.

13. Gard and Wright, *Obesity Epidemic*.

14. I cringed when Nestle, as a keynote speaker at the Ecological Farming Conference in January 2006, stated that the problem of obesity was "simple," using the very terminology that Gard and Wright refute (calories in–calories out). Most of this audience applauded wildly, for the obesity epidemic holds much marketing promise for those who stake their living in the production of organic fresh fruits and vegetables.

15. Paul Campos, *The Obesity Myth: Why America's Obsession with Weight Is Hazardous to Your Health* (New York: Gotham Press, 2004).

16. Michel Foucault, *History of Sexuality, an Introduction*, vol. I (New York: Vintage, 1985).

17. Pollan, *Omnivore's Dilemma*, 102.

18. Goodall et al., *Harvest for Hope*, 240.

19. Ibid.

20. Kathleen Lebesco, *Revolting Bodies? The Struggle to Redefine Fat Identity* (Amherst: University of Massachusetts, 2004).
21. Pollan, *Omnivore's Dilemma*, 9.
22. This is an activist strategy popular in Europe, intended presumably to incite public rancor about the unnecessary proliferation of genetic engineering, especially in light of the fact that the primary justification of such technologies is to improve productivity. In this way, such a strategy is surely germane to Pollan's point.
23. The quoted catchphrase is widely circulated in alternative-food-movement circles.

Analyze

1. How does Guthman struggle with the language used to define obesity? How does this struggle manifest itself, and what is the language that seems to vex her so?
2. In what ways does Guthman take issue with other writers, including Michael Pollan, Joel Salatin, and others? Why?
3. Guthman talks of a common, shared "rhetorical strategy" shared by other authors whom she opposes. What is a rhetorical strategy? What is, according to Guthman, these authors' rhetorical strategy?

Explore

1. Guthman says there is "much to criticize in the public conversation about obesity." Identify and explore a popular weight-loss campaign for either a product or a program. How does it perpetuate the problems Guthman notes in her article?
2. Guthman mentions philosopher Michel Foucault, suggesting that the philosopher might have cited on this topic the "productive power of obesity talk." What does this mean? How do we see it enacted not only in this article and in the other writers Guthman mentions, but also in daily life?
3. Explore what Guthman means when she writes of the "antiregulatory approach to food politics." What does she mean when she says it has "taken hold?" Why do these relate to ideas that Guthman believes are "privileged?"

Psyche Williams-Forson
"Suckin' the Chicken Bone Dry: African American Women, History, and Food Culture"

Professor and co-director of American studies at the University of Maryland, Psyche Williams-Forson's research interests often explore the intersections of food and cultural studies. This essay was originally part of a book, *Cooking Lessons: The Politics of Gender and Food*, which preceded her award-winning book, *Building Houses out of Chicken Legs: Black Women, Food, and Power.* Williams-Forson draws on her own experiences to examine stereotypes and food.

How is Williams-Forson's argument a sophisticated one? Why?

Chicken has always been an integral part of my life. Like that of other African Americans,[1] Sunday dinner at my house often included fried chicken, macaroni and cheese with plenty of paprika, collard greens with pork neck-bones (until diabetes hit my home, then it was smoked turkey or some other seasoning), potato salad, corn pudding, rolls, or corn bread. And, if it wasn't this meal, it was some variation of this theme. I remember those days very well with the familiar sounds of bones crackling under my mother's teeth as she sucked out the marrow. The bones were eaten clean, chewed, and marrow juices savored until nothing was left or what remained was completely bone dry. My mother always said, "Sunday isn't the same without some chicken. You need something you can go back to later on." Usually, long after the dishes had been washed, someone would be in the kitchen wrapping a piece of bread around a chicken leg or wing, dousing it with hot sauce, and washing it down with iced tea or Coca-Cola. In the confines of the safe space of home all stereotypes about Black folks and chicken were forgotten.

Recalling these personal experiences has led me to think more carefully about how stereotypes are underpinned by variables such as gender, power, and history. These same dynamics are often at work in food interactions. So, I began more seriously considering "what food means"; how do the foods we procure, prepare, present, and consume have an impact on our cultural identity? What are the symbolic messages encoded in the foods we consume? Moreover, given their socially sanctioned status as nurturers, caretakers, and preparers of food what is the role of women in interpreting how and what these foods mean? To begin, I explored African American/ Black/Negro foodways in an effort to unearth something about our foods and their meanings to our communities. I was shocked to learn that little existed to explain *and* interpret this history.[2] This lack of scholarly interpretation prompted me to seriously research foods consumed by Black people in the United States. I began by considering the gendered element of foodways. Taking as true Pamela Quaggiotto's notion that, "the mother determines when, what, and how much family members will eat. . . . She controls the symbolic language of food, determining what her dishes and meals will say about herself, her family, and world," made clear that women must be placed at the center of this analysis.[3] Armed with this notion in hand, I first set out to examine the food dynamics in my own home.

Investigating Connections

My research into the realm of African American foods was about more than merely locating and identifying them. It was about understanding the connections between the foods and the people who consume them. This went beyond the theory of "you are what you eat" to "how does what we eat reflect our cultural identity?" How does our historical, socioeconomic, and political space influence the foods that we consume? Black people are engaged in an ideological warfare between race, identity, and food. For example, stereotypes concerning Black people's consumption of fried chicken—stereotypes that have been around for centuries—still pervade the American psyche today. Consider, for instance, the ease with which pro golfer Fuzzy Zoeller could make the comment to the media about the assumed food practices of pro golfer Tiger Woods. It was shortly after Tiger Woods (assumed to be fully African American because of his skin color) won the Master's Golf Tournament in 1997 that Zoeller commented to the media: "That little boy is driving well and he's putting well. He's doing everything it takes to win. So, you know what you guys do when he gets in here? You pat him on the back and say congratulations and enjoy it and tell him not to serve fried chicken at next year's dinner. Got it? . . . or collard greens or whatever the hell those people eat."[4] Comments such as this one made by Zoeller are unfortunately commonplace, functioning continuously to thwart and deflate African American economic, political, and cultural success. As Doris Witt successfully argues,

> Woods had the temerity to reign supreme at a sport thought to be innately "white." . . . The situation demanded some form of redress, which Zoeller took it upon himself to provide. Smart enough not to acknowledge directly his apprehension that Woods' victory marked a significant incursion against the faltering forces of white racial supremacy, Zoeller had recourse to chicken and greens.[5]

The media's—particularly those commentators with Southern roots—attempt to dilute this recourse by suggesting, "they themselves certainly liked fried chicken and collard greens" did little to appease Zoeller's racist intentions or Woods' compliance with such behavior, his declaration of "Cablinasion" heritage, notwithstanding.[6] Yet, the introduction of his Asian heritage brings his mother into the fore as a mediator introducing the intersection of gender, race, and food. Bringing her Thai heritage and thus Woods' multiethnic roots serves, on some level to reduce the severity of the comments to little more than "Black people's overreacting." In reality, however, it seems that Zoeller's comments, Woods' reaction, and his mother's entree serve to heighten the relationship between food, race, nationality, and gender in today's society. My conjecture is that bringing Woods' mother into the debacle inadvertently illustrated the power of women at the center of mediating food interactions.

5   Black feminist scholar Patricia Hill Collins suggests the critical need for Black women to be aware of the importance of self-definition and self-valuation in historical and contemporary statements of Black feminist thought.[7] This assertion has utility for this discussion in that Black people also need to be aware of this importance in the statements used by White popular culture to describe and characterize Black cultural life. As Collins suggests, we need to be attuned to the way in which processes of power underlie our social interactions and more importantly, are involved in the process of external definition. These external definitions can, however, be challenged through a process known as "self-definition." These acts of "challenging the political knowledge-validation process that result[s] in externally defined stereotypical images" can be unconscious or conscious acts of resistance.[8] By utilizing and identifying symbols commonly affiliated with our cultural heritage, we engage in the process of self-definition or

refusing to allow the wider American culture to dictate what represents our expressive culture and thereby represents us as Black people. But, this process of defining one's self is fraught with complications and complexities particularly if the group fails to understand or acknowledge that there is a power structure at work behind the creation of the stereotype.

Collins explains these complications further in her delineation of self-valuation or the replacement of negative images with positive ones. This process of replacement can be equally as problematic as external definition if we fail to understand and to recognize the stereotype as a controlling image. This was illustrated at a recent conference where I pointed out the hip-hop voiceover that can be heard in some of KFC's (formerly Kentucky Fried Chicken) commercials. I suggested that this depiction had stereotypical undertones. I also suggested that the visual image of the Colonel doing the "hip hop dance" was as bedeviling an image as that of the Black-faced man with big, shiny, red lips used to symbolize the restaurants of the Coon Chicken Inn. While many in the audience agreed with my assessment, some of the elder Black attendees championed the cause of "moving on" and "not letting the past control us." Perhaps in their minds, the hip-hop Colonel was a much-improved image over those with which they had coming of age viewing. Yet, in my mind, Collins' caution is registered here. This exchange of one set of controlling images for another does little to eradicate the defining image itself. We as Black people need to attend to the ways in which historical, social, political, and economical contexts have established these images (or narratives as I have termed them) and how they are embedded in our process of food selection, preparation, and consumption.

Black independence from negative controlling images is further challenged by Collins' suggestion to "push the envelope" by examining the content or basis for these external definitions. She suggests that usually stereotypes are "actually distorted renderings of those aspects of Black female behavior seen as most threatening to White patriarchy."[9] This assertion has model utility for this discussion in that the same holds true of the stereotypes that assassinate the character of Black people.

Evolution of a Stereotype

Initially, it seems these stereotypes involving Black people's affinity for chicken began as ideologies shaped from laws and ordinances passed during the seventeenth and eighteenth centuries as a way to control the economic gains of enslaved and free men and women who bartered and traded in the marketplace. Market trading in some of the heaviest areas like Charleston, South Carolina; Wilmington, North Carolina; New Orleans, Louisiana; and, varying parts of Virginia, Maryland, and Georgia provided one of the greatest and most essential forms of social interaction between Whites and Blacks. Meat and poultry procurement required a number of social interactions both on and off the plantation. Many of these market activities involved enslaved and free women of African descent. Enslaved women were frequently allowed to trade and engage in business using the possessions given them by their masters or those foods cultivated in their own gardens. In his study of eighteenth-century Black culture in Chesapeake Virginia and the Lowcountry of the Carolinas, Phillip Morgan points to the records of market activity that suggest that in the latter part of the century slaves controlled the poultry trade.[10] Accordingly, travelers' accounts indicate that "flocks of poultry [are] numerous" and "there are very few [slaves] indeed who are denied the privilege of keeping dunghill fowls, ducks, geese, and turkeys."[11] Moreover, some Black people would often sit by the wharf for days on end waiting to buy foods like chicken and then sell them for exorbitant prices.[12] Morgan notes a similar practice whereby some travelers would instruct their stewards to hold in reserve various foods like bacon so they would have bartering power with "the Negroes who are the general Chicken Merchants [sic]."[13]

As a result of this monopoly over the sale of poultry as well as the continuous increase in the Black population in many of these towns, regulations appeared which sought to limit the hawking of items being sold door-to-door. Anne E. Yentsch says that in 1717, Annapolis town fathers moved to restrict the market activities of its "Negroes" by limiting door-to-door sales by "confining purchases of flesh or fish, living or dead, eggs, butter, or cheese (oysters excepted) to the market."[14] She suggests the reason for these activities being stalled was the ambiguous ownership of goods prior to sale. Food items were not supposed to be sold prior to passing through the town gates, and in particular customers were not supposed to purchase goods whose ownership might be difficult to trace. This included items such as chickens, which were often sold outside the market. Yentsch maintains that goods such as oysters, salted fish in large barrels or casks, cattle, sheep, and hogs that were alive could easily be traced because they were by-and-large produced by small farmers. However, given that numerous Blacks had chicken coops as did many of their masters, the suggestion was that in buying dead chickens no one knew for sure whose chickens they were buying.[15]

Yet, despite these laws and ordinances, Black monopoly over the sale   10 and trade of poultry increased and continued to cause numerous problems for customer and planter alike. Since the legal tactic failed, the town fathers began to accuse Blacks of theft. This accusation was fueled by Black people's use of trading practices like forestalling and extraplantation trading. Forestalling was the practice of anticipat[ing] the market by buying outside the city gates, which allowed sellers to place early bid on the goods which they in turn sold for higher prices within the market area.[16] The problem with this practice was that when Blacks were selling chickens, as many of them were, the goods were untraceable having been purchased (and possibly sold) well before the legal market trading activity began. Another practice described by Morgan, which had similar dire consequences for White planters, was extraplantation or offsite trading. According to Morgan, enslaved people took it upon themselves to branch out well beyond the neighboring plantation areas in search of more lucrative trading venues. Because it was hard to determine where the chickens and hens came from— the coffers of the enslaved or planters—these practices also proved to be an economic anathema.[17]

Legal ordinances did little to reduce the trading practices of Blacks. Many, both enslaved and free, continued to receive various gains from their trading acumen, furthering the ire of slaveowners. Thus, town managers instituted even newer laws as late as the mid-nineteenth century forbidding huckstering or the selling of day-old food at reduced prices in the market places, door-to-door or curbside.[18] Lastly, in part from truth as much as fiction, slaveowners—who considered any and all commodities, including the slave, to belong to them—began to associate Black trading practices with theft. Admittedly, some slaves did engage in pilfering and stealing of wares. Some scholars, however, have referred to these acts of pilfering as acts of skill and cunning. Eugene Genovese's study of African American life and culture, suggests this when he writes, "for many slaves, stealing from their own or other masters became a science and an art, employed as much for the satisfaction of outwitting Ole' Massa as anything else."[19] In *Weevils in the Wheat,* one slave affords us a glimpse at the "anything else." According to ex-slave Charles Grandy hunger was one motivating factor for the enslaved to use skill and cunning to steal food. He says, "I got so hungry

I stealed chickens off de roos'. . . . We would cook de chicken at night, eat him an' bu'n de feathers. . . . We always had a trap in de floor fo' de do' to hide dese chickens in."[20]

It is this notion of the "chicken thieving darky" that provides a valuable segue into helping us historicize our present day stereotypes of the "chicken loving darky." This ideology began to crystallize during the Reconstruction era as the need to reclaim the "Old South" and "The Lost Cause of Southern White heritage" plagued the minds of many White Americans. With the mass exodus North and West of many newly freed Blacks, the South suffered a devastating loss of free labor. Jobs in the South were few. Many Black men had joined the "Yankees" or fled to the North in search of employment often as cooks on railroads or ships, in hotels and restaurants. Most Black women entered domestic service, many marshaling their culinary experiences of cooking either in the Big House or in the slave quarters. What was once championed by many as talented cooking of the South quickly turned to an object of ridicule and defacement.

According to historian Kenneth Goings, the loss of control over Black people due to the ending of slavery, the emergence of political and Black political participation, and outward migration by Blacks registered a blow among White Southerners. Threatened by Black newfound freedom, Southern Whites used advancing communications to forge a means of reasserting control and reclaiming power.[21] In an attempt to subjugate Blacks and conjure memories of the Ole' South, White Americans vented their anger using artifacts of visual media like brochures, pamphlets, trading cards, greeting cards, and food products. Emerging from this "new White backlash" was an ideology of Black inferiority, which prompted the formulation of racist stereotypes. These stereotypes were perpetuated by advertisements, trading cards, and sheet music like that of Fred Fischer which pictures an old Black man with his hands in a hen house, caption reading: "If the Man in the Moon Were a Coon."

Goings, whose study *Mammy and Uncle Mose* historicizes the cultural and political economy of Black collectibles, maintains that the coon image was one of the most offensive stereotypes. Most prevalent from 1880 to 1930, Goings considers "Zip Coon" "the alter ego to Jim Crow." He elaborates,

> Zip Coon was a "citified," "dandified" slave, who wore a fashionable (but worn) morning coat and top hat. . . . The word "coon" comes

from the South, a shortening of "raccoon." This scavenger steals food at night, has enormous whites of the eye that contrast with its dark face, and is best when chased up a tree by dogs. . . . The "coon" like the "sambo" was an attempt to reduce African-American men to ridiculous, stupid, and even beastlike comic figures.[22]

M. L. Graham used this coon motif as the mascot for his little-known   15 "Coon Chicken Inn" restaurants. The emblem, a Black-faced man with large, extended red lips, was typically symbolic of how Whites would stereotype Black people with food to endorse various products like fried chicken. Considered a most affective advertising technique, images like this one reinforced the "stereotypical Old South/New South myth of the loyal, happy servant just waiting to be used by the master—and now the consumer." The restaurant with all of its accoutrements becomes a metaphor for Whites using and discarding Black service. When the meal was complete, the napkins, plates, and utensils bearing the Black-faced logo were discarded, White patrons were symbolically discarding Blacks (who had fulfilled their duty of seeing that their "White masters" were well fed). This act of physical disposal provided Whites with what Goings describes in a similar discussion as a sense of "racial superiority" and a "therapeutic sense of comfort." This motif served to be even more effective because it seared in the minds of many White Americans the notion that "under the cover of night, the darky would supposedly steal a chicken from the master's coop for a purloined Sunday dinner"; and thus, the stereotypical belief that Black people are "chicken loving" and "chicken thieving darkies."[23] Manipulating these objects of material culture enabled White Americans to not only forge an alliance between White people that surpassed class lines, but also enabled them to more collectively subjugate and vilify the lives and cultures of Blacks. This notion of Black inferiority provided a safeguard for White America during a time when their racial, economic, and political balance was perceived as threatened. From this, it seems that a distinct historical narrative developed and continues to evolve around Black folks' consumption of fried chicken.

However, this narrative and its accompanying stereotypes have produced a paradoxical response from many White people. On the one hand, they want to attribute Black consumption of fried chicken as normative; on the other hand, they want to equate this consumption with something negative. However, the issue becomes more complex when fried chicken—as one of the most heralded foods of the South—is listed among the many contributions of Black folks. At issue here is how to malign Black people and their consumption of fried chicken without crediting them with contributing the method of deep-frying to New World Cuisine. Well into the nineteenth century as Blacks in general continued to monopolize and control the distribution of poultry, Black women dominated the cooking of chicken, being widely credited with lining the "Southern groaning boards" with heaping platters of steaming fried chicken. Even though evidence has been garnered in support of these assertions, scholars and lay people alike often attempt to discredit these contributions.[24]

Some White people will go to any lengths to distance fried chicken and other "Southern-identified foods" from the culinary repertoire of Black people. Take for instance this anecdote from the 1998 American Studies Association Annual Meeting. Following the presentation of a similar argument about the "particularistic" relationship between fried chicken and Black people, one audience member vehemently exclaimed, "fried chicken is not African American food, it's Southern food."[25] This assertion begs the question of why White people find it necessary to distinguish foods eaten in the South from those prepared and consumed by Black people. If I had, for instance, written a paper on chit'lins or collard greens, I doubt that I would have met with the same resistance given that these are deemed "soul foods"—foods within my culinary boundary. However, to align myself with foods that are comfortably situated within the White Southern culinary repertoire is an invasion. This cultural demarcation becomes necessary for symbolically separating the domestic rituals of the South. As a Black woman, my cultural role was to prepare and cook fried chicken like the proverbial mammy or enslaved cook in the Big House. However, fried chicken is not mine to claim, lest I blur the lines between the "symbolic separations [of] those who prepare the food and those who consume it" according to literary theorist Mary Titus.[26] This relationship reveals fried chicken as a "complex cultural text," a Southern food that emerged out of a social institution shaped by racial complexities. Therefore, keeping the symbolic mental distance between cook and consumer is necessary for White Americans to maintain the purity of Southern cuisine, but it is also complicated by the consumption of fried chicken by Black people. It seems here that words are being used to convey coded messages, namely, Southern is a code word for White, while "soul food" is decoded as Black.[27] I never conveyed that fried chicken "belonged" to Black people; rather,

I explicitly argued that the relationship between Black people and fried chicken has to be considered in the context of the historical and economic circumstances of the South. This circumstance involves the creation of a national narrative that was in defense of a White Southern heritage—a heritage defined by food; indeed, one of the South's most prevalent defining characteristics.

Implicit in this illustration is a repetition of the genre contained in many White cookbooks—recipes contributed by Blacks, yet culturally robbed by Whites. Taking the illiteracy of Blacks for granted, many White women took the recipes of Black women and used them for their own pecuniary gain and acclaim. This practice was still taking place as late as the 1940s when Marjorie Rawlings wrote *Cross Creek Cookery* using many of the recipes created by Idella Parker. In her biographical account, Parker states:

> Many of the recipes in the book were mine, but she only gave me credit for three of them, including "Tdella's Biscuits." There were several others that were mine too, such as the chocolate pie, and of course it was me who did most of the cooking when we were trying all the recipes out. All I ever got from the cookbook was an autographed copy, but in those days I was grateful for any little crumb that white people let fall, so I kept my thoughts about the cookbook strictly to myself.[28]

This practice has occurred far too often to enumerate. It is, I believe, one of the ways that White people have been able to claim and reclaim Southern foods like fried chicken for their own. Diane Spivey has labeled this phenomenon, "Whites Only Cuisine" in her recently published book, *The Peppers, Cracklings, and Knots of Wool Cookbook: The Global Migration of African-Cuisine*. She says:

> The end of the [Civil] war also signaled the beginning of the redefining of southern white heritage. The "Lost Cause," or southern white elites' efforts to hold on to their old way of life, centered around food. Cooking and cuisine were remade to look uniquely southern. . . . Asserting that the recipes were "southern" made these cookbooks exclusionary, and therefore racist, because the cookbooks and recipes contained therein were heralded as the creations of elite southern white women. In an attempt to promote southern

white culture, therefore, the concept of "southern cooking" started out as *Whites Only Cuisine*.[29]

20   This concept of *whites only cuisine* seemingly remains today in the subconscious minds of many White Americans undergirded by a need to control most aspects of American cultural life.

This concept is another one of the propelling forces that has produced and shaped the stereotype surrounding Black consumption of fried chicken. This stereotype has left such an indelible imprint that some African Americans refuse to consume the food in public. According to a survey I conducted in relationship to another research project, many Blacks in corporate settings—particularly those between the ages of 29 and 35—refuse to eat chicken in the presence of White co-workers. As one informant said, "I don't even want my co-workers to get in their minds that whole stereotype thing of [fried] chicken and watermelon, you know?" This feeling suggests that these African Americans understand the ideology of racism and how it is deeply embedded in many White Western minds so as to make stereotypical comments commonplace. On the other hand, their resistance to eating chicken may suggest an uncomfortable feeling with being associated with this aspect of their food heritage and identity. Still others celebrate this aspect of the stereotype by acknowledging it as a part of their identity as African Americans in a racist society. Nowhere is this more evident than in Black churches where chicken is affectionately called, the "gospel bird" or the "preacher's bird."[30]

Resisting the Stereotype

It is in African American churches where the oppressed have taken an active role in the social process of cultural identification. In this arena, fried chicken has been and still remains a visible part of the expressive culture of African Americans and a useful tool in social action. An examination of its role in the process of collective self-help and racial uplift will delineate the ways in which Black women have used chicken—despite the stereotype—to construct parts of their cultural identity. In their discussion of the material expressions of culture, archaeologists Mary Beaudry, Lauren Cook, and Stephen Mrozowski argue that the use of objects and their symbolism in the process of constructing cultural identity is "first and foremost a public act of mediation between self and other."[31] They suggest that through an analysis of material items we can begin to understand the ways in which individuals used objects important to self-expression and self-definition in the construction of this identity. Borrowing from Mihaly Csikszentmihalyi and Eugene Rochberg-Holton, they further suggest that individuals and members of a "subculture" will create their identity by using "object[s] or sign[s] that [allow] a person to 'make his self manifest'"; a process that generally occurs through leisure or during off-work hours.[32] What this suggests, then, is that when Black women congregate in church kitchens, cooking, networking, and "strifing," they are building upon an integral part of the Black communities' cultural identity.

Many Black religious activities like the new minister's induction, funerals, homecomings or revivals, women's day, men's day, and youth day are replete with food. Black women (and men) "light up more stoves" and "grease more frying pans" in an attempt to feed congregations while asserting and maintaining their heritage and culture through the tradition of selling fried chicken dinners. For instance, Workman Memorial AME Zion Church in Hartford, Connecticut, made news in *The Hartford Courant,* with the headlines declaring, "Church to Have Soul Food Benefit." The article indicates that the church is ninety-eight years old and has been selling fried chicken dinners for as many years. With a global mission of "help[ing] in poor parts of Africa" the church has its annual "Soul Food to Go" dinner selling: "southern fried chicken, collard greens, candied yams, macaroni and cheese and corn bread." According to the pastor, Rev. Shelley D. Best, "you don't get soul food in Connecticut. . . . There's something to be said for the food—It's not Kentucky Fried Chicken. . . . Every item is an art form. It's part of the African American tradition."[33] These acts of resistance against the narrative put forth by White America can perhaps be considered unconscious; however, the constant use and reuse of fried chicken as a tool for social action might suggest otherwise. African Americans have used fried chicken to symbolize self-definition, self-expression, and celebration. Food identifies those who belong to the "in-group" and as Beaudry, Cook, and Mrozowski suggest, is "occasionally [used] as a weapon to annoy those who do not" [belong].[34]

Food as emblematic of culture and as a weapon of resistance has long been utilized in the Black community and in particular in our formal institutions like the church. Just after Emancipation when Black people were in need of a "safe space" to structure and organize their lives, the church provided this support.[35] It has been a mainstay in the Black community as a haven for social, political, and cultural expression. Though many White Southern families would also engage in preparing chicken on Sunday when the preacher came, for African Americans this ritual dates back to Emancipation when the church became the center of Black community life. It was during this period that Black people could construct lives consistent with being freed women and men and removing themselves from the controlling presence of White churches. In selecting their own preachers they no longer had to hear sermons of White masters who admonished them "don' steal f'om you' marser an' missus" among other things. In Black churches of this period, parishioners could hear messages of equality and social action. The minister was their spiritual leader and motivator. To show their gratitude and fondness for the minister, parishioners would take turns inviting him to their home for Sunday dinner and the hostess would excitedly engage in the labor-intensive process of cleaning, catching, killing, plucking, and cooking a chicken for the occasion. Nowhere is the excitement of the occasion captured more euphorically then in the autobiographical narrative of Sara Brooks. In illustrative detail Brooks recalls how her mother hustled to prepare a "big meal" for her preacher:

> My mother would fix a big meal . . . so they could have fried chicken for the preacher cause the preacher love fried chicken . . . and she'd clean the chickens out by givin em cornmeal—wet it and put bakin soda in it—and that would clean the chickens out. So my mother'd have fried chicken and she'd cook vegetables and cakes and pies. The preacher and my daddy would eat first; then we'd eat what was left.[36]

25   Numerous anecdotes and jokes in African American folklore detail stories about the preacher and fried chicken. Because the pastor is considered to hold the position of highest esteem and "cultural power" in the church, and often the community, it is considered a privilege to serve him the choicest pieces of chicken. Marvalene H. Hughes indicates, "whether on the church ground or in the Black home, the Black preacher is the first to choose his food."[37] So powerful is this object to the Black community that it has become associated with our folklore. In a recent church service, one minister suggested that chicken is one of the four Cs that could "bring the preacher down." As the saying goes, the Cs represent, "cash," "chicks," "cadillacs," and "chicken." For the preacher to praise one parishioner's

chicken over another can result in gender conflict resulting in ostracism and internal strife among the women known for cooking the best fried chicken. His open acknowledgment and praise of one sista's fried chicken over another suggests that he is enjoying something at that sista's house other than just the "preacher's bird."[38]

Strife over who cooks the best bird on Sundays is one of the many feelings engendered by fried chicken consumption. It is so central to many church functions that its absence can also arouse the displeasure of parishioners with savoring tongues. I recall one year I decided to fast on chicken beyond the Lenten season. Mother was used to my whimsical ever-changing dietary habits, so she asked what foods I preferred for the post-Lenten meal. Though I knew the meal was going to be openly shared by everyone after church service, I never thought that what my mother prepared for *me* would be shared as well. So, in the absence of this morsel of knowledge, I boldly exclaimed, "baked fish. I'm still fasting from chicken and fried foods." She said, "Fish? Aw, you've gone and messed up my dinner. I had a menu all laid out. All right." And, of course, she was right. I had, in fact, "gone and messed up her dinner." What I had not anticipated was the relative badge of cultural shame I brought to my mother, who, as a preacher's wife, had a certain expectant role to play in the culinary expose of the after-church meal. During the course of the meal, more than one parishioner commented, "Sista Williams you didn't cook any chicken this year? Umph, that's not like you. I just knew I was gonna have some of your chicken." In an effort to support my resolve and quell my temptation, my mother had all but violated one of the unspoken principles of food consumption within the Black church—she, a preacher's wife, had left out the chicken!

Black women have been gracing tables in the church with fried chicken for a long time. Like the present-day benefit held at the Workman Memorial AME Church in Hartford, Connecticut, churches during the latter part of the nineteenth century would often have church fairs and bazaars to raise money. Overlapping with mutual aid and benevolent societies, church institutions—as a venue for cooperative economics—relied upon the leadership of women in varying roles ranging from the Sunday school teacher to the kitchen cook. Using the proceeds from church lunch and dinner sales, Black women were able to assist in building baptismal pools, edifices, sanctuaries, and contribute to other church needs. This creative consciousness combined with spirituality, camaraderie and cooking imagination imbues chicken with polysemic meanings. These meanings exceed the obvious notion of food as nutritive; they also reflect ingenuity and creativity wrought by the historical circumstance of living gendered lives in a racist society.

Historically and in contemporary society, for many African American women cooking in the church not only offers an opportunity to provide sustenance, but also a time for networking "in the name of the Lord." Though women were often denied the status and power afforded men, they were able to carve out an alternative space of power in the microcosmic arena of the kitchen to provide their pecuniary contributions. The kitchen afforded Black women a level of "cultural authority" and "financial autonomy" as described by Doris Witt, wherein they could exercise a modicum of power by contributing to the campaign of racial uplift. In the microcosmic "safe space" of the kitchen, they could engage the macro space of the Black church to explore and validate expressions of the self even as the wider American culture issued assault. In her discussion of the women's movement in the Black Baptist Church, African American religious historian Evelyn Brooks Higgenbotham contextualizes Black women's involvement in the church from the perspective of the larger racial struggle. With a focus on "racial solidarity" and "racial self-determination" they operated out of a "paradox of opposition": male domination/racial cooperation; White control/collaboration. This "amalgam of separatist leanings" was "inspired by the nexus of race and gender consciousness."[39]

This "nexus of race and gender consciousness" operated out of the context of W. E. B. DuBois' "double consciousness" to form what Higgenbotham calls, "double gender consciousness," which blurred the lines between Black women as "homemakers and soldiers." Black women were doing more than merely frying chicken in the kitchen to "raise a little bit o' money." These collective efforts forged from "separatist leanings" were assaulted by varying degrees of opposition and conflict including Black men, White Baptist women, and sometimes each other. These conflicts notwithstanding, they were also engaged on a larger scale in redefining their expressions of self for themselves and for the larger American society who sought assiduously to subjugate and oppress them with negative stereotypes. Working "under siege," Black women were burdened with the task of not only procuring, preparing, and presenting foods like fried chicken for consumption, sustenance, and economic gain, but also, they were challenged with the task of teaching and conveying "respectable behavior" in all forms of expression, particularly table manners. Working against demeaning caricatures and icons in popular culture and academic discourse, like the "Coon" or the physically deviant Hottentot Venus, Black women resisted these depictions by emphasizing an air of respectability. They believed that proper adherence to manners and morals would negate the claims of racial and gender inferiority and give rise to social acceptance.

This goal notwithstanding, these assertions brought with them class 30 and status implications that manifested themselves most assuredly during mealtimes. Aimed in large part at the Black working-class poor, these edicts found expression in most of the major newspapers, magazines, church sermons and cookbooks/self-help guides of the period. For example, in *The Correct Thing to Do—To Say—To Wear*, Charlotte Hawkins Brown advocated the proper rules for presenting a dining room that creates an atmosphere that appeals to the eyes as well as to the taste" inasmuch as each meal should be "conducive to harmonious social intercourse."[40] Instructions were given on the proper way to use a fork and knife, including how the tines should be held when food is being carried to the mouth. Chicken, in any form, is absent from the menu. Rather, foods like "stuffed tomatoes in Aspic," "Cheese and Jelly Sandwiches," and "Celery Hearts" are among the delicacies. Of course, it is not surprising that fried chicken is not mentioned among the offerings given the assimilationist intent of these self-help manuals. In this context, Brown's "harmonious social intercourse" could not be obtained while eating fried chicken—a practice performed sans utensils—because this form of eating replicated an element of barbarism left over from the colonial past when tableware was scarce or nonexistent.

These edicts aside, among the working poor and middle-class Blacks, fried chicken was a constant. Few written documents of the Black middle class make note of its appearance at gatherings not wanting to associate themselves with foods or other acts of "barbarism" that would reduce their social acceptance in the eyes of the larger White society. The Black middle class often maintained a code of silence about the everyday lives of the Black working class for fear that *all* Black people would be subjected to the humiliation and economic despair that accompanied second-class citizenship. Yet, anecdotes and oral histories tell the story of how fried chicken was and continues to be a steady survival food among most African Americans. Big boxes of fried chicken packed neatly for the Northern journey, rent parties where fried chicken dinners sold for a dollar, juke joints where fried chicken flows like the whiskey and music, all reflect spaces where African American culture, community, and history can be expressed. Even the metaphorical "chicken bone express" is celebrated in the folklore of Black people to describe the days of segregation when travelers would carry shoeboxes full of food to sustain them on their journey because White food establishments were inhospitable to Blacks. As the saying goes, you could identify the travel route of Black folks by following the trail of chicken bones along the highway or the railroad track. Norma Jean Darden recounts similar travel experiences in her family memoir and cookbook, *Spoonbread and Strawberry Wine*:

> These trips took place during the fifties, and one never knew what dangers or insults would be encountered along the way. Racist policies loomed like the unidentified monsters in our childish imaginations and in reality. After the New Jersey Turnpike ended, we would have to be on the alert for the unexpected. So, as we approached that last Howard Johnson's before Delaware, our father would make his inevitable announcement that we had to get out, stretch our legs, and go the bathroom, whether we wanted to or not. This was a ritualized part of every trip, for, although there would be many restaurants along the route, this was the last one that didn't offer segregated facilities. From this point on, we pulled out our trusty shoe-box lunches.[41]

Listed first on the menu of foods found in those "trusty shoe-box lunches" was fried chicken accompanied by peanut butter and jelly sandwiches, deviled eggs, carrot and celery sticks, salt and pepper packets, chocolate layer cake, and a thermos of lemonade. Though negative and unwelcome at the time, experiences such as these are a part of the African American legacy of living in America. These experiences become a filter through which objects, like fried chicken, take on meanings that fashion a collective memory of resistance. These are also experiences through which Patricia Hill Collins' process of self-valuation—understanding and resisting the controlling images and then replacing them with more positive ones—takes place. As I think about the comfort foods of my youth I recognize my own memories as a part of this self-valuation experience. Traveling to Virginia with picnic baskets full of food were fun times for me. I always remember wanting to be the one to stay awake and help my father, "watch the road" just in case he needed my navigational *help*. Staying awake through most of the journey also entitled me to knowing when we were ready to eat. When we traveled to the South in the '60s and '70s my mother would prepare a big picnic basket with fried chicken, Vienna sausages, white bread (which was later replaced by wheat), fruit, juicy juices, cookies, and potato chips. This was the economy lunch for a family of five. I was always excited when it was announced that we were going on a trip. I couldn't wait; sleep was elusive. The combination of sightseeing, helping my father watch the road, and considering the contents of the picnic basket always kept me wide awake.

On the morning of our trip I vividly recall waking to the smells of chicken frying in the kitchen. I would usually be the first one awake and into the kitchen climbing up on the stool beside the stove to watch my mother deep fry chicken and gather foodstuffs for our trip. Sometimes she let me season the chicken (after I washed my hands of course). At first she used only salt, pepper, and a dash of paprika. Later she began to use garlic powder, an aroma I still love to smell. When the chicken was well floured, she lowered it into the hot and sizzling frying pan or pot filled with Wesson oil. As I got older and began cooking my own fried chicken—when I still cooked and ate chicken—I would add my own twist with cayenne to give it an extra spicy taste. These were fun times. My feelings about these times were slightly hampered, however, when I later learned the reasons we traveled with our own food. In part, it was economics. Feeding a family of five at every stop would prove to be very expensive. The other reason, it turns out, was the lack of eating establishments hospitable to African Americans. The 1970s were not far enough removed from the feelings of hostility surrounding the Civil Rights confrontations. To avoid these encounters, we stopped to use the restrooms and order food at places that served and catered to Black people. Understanding these circumstances and their social and political implications was turned into acts of agency by my parents who exposed us to the racism while simultaneously displaying tactics of resistance.

These displays of self-support and collective memory continue to exist—consciously or unconsciously—every time a kitchen fills with the smells of fried chicken, candied sweet potatoes, black-eyed peas, greens, and macaroni and cheese because somewhere nearby there is probably a Black woman. Through her double gendered consciousness of being Black and a woman in the United States, she brings to bear on the food she cooks the act of positive self-expression and self-valuation. It is usually through her that proper morals and manners of mealtime behaviors are instilled and executed, not necessarily to accommodate racial discourses as such, but to foster individuals imbued with a social and cultural history of African American struggle.

35   For some people, fried chicken may still simply suggest the presence of Southern culinary culture. But for many African Americans fried chicken is a symbolic icon of the African American struggle and survival. Foods like fried chicken, collard greens, deviled eggs, potato salad, macaroni and cheese, and corn bread are more than "soul food" or what Vertamae Grosvenor calls, "get down foods." For many Black people, these foods also reflect certain times and places in history when food choices and establishments were limited or inaccessible; when these foods provided a way to pay rent; and when they offered a temporary safe haven away from the complexities of the urban landscape by being served at the chicken shack up the road.

Though many of these foods have been modified and adapted to include a number of ethnic and regional cooking variations, there still exists a solid link between fried chicken and African American history. Through the sharing of stories with elders and siblings, younger generations can come to understand the traditions and legacies that comprise these histories and life experiences. In this way, they can arm themselves with the knowledge of how negative controlling images creep into our psyches and slowly eat away at our self-esteem and cultural identity as Black people. We must never forget that we live in a society that espouses "liberty and justice for all" but fails in reality to live up to this enormous undertaking. It is, in part, out of this contradiction that African American women as survivalists generation after generation have used their "soulful creativity" to transmit cultural practices of food through their networks in the home, the labor market, and the community. Through their culturally sanctioned roles as nurturers and caretakers, African American women make food a major aspect of the expressive culture of the Black community. During times of economic despair, African American women create a big pot of chicken stew, or fry chicken backs and feet adding rice to make a meal. When the economic condition improves, chicken still may be fried, or steamed, barbecued, curried, eaten alone or with a host of side dishes to complete a dinner. Whether pilfering, borrowing, or sharing, African American women along with their men have insured that our heritage and history are present through the continued presence of these foods at almost every major family gathering. More importantly, Black women have manipulated fried chicken to serve as a weapon of resistance in repudiating the negative connotations and denigrating ideologies espoused in the image of "chicken eating Black folks."

Notes

I am grateful to the Smithsonian Institute's Anacostia Museum and the Center for African American Life and History, specifically Portia James for helping to support some of the research for this chapter. I also wish to thank Sherrie A. Inness, Philipia L. Hillman, Doris Witt, Donna Rowe, Shireen Lewis, Warren Belasco, and Lyllie B. Williams for their helpful comments and encouragement. I would especially like to thank my husband, Akai Kwame Forson, for sharing his Diasporic experiences and perspectives.

1. I wrestled with whether to use the prevailing term *African American* or to use the almost nonexistent *Black*. I decided that I would use the terms interchangeably and risk debate. It seemed that regardless of whether people were born in America and are, therefore, "African American" or if they have migrated to the United States from around the African Diaspora, they are considered "chicken loving darkies." See the comments regarding the Tiger Woods debacle.

2. At that time, scholarly work was scant. There were several cookbooks including Jessica Harris's *The Welcome Table* and *Iron Pots and Wooden Spoons*, and Vertamae Grosvenor's *Vibration Cooking*. Archaeological work about faunal remains and slave artifacts were also prevalent. However, little scholarly work had been completed that went beyond historical explanations to include interpretations and meanings. One of the most recent scholarly works to explore these domains is Doris Witt's *Black Hunger* (New York: Oxford University Press, 1999).

3. This discussion in no way attempts to negate the contributions of Black men to this negotiation process. However, if women are prescribed socially to undertake the cooking for and nurturing of the family, we can readily accept Quaggiotto's argument. See Carole M. Counihan, "Female Identity, Food, and Power in Contemporary Florence," *Anthropological Quarterly* 61 (1988): 52.

4. Harry Blauvelt, "Zoeller Says His Comments about Woods Made 'In Jest,'" *USA Today*, 22 April 1997, sec. 2C.

5. Witt, *Black Hunger*, 4.

6. I borrow quite loosely here from Witt, *Black Hunger*, who discusses this incident in relation to African American women, food, and masculinity. See in particular 3–5.

7. Patricia Hill Collins, "Learning from the Outsider Within: The Sociological Significance of Black Feminist Thought," *Social Problems* 33, no. 6 (1986): 516.

8. Collins, "Learning from the Outsider Within," 516–17.

9. Collins, "Learning from the Outsider Within," 516–17.

10. Some sources indicate that chicken started to become a mass-produced commodity around the year 1800, but travelers' accounts and planters records date the trading and bartering activities of enslaved Blacks to earlier periods. Phillip D. Morgan, *Slave Counterpoint: Black Culture in the Eighteenth-Century Chesapeake and Lowcountry* (Chapel Hill: University of North Carolina Press for the Omohundro Institute of Early American History and Culture, Williamsburg, Virginia, 1998).

11. Scholars have argued that chicken was a semiluxury item for plantation owners, relegated primarily to Sunday dinner or for the arrival of visitors; see Sam Hilliard's, *Hog Meat and Hoecake* (1972) and Joe Gray Taylor's, *Eating, Drinking & Visiting in the South* (1982). However, Hilliard also points out the frequency with which many enslaved people kept chickens and other poultry and would supplement planter's coffers when flocks were low. Southern Black and poor White families have always eaten what anthropologist Tony Whitehead refers to as "low status" chicken: necks, feet, giblets, and backs. The participants in his study refer to these items as "poor people's food" or "black people's food." See Whitehead's "Sociocultural Dynamics and Food Habits in a Southern Community," *Food in the Social Order: Studies of Food and Festivities in Three American Communities*, ed. Mary Douglas (New York: Russell Sage Foundation, 1984), 115. My own research has yielded that fried chicken fat (the chicken butt) supplied an additional meat source as well as a source of cooking oil in lieu of traditional pork sources (fatback, lard, bacon). The chicken bones are often used to season soups and broths and then sucked dry to savor the seasoned marrow.

12. Anne E. Yentsch, *A Chesapeake Family and Their Slaves: A Study in Historical Archaeology* (Cambridge, U.K.: Cambridge University Press, 1994), 242.

13. Morgan, *Slave Counterpoint,* 359.
14. Yentsch, *A Chesapeake Family and Their Slaves,* 245.
15. Yentsch, *A Chesapeake Family and Their Slaves,* 245.
16. Yentsch, *A Chesapeake Family and Their Slaves,* 244.
17. Morgan, *Slave Counterpoint,* 360.
18. Yentsch, *A Chesapeake Family and Their Slaves,* 248.
19. Eugene Genovese, *Roll, Jordan, Roll: The World the Slaves Made* (New York: Vintage, 1976), 606.
20. Charles L. Perdue Jr., Thomas E. Barden, and Robert K. Phillips, eds., *Weevils in the Wheat* (Charlottesville: University of Virginia Press, 1976), 116.
21. Kenneth W. Goings, *Mammy and Uncle Mose: Black Collectibles and American Stereotyping* (Bloomington: Indiana University Press, 1994), 4–7.
22. Goings, *Mammy and Uncle Mose,* 43–44.
23. Goings, *Mammy and Uncle Mose,* 47.
24. This debate is a highly contentious one among scholars of Southern and African American foodways. Since few references to fried chicken appear in Southern cookbooks prior to 1850, numerous scholars have attributed the technique of frying to West African women—this coupled with West African use to palm oil. However, another body of scholars suggests that the English made this contribution to New World cuisine. As Yentsch suggests, there was such amalgamation that true origins of some food practices are hard to pinpoint. See Yentsch, *A Chesapeake Family and Their Slaves,* 196–215; Jessica Harris, *The Welcome Table: African American Heritage Cooking* (New York: Simon & Schuster, 1995); Michael Krondl, *Around the American Table: Treasured Recipes and Food Traditions from the American Cookery Collections of the New York Public Library* (Holbrook, Mass.: Adams Publishing, 1995); Sam Hilliard, *Hog Meat and Hoecake: Food Supply in the Old South, 1840–1860* (Carbondale: Southern Illinois University Press, 1972).
25. These observations must be attributed to Doris Witt who actually read the paper in my absence during the conference. However, any misrepresentations of the incident are mine.
26. Mary Titus, "'Groaning Tables and Spit in the Kettles': Food and Race in the Nineteenth-Century South," *Southern Quarterly* 20, no. 2–3 (1992), 15.

27. This notion of coding was suggested by Witt during comments on earlier drafts of this chapter.

28. Idella Parker and Marjorie Keating, *Idella: Marjorie Rawlings' 'Perfect Maid.'* (Gainesville: University Press of Florida, 1992), 69.

29. Diane M. Spivey, "Economics, War, and the Northern Migration of the Southern Black Cook," in *The Peppers, Crackling, and Knots of Wool Cookbook: The Global Migration of African Cuisine* (New York: State University of New York Press, 1999), 263.

30. See Jualynne E. Dodson and Cheryl Townsend Gilkes, "There's Nothing Like Church Food," *Journal of the American Academy of Religion* 63, no. 3 (1995): 523; and Helen Mendes, *The African Heritage Cookbook* (New York: MacMillan, 1971), 82.

31. Mary C. Beaudry, Lauren J. Cook, and Stephen A. Mrozowski, "Artifacts and Active Voices: Material Culture as Social Discourse," in *The Archaeology of Inequality*, ed. Robert Paynter and Randall H. McGuire (Oxford: Basil Blackwell, 1991), 154.

32. This is not to suggest that Black women's church work, including cooking, is "leisure" or "nonwork." To the contrary, it is important social work; however, for the purposes of this discussion, church activities are considered in addition to the formal production of labor.

33. Jill Storms, "Church to Have Soul Food Benefit," *The Hartford Courant* 1998, 16 November 1986, sec. B1.

34. Beaudry et al., "Artifacts and Active Voices," 156.

35. Farah Jasmine Griffin uses the term *safe space* to designate "spaces of resistance" which are by no means hegemonic but where "the South is evoked . . . the site of African American culture, community, and history." See Griffin, "Safe Spaces and Other Places: Navigating the Urban Landscape," in *Who Set You Flowin'? The African-American Migration Narrative* (New York: Oxford University Press, 1995), 110–11.

36. Thordis Simonsen, *You May Plow Here: The Narrative of Sara Brooks* (New York: W. W. Norton, 1986), 78–79.

37. Marvalene H. Hughes, "Soul, Black Women, and Food," *Food and Culture*, ed. Carole Counihan and Penny Van Esterik (New York: Routledge, 1997), 277.

38. I am grateful to Philipia L. Hillman for providing me with this observation. Dr. G. Martin Young, "Hold on Help Is on the Way." Sermon preached at Florida Avenue Baptist Church, Washington, D.C., 29 March 1998.

39. Evelyn Brooks Higgenbotham, *Righteous Discontent: The Women's Movement in the Black Baptist Church, 1880–1920* (Cambridge, Mass.: Harvard University Press, 1993), 50.

40. Charlotte Hawkins Brown, "At Mealtime," *The Correct Thing to Do— To Say—To Wear* (New York: G. K. Hall, 1995), 47.

41. Norma Jean Darden, *Spoonbread and Strawberry Wine* (New York: Doubleday, 1994), 291.

Analyze

1. How does the author employ historical, cultural, and personal references to reveal the nature and implications of a stereotype? For what purpose? In fact, what is that stereotype?

2. Look at the historical trajectory for the particular stereotype that Williams-Forson explores. Analyze the changing contexts that accompany the evolution of the stereotype. What do you find? Why?

3. How does the author analyze the language of others as a way to further understand the genesis and impact of her subject? What is the effect? For what purpose?

Explore

1. The author asks, "How does our historical, socioeconomic, and political space influence the foods that we consume?" Consider this question in relation to your own life and that of your family; what do you discover?

2. Williams-Forson also uses photographs and other images to evidence the ways in which pervasive stereotypes are communicated without alphabetic text. What other, similar examples can you find in popular culture? In the case of this article, how and why do the images enhance the text?

3. How does Williams-Forson's own positive personal experience— which start the article—serve as a gateway to revealing the negative? How does this discussion become a more complex, scholarly inquiry than it initially seems? As you've considered before, how can positive personal experiences you have had with food lead to discussions that are less positive? Why would this negative turn take place?

William Roseberry
"The Rise of Yuppie Coffees and the Reimagination of Class in the United States"

William Roseberry was known as a scholar-teacher focusing on the intersection of history and anthropology. Although Roseberry is not remembered as a food writer per se, this particular piece has been widely read as a concise but incisive reading of the impact of class and consumption on everyday life. The primary argument in the article is that coffee is the "beverage of postmodernism."

This 1996 piece might seem a bit dated. However, in what ways is this conversation still relevant?

Let us begin at Zabar's, a gourmet food emporium on Manhattan's Upper West Side. We enter, make our way through the crowd waiting to place orders in the cheese section, move quickly past the prepared foods, linger over the smoked fish, then arrive at the coffees. There, in full-sized barrels arranged in a semicircle, we find a display of roasted coffee beans for sale—Kona style, Colombian Supremo, Gourmet Decaf, Blue Mountain style, Mocha style, "French Italian," Vienna, Decaf Espresso, Water Process Decaf, Kenya AA—and a helpful clerk waiting to fill our order, grind the beans to our specification, and suggest one of a small selection of flavored syrups.

Given Zabar's reputation for quality and excess, this is a rather modest selection as coffee now goes. The evidence of plenty and waste can be found in the size of the barrels and the quantity of roast beans available for sale and spoilage. But the real spot to spend money is upstairs, where the brewers, grinders, and espresso coffeemakers are sold—from simple Melitta drip cones and carafes to the more serious Krups Semiprofessional Programmatic ($349) or the Olympia Caffarex ($1,000). Zabar's collection of coffee is not especially distinguished. They eschew the trend toward flavors (raspberry, almond, chocolate, amaretto, vanilla, and the like, in various combinations), offering instead a few prepackaged coffees in flavors and small bottles of flavored syrups for those customers who prefer them. But only two of their coffees are sold as specific varietals, Colombian Supremo and Kenyan AA. The rest are "styles" that suggest a geographic place without having anything to do with it. Kona style can include beans from El Salvador, Blue Mountain style, beans from Puerto Rico, and so on.

If I visit the deli across the street from my apartment, I can choose from a much wider variety of coffees, 43 in all, including Jamaican Blue Mountain, Venezuela Maracaibo, German Chocolate, Swedish Delight, Double Vanilla Swedish Delight, Swiss Mocha Almond, and Decaf Swiss Mocha Almond, to name just a few. These are displayed in burlap bags that take up much more space than coffee sections used to occupy when my only choices were Maxwell House, Folgers, Chock Full o' Nuts, El Pico, and Medaglia d'Oro. And they require the assistance of a clerk to weigh, bag, and grind the coffee.

As I walk down the street, virtually every deli offers a similar variety, generally in minibarrels, though sometimes the barrels are distributed in apparently casual abundance throughout the store so that I can also select breads, spreads, teas, chocolates, and cheeses as I decide which among the many roasts, varietals, styles, or flavors I will choose this week. I no longer need the gourmet shop—though such shops, which proliferated in the 1980s, continue to thrive, concentrated in cities but also present in suburban towns and shopping malls—to buy what coffee traders call "specialty" coffees; nor do I need to be a gourmet to buy and enjoy them (or better said, I need not be a gourmet to look, act, and feel like one). I can go to the corner deli or the major supermarket, where even Maxwell House and A&P have joined the "specialty" trend.

Surely these developments are "good." Specialty coffees taste better than   5 mass-market coffees. They offer pleasure in many ways: the aroma, ambience, and experience of the coffee shop or even the deli itself (indeed, part of the experience of a place like Zabar's is the succession of smells); the casual conversation with the shop owner or dinner guest about varietals, roasts, preparation methods; the identification with particular places through consumption—Copenhagen or Vienna, Jamaica or the Celebes; or the inclusion of coffee purchasing, preparation, and consumption in a widening spectrum of foods—including wines, beers, waters, breads, cheeses, sauces, and the like—through which one can cultivate and display "taste" and "discrimination." Moreover, the expansion of specialty coffees marks a distinct break with a past characterized by mass production and consumption. The move toward these coffees was not initiated by the giants that dominate the coffee trade but by small regional roasters who developed new sources of supply, new modes and networks of distribution that allowed, among other things, for consumers to buy coffee directly (well, not *directly*) from a peasant cooperative in Chiapas or Guatemala. New coffees, more choices, more diversity, less concentration, new capitalism: the beverage of postmodernism.

Proper understanding of the proliferation of specialty coffees requires consideration of the experiences and choices of the consumer in the coffee shop and at the dinner table, but it also requires consideration of the methods, networks, and relations of coffee production, processing, distribution, and sale in the 1980s, as well as a placement of those methods, networks, and relations within a wider history.

This essay concentrates on that second range of questions, on what might be termed the *shaping* of taste. I begin with two historical issues—first, the complex relation between the recent rise of specialty coffees and an earlier period characterized by standardization and mass-marketing, and second, the specific history of specialty coffees themselves. In considering both, I deal with coffee in particular, but what was happening with coffee marketing and consumption was not at all unrelated to what was happening with many other food commodities. I then turn to a range of questions that might be termed sociological: How has the turn toward specialty coffees been organized? What has been the position and role of the giant corporations that dominated the coffee trade during the period of standardization? Who have been the innovators and "agents" of change in the move toward specialty coffees? How have they organized themselves? How have they reimagined and reorganized the market? What kinds of class and generational maps of United States society have they used in their reimagination of the market? How have they imagined themselves, and the class and generational segments they target as their market niche, in relation to a wider world of coffee producers?

These more historical and sociological questions raise issues for anthropological interpretation. Can the study of changing marketing and consumption patterns of a single commodity at a particular moment—even a mundane commodity produced for everyday and routine consumption—shed some light on a wider range of social and cultural shifts? We have a good example of such an analysis in Sidney Mintz's *Sweetness and Power* (1985), an exploration of the growing and changing presence of sugar in the English diet from the 17th through 19th centuries, linked—explicitly and necessarily—to industrialization and the growth of a working class, changing modes of life, consumption, and sociality in growing cities in England, and to the establishment of colonial power, plantation economies, and slave labor in the Caribbean. The range of issues considered here is more modest, but it shares Mintz's conviction that "the social history of the use of new foods in a western nation can contribute to an anthropology of modern life" (1985: xxviii).

A distinctive feature of the essay is that the data come largely from two trade journals, *World Coffee and Tea (WC&T)* and *Coffee and Cocoa International (C&CI)*. These journals raise several questions, the first of which is methodological—the use of trade journals in relation to other possible methods and sources, including ethnographic ones. The journals give us access to the preoccupations, diagnoses, and strategies of a range of actors in the coffee trade—growers, traders, roasters, distributors, and retailers large and small, in producing as well as consuming countries. In one sense, they share a common interest: to increase coffee consumption and maximize profits. In many other senses, their interests and their stakes in the coffee trade differ.

If we are trying to understand these actors—their interpretations and intentions, their images of the social world in which they act, their disagreements and disputes, and their actions—trade journals constitute a central, readily available, and underused source. But their use raises a second related and interesting issue of the trade journal as text. The articles in the journals speak to a particular kind of public—in this case, to an assumed community of "coffeemen." The anthropologist who would use these articles for other purposes has the strong sense that he (in this case) is eavesdropping, or—to return to the text—peering over the shoulder of the intended reader.

10

Connections and Contrasts

We understand and value the new specialty coffees in relation to "the past," though in fact more than one past is being imagined. On the one hand, specialty coffees are placed in positive relation to the past of, say, two decades ago, when most coffee in the United States was sold in cans in supermarkets, the roasts were light and bland, the decaffeinated coffees undrinkable, the choices limited to brand and perhaps grind, and the trade dominated by General Foods and Procter and Gamble. On the other hand, the new coffees seem to connect with a more genuine past before the concentration and massification of the trade. The identification of particular blends and varietals recalls the glory days of the trade; the sale of whole beans in barrels or burlap bags recalls that past (for a present in which the "containerization" in international shipping has rendered such bags obsolete) at the same time that it gives the late-20th-century gourmet shop the ambience of the late-19th-century general store. This identification is further effected with the tasteful display of old coffee mills, roasters, and brewing apparatus on the store shelves. Coffee traders themselves share these identifications. Alan Rossman, of Hena "Estate Grown" Coffee, explained to *World Coffee and Tea* in 1981:

> I am a second generation coffeeman and, through direct experience, remember when there was a certain pride in the coffee business. We used to wonder why, in earlier days, there were so many second generation coffeemen around. And it was because there was an art to coffee then. . . . . Today, the ballgame has changed and suddenly the password in coffee has become "cheaper, cheaper!"
>
> All of a sudden . . . comes along somebody who's interested in quality. He doesn't care that he may have to sell it at twice the price of canned coffee, he's only interested in quality. All we're doing today is copying what our fathers and grandfathers did years and years ago. . . . Specialty coffee has revived the pride that was lost somewhere along the line and it is the main reason why I, who was born and raised in the coffee business, really enjoy now being part of that business. [*WC&T* 1981b:12]

In the same issue of *World Coffee and Tea*, the journal enthused:

> And so it seems that the coffee trade in the U.S. has come full circle, returning to its roots and the uncomplicated marketing of coffee in bins, barrels and the more modern method of lucite containers. As they did in the early days of coffee consumption, American consumers, in ever-growing numbers, are blending their own coffee, grinding it at home and brewing it fresh each day. [*WC&T* 1981b:12]

Similarly, the journal notes that specialty coffees appeal to consumers who prefer "natural," "whole," and "fresh" foods. Imagining yet another past, the same journal nervously tracks the latest government reports on the effects of caffeine or methylene chloride. But to what extent is the new also a return? Upon what pasts have the specialty coffees actually built?

In an important essay, Michael Jimenez (1995) describes the processes through which coffee was transformed from an elite and expensive beverage, with annual per capita consumption in the United States at three pounds in 1830, to a relatively inexpensive drink consumed in working-class homes and at factory "coffee breaks" across the country by 1930. Much of his analysis concerns the first three decades of the 20th century, by which time coffee was widely distributed and consumed.

Of special relevance is Jimenez's analysis of the emergence of a more con-   15
centrated and consolidated coffee trade in the first three decades of this century, one that had developed a central directing (though not controlling) authority and imposed standardized notions of quality and taste in the creation of a national market. Jimenez shows that we cannot understand transformations in the coffee trade without understanding a broad range of economic and social transformations in the history of American capitalism—the industrial revolution of the late 19th century and the creation of a more homogeneous proletariat; the development of national markets and modes of distribution; the revolution in food production, processing, and distribution that resulted in the creation of the supermarket, among other things (indeed, the histories of the supermarket and of standardization in the coffee trade are contingent); the revolution in advertising; the concentration and consolidation of American industry; and so on. In all this, the particular history of the standardization of coffee for mass markets is not unrelated to the history of standardization, indeed "industrialization," of foods in general in the 19th and 20th centuries (see Goody 1982:154–174).

The process of standardization and concentration begun before the depression was consolidated over the succeeding decades, especially after World War II, during which we can locate two new developments. The first involved the creation of international control instruments and agreements, beginning in World War II and culminating in the creation of the International Coffee Organization and an International Coffee Agreement signed by producing and consuming countries, through which export quotas were imposed upon producing countries. Though room was allowed for new producers (especially from Africa) to enter the market, entry and participation were controlled. With such instruments, and with the widening production and consumption of solubles, the trend toward coffee of the lowest common denominator continued.

The second postwar development involved the long-term decline in consumption beginning in the 1960s. Through the 1950s, consumption was essentially flat, with minor fluctuations. From 1962, one can chart a consistent decline. In that year, 74.7 percent of the adult population was calculated to be coffee drinkers; by 1988 only 50 percent drank coffee

TABLE 3.1 Percentage of U.S. population drinking coffee, 1962–88. Redrawn and simplified after *WC&T* 1989a.

Year	Percentage Drinking
1962	74.7
1974	61.6
1975	61.6
1976	59.1
1977	57.9
1978	56.7
1979	57.2
1980	56.6
1981	56.4
1982	56.3
1983	55.2
1984	57.3
1985	54.9
1986	52.4
1987	52.0
1988	50.0

(see Table 3.1). Even those who drank coffee were drinking less. In 1962, average coffee consumption was 3.12 cups per day; by 1980 it had dipped to 2.02 cups and by 1991 had dropped to 1.75, which represented a slight increase over the 1988 low of 1.67 (*WC&T* 1991:14). Worse, in the view of "coffeemen," consumption was increasingly skewed toward an older set. At the beginning of the 1980s, they worried that they had not been able to attract the 20- to 29-year-old generation, who seemed to identify coffee drinking with the settled ways of their parents and grandparents. According to their calculations, 20- to 29-year-olds drank only 1.47 cups per day in 1980, while 30- to 59-year-olds drank 3.06 cups, and those over 60 drank 2.40 (*WC&T* 1980:22).

Differentiation and the Identification of Market Niches
The long-term trend toward decline was exacerbated by the effects of the July 1975 frost in Brazil, after which wholesale and retail prices rose precipitously. In response, various consumer groups began to call for boycotts,

and coffee purchases declined sharply. Congressional hearings were called to investigate the coffee trade, and the General Accounting Office conducted an official inquiry and published a report.

At the beginning of the 1980s, then, many "coffee-men" had reason to worry. Kenneth Roman Jr., president of Ogilvie and Mather, a major advertising and public relations firm which carried the Maxwell House account, offered them some advice. In an interview with the editors of *World Coffee and Tea*, he commented,

> Coffee is a wonderful product. I believe, however, that we have got to stop selling the product on price. We must sell coffee on quality, value and image. I believe coffee has a potential for this marketing approach and I know we can do it. But we must get started now. . . .
>
> Once you start selling a product on price, you end up with a lot of money being put into price promotions . . . and you forget the basic things like the fact that coffee tastes good, that it smells and looks nice, that it's unique. . . .
>
> We are entering the "me" generation. The crucial questions "me" oriented consumers will ask, of all types of products, are: What's in it for me? Is the product "me"? Is it consistent with my lifestyle? Does it fill a need? Do I like how it tastes? What will it cost me? Is it necessary? Can I afford it? Is it convenient to prepare? How will it affect my health? [*WC&T* 1981a:35]

In a speech to the Green Coffee Association of New York, Roman suggested fictitious couples and individuals who could serve as markers of distinct market niches and suggested that "coffeemen" should develop different coffees to appeal to specific niches. The first couple was "the Grays," a dual-income couple in their mid-thirties, for whom coffee is a "way of life" and who prefer to buy their coffee in a gourmet shop. Others included "the Pritchetts," in their late fifties and watching their pennies, for whom price is the most important question; "Karen Sperling," a single working woman in her thirties who does not want to spend much time in the kitchen and for whom a better instant coffee should be developed; "the Taylors," in their sixties and worried about caffeine, for whom better decaffeinated coffees should be developed; and "Joel," a college student who does not drink coffee. "We don't know yet what to do about Joel. . . . Finding the right answer to that question will be the toughest, and probably the

20

most important task coffee marketers will face in the 80s" (*WC&T* 1981a:76–77).

Kenneth Roman was inviting "coffeemen" to envision a segmented rather than a mass market, and to imagine market segments in class and generational terms. In his scheme were two groups that were to be the targets of specialty coffee promotions—the yuppie "Grays" and the mysterious "Joel," who prefers soft drinks. These two segments mark what were to become two strains of an emerging specialty business—the marketing of quality varietals, on one hand, and the promotion of flavored coffees, the equivalent of soft drinks, on another.

Roman was describing the virtues of product diversification to a trade that had grown on the basis of standardization. Yet the standardization itself was a bizarre development, having been imposed upon a product that "naturally" lends itself to diversity. Even during the period of concentration among roasters and packagers, the export–import trade was organized around a complex grading hierarchy, first according to type (arabica or robusta), then according to place, processing methods, and shape, size, and texture of the bean. Coffees are graded first according to a hierarchy from Colombian arabica, other milds, Brazilian, to robustas. They are traded and may be sold by the place of their origin or export (varietals such as Guatemalan Antigua, Kona, Blue Mountain, Maracaibo); once traded, they may be blended with coffees from other locales or of other grades. Both varietals and blends can then be subjected to different roasts, imparting different, more or less complex aromas and tastes to the coffee. From the point of production through traders, export firms, importers, warehousers, roasters, and distributors, the grading hierarchy with significant price differentials prevails. In their attempt to capture and service a mass market in the 20th century, the giant roasters had bought their coffee through these grading differentials, then proceeded to obliterate them in the production of coffee of the lowest common denominator.

The giants had never controlled the whole trade, however. In addition to the major roasters and their distribution network through grocery stores, smaller "institutional" roasters were scattered throughout the country, servicing restaurants, cafes, offices, vendors, and the like. At the beginning of the 1980s, fewer than 200 roasting and processing companies operated in the United States, with four of them controlling 75 percent of the trade (*C&CI* 1982:17). In addition, a small network of specialty, "gourmet" shops could be found, primarily in coastal cities like New York and

San Francisco. In the retrospective view of "coffeemen," these shops began to attract new customers and expand business in the wake of the 1975 freeze, when coffee prices expanded across the board and consumers faced with paying $3 a pound for tasteless coffee began searching for something "better" and found that "quality" coffee that used to cost three times super-market prices was now only about a dollar more.

This, in turn, provided stimulus for others to enter the gourmet trade, perhaps including specialty coffees as one of a range of foods in a gourmet shop. For this expanding number of retailers, supply was a problem. They were dealing in small lots of a product that was imported, warehoused, and sold in bulk, and were entering a trade that was highly concentrated. As the specialty trade expanded, the critical middlemen were the roasters, who could develop special relationships with importers willing to deal in smaller lots. The roasters, in turn, would supply a network of specialty stores. Loca-tion mattered, as a relatively dense concentration of specialty traders, roast-ers, retailers, and customers developed on the West Coast, especially in Seattle and the San Francisco Bay Area. The roasters best situated to take advantage of the situation were institutional roasters who began to develop specialty lines as subsidiaries of their restaurant supply business. These re-gional roasters, and others new to the trade, quickly became the control points of an expanding gourmet trade, developing new supplies, roasts, and blends; taking on regular customers among shop owners; running "educa-tional" seminars to cultivate a more detailed knowledge of coffee among re-tailers, expecting that they in turn would educate their customers; and so on. An early gourmet-market idea popular with retailers was the "gourmet coffee of the day," sold by the cup, allowing the retailer to drain excess inventory and acquaint customers with different blends and roasts at the same time.

One of the most important difficulties for the roaster was the establish-   25
ment of a regular supply of green coffee. Here the problem was less one of quality than of quantity: major importers and warehousers were reluctant to break lots into shipments below 25 to 50 bags (of 60 kilograms each), but a small to medium-sized roaster dealing with several varietals needed to buy in lots of about 10 bags each. While a collection of green coffee traders in the Bay Area (B. C. Ireland, E. A. Kahl, Harold L. King, Royal Coffee) specialized in the gourmet trade and traded in smaller lots, New York trad-ers were slow to move into the new markets (Schoenholt 1984a:62). As late as 1988, Robert Fulmer of Royal Coffee complained, "Demand for quality has happened faster than producers can react. The New York 'C' market is

becoming irrelevant, because it's not representative of what people want" (*C&CI* 1988a: 18–22).

Although the trend still represented a very small percentage of total coffee sales in the United States by the early 1980s, traders and roasters had begun to take notice. A scant seven months after Kenneth Roman discussed the need to identify a segmented market and diversify coffee products, *World Coffee and Tea* issued a report on "the browning of America," pointing to an exponential growth in the segment of the coffee trade devoted to specialty lines, with annual growth rates approaching 30 to 50 percent. The journal estimated total U.S. sales of specialty coffees for 1980 to be 14 million pounds (*WC&T* 1981b:12). Over the 1980s growth was phenomenal: *Coffee and Cocoa International* reported sales of 40 million pounds in 1983 (*C&CI* 1985), after which further reports were presented in value of the trade rather than the number of bags—$330 million in 1985 (*C&CI* 1986), $420 million in 1986, $500 million in 1987, by which time specialty coffee constituted 8 percent of total trade, and so on (*C&CI* 1988b).

The expansion of specialty coffees was coincident with a number of technological and commercial developments that require brief mention. First, the "containerization" revolution in international shipping has drastically cut the amount of time coffee is in transit from producing countries to consuming countries (from 17 to 10 days for a typical Santos–to–New York run), and has transformed warehousing practices in the United States, cutting warehouse storage times from an average of six months to an average of 10 to 14 days. Speed in transfer and the development of direct and immediate relationships with roasters have become critical, and the widespread use of containers has allowed distributors to relocate from the coasts to interior cities, enhancing flexibility in supply and distribution (Coe 1983).

Changing relationships between roasters, traders, and bankers were also involved in the gourmet boom. The combination of high inflation and interest rates of the late 1970s and early 1980s affected the way in which "coffeemen" could think about financing their trade. By the early 1980s, banks were less willing to finance purchases of large lots that would be warehoused for several months and encouraged their clients to buy smaller lots and maintain lower inventories. "It's a different world now," Mickey Galitzine of the Bank of New York commented to *World Coffee and Tea* (1983a:21), "and I'm not sure we can go back. People have adjusted to this new situation and are now buying in a different pattern. They're simply used to buying less."

They were buying less, but still buying in lots that were large and risky enough to concern the specialty roaster. Institutional roasters could roast, grind, and package large lots and not worry about freshness. Specialty roasts, to be sold in whole beans, required freshness and had to be distributed and sold quickly. The roaster therefore had to develop an extensive network of retailers but was limited to particular regions because of the difficulties in shipping whole roast beans and maintaining freshness. Here the development of valve packaging made it possible for roasters to keep roasted beans fresh longer, extending the time available for shipping, storage, and selling. The beans could be packed in 250-gram bags for direct retail sale or in 15- or 25-pound bags for retail storage. Indeed, the deli across the street from me buys its 43 varieties from a single roaster in 15-pound valve bags, transferring the coffee to burlap bags for presentation and sale.

New Actors, New Institutions

Throughout the 1980s, the "quality" segment of the coffee market, highest   30 in prices and profit margins, was booming while total coffee consumption declined. This constitutes such a perfect response to market decline, and such an obvious response to the suggestions of Kenneth Roman, that we might expect a central directing power—"Capital," or at least "The Coffee Interest." But the initiative toward specialty coffees occurred outside of and despite the controlling interests of the giants like General Foods, Procter and Gamble, and Nestle, who ignored the growth of specialty coffees and seemed to regard them as a fad until they captured a significant percentage of the market. Their reticence might be explained by the fact that the giants were part of large food conglomerates likely to be less threatened by a long-term decline in coffee consumption than the smaller institutional roasters, who were forced to develop new markets in order to survive.

This is not to say that the emergence of specialty coffees was completely free from direction and organization. I have pointed to *some* of the larger commercial, financial, and technological changes with which the move to specialty coffees was associated. In addition, the coffee trade viewed the new developments with interest and excitement. We have seen the notice taken by trade journals from the early 1980s. *World Coffee and Tea* began tracking developments quite closely, with frequent reports on the trade and profiles of particular roasters or retailers. In 1984, the journal also began an irregular column, "The Gourmet Zone," by Donald Schoenholt, followed in the early 1990s by a regular column with various contributors, "The Specialty Line." *Coffee and Cocoa International* viewed developments from a greater distance but enjoyed profiling particular gourmet retailers for their readers. Most importantly, a group of roasters and retailers formed the Specialty Coffee Association of America (SCAA) in 1982. As with the earlier formation of the National Coffee Association (and later the International Coffee Organization), the importance of such trade associations needs to be emphasized. They provide an important directing organization that can lobby the government, speak for the trade, identify economic and political trends, engage in promotional campaigns, provide information and training for entrepreneurs entering the trade, and so on.

In association with the National Coffee Service Association, the SCAA appealed to the Promotion Fund of the International Coffee Organization and received a $1.6 million grant to promote specialty coffees, especially among the young (*WC&T* 1983b). The money was funneled through the Coffee Development Group (CDG), which promoted specialty coffees throughout the 1980s. One of their early activities involved joint sponsorship of coffeehouses on college campuses (Columbia University being one of the first), at which coffee brewed from specialty roasts and blends would be sold. The CDG would specify the amount of coffee that had to be included in each pot brewed (*WC&T* 1988). Some, such as the shop at the University of Southern California, even experimented with iced cappuccino, sold in cold drink "bubblers" (*WC&T* 1989b).

In addition to promotional efforts, the SCAA has pursued other goals as well, including the dissemination of information on green market conditions and the development of networks among roasters, retailers, and traders. By 1989, the group held its first convention, and each annual convention demonstrates the phenomenal growth of the association. Its conventions now attract over 3,000 people, and it claims to be the largest coffee association in the world.

Many of the association's members are new to the coffee trade, and they bring with them a formation quite unlike that which characterized second- and third-generation "coffeemen." For one thing, many begin with a lack of knowledge about the basics of coffee production, processing, and marketing. This is reflected in a new tone in *World Coffee and Tea*, which increasingly offers articles giving basic and introductory information of various aspects of the coffee trade, recently advising new entrepreneurs that

"historic and geographic background is an essential element to a comprehensive knowledge of coffee. If you're selling Colombian coffee, you should
have some idea about where Colombia is located and what kinds of coffee
it produces" (McCormack 1994:22). It is also reflected in the kinds of
workshops and training sessions offered at annual conventions of the
SCAA, popularly known as Espresso 101 or Roasting 101 or Brewing 101.

The presence of new entrepreneurs is also reflected in new sets of social,   35
political, and ethical concerns that would have been anathema to earlier
generations of "coffeemen." Among them is a growing interest in social and
environmental issues and the creation by coffee roasters of such organizations as Equal Exchange and Coffee Kids, and companies like Aztec
Harvests ("owned by Mexican co-op farmers"). As the founder of Coffee
Kids, Bill Fishbein, expresses the problem:

> This disparity that exists between the coffee-growing world and the
> coffee-consuming world is rooted in the centuries and remains the
> true inheritance of 500 years of colonialism. Although no one in
> today's coffee industry created the existing situation, everyone, in-
> cluding importers, brokers, roasters, retailers, and consumers are
> left with this legacy either to perpetuate or address. [Fishbein and
> Cycon 1992:14]

William McAlpin, a plantation owner in Costa Rica, gives voice to an
older generation that dismisses these concerns along the paternalistic lines
one expects from a plantation owner proud of the livelihood he has provided for "our residents," but also observes:

> I am always amused to see that many of these same people, who are
> involved in the final stages of selling specialty coffee, while pro-
> claiming that they support this or that charity or political action
> squad, are careful to avoid mentioning that the usual mark-up by
> the specialty coffee trade is from 400% to 600% of the price paid
> for delivered green coffee....
>
> From the producer's point of view, it seems truly ironic that a
> product that takes a year to grow, and that requires thousands of
> worker hours of difficult, delicate, and often dangerous work,
> should be so remarkably inflated by someone who simply cooks and
> displays the coffee. [McAlpin 1994:7]

In any case, both dimensions of the formation of the new coffee men and women find expression and are given direction by the SCAA. In addition to the workshops and training seminars, one can see this in their annual choice of a plenary speaker. At its second convention, held in San Francisco, the SCAA arranged a group tour of wineries and invited a wine merchant to give the plenary address, in which he offered advice based on the success of a beverage that the trade journals have most frequently taken as the model to be emulated. For the 1993 convention, the association invited Ben Cohen of Ben and Jerry's Ice Cream. Of his address, *World Coffee and Tea* reported:

> Ben Cohen urged the members of the coffee industry to integrate the 1960s values of peace and love with running their businesses....
>
> Cohen pointed out that coffee is a very political commodity and called on the members of the special coffee industry to:
>
> • purchase coffee from the Aztec Cooperative because a high percentage of the money goes back to the farmers; "buy it, tell your customers about it, and let them choose whether or not they want to pay the higher price," Cohen said.
>
> • buy organic coffees; and
>
> • participate in Coffee Kids by using a coin drop or donating a percentage of sales.
>
> "Use these steps to build your image as a socially conscious business," Cohen explained, "and make it your point of difference in a highly competitive business." [*WC&T* 1993:7]

Flexibility and Concentration

As the smaller roasters captured the new market niche, they expressed both surprise and concern about the activities of the giants, sometimes assuming that the market was theirs only as long as the giants stayed out (e.g., *WC&T* 1984:12). Some of the roasters' and retailers' fears were realized in September 1986 when both General Foods and A&P introduced specialty lines for sale in supermarkets—General Foods with Maxwell House Private Collection and A&P with Eight O'Clock Royale Gourmet Bean in 14 varieties, "all designed to appeal to the former soft drink generation." At the time, Karin Brown of General Foods commented,

"Gourmet is the fastest-growing segment of the market—large enough to make sense for General Foods' entry now" (*C&CI* 1986:9).

By the time the giants began to enter the market, the groundwork for a certain kind of standardization and concentration among the newcomers had already been laid. In coastal cities, the isolated gourmet food shop was already competing with chains of gourmet shops operating in minimalls, which could, if they chose, develop their own roasting capacities. In addition, some roasters (the best known and most aggressive of which has been Starbucks of Seattle) had begun to move beyond regional distribution chains and develop national markets. While structural changes, from the technologies of shipping, warehousing, and packaging to the credit policies of banks, were significant, we need to also consider some of the characteristics of the gourmet beans themselves.

As the gourmet trade expanded, participants viewed two new developments with excitement or alarm, depending on their respective commitment to traditional notions of "quality." As noted above, the quality of coffee "naturally" varies according to several criteria—type of coffee tree and location of cultivation (varietals), method of processing, size and texture of bean, and degree of roasting. With the expansion of the specialty trade, two new modes of discrimination were introduced—"styles" and "flavors." Because the availability of particular varietals is uncertain (a hurricane hits Jamaica, wiping out Blue Mountain coffee, or a trader cannot provide Kenya AA in lots small enough for a particular roaster because larger roasters can outcompete, and so on), and the price of varietals fluctuates accordingly, roasters attempt to develop blends that allow them flexibility in using a number of varietals interchangeably. "Peter's Blend" or "House Blend" says nothing about where the coffee comes from, allowing the roaster or retailer near perfect flexibility, but so again does the sale of "Mocha style" or "Blue Mountain style." At the beginning of this trend, J. Gill Brockenbrough Jr. of First Colony Coffee and Tea complained, "It is more and more difficult all the time to find the green coffee we need. . . . But there really is no such thing as a 'style' of coffee, either it *is* or it *isn't* from a particular origin" (*WC&T* 1981b:15). Donald Schoenholt of Gillies 1840 elaborated in his column, "The Gourmet Zone," in *World Coffee and Tea*:

> In the past I have pointed out the practice of labeling "varietals" with the code word "style," a habit which has come to replace good judgment too often these days. But now it appears we have a new

phenomenon added to the good-humored diversity of specialty coffee labeling: the gentle art of selling the same coffee by whatever varietal label the customer orders.

One well-known trade executive states his customers understand that substitutions are made from time-to-time when varietals are unavailable. A well-known roaster/retailer avoids buying varietal selections, following instead the accepted tradition of buying for cup qualities alone. He offers his patrons distinctive tastes in varietal labeled blends—Colombian Blend, Kenya Blend, Jamaica Blue Mountain style, etc.

Where the wholesale or retail clientele understand a merchant's practices and honorable intent, both the above-mentioned methods of labeling have been accepted. The problem arises where a merchant's intent is to mislead, through unbridled use of a stencil machine, creating labels just for the sake of inventing variety where none exists. Where no effort or skill is used, the public is presented with cut-rate mislabeled coffees.

A recent inspection of a grocer in the New York area sadly proved a point: Virtually every American roast coffee on display was the same item under different label, purchased from a discount roaster offering all American roast beans, regardless of origin, in the same $2.60 per lb. price range. [Schoenholt 1984b:39]

A second, related development was the emergence of coffee flavors that can be sprayed on recently roasted beans. C. Melchers and Company of Bremen began operating in the United States in 1982, offering an ever-expanding variety of liquid flavors for coffee and tea. Each flavor is composed of 20 to 60 "natural" and "artificial" (chemical) ingredients, and Melchers is adept at developing different combinations to produce "unique" flavors for particular roasters (*WC&T* 1983c:16, 18). Viewing this trend, Larry Kramer of Van Cortland Coffee observed, "Specialty coffee is becoming the Baskin Robbins of the specialty food trade." Actually, as we have seen, it turned out that Ben and Jerry's would have been more to the point. Some roasters and retailers refused to deal in such coffees. Complained Paul Katzeff of Thanksgiving Coffee, "People who drink good coffee drink it because they enjoy the flavor of real coffee. . . . I doubt that flavored coffees bring in drinkers who never drank coffee before" (*WC&T* 1982:20). Despite such expressions of dismay, the move toward flavored coffees has continued apace; roasters and retailers alike recognize that flavors are popular, that they are attracting new coffee drinkers, especially among the "former soft drink generation" that had seemed lost to coffee consumption at the beginning of the 1980s—Kenneth Roman's "Joel," about whom "we don't know yet what to do." Increasingly popular in both retail shops and espresso bars are flavored syrups that, in addition to imparting an apparent "Italian" elegance, grant the small retailer more flexibility. A smaller number of blends, varietals, and roasts can be kept in stock, along with a few bottles of syrup, and customers can add or mix their own flavors.

Style and flavor can, in turn, be combined in various ways, so that one can buy Blue Mountain style vanilla or almond, Mocha style chocolate cream or amaretto, and so on. If we further combine with different roasts, throw in the possibility of caffeinated or water process decaffeinated, the possibilities for variety are almost endless. Critically important, however, is that the variety is *controllable*. To the extent that roasters and retailers are able to create criteria of variability and quality that are removed from the "natural" characteristics and qualities of the coffee beans themselves, they generate for themselves extraordinary flexibility. In extreme cases, they "invent variety where none exists," as Schoenholt complains. Here we find a consumer who acts and feels like a gourmet but is buying coffee that is not far removed from Maxwell House Private Collection. More generally, they create, define, and control their own forms of variety. Specialty "coffeemen" constantly emulate and consult wine merchants and hope that consumers will select coffee with the same discrimination and willingness to spend money they demonstrate when buying wine, but the Baskin Robbins (or Ben and Jerry's) model may not be too much of an exaggeration.

Ironically, controllable variety also makes the specialty trade subject to concentration, whether from the outside as giants create their own "Private Collection" and "Royale Gourmet Bean" lines or from internal differentiation, expansion, and concentration among smaller roasters. Variety, too, can be standardized, especially if the varieties have little to do with "natural" characteristics.

The Beverage of Postmodernism?

In his study of the transformation of coffee production and consumption in the early 20th century, Michael Jimenez suggests that coffee is the beverage of U.S. capitalism. Indeed, as we consider the place of coffee as a beverage of choice in working- and middle-class homes and in factory canteens, the role of coffee traders in the emergence of a practical internationalism, and the processes of standardization and concentration that restructured the coffee market, we see that the coffee trade was subject to and participant in the same processes that made a capitalist world.

45   This is not to suggest, of course, that coffee exists in some sort of unique relationship with capitalism, but that it provides a window through which we can view a range of relationships and social transformations. The processes of standardization and industrialization were common to many foods in the 20th-century United States, and coffee would therefore be one of many foods through which one could examine the transformation industrialization wrought in such broad areas as the structure of cities, the remaking of work and domestic life and organization, or more specific concerns, such as the rise of advertising or the supermarket. Here, Jimenez's work on coffee in the United States complements Mintz's work on sugar in England (1985). Yet coffee and sugar belong to a small subset of commodities that can illuminate capitalist transformations in other ways in that they link consumption zones (and the rise of working and middle classes that consumed the particular products in ever increasing numbers) and production zones in Latin America, the Caribbean, Africa, and Asia (and the peasants, slaves, and other rural toilers who grew, cut, or picked the products). For these commodities once inadequately termed "dessert foods" and now increasingly called "drug foods," Sidney Mintz offers a more arresting phrase—coffee, sugar, tea, and chocolate were "proletarian hunger killers" (1979).

Might we, in turn, now consider coffee to be the beverage of postmodernism? That is, can an examination of shifts in the marketing and consumption of one commodity provide an angle of vision on a wider set of social and cultural formations and the brave new world of which they are a part? That I can walk across the street and choose among a seemingly endless variety of cheeses, beers, waters, teas, and coffees places me in a new relationship to the world: I can consume a bit of Sumatra, Darjeeling, France, and Mexico in my home, perhaps at the same meal. Such variety stands in stark contrast to the stolid, boring array of goods available two decades ago. We live now in an emerging era of variety and choice, and the revolution in consumption seems to indicate, and in some ways initiate, a revolution in production. As with coffee, so with other food products: the moves toward product diversification often came not from the established and dominant corporations but from independents whose initiatives have undercut and undermined the established practices and market share of those corporations. We might see this as the extension of the Apple Computer model of entrepreneurialism to other realms.

David Harvey elaborates:

> The market place has always been an "emporium of styles" . . . but the food market, just to take one example, now looks very different from what it was twenty years ago. Kenyan haricot beans, Californian celery and avocados, North African potatoes, Canadian apples, and Chilean grapes all sit side by side in a British supermarket. This variety also makes for a proliferation of culinary styles, even among the relatively poor. . . .
>
> The whole world's cuisine is now assembled in one place in almost exactly the same way that the world's geographical complexity is nightly reduced to a series of images on a static television screen. This same phenomenon is exploited in entertainment palaces like Epcot and Disney-World; it becomes possible, as the U.S. commercials put it, "to experience the Old World for a day without actually having to go there." The general implication is that through the experience of everything from food, to culinary habits, music, television, entertainment, and cinema, it is now possible to experience the world's geography vicariously, as a simulacrum. The interweaving of simulacra in daily life brings together different worlds (of commodities) in the same space and time. But it does so in such a way as to conceal almost perfectly any trace of origin, of the labour processes that produced them, or of the social relations implicated in their production. [1989:299, 300]

A more complete understanding of coffee marketing and consumption in the 1980s and 1990s requires that we make some attempt to examine the world of production concealed by the emporium of styles. We might begin by maintaining an understanding of coffee as "the beverage of United States capitalism" but placing the history of that beverage within two periods of capitalist accumulation.

In David Harvey's view, much of 20th-century capitalism was dominated by a "Fordist" regime of accumulation; since the mid-1970s a new regime has emerged, which he labels "flexible accumulation." The Fordist regime can be seen to begin in 1914, with the imposition of assembly line production, and it has dominated the post–World War II period. The Fordist regime was founded on mass production and industrial modes of organization, based in a few key industries (steel, oil, petrochemicals, automobiles), characterized by the presence of both organized management and organized labor with negotiated, relatively stable pacts between them. These industries, in turn, were subject to state regulation and protection of markets and resources, and they produced standardized commodities for mass markets. With the financial crises of the 1970s, the stabilities of the Fordist regime came to be seen as rigidities. Harvey sees the regime of flexible accumulation emerging in partial response. His description of the innovations characteristic of flexible accumulation concentrates on many features that we have already encountered in our discussion of specialty coffees—the identification of specialized market niches and the production of goods for those niches as opposed to the emphasis on mass-market standardized products; the downsizing of plants and production processes; the shrinking of inventories so that producers purchase smaller quantities and practice just-in-time production; the revolution in shipping and warehousing technologies to cut shipping times; the reconfiguration of financial markets; and so on.

50   In this regard, it is interesting to place the period considered by Jimenez and the period examined in this essay next to each other. Both concern decades that saw, if we follow Harvey's analysis, experimentation with new regimes of accumulation. But if we return to a history more specific to coffee, both also began with a perceived problem—stagnation in consumption in the first, long-term decline in the second. Both began with evident consumer dissatisfaction and governmental investigation (in the form of congressional hearings). In both, the coffee trade, in the individual actions of its fragmented members and in the programs of its directing centers, devised strategies to respond to perceived crises that, as it happens, neatly correspond with the forms, methods, and relations of emerging regimes of accumulation.

As I visit the gourmet shop, it might be a bit disconcerting to know that I have been so clearly targeted as a member of a class and generation, that the burlap bags or minibarrels, the styles and flavors of coffee, the offer of a "gourmet coffee of the day," have been designed to appeal to me and others in my market niche. But such are the circumstances surrounding my freedom of choice. In an influential essay on the global cultural economy, Arjun Appadurai has suggested the emergence of a new "fetishism of the consumer" and claims that commodity flows and marketing strategies "mask . . . the real seat of agency, which is not the consumer but the producer and the many forces that constitute production. . . . The consumer is consistently helped to believe that he or she is an actor, where in fact he or she is at best a chooser" (1990:307). While I think Appadurai's larger claims regarding the radical disjuncture between the present global cultural economy and earlier moments and forms require careful and skeptical analysis (Roseberry 1992), the recent history of coffee marketing and consumption seems to support his understanding of consumer fetishism.

That is to say, my newfound freedom to choose, and the taste and discrimination I cultivate, have been shaped by traders and marketers responding to a long-term decline in sales with a move toward market segmentation along class and generational lines. While I was thinking of myself as me, Kenneth Roman saw me as one of "the Grays." How many readers of this essay have been acting like "Joels"? This is not, of course, to say that we enter the market as mere automatons; clearly, we have and exercise choices, and we (apparently) have more things to choose from than we once did. But we exercise those choices in a world of structured relationships, and part of what those relationships structure (or shape) is both the arena and the process of choice itself.

Another, inescapable part of that world of structured relationships is a set of connections with the world of production and of producers. My vicarious experience of the world's geography is not *just* a simulacrum; it depends upon a quite real, if mediated and unacknowledged, relationship with the rural toilers without whom my choice could not be exercised. How has the brave new world of choice and flexibility affected them?

For both Fordist and flexible accumulation regimes, the mode of mobilizing labor is critical—the importance of a stable core of organized labor and labor relations under Fordism and its virtual opposite under flexible accumulation, which seems to remove labor as much as possible from core to peripheral (temporary, seasonal, occasional, or contracted) labor supplies that can be engaged and disengaged as needed. Some of the innovations that I have discussed in relation to the coffee market have involved such shifts in labor relations (e.g., the move toward containerization in international shipping, which revolutionized distribution in the United States and allowed importers to bypass the docks and warehouses of coastal cities, cutting the need for labor and the power of the unions of longshoremen and warehousemen).

55   As we turn from the United States to the manifold points of production, we find that the changes can be quite dramatic, though their shape and consequences remain uncertain and can only be suggested here. Throughout the post–World War II period, the coffee trade was regulated by a series of international coffee agreements, the first of which was the Pan American agreement during the war, and the longest lasting of which was the International Coffee Agreement (ICA) administered by the International Coffee Organization (ICO), formed in 1963. Through the agreements, producing and consuming countries submitted to a series of quotas that could be adjusted and even suspended from year to year—as particular countries suffered hurricanes, droughts, or frosts or other countries entered the market and signed the agreement—but that nonetheless imposed a series of (let us call them Fordist) rigidities on international trade. They also provided a series of protections for individual producing countries and regions, regulating both prices (which fluctuated but with highs and lows that were less dramatic) and market share.

The agreements were never especially popular among "coffeemen," who profess a free trade philosophy, and they encountered increasing opposition in the 1980s. Specialty traders wanted to develop new sources of supply, emphasizing arabicas and deemphasizing robustas, which had an important place in mass-market blends and soluble (instant) coffees but found little acceptance in specialty markets. Unfortunately for the specialty traders, the percentages of arabicas and robustas offered on the world market were fixed by the ICA; fortunately for robusta producers, their livelihoods were relatively protected by that same agreement.

The ICA was due for renewal and extension in 1989, but the various members of the ICO encountered difficulties in resolving their differences. Two countries were especially insistent on their needs—Brazil, which wanted to maintain its 30 percent share, and the United States, which pressed two concerns: (1) the troublesome practice among producing countries of discounting prices to nonmember consuming countries (essentially those within the then-existing socialist bloc), and (2) the inflexibility of the quotas that, they argued, prevented traders and consumers from acquiring more of the quality arabicas. Because the differences could not be resolved, the ICA was suspended in mid-1989, ushering in a free market in coffee for the first time in decades.

The immediate effects were dramatic for producing countries. Prices plummeted and quickly reached, in constant dollar terms, historic lows.

Exporting countries that could do so expanded exports in an attempt to maintain income levels in the face of declining unit prices, and importers took advantage of the low prices and expanded stocks. In addition to the general price decline, robusta producers were especially disadvantaged, as prices for robusta dipped below $.50 per pound and farmers faced a world market that no longer wanted their product. Robusta is grown primarily in Africa, and African producers and economies were devastated.

By 1993, under the leadership of Brazil and Colombia, along with Central American arabica producers, a coffee retention plan was signed that called for the removal of up to 20 percent of production by participants in the plan. The plan was the first step toward a new Association of Coffee Producing Countries in which both Latin American and African countries participated, and it has succeeded in spurring a price recovery. It remains a fragile coalition, however, and by the time it had been formed the market had been completely restructured. Most importantly, because market prices had fallen below the level of production costs, only the strong—those who could weather a prolonged depression—survived. The weak disappeared from the coffee scene.

The free market vastly increased the flexibility of coffee traders and   60 "peripheralized" the labor of coffee growers in a direct and immediate way. My freedom to choose in the deli across the street or the gourmet shop a few blocks away is implicated with the coffee trader's freedom to cut off the supply (and therefore the product of the laborer) from, say, Uganda or the Ivory Coast. To the extent that "coffeemen" have been successful in creating styles, so that I think I am drinking coffee from a particular place but the coffee need not have any actual association with that place, I will not even be aware of the processes of connection and disconnection in which I am participating. "The beverage of U.S. capitalism," indeed!

Conclusion

Resolution of the issues raised by this analysis would take us beyond our sources. My aim is to draw out certain implications and perspectives resulting from the angle of vision pursued herein, but also to point toward questions and perspectives that could be pursued in supplementary and complementary analyses—other chapters, so to speak.

This essay's perspective on the shaping of market trends and taste may raise the specter of manipulation by unseen, but powerful, forces. In an important discussion of the Frankfurt School's approach to culture industries in general and to consumption patterns in particular, Stephen Mennell observes:

> The problem with the use of words like "manipulation" by the Frankfurt School and other critics is that it suggests that those in powerful positions in industry—the culture industry or the food and catering industries—*consciously* and with malevolent intent set out to persuade people that they need and like products of inferior or harmful quality. It fails to draw attention to the unplanned, unintended, vicious spiral through which supply and demand are usually linked. [1996:321]

There is, of course, plenty of evidence from the trade journals that conscious action on the part of a range of actors in the coffee trade to persuade people that they need and like certain products—leaving aside the question of intent and the quality of the products—is *precisely* what they do. But it is also clear from the sources that they do not act in concert, that there is no single controlling interest (despite obvious power relations), that there has been ample room for new interests and actors, that these actors, big and small, often do not know what they are doing, and that in their bumbling experimentation they have stumbled on some strategies that work. They work not because there is a manipulable mass out there waiting to be told what to drink but because there is a complex, if specific, intersection between the shaping actions of various actors in the coffee trade and the needs, tastes, and desires of particular groups of consumers and potential consumers.

We gain access to that intersection by means of a discussion of *class*. We have seen that Kenneth Roman preached market segmentation along class and generational lines. His own suggestion of segments was relatively simple, even crude—divided by very broad distinctions of class and generation, with some sense of gender differentiation, but each of the segments was implicitly white. Theorists of niche marketing have since gone much further in dividing national populations into class, racial, ethnic, and generational groups than Roman would have imagined in the early 1980s, as books like *The Clustering of America* (Weiss 1988) make clear. That these distinctions, however crude, are being made, and that they *work* for the purposes for which they are intended, is worth some reflection.

The point, of course, is that when market strategists *imagine* a class and   65
generational map that includes people like "the Grays" and "Joel," they are
not trying to create categories out of thin air. They are doing—for different
purposes—what sociologists and anthropologists used to do: trying to describe a social and cultural reality. The imagined map works only if there
are indeed such groups "out there," so to speak, and that the map needs to
work is the whole point.

That there is a complex relationship between class and food consumption is often remarked, first in the obvious sense that particular groups
occupy differential market situations in terms of their ability to purchase
certain foods, and second in the uses various groups make of foods and
food preferences in marking themselves as distinctive from or in some sense
like other groups. In the case of specialty coffee, one of its interesting features is that it is *not,* or is not meant to be, a "proletarian hunger killer."
Looking further afield, it is worth comment that the other proletarian
hunger killers of the 19th and 20th centuries—with the exception of
sugar, which does not lend itself to such multiple distinctions except in
combination with other substances—are also caught up in the move toward
variety and at least the illusion of quality. In one sense this signals the
return to "dessert food" status, but there are other senses that need to be
considered.

The original market segment toward which specialty coffee, tea, and
chocolate were directed was that of "the Grays"—urban, urbane, professional men and women who distinguished themselves through consumption and who consumed or hoped to consume variety and quality, as well
as quantity. If they fashioned themselves through consumption, an interesting feature of the movement is that among the commodities in which
they demanded variety and quality were the old proletarian hunger killers.
In doing so, they almost certainly did not imagine themselves in connection either with proletarians or with the rural toilers who grew, cut, or
picked what the yuppies chose to consume.

The identifications they were making were rather more complex and
may connect with the commodities' "prehistory," as it were, representing
a kind of preindustrial nostalgia. Each of the proletarian hunger killers
entered European social history as expensive goods from exotic locales,
affordable and consumable only by a privileged few, not in homes but in the
courts, or, increasingly in the 17th and 18th centuries, in coffee houses
(Schivelbusch 1992; Ukers 1935). They became proletarian hunger killers

as their costs of production, processing, and shipping dropped, as available quantities increased dramatically, and as they became items of domestic and routine consumption. The class and cultural identification of this yuppie segment, then, is not so much bourgeois as courtly, genteel, cosmopolitan. It could be seen to represent an attempt to re-create, through consumption, a time before mass society and mass consumption. It could be seen, then, as a symbolic inversion of the very economic and political forces through which this particular class segment came into existence. Here, close attention to class-conditioned patterns of consumption can provide another window onto the cultural history of U.S. capitalism.

But the story does not end here. Over the past decade, the consumption of yuppie coffees has broken free from its original market segment, as the coffees are more widely available in supermarkets and shopping malls and are more widely consumed. We have seen that the processes of production and distribution have been subject to concentration and centralization from above and below as Maxwell House and Eight O'Clock Coffee have introduced gourmet coffees and as new chains as different from each other as Starbucks and Gloria Jean's move into central positions at the coffee shop end. This movement, in which a class-conditioned process of marketing, promotion, and consumption escapes class locations, and apparent variety and quality are standardized and mass-marketed, has obvious limits. Gourmet coffees can be standardized, and their processes of production and marketing concentrated, but it is unlikely that these coffees will ever become truly mass-market coffees. Their continued success will depend upon the processes of social and cultural differentiation they mark, even as the social locations of groups of consumers are blurred. It will also depend upon the continued existence, at home and abroad, of a world of exploitative relationships, evidenced in the social relations through which coffee is produced, the engagement and disengagement of coffee-producing regions under free-market conditions, and the processes of standardization and concentration to which gourmet coffee production and marketing have been subjected. Coffee remains, as Ben Cohen expressed it, a "very political commodity."

70   *Acknowledgments.* An early version of this article was presented at the session "Histories of Commodification: Papers in Honor of Sidney Mintz," at the 91st Annual Meeting of the American Anthropological Association, San Francisco, November 1992. I thank Ashraf Ghani for inviting me to participate in the session and Richard Fox for his astute commentary.

I have also benefited from a stimulating discussion among sociologists and anthropologists at the University of California at Santa Barbara, for which I thank Elvin Hatch and Roger Friedland, and a discussion among historians at the State University of New York at Stony Brook, for which I thank Brooke Larson and Paul Gootenberg. For their useful suggestions, I thank as well the reviewers for *American Anthropologist* and Talal Asad, Kate Crehan, Nicole Polier, Deborah Poole, Rayna Rapp, and Kamala Visweswaran.

References Cited

Appadurai, Arjun. 1990. Disjuncture and Difference in the Global Cultural Economy. *Theory, Culture and Society* 7:295–310.

Coe, Kevin. 1983. Changes in Store. *Coffee and Cocoa International* 10(5):39–41.

C&CI (Coffee and Cocoa International). 1982. High Hopes for the Promotion Drive. *Coffee and Cocoa International* 9(2):14–17.

C&CI (Coffee and *Cocoa International). 1985. Major Growth Seen for Gourmet Coffee Market. Coffee and Cocoa International* 12(1):5.

C&CI (Coffee and Cocoa International). 1986. Giants Clash in Specialty Brands War. *Coffee and Cocoa International* 13(5):9.

C&CI (Coffee and Cocoa International). 1988a. The California Trade: A West Coast View. *Coffee and Cocoa International* 15(5):18–22.

C&CI (Coffee and Cocoa International). 1988b. $500m Gourmet Market to Expand, Says Study. *Coffee and Cocoa International* 15(6):6.

Fishbein, Bill, and Dean Cycon. 1992. Coffee Kids. *World Coffee and Tea*, October: 14–15, 28.

Goody, Jack. 1982. *Cooking, Cuisine, and Class: A Study in Comparative Sociology*. Cambridge: Cambridge University Press.

Harvey, David. 1989. *The Condition of Postmodernity*. Oxford: Basil Blackwell.

Jimenez, Michael. 1995. From Plantation to Cup: Coffee and Capitalism in the United States, 1830–1930. In *Coffee, Society, and Power in Latin America*. William Roseberry, Lowell Gudmundson, and Mario Samper Kutschbach, eds. Pp. 38–64. Baltimore, MD: Johns Hopkins University Press.

McAlpin, William J. 1994. Coffee and the Socially Concerned. *World Coffee and Tea*, July: 6–7.

McCormack, Tim. 1994. Teaching Consumers about Coffee. *World Coffee and Tea*, July: 21–23.

Mennell, Stephen. 1996. *All Manners of Food: Eating and Taste in England and France from the Middle Ages to the Present*. 2nd edition. Urbana: University of Illinois Press.

Mintz, Sidney. 1979. Time, Sugar, and Sweetness. *Marxist Perspectives* 2:56–73.

Mintz, Sidney. 1985. *Sweetness and Power: The Place of Sugar in Modern History*. New York: Viking.

Roseberry, William. 1992. Multiculturalism and the Challenge of Anthropology. *Social Research* 59:841–858.

Schivelbusch, Wolfgang. 1992. *Tastes of Paradise: A Social History of Spices, Stimulants, and Intoxicants*. New York: Vintage.

Schoenholt, Donald N. 1984a. The Gourmet Zone. *World Coffee and Tea*, September: 62–63.

Schoenholt, Donald N. 1984b. The Gourmet Zone. *World Coffee and Tea*, November: 39.

Ukers, W. H. 1935. *All about Coffee*. 2nd edition. New York: The Tea and Coffee Trade Journal Company.

Weiss, Michael J. 1988. *The Clustering of America*. New York: Harper and Row.

WC&T (World Coffee and Tea). 1980. U.S. Coffee Drinking Slips after Slight Gain; Young Still Not Drinking. *World Coffee and Tea*, November: 21–22.

WC&T (World Coffee and Tea). 1981a. Ad Man Cautions Coffee Men to Modernize Coffee's Image; Sees Coffee as Drink of '80s. *World Coffee and Tea*, January: 35, 76–78.

WC&T (World Coffee and Tea). 1981b. America's Coffee Renaissance Explodes with Excitement as Specialty Coffee Trade Booms. *World Coffee and Tea*, August: 10–15.

WC&T (World Coffee and Tea). 1982. Specialty Coffee '82: A Look at Some Trends. *World Coffee and Tea*, August: 16–28.

WC&T (World Coffee and Tea). 1983a. Bankers Cite Changes in Coffee Business Due to World Economy. *World Coffee and Tea*, November: 20–22.

WC&T (World Coffee and Tea). 1983b. CDG Receives ICO Grant: Specialty Coffee Task Force Formed. *World Coffee and Tea*, August: 11.

WC&T (World Coffee and Tea). 1983c. Coffee, Tea Flavorings Play Important Role in U.S. Gourmet Scene. *World Coffee and Tea,* August: 16–18.

WC&T (World Coffee and Tea). 1984. Quality, Fresh Product Keep Sales Booming in the Gourmet Segment. *World Coffee and Tea,* August: 8–14.

WC&T (World Coffee and Tea). 1988. College Coffeehouses Flourish. *World Coffee and Tea,* August: 10.

WC&T (World Coffee and Tea). 1989a. United States of America, Percentage Drinking Coffee, 1962 to 1988. *World Coffee and Tea,* March: 14.

WC&T (World Coffee and Tea). 1989b. Decaffeinated and Soluble Constantly Experiment to Improve Market Share. *World Coffee and Tea,* March: 11–15.

WC&T (World Coffee and Tea). 1991. Depressed Prices Lead to Continued Building of Stocks by Consumers. *World Coffee and Tea,* September: 12–16.

WC&T (World Coffee and Tea). 1993. SCAA '93–The Largest Coffee Event in History! *World Coffee and Tea,* June: 6–7.

Analyze

1. From this piece we can tell that Roseberry loved to focus on the marriage of history and anthropology. How does his language reveal both disciplines? To what effect?

2. At one point early in the article, Roseberry says, "Surely these developments are 'good,'" and he puts "good" in quotation marks. Why does he do this? How does it frame the rest of the article? Explain.

3. Roseberry's argument is situated about fifteen years after the first Starbucks opened in Seattle. How does his argument hold up this many years later? Why or why not?

Explore

1. As do other articles in this volume, Roseberry's piece examines the intersections of food and class. Using this essay as a model, construct a similar historical and economic timeline for a different product whose fate and implications you see as being similar to that of coffee.

2. What does Roseberry mean when he says that coffee is "the beverage of postmodernism?" What sense do you make of his explanation? What information can you find through other sources to make Roseberry's point clearer than it might seem?

3. "That there is a complex relationship between class and food consumption is often remarked . . ." How does Roseberry explore this relationship? What types of examples does he use, and which do you find most persuasive and effective? Find other articles of this type—more academic, perhaps, in scope than others—and compare.

Riddhi Shah
"Men Eat Meat, Women Eat Chocolate: How Food Gets Gendered"

A regular contributor to Salon.com and the editorial director at the *Huffington Post*, Riddhi Shah was educated at New York University. Shah specializes in "good news and social impact platforms," according to the *Post*, and regularly writes about food and its impact on cultural politics. With lively titles for her pieces that include "The Psychological Jujitsu of 'Xtreme Baby Carrots,'" the article that follows begins a conversation about what she calls "America's gender-segregated eating culture."

As you read this article, consider that its online publication allows the reader to link to a variety of sites that enhance its meaning. What do you glean from the article itself as published here as self-contained information?

Bros may have stopped icing bros, but we've yet to see the last of the sexist idea behind the game—that a man can be humiliated by being forced to chug a drink associated with girls. Girls soon started Busching girls, replacing the bottle of Smirnoff Ice with cans of Busch beer. This time, the idea was to embarrass women by making them drink bottles of a vile brew otherwise seen in the hands of manly men.

So what is it with certain foods (and drinks) getting the boys vs. girls treatment? There may be a few male stars—like Joaquin Phoenix and Tobey Maguire—who are vegetarians, and women may be joining the ranks of bloody-aproned butchers, but in the American consciousness, real men still don't eat quiche and women stick with chocolate, tofu and yogurt. This could easily be the handiwork of the evil geniuses on Madison Avenue, but might these clichés also arise from some long-buried grain of truth? Are genetic differences responsible for our gendered eating? How many of our eating patterns come from gender socialization, and how many are hereditary? And why is it that food rarely seems to be categorized this way outside the U.S.?

Marcia Pelchat is a sensory psychologist specializing in food and beverage selection at the Monell Chemical Senses Center. Women, she said, are genetically predisposed to prefer sweeter tastes, with greater sensitivity to bitterness. As a result, cocktails and alcoholic drinks aimed at women tend to be sweet—as an attempt to mask the burn—and colorful (because, you know, pink will make anything more palatable). Drinks for men, on the other hand, tend to let the bitterness take the fore: "Men who drink hoppy drinks don't just not notice the bitter taste, they actually like it," Pelchat said.

Others, like Yale University's David Katz, said some of our gender-driven eating can be explained by evolution. Men, as hunters, see meat as a reward and also need more protein than women in order to build muscle mass. "Men and women have differences in physiology which might have to do with access to different kinds of food," said Katz, who is the director of Yale's Prevention Research Center. That is, the different caloric requirements of men and women may be because we had differing access to foods as cavemen and cavewomen. We're only continuing along those patterns today.

Another factor, Katz said, is the different hormonal composition of men   5
and women. Women's craving of certain foods during pregnancy, and, in some cases, before their periods, might also explain why they prefer to eat different foods throughout the year.

One of the foods that's classically gendered—and adheres to both Pelchat's theory of the feminine sweet tooth and Katz's explanation of hormone-related food cravings—is chocolate. In the American imagination, in particular, a craving for chocolate has always been the exclusive preserve of premenstrual women and post-breakup slumber parties. (Really, how many times have you heard a man say he's dying for a box of Kisses?) A 1999 study by Debra Zellner, a psychologist at Montclair University, found that 50 percent of American women craved chocolate, while only 20 percent of men reported doing so.

But beyond the borders of the United States, the story is different. The same study found that in Spain, men and women craved chocolate equally—about 25 percent, while in Egypt, neither sex craved chocolate, with both sexes showing a high preference for salty foods.

Elsewhere in the world, studies have found that instead of girls, it is boys who like candy and sweets. Lucy Cooke, a researcher at the University College in London, found that school-age British boys showed a clear preference for sugary and fatty foods, meats, and eggs, while girls were more willing to eat fruits and vegetables.

And when I took my work home, I realized that my husband and I—both of us grew up in India—have eating habits that fly in the face of all these studies. My husband has an insatiable sweet tooth, can't go to bed without his nightly Mars bar, and diligently spends hours in the fruit aisle. I, on the other hand, am a complete dairy fiend, love my protein, adore a good whisky, and wouldn't notice if Ben & Jerry's stopped producing Cherry Garcia tomorrow (my husband would react with some emotion). And when I tried to think of differences in eating habits between men and women in India, I was unable to come up with anything conclusive—for every woman who likes chocolate, there's a man who likes it too, and for every man who is rabidly carnivorous, there's a woman who can out-meat him.

10   As I thought more about global dietary practices, it occurred to me that the U.S. has perhaps one of the more gender-segregated eating cultures in the world. (Can you imagine a French woman saying she stays away from red meat or a French man saying that chocolate is chick food?)

So while it seems possible that some food preferences could be put down to gender, it's obvious that American culture has a way of exacerbating them.

Brian Wansink is the director of Cornell University's Food and Brand Lab, the author of Mindless Eating: Why We Eat More Than We Think, and all-around food psychology genius. People, he said, are more likely to eat a food when they associate with it qualities they'd like to see in themselves. So a man who wants to be strong and masculine is more likely to eat a food described as strong and masculine—hence the prevalence in American culture of meat as a manly food. Besides, he said, America has some of the most psychographically segmented advertising in the world—all messages that the food we eat is subconsciously saying something about us. "The reason we can view food as a commercial product is because we've never had a major starvation or a food shortage. We've always had an abundance of food," he said. In India, it occurred to me, food was sacred, an elemental life force that provided sustenance, a resource we rarely took for granted. In the U.S., instead, it was an extension of one's identity, a phenomenon made possible by the United States' unique history of unrivaled luxury.

Despite the current obesity epidemic, American women, and specifically rich American women, tend to be very weight conscious—yet another factor that affects eating choices across genders. The same calorie consciousness is not societally required of men, said Paul Rozin, a psychology professor at the University of Pennsylvania.

But might things be changing? After all, women are charting brave new culinary landscapes—they're brewing beer and drinking it in larger quantities than ever before, and meat, say many women, is the new black. Rozin didn't seem to think so. The family meal, he said, is important in terms of men and women eating the same food. "And as the family continues to splinter, or as people continue to eat out more often, men and women will order different foods." But ever the optimist, I'll continue to wish for advertisements that see me as belly first and boobs later.

Analyze

1. Shah's essay is written in a very lively, particular style. How would you describe her use of language and image? What effect does it have?
2. Much is said these days about the blurring of the line between news and entertainment. Does this piece seem to blur the same line? If so, how? Or not? Why? What effect does this type of writing have? Is it persuasive or just entertaining?
3. Shah argues that America is one of the more "gender-segregated eating cultures in the world." Analyze Shah's argument. What evidence does she give? Is her premise true to begin with? Why or why not?

Explore

1. Shah's topic is one that could also be discussed in a more formal, scholarly, or academic fashion. Taking Shah's original argument, find credible sources and examine her premise that "men eat meat, and women eat chocolate."

2. Apply Shah's logic to understand the motivations behind certain brands and marketing campaigns. (Think of Hooters and Dove Chocolate, for instance.) How do these and other brands reveal forms of gender-based marketing? Why and how?

3. If you find this article online—and we encourage you to do so—you might see a variety of related links that will take you, immediately, to other resources that may enhance Shah's article. Are these helpful? To what extent do these hypertextual sources serve as a type of bibliography or set of footnotes? How do they enhance Shah's article—or do they?

B. R. Myers
"The Moral Crusade against Foodies"

B. R. Myers is, among other accomplishments, a contributing editor to *The Atlantic,* where the following essay first appeared; an opinion columnist at the New York *Times;* and associate professor of international studies at Dongseo University in South Korea. Myers started an online war among foodies, of sorts, and this article, which Slate.com calls "the most widely-read take-down of foodie-ism," exemplifies Myers's perspective on ideologies of the elite.

 Why do you think this article started an online war?

We have all dined with him in restaurants: the host who insists on calling his special friend out of the kitchen for some awkward small talk. The publishing industry also wants us to meet a few chefs, only these are in no hurry to get back to work. Anthony Bourdain's new book, his 10th, is *Medium Raw: A Bloody Valentine to the World of Food and the People*

Who Cook. In it he announces, in his trademark thuggish style, that "it is now time to make the idea of *not* cooking 'un-cool'—and, in the harshest possible way short of physical brutality, drive that message home." Having finished the book, I think I'd rather have absorbed a few punches and had the rest of the evening to myself. No more readable for being an artsier affair is chef Gabrielle Hamilton's memoir, *Blood, Bones and Butter.*

> It's quite something to go bare-handed up an animal's ass . . . Its viscera came out with an easy tug; a small palmful of livery, bloody jewels that I tossed out into the yard.

Then there's Kim Severson's *Spoon Fed: How Eight Cooks Saved My Life,* which is the kind of thing that passes for spiritual uplift in this set. "What blessed entity invented sugar and cacao pods and vanilla beans or figured out that salt can preserve and brighten anything?" And I thought I knew where that sentence was going. The flyleaf calls *Spoon Fed* "a testament to the wisdom that can be found in the kitchen." Agreed.

To put aside these books after a few chapters is to feel a sense of liberation; it's like stepping from a crowded, fetid restaurant into silence and fresh air. But only when writing such things for their own kind do so-called foodies truly let down their guard, which makes for some engrossing passages here and there. For insight too. The deeper an outsider ventures into this stuff, the clearer a unique community comes into view. In values, sense of humor, even childhood experience, its members are as similar to each other as they are different from everyone else.

For one thing, these people really do live to eat. *Vogue*'s restaurant   5 critic, Jeffrey Steingarten, says he "spends the afternoon—or a week of afternoons—planning the perfect dinner of barbecued ribs or braised foie gras." Michael Pollan boasts in *The New York Times* of his latest "36-Hour Dinner Party." Similar schedules and priorities can be inferred from the work of other writers. These include a sort of milk-toast priest, anthologized in *Best Food Writing 2010*, who expounds unironically on the "ritual" of making the perfect slice:

> The things involved must be few, so that their meaning is not diffused, and they must somehow assume a perceptible weight. They attain this partly from the reassurance that comes of being "just so," and partly by already possessing the solidity of the absolutely familiar.

And when foodies talk of flying to Paris to buy cheese, to Vietnam to sample *pho*? They're not joking about that either. Needless to say, no one shows much interest in literature or the arts—the real arts. When Marcel Proust's name pops up, you know you're just going to hear about that damned madeleine again.

It has always been crucial to the gourmet's pleasure that he eat in ways the mainstream cannot afford. For hundreds of years this meant consuming enormous quantities of meat. That of animals that had been whipped to death was more highly valued for centuries, in the belief that pain and trauma enhanced taste. "A true gastronome," according to a British dining manual of the time, "is as insensible to suffering as is a conqueror." But for the past several decades, factory farms have made meat ever cheaper and—as the excellent book *The CAFO* [Concentrated Animal Feeding Operations] *Reader* makes clear—the pain and trauma are thrown in for free. The contemporary gourmet reacts by voicing an ever-stronger preference for free-range meats from small local farms. He even claims to believe that well-treated animals taste better, though his heart isn't really in it. Steingarten tells of watching four people hold down a struggling, groaning pig for a full 20 minutes as it bled to death for his dinner. He calls the animal "a filthy beast deserving its fate."

Even if gourmets' rejection of factory farms and fast food is largely motivated by their traditional elitism, it has left them, for the first time in the history of their community, feeling more moral, spiritual even, than the man on the street. Food writing reflects the change. Since the late 1990s, the guilty smirkiness that once marked its default style has been losing ever more ground to pomposity and sermonizing. References to cooks as "gods," to restaurants as "temples," to biting into "heaven," etc., used to be meant as jokes, even if the compulsive recourse to religious language always betrayed a certain guilt about the stomach-driven life. Now the equation of eating with worship is often made with a straight face. The mood at a dinner table depends on the quality of food served; if culinary perfection is achieved, the meal becomes downright holy—as we learned from Pollan's *The Omnivore's Dilemma* (2006), in which a pork dinner is described as feeling "like a ceremony . . . a secular seder."

10   The moral logic in Pollan's hugely successful book now informs all food writing: the refined palate rejects the taste of factory-farmed meat, of the corn-syrupy junk food that sickens the poor, of frozen fruits and vegetables transported wastefully across oceans—from which it follows that to serve one's palate is to do right by small farmers, factory-abused cows, Earth

itself. This affectation of piety does not keep foodies from vaunting their penchant for obscenely priced meals, for gorging themselves, even for dining on endangered animals—but only rarely is public attention drawn to the contradiction. This has much to do with the fact that the nation's media tend to leave the national food discourse to the foodies in their ranks. To people like Pollan himself. And Severson, his very like-minded colleague at *The New York Times*. Is any other subculture reported on so exclusively by its own members? Or with a frequency and an extensiveness that bear so little relation to its size? (The "slow food" movement that we keep hearing about has fewer than 20,000 members nationwide.)

The same bias is apparent in writing that purports to be academic or at least serious. The book *Gluttony* (2003), one of a series on the seven deadly sins, was naturally assigned to a foodie writer, namely Francine Prose, who writes for the gourmet magazine *Saveur*. Not surprisingly, she regards gluttony primarily as a problem of overeating to the point of obesity; it is "the only sin . . . whose effects are visible, written on the body." In fact the Catholic Church's criticism has always been directed against an inordinate *preoccupation* with food—against foodie-ism, in other words—which we encounter as often among thin people as among fat ones. A disinterested writer would likely have done the subject more justice. Unfortunately, even the new sociological study *Foodies: Democracy and Distinction in the Gourmet Foodscape* is the product of two self-proclaimed members of the tribe, Josée Johnston and Shyon Baumann, who pull their punches accordingly; the introduction is titled "Entering the Delicious World of Foodies." In short, the 21st-century gourmet need fear little public contradiction when striking sanctimonious poses.

The same goes for restaurant owners like Alice Waters. A celebrated slow-food advocate and the founder of an exclusive eatery in Berkeley, she is one of the chefs profiled in *Spoon Fed*. "Her streamlined philosophy," Severson tells us, is "that the most political act we can commit is to eat delicious food that is produced in a way that is sustainable, that doesn't exploit workers and is eaten slowly and with reverence." A vegetarian diet, in other words? Please. The reference is to Chez Panisse's standard fare—Severson cites "grilled rack and loin of Magruder Ranch veal" as a typical offering—which is environmentally sustainable only because so few people can afford it. Whatever one may think of Anthony Bourdain's moral sense, his BS detector seems to be working fine. In *Medium Raw* he congratulates Waters on having "made lust, greed, hunger, self-gratification and fetishism look *good*." Not to everyone, perhaps, but okay.

The roman historian Livy famously regarded the glorification of chefs as the sign of a culture in decline. I wonder what he would have thought of *The New York Times'* efforts to admit "young idols with cleavers" into America's pantheon of food-service heroes.

With their swinging scabbards, muscled forearms and constant proximity to flesh, butchers have the raw, emotional appeal of an indie band . . . "Think about it. What's sexy?" said Tia Keenan, the fromager at Casellula Cheese and Wine Café and an unabashed butcher fan. "Dangerous is sometimes sexy, and they are generally big guys with knives who are covered in blood."

15   That's Severson again, by the way, and she records no word of dissent in regard to the cheese vendor's ravings. We are to believe this is a real national trend here. In fact the public perception of butchers has not changed in the slightest, as can easily be confirmed by telling someone that he or she looks like one. "Blankly as a butcher stares," Auden's famous line about the moon, will need no explanatory footnote even a century from now.

But food writing has long specialized in the barefaced inversion of common sense, common language. Restaurant reviews are notorious for touting $100 lunches as great value for money. The doublespeak now comes in more pious tones, especially when foodies feign concern for animals. Crowding around to watch the slaughter of a pig—even getting in its face just before the shot—is described by Bethany Jean Clement (in an article in *Best Food Writing 2009*) as "solemn" and "respectful" behavior. Pollan writes about going with a friend to watch a goat get killed. "Mike says the experience made him want to honor our goat by wasting as little of it as possible." It's teachable fun for the whole foodie family. The full strangeness of this culture sinks in when one reads affectionate accounts (again in *Best Food Writing 2009*) of children clamoring to kill their own cow—or wanting to see a pig shot, then ripped open with a chain saw: "YEEEEAAAAH!"

Here too, though, an at least half-serious moral logic is at work, backed up by the subculture's distinct body of myth, which combines half-understood evolutionary theory with the biblical idea of man as born lord of the world. Anthropological research, I should perhaps point out, now indicates that *Homo sapiens* started out as a paltry prey animal. Clawless, fangless, and slight of build, he could at best look forward to furtive boltings of carrion until the day he became meat himself. It took humans quite a while to learn how to gang up for self-protection and food acquisition, the latter usually a hyena-style affair of separating infant or sick animals from their herds. The domestication of pigs, cows, chickens, etc. has been going on for only about 10,000 years—not nearly long enough to breed the instincts out of them. The hideous paraphernalia of subjugation pictured in *The CAFO Reader*? It's not there for nothing.

Now for the foodie version. The human animal evolved "with eyes in the front of its head, long legs, fingernails, eyeteeth—so that it could better chase down slower, stupider creatures, kill them, and eat them" (Bourdain, *Medium Raw*). We have eaten them for so long that meat-eating has shaped our *souls* (Pollan, *The Omnivore's Dilemma*). And after so many millennia of domestication, food animals have become "evolutionarily hard-wired" to depend on us (chef-writer Hugh Fearnley-Whittingstall, *The River Cottage Meat Book*). Every exercise of our hungry power is thus part of the Great Food Chain of Being, with which we must align our morals. Deep down—instinctively if not consciously—the "hardwired" pig understands all this, understands why he has suddenly been dragged before a leering crowd. Just don't waste any of him afterward; that's all he asks. Note that the foodies' pride in eating "nose to tail" is no different from factory-farm boasts of "using everything but the *oink*." As if such token frugality could make up for the caloric wastefulness and environmental damage that result from meat farming!

Naturally the food-obsessed profess as much respect for tradition as for evolution. Hamilton, in *Blood, Bones and Butter*, writes of her childhood dinners: "The meal was always organized correctly, traditionally, which I now appreciate." Even relatively young traditions like the Thanksgiving turkey must be guarded zealously against efforts to change or opt out of them. Foreign traditions destigmatize every dish even for the American. In *Best Food Writing 2010*, one foie gras lover asks another whether he would eat tortured cat if there were sufficient Mongolian history behind the dish; the answer is yes.

So tradition is an absolute good? No. When it dictates *abstention* from a certain food, it is to be rejected. Francine Prose shows how it's done in her prize-winning *Saveur* article, "Faith and Bacon." I need hardly explain which of those two she cannot live without. Prose concedes that since pigs compete ravenously with humans for grain, her Jewish forefathers' taboo against pork may well have derived from ecological reasons that are even more valid today. Yet she finds it unrealistic to hope that humans could ever suppress their "baser appetites . . . for the benefit of other humans, flora, and fauna." She then drops the point entirely; foodies quickly lose interest in any kind of abstract discussion. The reader is left to infer that since baser appetites are going to rule anyway, we might as well give in to them.

But if, however unlikely it seems, I ever find myself making one of those late-life turns toward God, one thing I can promise you is that this God will be a deity who wants me to feel exactly the way I feel when the marbled slice of pork floats to the top of the bowl of ramen.

Yes, I feel equally sure that Prose's God will be that kind of God. At least she maintains a civil tone when talking of kashrut. In "Killer Food," another article in *Best Food Writing 2010*, Dana Goodyear tells how a restaurant served head cheese (meat jelly made from an animal's head) to an unwitting Jew.

One woman, when [chef Jon] Shook finally had a chance to explain, spat it out on the table and said, "Oh my fucking God, I've been kosher for thirty-two years." Shook giggled, recollecting. "Not any more you ain't!"

We are meant to chuckle too; the woman (who I am sure expressed herself in less profane terms) got what she deserved. Most of us consider it a virtue to maintain our principles in the face of social pressure, but in the involuted world of gourmet morals, constancy is rudeness. One must never spoil a dinner party for mere religious or ethical reasons. Pollan says he sides with the French in regarding "any personal dietary prohibition as bad manners." (The American foodie is forever projecting his own barbarism onto France.) Bourdain writes, "Taking your belief system on the road—or to other people's houses—makes me angry." The sight of vegetarian tourists waving away a Vietnamese *pho* vendor fills him with "spluttering indignation."

25   That's right: guests have a greater obligation to please their host—and passersby to please a vendor—than vice versa. Is there any civilized value that foodies cannot turn on its head? But I assume Bourdain has no qualms about waving away a flower seller, just as Pollan probably sees nothing wrong with a Mormon's refusal of a cup of coffee. Enjoinders to put the food provider's feelings above all else are just part of the greater effort to sanctify food itself.

So secure is the gourmet community in its newfound reputation, so sure is it of its rightness, that it now proclaims the very qualities—greed, indifference to suffering, the prioritization of food above all—that earned it so much obloquy in the first place. Bourdain starts off his book by reveling in the illegality of a banquet at which he and some famous (unnamed) chefs dined on ortolan, endangered songbirds fattened up, as he unself-consciously tells us, in pitch-dark cages. After the meal, an "identical just-fucked look" graced each diner's face. Eating equals sex, and in accordance with this self-flattery, gorging is presented in terms of athleticism and endurance. "You eat way past the point of hitting the wall. Or I do anyway."

If nothing else, Bourdain at least gives the lie to the Pollan–Severson cant about foodie-ism being an integral part of the whole, truly sociable, human being. In Bourdain's world, diners are as likely to sit solo or at a countertop while chewing their way through "a fucking Everest of shellfish." Contributors to the *Best Food Writing* anthologies celebrate the same mindless, sweating gluttony. "You eat and eat and eat," Todd Kliman writes, "long after you're full. Being overstuffed, for the food lover, is not a moral problem." But then, what is? In the same anthology, Michael Steinberger extols the pleasure of "joyfully gorging yourself . . . on a bird bearing the liver of another bird." He also talks of "whimpering with ecstasy" in a French restaurant, then allowing the chef to hit on his wife, because "I was in too much of a stupor . . . [He] had just served me one of the finest dishes I'd ever eaten." Hyperbole, the reader will have noticed, remains the central comic weapon in the food writer's arsenal. It gets old fast. Nor is there much sign of wit in the table talk recorded. Aquinas said gluttony leads to "loutishness, uncleanness, talkativeness, and an uncomprehending dullness of mind," and if you don't believe him, here's Kliman again:

> I watched tears streak down a friend's face as he popped expertly cleavered bites of chicken into his mouth . . . He was red-eyed and breathing fast. "It hurts, it hurts, but it's so good, but it hurts, and I can't stop eating!" He slammed a fist down on the table. The beer in his glass sloshed over the sides. "Jesus Christ, I've got to stop!"

We have already seen that the foodie respects only those customs, traditions, beliefs, cultures—old and new, domestic and foreign—that call on him to eat more, not less. But the foodie is even more insatiable in regard to variety than quantity. Johnston and Baumann note that "eating unusual foods is part of what generates foodie status," and indeed, there appears to be no greater point of pride in this set than to eat with the indiscriminate omnivorousness of a rat in a zoo dumpster. Jeffrey Steingarten called his first book *The Man Who Ate Everything*. Bourdain writes, with equal swagger, "I've eaten raw seal, guinea pig. I've eaten bat." The book *Foodies* quotes a middle-aged software engineer who says, "Um, it's not something I would be anxious to repeat but . . . it's kind of weird *and cool* to say I've had goat testicles in rice wine." The taste of these bizarre meals—as researchers of oral fixation will not be surprised to learn—is neither here nor there. Members of the Gastronauts, a foodie group in New York, stuff live, squirming octopuses and eels down their throats before posting the carny-esque footage online.

Such antics are encouraged in the media with reports of the exotic foods that can be had only overseas, beyond the reach of FDA inspectors, conservationists, and animal-rights activists. Not too long ago MSNBC.com put out an article titled "Some Bravery as a Side Dish." It listed "7 foods for the fearless stomach," one of which was ortolan, the endangered songbirds fattened in dark boxes. The more lives sacrificed for a dinner, the more impressive the eater. Dana Goodyear: "Thirty duck hearts in curry . . . The ethos of this kind of cooking is undeniably macho." Amorality as ethos, callousness as bravery, queenly self-absorption as machismo: no small perversion of language is needed to spin heroism out of an evening spent in a chair.

30   Of course, the bulk of foodie writing falls between the extremes of Pollanesque sanctimony and Bourdainian oafishness. The average article in a *Best Food Writing* anthology is a straightforward if very detailed discussion of some treat or another, usually interwoven with a chronicle of the writer's quest to find or make it in perfect form. Seven pages on sardines. Eight pages on marshmallow fluff! The lack of drama and affect only makes the gloating obsessiveness even more striking. The following, from a man who travels the world sampling oysters, is typical.

> Sitting at Bentley's lustrous marble bar, I ordered three No. 1 and three No. 2 Strangford Loughs and a martini. I was promptly set up with a dark green and gold placemat, a napkin, silverware, a bread plate, an oyster plate, some fresh bread, a plate of deep yellow butter rounds, vinegar, red pepper, Tabasco sauce, and a saucer full of lemons wrapped in cheesecloth. Bentley's is a very serious oyster bar. When the bartender asked me if I wanted olives or a twist, I asked him which garnish he liked better with oysters. He recommended both. I had never seen both garnishes served together, but . . . (Robb Walsh, "English Oyster Cult," *Best Food Writing 2009*)

I used to reject that old countercultural argument, the one about the difference between a legitimate pursuit of pleasure and an addiction or pathology being primarily a question of social license. I don't anymore. After a month among the bat eaters and milk-toast priests, I opened Nikki Sixx's *Heroin Diaries* (2008) and encountered a refreshingly sane-seeming young man, self-critical and with a dazzlingly wide range of interests. Unfortunately, the foodie fringe enjoys enough media access to make daily claims for its sophistication and virtue, for the suitability of its lifestyle as a model for the world. We should not let it get away with those claims. Whether gluttony is a deadly sin is of course for the religious to decide, and I hope they go easy on the foodies; they're not all bad. They are certainly single-minded, however, and single-mindedness—even in less obviously selfish forms—is always a littleness of soul.

Analyze

1. What does Myers mean when he writes, "Gluttony dressed up as foodie-ism is still gluttony?" How does this relate to his larger point? What is his larger point?

2. Myers seems inspired by what began as a review of Anthony Bourdain's book, *Medium Raw*. According to Myers, what part of Bourdain's narrative best epitomizes that against which Myers rails? What else in Myers's piece supports his argument?

3. First, define "tone." What is the tone of Myers's piece? What evidence do you find that supports your contention? How does Myers's language and tone contribute to or detract from your sense of Myers's ethos? (Define *ethos*.)

Explore

1. There are numerous, widely read responses to Myers's review, which can be found easily with online search engines. Compare and contrast them. Once you have weeded through the arguments that aren't well thought-out, what arguments for and against Myers seem to be the most credible? Why? What are their common characteristics?

2. This book contains articles by several of the writers whom Myers attempts to discredit. Construct your own response to Myers's argument in support of the culture of "foodie-ism," even if you personally believe that Myers is on point.

3. How does Myers attack—for want of a better word—other writers besides Anthony Bourdain? Explore his rhetorical strategies for using the work of others to support his arguments. Consider Myers's contention that these writers seem (or not) to specialize in the "barefaced inversion of common sense." Is this the case? How so, and how not?

Forging Connections

1. How do the essays in this section demonstrate that food is, indeed, political? Taking two of the essays in this chapter as your starting points, how would you define the politics of food?

2. Throughout this book and especially in the first chapter, we explore the ways in which food can serve as a means by which people come together. However, as evidenced in this chapter, food—or the issues raised by context of eating and procuring food—can also prove decidedly divisive. Referring to several of these essays as the bases for your discussion, think of ways in which food, its cultures, and its contexts have been divisive in your experience.

Looking Further

1. Select one essay from this chapter and one with a contrasting tone and purpose from the chapter entitled "Food as Memory and Identity." Then, look elsewhere for an article with a completely different point of view and tone about food, its contexts, and potential to divide or unite people. Contrast the three, creating your own argument regarding the complexities of food.

2. Many of the political issues identified in this chapter have national or global implications. Research to find a politically contentious, food-related issue that is particularly relevant to your local community. Craft a paper or multimedia presentation that introduces your argument with its supporting evidence.

Food and
Health

4

There is, of course, a natural connection between our bodies and what we eat. As our questions in "Looking Further" will reveal at the end of this chapter, the readings throughout this chapter demonstrate our national concern—some would say obsession—with too much or too little food.

The conversation about food and health is at once very personal and highly political. As you go through this chapter, consider the policy, political, and economic implications of the too-little-versus-too-much food debates, looking at the validity of arguments, the intended audience for the arguments, and the language used to make the arguments.

David Zinczenko
"Don't Blame the Eater"

Author of the best-selling *Eat This, Not That* series, David Zinczenko is president and CEO of Galvanized Brands, a company launched in 2013 that seeks to bring awareness to issues surrounding global health and wellness. Zinczenko is a past editor in chief of *Men's Health* magazine, where the feature "Eat This, Not That" was a popular mainstay of the magazine. "Don't Blame the Eater" was originally published in *The New York Times*.

If the eater is not to blame, then who is?

If ever there were a newspaper headline custom-made for Jay Leno's monologue, this was it. Kids taking on McDonald's this week, suing the company for making them fat. Isn't that like middle-aged men suing Porsche for making them get speeding tickets? Whatever happened to personal responsibility?

I tend to sympathize with these portly fast-food patrons, though. Maybe that's because I used to be one of them.

I grew up as a typical mid-1980's latchkey kid. My parents were split up, my dad off trying to rebuild his life, my mom working long hours to make the monthly bills. Lunch and dinner, for me, was a daily choice between McDonald's, Taco Bell, Kentucky Fried Chicken or Pizza Hut. Then as now, these were the only available options for an American kid to get an affordable meal. By age 15, I had packed 212 pounds of torpid teenage tallow on my once lanky 5-foot-10 frame.

Then I got lucky. I went to college, joined the Navy Reserves and got involved with a health magazine. I learned how to manage my diet. But most of the teenagers who live, as I once did, on a fast-food diet won't turn their lives around: They've crossed under the golden arches to a likely fate of lifetime obesity. And the problem isn't just theirs—it's all of ours.

5   Before 1994, diabetes in children was generally caused by a genetic disorder—only about 5 percent of childhood cases were obesity-related, or Type 2, diabetes. Today, according to the National Institutes of Health, Type 2 diabetes accounts for at least 30 percent of all new childhood cases of diabetes in this country.

Not surprisingly, money spent to treat diabetes has skyrocketed, too. The Centers for Disease Control and Prevention estimate that diabetes accounted for $2.6 billion in health care costs in 1969. Today's number is an unbelievable $100 billion a year.

Shouldn't we know better than to eat two meals a day in fast-food restaurants? That's one argument. But where, exactly, are consumers— particularly teenagers—supposed to find alternatives? Drive down any thoroughfare in America, and I guarantee you'll see one of our country's more than 13,000 McDonald's restaurants. Now, drive back up the block and try to find someplace to buy a grapefruit.

Complicating the lack of alternatives is the lack of information about what, exactly, we're con- **Complicating the** suming. There are no calorie information charts **lack of alternatives is** on fast-food packaging, the way there are on **the lack of information** grocery items. Advertisements don't carry warn- **about what, exactly,** ing labels the way tobacco ads do. Prepared foods **we're consuming.** aren't covered under Food and Drug Administration labeling laws. Some fast-food purveyors will provide calorie information on request, but even that can be hard to understand.

For example, one company's Web site lists its chicken salad as containing 150 calories; the almonds and noodles that come with it (an additional 190 calories) are listed separately. Add a serving of the 280-calorie dressing, and you've got a healthy lunch alternative that comes in at 620 calories. But that's not all. Read the small print on the back of the dressing packet and you'll realize it actually contains 2.5 servings. If you pour what you've been served, you're suddenly up around 1,040 calories, which is half of the government's recommended daily calorie intake. And that doesn't take into account that 450-calorie super-size Coke.

Make fun if you will of these kids launching lawsuits against the fast-   10 food industry, but don't be surprised if you're the next plaintiff. As with the tobacco industry, it may be only a matter of time before state governments begin to see a direct line between the $1 billion that McDonald's and Burger King spend each year on advertising and their own swelling health care costs.

And I'd say the industry is vulnerable. Fast-food companies are marketing to children a product with proven health hazards and no warning labels. They would do well to protect themselves, and their customers, by providing the nutrition information people need to make informed choices about their products. Without such warnings, we'll see more sick, obese children and more angry, litigious parents. I say, let the deep-fried chips fall where they may.

Analyze

1. In what ways does Zinczenko argue that fast-food companies deliberately complicate the decision-making processes for consumers, particularly young adult consumers?
2. What function does the personal story at the start of the article serve? To what effect?
3. Zinczenko equates the manipulative marketing of fast-food industries to that of the tobacco industry. Using examples from the article, to what extent is this convincing? How or how not?

Explore

1. The author uses examples from fast-food industry websites and marketing materials as a way to illustrate the ways in which these industries intentionally obscure nutritional information. Using the Internet as one of your resources, gather information apart from the author's to prove—or disprove—his point.
2. Research and examine marketing campaigns for food products and tobacco products. See if you can find one advertisement for each type of industry from several time periods. What does an analysis of these advertisements tell you? Have they changed over the years? How so? How not?
3. Zinczenko notes that "Before 1994, diabetes in children was generally caused by a genetic disorder—only about 5 percent of childhood cases were obesity-related, or Type 2, diabetes." The author goes on to say that today "Type 2 diabetes accounts for at least 30 percent of all new" childhood instances of diabetes. Using your research skills to gather additional resources, write an essay in which you trace the evolution or progression of Type 2 diabetes in children as it correlates with increased fast-food consumption.

Michael Pollan
"Our National Eating Disorder"

Michael Pollan is not only a noted food writer; you will note that he is also frequently mentioned in the articles and essays in this volume. He is a professor of journalism at the University of California at Berkeley, and he has published several best-selling books about food, including *The Omnivore's Dilemma: A Natural History of Four Meals* (2006), and *Food Rules: An Eater's Manual* (2009). Pollan's articles and essays about food also appear regularly in the New York *Times.* In "Our National Eating Disorder" Pollan looks at the natural and fraught history of corn.

Why does Pollan indicate that the United States has an "Eating Disorder?"

Carbophobia, the most recent in the centurylong series of food fads to wash over the American table, seems to have finally crested, though not before sweeping away entire bakeries and pasta companies in its path, panicking potato breeders into redesigning the spud, crumbling whole doughnut empires and, at least to my way of thinking, ruining an untold number of meals. America's food industry, more than happy to get behind any new diet as long as it doesn't actually involve eating less food, is still gung-ho on Low Carb, it's true, but in the last few weeks, I can report some modest success securing a crust of bread, and even the occasional noodle, at tables from which such staples were banned only a few months ago.

Surveying the wreckage of this latest dietary storm makes you wonder if we won't someday talk about a food fad that demonized bread, of all things, in the same breath we talk about the all-grape diet that Dr. John Harvey Kellogg used to administer to patients at his legendarily nutty sanitarium at Battle Creek, Mich., or the contemporaneous vogue for "Fletcherizing"—chewing each bite of food as many as 100 times—introduced by Horace Fletcher (also known as the Great Masticator) at the turn of the last century. That period marked the first golden age of American food faddism, though of course its exponents spoke not in terms of fashion but of "scientific eating," much as we do now.

Back then, the best nutritional science maintained that carnivory promoted the growth of toxic bacteria in the colon; to battle these critters, Kellogg vilified meat and mounted a two-fronted assault on his patients' alimentary canals, introducing quantities of Bulgarian yogurt at both ends. It remains to be seen whether the Atkins-school theory of ketosis, the metabolic process by which the body resorts to burning its own fat when starved of carbohydrates, will someday seem as quaintly quackish as Kellogg's theory of colonic autointoxication.

What is striking is just how little it takes to set off one of these applecart-toppling nutritional swings in America; a scientific study, a new government guideline, a lone crackpot with a medical degree can alter this nation's diet overnight. As it happened, it was an article in this magazine two years ago that almost singlehandedly ushered in today's carbophobia, which itself supplanted an era of lipophobia dating back to 1977, when a controversial set of federal nutritional guidelines ("Dietary Goals for the United States," drafted by a Senate committee led by George McGovern) persuaded beef-loving Americans to lay off the red meat. But the basic pattern was fixed decades earlier: new scientific research comes along to challenge the prevailing nutritional orthodoxy; some nutrient that Americans have been happily chomping for years is suddenly found to be lethal; another nutrient is elevated to the status of health food; the industry throws its marketing weight behind it; and the American way of dietary life undergoes yet another revolution.

5   If this volatility strikes you as unexceptionable, you might be interested to know that there are other cultures that have been eating more or less the same way for generations, and there are peoples who still rely on archaic criteria like, oh, taste and tradition to guide them in their eating decisions. You might also be interested to know that some of the cultures that set their culinary course by the lights of pleasure and habit rather than nutritional science are actually healthier than we are—that is, suffer a lower incidence of diet-related health troubles. The "French paradox" is the most famous such case, though it's worth keeping in mind the French don't regard the matter as a paradox at all; we Americans resort to that word simply because the French experience—a population of wine-swilling cheese eaters with lower rates of heart disease and obesity?!—confounds our orthodoxy about food. Maybe what we should be talking about is an American paradox: that is, a notably unhealthy people obsessed by the idea of eating healthily.

This obsession has been recognized as a distinctly American phenomenon at least since the early decades of the 20th century. Harvey Levenstein, a Canadian historian who has written two fascinating social histories of

American foodways, neatly sums up the beliefs that have guided the American way of eating since the heyday of William Sylvester Graham and John Kellogg: ". . . that taste is not a true guide to what should be eaten; that one should not simply eat what one enjoys; that the important components of food cannot be seen or tasted, but are discernible only in scientific laboratories; and that experimental science has produced rules of nutrition that will prevent illness and encourage longevity." The power of any orthodoxy resides in its ability not to seem like one, and, at least to a 1904 or 2004 genus American, these beliefs don't seem controversial or silly. The problem is, whatever their merits, this way of thinking about food is a recipe for deep confusion and anxiety about one of the central questions of life: what should we have for dinner?

That question, to one degree or another, assails any creature faced with a wide choice of things to eat: call it the omnivore's dilemma. The koala bear certainly doesn't worry about what's for dinner; if it looks and smells like a eucalyptus leaf, then it is dinner. His culinary preferences are hard-wired. But for omnivores like us, a vast amount of brain space and time must be devoted to figuring out which of all the many potential dishes nature offers are safe to eat. We rely on our prodigious powers of recognition and memory to guide us away from poisons (isn't that the mushroom that made me sick last week?) and toward nutritious plants (the red berries are the juicier, sweeter ones). Our taste buds help, too, predisposing us toward sweetness, which signals carbohydrate energy in nature, and away from bitterness, which is how many of the toxic alkaloids produced by plants taste. Some anthropologists believe that one reason we evolved such big and intricate brains was precisely to help us deal with the omnivore's dilemma. (Scientists theorize that as the koala, which once ate a variety of foods, evolved to eat a circumscribed diet, its brain actually shrank; food faddists take note.)

Being a generalist is, of course, a great boon as well as a challenge; it is what allowed humans to adapt to a great many different environments all over the planet and to survive in them even after favored foods were driven to extinction. Omnivory offers the pleasures of variety too. But the surfeit of choice brings a lot of stress with it and can lead to a kind of Manichaean view of food, a division of nature into the Good Things to Eat and the Bad.

While our senses can help us to draw the first, elemental distinctions between good and bad foods, we humans rely heavily on culture to keep it all straight. So we codify the rules of wise eating in an elaborate structure of taboos, rituals, manners and culinary traditions, covering everything from the proper size of portions to the order in which foods should be consumed to the kinds of animals it is O.K. to eat. Anthropologists may argue whether all these rules make biological sense, but certainly a great many of them do, and they keep us from having to re-enact the omnivore's dilemma at every meal.

10   One way to think about America's national eating disorder is as the return, with an almost atavistic vengeance, of the omnivore's dilemma. The cornucopia of the American supermarket has thrown us back onto a bewildering food landscape where we once again have to worry that some of those tasty-looking morsels might kill us. At the same time, many of the tools with which people historically managed the omnivore's dilemma have lost their sharpness, or simply failed, in the United States today. As a relatively new nation drawn from many different immigrant populations, each with its own culture of food, we Americans find ourselves without a strong, stable culinary tradition to guide us.

I recently asked my mother what her mother served for dinner when she was a child. The menu, full of such Eastern European Jewish delicacies as stuffed cabbage, cheese blintzes, tripe and spleen, bore absolutely no resemblance to the dinners my mother cooked for us. When I asked her why, she just laughed: "You kids wouldn't have touched that stuff!" True enough, and so for us—this being suburban New York in the mid-60's—she cooked a veritable world's fair of dishes: spaghetti and meatballs; beef Wellington; Chinese pepper steak; boeuf bourguignon. I remember all of these dinners fondly, and yet I've never cooked a single one of them myself. In America, each generation has been free to reinvent its cuisine, very often more than once. (My mother has herself long since moved on to more up-to-date, less beefy fare, lighter dishes influenced by Japanese, Indian and Californian styles of cooking.)

Whether this culinary open-endedness is a good thing or not, it does create a powerful vacuum into which flows the copious gas of expert opinion, food journalism and advertising. What other nation wages political war over a government graphic called the food pyramid? Or lionizes diet doctors, a new one every few months?

Food marketing in particular thrives on dietary instability and so tends to heighten it. Since it's difficult to sell more food to such a well-fed population (though not, as we're discovering, impossible), food companies put their efforts into grabbing market share by introducing new kinds of processed food, which has the virtue of being both highly profitable and infinitely adaptable. Food technologists can readily re-engineer processed foods to be low-fat or low-carb or high in omega-3's, whatever the current nutritional wisdom requires. So while the potato growers shudder before the carbophobic tide, the chip makers have been quick to adapt, by dialing down the spud content in their recipes and cranking up the soy.

Yet the success of food marketers in exploiting shifting nutritional fashions has a cost. Getting us to change how we eat over and over again tends to undermine the various social structures that surround (and steady) our eating habits: things like the family dinner and taboos on snacking between meals or eating alone. Big Food (with some help from the microwave oven) has figured out how to break Mom's choke hold on the American menu by marketing directly to every demographic, children included. The result is a nation of antinomian eaters, each of us trying to work out our dietary salvation on our own.

So we've learned to choose our foods by the numbers (calories, carbs,   15 fats, R.D.A.'s, price, whatever), relying more heavily on our reading and computational skills than upon our senses. Indeed, we've lost all confidence in our senses of taste and smell, which can't detect the invisible macro- and micronutrients science has taught us to worry about, and which food processors have become adept at deceiving anyway. Most processed foods are marketed less on the basis of taste than on convenience, image, predictability, price point and health claims—all of which are easier to get right in a processed food product than its flavor. The American supermarket— chilled and stocked with hermetically sealed packages bristling with information—has effectively shut out the Nose and elevated the Eye.

No wonder we have become, in the midst of our astounding abundance, the world's most anxious eaters. A few years ago, Paul Rozin, a University of Pennsylvania psychologist, and Claude Fischler, a French sociologist, began collaborating on a series of cross-cultural surveys of food attitudes. They found that of the four populations surveyed (the U.S., France, Flemish Belgium and Japan), Americans associated food with health the most and pleasure the least. Asked what comes to mind upon hearing the phrase "chocolate cake," Americans were more apt to say "guilt," while the French said "celebration"; "heavy cream" elicited "unhealthy" from Americans, "whipped" from the French. The researchers found that Americans worry more about food and derive less pleasure from eating than people in any other nation they surveyed.

Compared with the French, we're much more likely to choose foods for reasons of health, and yet the French, more apt to choose on the basis of pleasure, are the healthier (and thinner) people. How can this possibly be? Rozin suggests that our problem begins with thinking of the situation as paradoxical. The French experience with food is only a paradox if you assume, as Americans do, that certain kinds of foods are poisons. "Look at fat," Rozin points out. "Americans treat the stuff as if it was mercury." That doesn't, of course, stop us from guiltily gorging on the stuff. A food-marketing consultant once told me that it's not at all uncommon for Americans to pay a visit to the health club after work for the express purpose of sanctioning the enjoyment of an entire pint of ice cream before bed.

Perhaps because we take a more "scientific" (i.e., reductionist) view of food, Americans automatically assume there must be some chemical component that explains the difference between the French and American experiences: it's something in the red wine, perhaps, or the olive oil that's making them healthier. But how we eat, and even how we feel about eating, may in the end be just as important as what we eat. The French eat all sorts of "unhealthy" foods, but they do it according to a strict and stable set of rules: they eat small portions and don't go back for seconds; they don't snack; they seldom eat alone, and communal meals are long, leisurely affairs. A well-developed culture of eating, such as you find in France or Italy, mediates the eater's relationship to food, moderating consumption even as it prolongs and deepens the pleasure of eating.

"Worrying about food is not good for your health," Rozin concludes—a deeply un-American view. He and Fischler suggest that our anxious eating itself may be part of the American problem with food, and that a more relaxed and social approach toward eating could go a long way toward breaking our unhealthy habit of bingeing and fad-dieting. "We could eat less and actually enjoy it more," suggests Rozin. Of course this is easier said than done. It's so much simpler to alter the menu or nutrient profile of a meal than to change the social and psychological context in which it is eaten. (There's also a lot more money to be made fiddling with ingredients and supersizing portions.) And yet what a wonderful prospect, to discover that the relationship of pleasure and health in eating is not, as we've been hearing for a hundred years, necessarily one of strife, but that the two might again be married at the table.

20   Will you pass the chocolate cake, please?

Analyze

1. On the website for the Smithsonian Institute, the tagline for this article is as follows: "Corn is one of the plant kingdom's biggest successes. That is not necessarily good for the United States." Using evidence from the article, what are corn's successes and what implications do those successes have for those of us who depend on it for food?

2. Looking carefully at the article, analyze the ways in which Pollan's language reveals the ecological and historical lenses through which he approaches this subject.

3. How does the use of work by Haber, Bosch, and Smil enhance Pollan's arguments? What effect does the use of these scientists have on this argument?

Explore

1. Watch the documentary partly inspired by Pollan's work: "King Corn: You Are What You Eat." How does it illuminate the ways in which small family farms are being replaced by large, industrialized farms? How does it enhance your reading of this article—or not?

2. It is not uncommon for authors to attempt to vilify others whose arguments they wish to debunk. But how is the story of Fritz Haber particularly ironic? In class discussion, consider the topic of someone doing what he felt was patriotic—if reprehensible—for his country and then having his work, in effect, turned against him.

3. While this article is ostensibly about environment, there are in Pollan's exposition some clearly significant implications for our health. Research the issues related to the need to "fix" nitrogen to issues of environment and health. What do you discover?

Jennifer Wehunt
"The Food Desert"

A senior editor at *Chicago Magazine*, Jennifer Wehunt is also a frequent contributor to Homegrown.org. A self-described "avid, if amateur, backyard gardener," Wehunt has also written for the Chicago *Tribune*. She is particularly focused in her writing on local and sustainable food. "The Food Desert" captures an issue prevalent in many larger cities.

How does Wehunt's description of a food desert in Chicago suggest that this situation is not unique to that city?

I n the northeast corner of 101st Street and Princeton Avenue, a peeling sign lists activities forbidden by the 100th South Princeton Block Club: loitering, drug dealing, loud music. When Edith Howard moved from the projects to this block of brick bungalows in 1964, the neighborhood—Roseland—seemed a promising place to give her growing family a better life. But the Roseland of today is much changed: The block club hasn't been active for years, and drug and gang activity is common. What's more, Roseland lacks many of the basic resources that stabilize a neighborhood, including a good place to buy food. For groceries, Howard, 78, relies on her daughter to drive her the two and a half miles up to Chatham or down to the border of Morgan Park. "I used to shop in Roseland, but I never go over there now," Howard says of the string of sneaker shops and discount clothing stores.

Howard is one of the 609,034 Chicagoans who live in what's known as a food desert, a concentrated area short on access to fresh meat and produce, but flush with the packaged and fried yield of convenience stores and fast-food outlets. Mari Gallagher, of Mari Gallagher Research & Consulting Group and the National Center for Public Research, popularized the term in 2006, when she released a report on the phenomenon for LaSalle Bank. In the three years since, much has changed in the desert: The number of Chicagoans living within its boundaries has decreased, albeit slightly; at least one retailer is finding opportunity for growth in the affected areas; the green movement is taking hold, with farmers' markets and backyard gardens blooming; and leaders are recognizing that community education—on eating healthfully, on creating a demand for grocery stores—is critical. And yet, the desert remains.

What qualifies as a food desert? A cluster of blocks without a corner grocery doesn't by itself warrant the label; an entire neighborhood, or a cluster of neighborhoods, without a mainstream grocery store—such as a Jewel, a Treasure Island, or an Aldi—almost certainly does. Gallagher has identified three separate expanses within the city limits totaling 44 square miles where access to fresh and healthful food falls notably short: an elongated ring connecting the Near North Side with Lawndale and Austin; an upside-down Y stretching from the Near South Side to Ashburn and Greater Grand Crossing; and a meandering mass swallowing most of the Far South Side (see map in p. 219).

While portions of neighborhoods such as West Town fall within these boundaries, Chicago's food desert lies entirely below Division Street, affecting a population that is overwhelmingly African American: about 478,000 blacks, compared with some 78,000 whites and 57,000 Latinos, according to Gallagher's calculations. For her 2006 report, Gallagher measured the distance from the geographic center of each of the city's 18,888 inhabited blocks and found that not only do residents living in majority African American blocks travel the farthest on average to reach any type of grocery store—0.59 miles as opposed to 0.39 miles for majority-white blocks or 0.36 miles for Latinos—but they must travel twice as far to reach a grocery store as a fast-food restaurant.

What does it mean for a community to lack access to adequate fresh   5
food? Several things—and none of them good. Day to day, residents must leave their neighborhoods for basics such as raw meat and fresh vegetables. Edith Howard, whose daughter drives her to the store, is better off than many. An estimated 64,000 households in food deserts don't have cars, so a weekly shopping trip can require cobbling together a multibus route. If the hassle of schlepping grocery bags on the CTA sounds tiring—especially given that 109,000 food desert residents are single mothers—that's because it is. Many simply opt out, ducking into a fast-food outlet or a convenience store instead, where the inventory often runs more toward potato chips and liquor than spinach and oranges, and where a banana that would cost 29 cents at Dominick's goes for around 70 cents, if it's even available.

"Diet has a direct link to obesity, diabetes, and other diseases, and you can't choose a healthy diet if you don't have access to it," Gallagher says. "Many in the food desert who suffer are children who already have diabetes but who have yet to be diagnosed and treated."

Although other factors such as poor health care and stress are likely contributors, Gallagher found that, among those living in neighborhoods with the worst access to fresh food, ten out of every 1,000 people die from cancer, as opposed to fewer than seven per 1,000 in neighborhoods with the best food availability. The comparison is even bleaker when it comes to deaths from cardiovascular disease: 11 per 1,000 in the hardest-hit neighborhoods, compared with fewer than six per 1,000 among the best off. And because nearly one-third of Chicago's food-desert residents are children, these latent repercussions have years to germinate.

Gallagher has found one small reason for hope: The desert has shrunk. When she first canvassed the city in 2006, she counted 632,974 Chicagoans living within the boundaries she established. Last fall she revisited the data, recalculating food access for each city block, taking into account every grocery store opening and closing since 2006. The result? A modest but encouraging 23,940 fewer Chicagoans living in the desert.

The decline doesn't necessarily signal a trend, however. Much like a literal desert, a food desert is an ever-shifting organism, constantly claiming a few blocks here as it cedes a few blocks there. A Food-4-Less that opened in September 2006 in West Englewood positively impacted some 307 city blocks—or 40,712 residents, 13,626 of them children—but the closing of a Dominick's and a Cub Foods in neighboring Chatham adversely affected 16,032 residents, worsening food access for 142 city blocks. (Wal-Mart has eyed Chatham as a potential area for development, but as long as the city vetoes the nonunion megastore's expansion beyond its one Chicago site, additional locations remain off the table.) In total, between summer 2006 and fall 2008, the boundaries of the city's food desert withdrew in certain areas, leaving 52,836 residents with improved food access, but elsewhere grew to encompass another 28,896 Chicagoans who previously were not classified as living within the desert.

10   "The food desert is not one single problem with one single solution," Gallagher says, but one clear strategy, developing new stores, could have broad impact on Chicago's food access. That's why the Chicago Grocer Expo project—a group including Gallagher and city representatives—identified six priority sites, many city-owned and vacant, on the South and West sides best suited for new-store development. Unfortunately, the group released its list in September 2008, just in time for the economy's free fall. Molly Sullivan of the Chicago Department of Community Development says that while the city has held preliminary discussions with retailers regarding the targeted locations and has appointed its own task force to streamline the process for launching new stores, no lease has been signed on any of the six sites.

Recession aside, opening new grocery stores is not as simple as identifying a promising site. "The food desert is only part of the story—these are

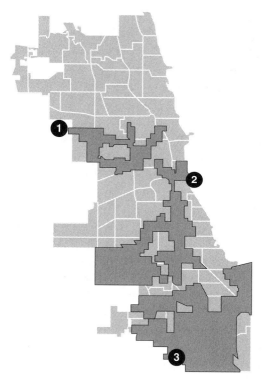

Figure 4.1 "Dry cells" in the city of Chicago.

business deserts," says Dr. Terry Mason, commissioner of the Chicago Department of Public Health, who recalls three nearby grocery stores—now long departed—when he was growing up in Englewood. "These neighborhoods are blighted and unsafe. There's a poor tax: Things in these neighborhoods cost more, and it's more difficult for businesses to operate there."

Salim Al Nurridin, a Roseland resident for more than 30 years, acknowledges that insurance costs can be higher in a troubled neighborhood like his, and even locals can be wary of shopping in places they consider dangerous. "If we cannot get crime, or the appearance of crime, off [our streets], then we cannot convince folks that this is a safe place to shop," he says. "In the greater Roseland area, we [spend] $90 million a year [on] groceries outside of the community. There's no reason a grocery store can't come into the greater Roseland area and make money."

Home to some 52,000 inhabitants, Roseland has been identified by Gallagher as the Chicago neighborhood where a supermarket could have the most significant impact. "Going on ten years now, I've been working aggressively to bring a store—a full-fledged national chain—to my community," says Alderman Anthony Beale (Ninth Ward), whose district includes much of Roseland. "I've done everything so far as to mark land down to one dollar, and for some reason, the big chains are redlining the African American community. When you go into stores in the suburban areas, they'll ask you for your ZIP Code, because they want to see where the money is coming from. If you analyze the data, you'll see that [much of it] is coming from African American communities. So why not bring a store into a community that's already providing your income?"

15   When that question is put to Jewel—a chain that has an established presence on the city's South Side—it elicits the following response: "We are committed to serving the needs of our customers," Jewel's communications manager Karen May writes in an e-mail. "However, it is not company policy to comment on current or future company operations."

At least one grocery chain has seen opportunity in underserved areas. The privately held Batavia-based discounter Aldi, which keeps its prices low by limiting the size of its no-frills stores as well as the scope of its generic-brand inventories, opened a store in Woodlawn in October, broke ground on another on the border of Englewood and Auburn Gresham in May, and is awaiting a permit for yet another store slated to open in Chatham in 2010. "It's typical for us to see an influx of customers when there's an economic downturn," says Martha Swaney, an Aldi spokeswoman. In fact, the chain's nationwide traffic increased from 15 million customers a month in 2008 to 18 million in 2009. "From a real-estate perspective, as some retailers are rolling back their expansions or even pulling out of existing properties, it increases the number of properties we have to choose from," Swaney says, sounding a bit like a kid in a candy store.

Some Chicagoans aren't waiting for grocery stores to come to the rescue. The nonprofit God's Gang, started in the 1970s by residents of Grand Boulevard, a neighborhood classified in part today as a food desert, provides training in urban agriculture to fellow citizens. Last year at least three underserved communities—Bronzeville, Englewood, and Woodlawn—launched farmers' markets. All over the city, in a move reminiscent of the "victory gardens" of World War II, industrious citizens are putting spare land to use, planting strawberries and tomatoes in backyards and side lots.

And in West Englewood, the nonprofit Growing Home hosts weekly farm-stand hours at its urban garden, giving people the chance to buy greens and tomatoes harvested on demand from the vine.

For Growing Home's Orrin Williams, a 2009 Chicago magazine Green Award recipient, the farm stand and farmers' market are just the beginning. "[Food desert] is a good PR term, but it doesn't begin to outline the issues involved," he says; as long as change is needed, why not think broader—and greener? "Some people are loyal to the grocery store, and that's fine. Other folks don't like big-box stores; they like smaller venues. And they should have a place, too." He sees greater Englewood as ripe for community-friendly, locally owned development, making the area south of 55th Street a destination for food- and green-related businesses. Possibilities range from mobile produce units (think ice cream trucks stocked with parsnips instead of popsicles) to veggie kiosks, or prestocked produce bins that could be installed daily in otherwise produce-poor convenience stores.

Like Williams, Angela Odoms-Young, an instructor in UIC's College of Applied Health Sciences who lives on the border between Chatham and Roseland, isn't enamored of the term "food desert." But, like Gallagher, she has studied food access for years, and her thoughts on the subject are as complicated as the issue itself. "When I first saw that term, I really paid attention," she says. "But it didn't affect me in the same way until I heard it used in relation to these communities that I really know and care about. As a researcher, if 'food desert' is something policymakers hear and want to do something about, I'm in support of it. But as a community member, it's another negative thing about the place where I live." There's an undertone of victimization, she says, that can do more harm than good; focusing on what's lacking won't necessarily attract grocery stores to the South Side. "Nobody says Lincoln Park needs more cupcake places, and yet there's a cupcake place on every corner," Odoms-Young says. "It's not the need that brings in the resources. There's got to be that 'and': There's a need and there's an economic opportunity."

"I wonder sometimes, What is the problem? Even in my own mind, as a highly educated, logically thinking person, I still cannot imagine [the resources that exist in Lincoln Park] on the South Side of Chicago. What will bring these places into low-income communities, and if they come, will they do well? I don't know."

Meantime, everyone agrees on the necessity for more education—the sort of learning that would change eating and cooking habits and encourage residents to shop at the grocery stores when, or if, they open. "What we need, we have to support," says A. Edward Davis Jr., pastor of Roseland's St. John Missionary Baptist Church, who gathered with fellow community members in late March to discuss the neighborhood's lack of fresh food.

"Once we get the stores back, we've still got to understand that we're losing people in these communities, and African Americans in particular, because we're not eating enough fruits and vegetables, and we're not cooking," says the public health department's Mason.

Robert L. House Sr., pastor of Roseland's New Life Baptist Church, agrees: "If you don't know how to wisely shop and wisely eat, you're still going to be battling yourself, no matter what grocery store is in town."

Several weeks after the community meeting in Roseland, word filtered down that Aldi was considering a site in the neighborhood—one of the six identified by the Chicago Grocer Expo project—at 115th Street and Michigan Avenue. This summer, the city will almost certainly approve the sale of the property to a developer, a significant step in the laborious process of opening a new store. It's not the Jewel or Dominick's some residents might have had their eye on, but, as Roseland's Salim Al Nurridin points out, "in these hard times, the affluent community is [shopping] at the Aldi." Today the lot is a vacant swath of broken concrete dotted with dandelions, but planners envision a $17.6 million LEED-certified shopping plaza anchored by the Aldi; the developer is even in talks to accommodate an adjoining el station if the CTA's prospective Red Line expansion moves forward. The project would bring not only fresh food to the neighborhood, but also 250 permanent jobs.

25   "I'm definitely excited," Alderman Beale says. "It's been hard getting to this point, but we're almost there. I'm also working on another grocery chain for a 270-acre-plus site on the Bishop Ford Freeway. In another two years, we'll have two quality grocery stores in the community, maybe three."

Three grocery stores in Roseland, a neighborhood that has gone without for years? As Odoms-Young says, the possibility is difficult to imagine: a real oasis—not just another mirage—in the food desert.

Analyze

1. Using evidence from this article, what constitutes a food desert? What are the conditions that create a food desert?

2. What are the multiple perspectives that Wehunt uses to make her argument? How does each contribute to the overall point of the article? How would you characterize the unique contribution of each? Consider language, style, and other factors.

3. "There's an undertone of victimization . . . that can do more harm than good; focusing on what's lacking won't necessarily attract grocery stores to the South Side." Examine this quote, looking at the language that is used to talk about marginalized or "disadvantaged" populations. What do you conclude?

Explore

1. Research the ways in which this issue manifests in your own, local communities, if it does. What conclusion do you come to and based on what evidence that describes your community?

2. Explore what Wehunt means by "a thicket of related problems that researchers, activities, and public officials are struggling to resolve." Identify one of these issues—transportation, for instance—and re-search the problem of food deserts from that one perspective.

3. Wehunt begins to explore the ways in which socioeconomic status can have a direct impact on health. Using other resources to complement the details in Wehunt's article, begin to explore the complex relation-ship between health and access.

Patricia Allen
"The Disappearance of Hunger in America"

Chair of the Department of Food Systems and Society at Marylhurst University in Portland, Oregon, Patricia Allen has made a career of studying political economic structures that constrain or allow social parity in sustainable food systems. She has published widely about food sustainability, including *Together at the Table: Sustainability and Sustenance in the American Agrifood System* (2004). "The Disappearance of Hunger in America" is a direct response to the USDA's announcement that they would no longer be using the word "hunger."

> How might Allen argue that "hunger" is the appropriate word to use to
> describe the condition of many Americans (and others) today?

The timing of the announcement could not have been worse. Last fall, a few days before the American feast of Thanksgiving, the United States Department of Agriculture (USDA) announced that it was eliminating the word *hunger* from its official assessment of food security in America and replacing it with the term *very low food security*. Not surprisingly, anti-hunger advocates condemned this decision, as did the press. An article in the *Sarasota Herald-Tribune* called it "a shallow attempt to sugarcoat a serious national health problem,"[1] while an editorial in the *Winston-Salem Journal* suggested it was "an effort to satisfy either some silly bureaucratic or sinister political motive."[2] An *Augusta Chronicle* columnist accused the USDA of using "semantics to sweep a dirty problem under the rug."[3]

The media portrayed the substitution of *food insecurity* for *hunger* as a political maneuver to deflect attention from the persistence of hunger in the face of plenty. In fact, the story is both more complicated and subtle than that. It's not that the United States has become less interested in food and politics. The popularity of books such as Eric Schlosser's *Fast Food Nation,* Michael Pollan's *The Omnivore's Dilemma*, and Greg Critser's *Fat Land,* and films such as Morgan Spurlock's *Supersize Me*, demonstrates that Americans are increasingly interested in, and conversant with, food issues.[4] If sales figures are any indication, we are ready to pay attention to the character of our food system and find ways to improve it. Although much recent food writing is celebratory, many titles also point to problems in the food system, such as food safety, nutrition, and environmental degradation. Yet very little is said about social justice issues, including the most obvious of all, which is hunger in America.[5]

Nevertheless, the hiding of hunger is not a government conspiracy. By eliminating the term *hunger,* the USDA was simply announcing an "innocent" statistical realignment. Specifically, USDA guidelines state that food insecurity is a social condition of limited or uncertain access to adequate food, whereas hunger is an individual physiological condition.[6]

In any case, since measuring hunger as an individual condition requires the collection of different data from that provided in the Current

Population Survey, the USDA decided to eliminate the term rather than collect different data.

On the face of it, and as the editorials claim, this move does look like a   5
political decision to hide the shame of hunger in the United States. However, it is more likely a methodological decision, albeit one based on an arbitrary distinction that appears to have no logical, etymological, or historical basis. Ironically, the lack of conspiracy actually makes the USDA's redefinition even more damaging, insidious, and difficult to combat, because it stalls, and perhaps reverses, the progress that has been made over the past several decades in the conceptualization of hunger and food security. The new terminology defuses the outrage that the term *hunger* elicits while disrupting the social progress that has been made over the last few decades as the term *food security* was developed and put into use.

The statistical elimination of the term *hunger* does violence to hungry people and to the efforts to end hunger in America. At the same time, the term *food security* should not be dismissed. It is real and important, and it needs to remain as a conceptual category when we talk about inequalities surrounding food.

A Brief History of the Discourse on Food Security

There has always been hunger. In some cases, hunger has been the result of food shortages due to crop failures. More often it is the result of poverty and the inability of people to pay for the food they need. This fact is what makes the issue of food justice so highly charged. Not only is food a basic requirement for life but there is no reason for people to go without it. This belief put the problem of hunger on the international agenda in 1933 and led to the development of food assistance programs in the United States during the Depression, when agricultural surpluses and hunger coexisted.[7]

Although food security issues in one form or another have been around since the beginning of time, contemporary approaches to food security emerged during the world food crisis of the early 1970s when the price of staple foods skyrocketed. The term *food security* was introduced in 1974 at the United Nations World Food Conference, though the change in discourse was not intended to diminish hunger as a problem—quite the opposite. Food security became a clear and central policy goal of most developing countries as the World Food Conference proclaimed people's inalienable right to freedom from hunger and resolved to eliminate hunger and malnutrition completely.[8] As poverty increased in the United States during the 1980s,[9] the US government also adopted the term *food security*, defining it as "a condition in which all people have access at all times to nutritionally adequate food through normal channels."[10] However, the United States did not adopt a statement about the inalienable human right to food.

In the 1990s, changes in economic and ideological conditions spurred new efforts to conceptualize food security. At the international level, this led to attempts to expand and deepen the concept of food security. The 1996 World Food Summit paid increased attention to the right to food. It also broadened the scope of the analytical unit used to measure food insecurity and for the first time considered not only the quantity but also the quality of food.[11] But it became clear that defining food security on a national or global scale resulted in aggregate measures that missed instances of food insecurity within households, communities, and regions. New approaches were needed to address these problems.

The combination of deteriorating food security conditions, the insufficiency of private and public efforts to combat hunger, and the conceptual innovations at the international level led in the United States to the development of the concept of *community* food security. Within this context, the food-system vulnerabilities revealed in Los Angeles following the Rodney King verdict in 1992 prompted a group of environmental justice students from the University of California at Los Angeles, led by Robert Gottlieb, to assess the core issues facing the South Central Los Angeles community.[14] What they discovered was that people's greatest concerns centered on food access, quality, and price. Of course, many people had been working for decades to improve local food security, but the group's study, *Seeds of Change: Strategies for Food Security for the Inner City*, provided a catalyst for taking food security work to a new level.[15]

10   In 1994 thirty organizations and individuals hoping to influence upcoming farm bill legislation (which authorizes funding for food and agriculture programs in the United States) met to discuss new approaches to food security. This group developed the 1995 Community Food Security Empowerment Act, which proposed community food security as the conceptual basis for solving food-system problems. Endorsed by more than 125 organizations, the act defined *community food security* as "all persons

obtaining at all times a culturally acceptable, nutritionally adequate diet through local non-emergency sources."[16]

A new social movement was born. The national Community Food Security Coalition was established in 1996, and it continues to grow (the number of participants at its annual conference has increased from a couple hundred to more than one thousand in 2006). Part of what makes community food security so compelling is that it is an integrated approach that focuses not only on meeting people's food security needs in the present but also on a broad range of food-system issues, including farmland loss, agriculture-based pollution, urban and rural community development, and transportation. The goal is to work toward the systematic and long-term elimination of food insecurity.

This approach has been supported by the USDA, which responded to the movement by establishing the Community Food Projects Program in 1996. Congress authorized a program of federal grants to support the development of community food projects. Under this legislation, *community food security* is defined as "all persons obtaining at all times an affordable, nutritious and culturally appropriate diet through local, non-emergency food sources (or through normal economic channels)."[17] The USDA and the Community Food Security Coalition are working together to build collaborative relationships.

This partnership was the latest chapter in the story of food security in the United States—until the USDA's November 2006 announcement, that is. Until then, the trend had been to expand and deepen the concept of food security, in both public and private efforts. But the latest iteration of the USDA's fight against hunger in America—its call for the elimination of hunger as a category—works against all of these efforts.

The Violence of Science in Measuring Hunger

As I previously noted, the motivation for eliminating *hunger* from the USDA vocabulary had more to do with statistics than politics. I do not mean to imply that science and politics are separable; they aren't. I mean that the decision was probably *not* made in an overt attempt to hide a politically unpalatable situation. Yet the redefinition damages the struggle against hunger by swaddling the issue in the cloak of science, which serves to make the semantic choice seem rational, sensible, even common sense, and not cruel or mean-spirited at all. The new USDA terminology eliminates a crucial rhetorical weapon of the weak—the word *hunger*—in their fight against injustice and makes it seem as though this choice is the only reasonable one for educated, scientific people.

15   Indeed, an editorial in the *Washington Post* makes precisely this point in its criticism of editorials that had appeared earlier in the newspaper. Herb Reed writes that, "The USDA made this change for scientific reasons based on advice from the Committee on National Statistics of the National Academies. The National Academies are made up of the top scientists in the United States . . . Who is more qualified to advise on how to write scientific reports, *Post* editors or top US scientists?"[18] The message is that you have no right to an opinion if you are not a scientist. Since chronically hungry people are unlikely to be scientists, the implication is that they have no right to claim they are hungry or to seek political redress for hunger.

This attempt to scientize hunger takes us back to an earlier time and seems to negate whatever progress has been made in the intervening period, such as the expanded definition of food security and the USDA's cooperation with the community food security movement. Indeed, the USDA has come full circle since it began collecting data on hunger. When government food-assistance programs were instituted in the 1960s, hunger was medicalized and defined in clinical terms in order to facilitate measurement techniques that would "presumably provide the hard evidence from which to draw conclusions about the incidence of hunger."[19] This measurement approach was criticized during the 1980s as having little policy relevance, because by the time hunger is clinically detectable, the damage may be irreversible.[20] Additionally, it was recognized that hunger is a community and household problem, not just an individual one.

The 1994 President's Task Force on Food Assistance included two definitions of hunger. One was clinical and related to nutritional deficiencies; the other was social, whereby *hunger* was defined as the inability to obtain sufficient food and nourishment. While the United States did not embrace the international efforts in the 1990s to assert food as a human right, it did move away from a strict physiological definition of hunger. Since then several national studies, such as the Community Childhood Hunger Identification Project (CCHIP), have estimated the extent of hunger.

In their efforts to document hunger, statisticians have been frustrated by the use of inconsistent measures in different research instruments, as well as by the use of proxy measures of hunger, such as poverty. Recently, the leaders of two USDA agencies, the Economic Research Service and the

Food and Nutrition Service, requested that the Committee on National Statistics (CNSTAT) of the National Academies review the USDA's measurement methods for food security. There is nothing necessarily sinister in this request. Reviews of statistical methodologies are conducted regularly, as all researchers want to be sure that they are using accurate terminology for what they are counting or describing.

However, the way in which issues are framed determines the importance attached to them and how they are addressed; data defines and delimits the problem. Essentially, because hunger is not assessed in the USDA's food security survey, the CNSTAT decided that it does not exist. Criticisms of this methodological change point out that this shift does nothing to actually make the problem of hunger go away; hunger is still with us. However, in a very real sense, it does exactly that—eliminate hunger. If hunger is no longer an analytical category, how does one talk about it or advocate for its elimination? How does one make policy claims about something for which there is no data and which, therefore, does not exist in policy science terms?

The discursive shift from *hunger* to *very low food security* also takes away the sharp edge of the word *hunger.* As the report states,[21] "Hunger is a very politically sensitive word." *Food insecurity*, on the other hand, sounds less urgent, less important, less shameful, and less embarrassing. When advocates don't have the word *hunger* in their arsenal to fight against it, the suffering of those who are, in fact, hungry is diminished. The violence of hunger is compounded by the violence of a science that claims hunger does not exist.

This is not to say that we don't need conceptual clarity in solving social problems. But we have to ask what is to be gained by working to create more accurate and precise measures of hunger. True, programs and policies need to be targeted toward those who need them, and in ways that are most effective. We already know, however, that far more children than adults are food insecure. We know that far more African Americans and Latinos are hungry than European-Americans. We know that there are many, many people who don't have enough or the right kinds of food to eat.

What the USDA's statistical shift does is make hunger disappear from the public agenda and give people the impression that it no longer exists in the United States. It also trivializes the experiences of the hungry. What it does not do is contribute to resolving food security problems, even though that is the USDA's goal.

20

The disappearance of hunger may simply be an unfortunate product of the distant gaze of experts who are far removed from the situation they study. Certainly, government statisticians can have only a partial and privileged perspective on food insecurity. The voices and experiences of the hungry must be included in any determination of the USDA's food security programs, measurements, and methods. Otherwise, the statisticians should meet with food-insecure parents and their children to explain to them why they are not hungry. In the meantime, the rest of us can do our part to make food justice issues visible, audible, and palpable. Solvable.

Notes

1. "Hunger by Any Other Name: Government Shouldn't Sugarcoat 'Involuntary Lack of Food,'" *Sarasota Herald-Tribune*, 24 November 2006, A18.
2. "Mumbo Jumbo," *Winston-Salem Journal*, 30 November 2006, A10.
3. Rhonda Chriss Lokeman, "Leave It to Bureaucrats to Desensitize Hunger," *The Augusta Chronicle*, 29 November 2006, A05.
4. Eric Schlosser, *Fast Food Nation: The Dark Side of the All-American Meal* (Boston: Houghton Mifflin, 2001); Michael Pollan, *The Omnivore's Dilemma: A Natural History of Four Meals* (New York: Penguin Press, 2006); Greg Critser, *Fat Land: How Americans Became the Fattest People in the World* (Boston: Houghton Mifflin, 2003); Morgan Spurlock, *Supersize Me* [video recording], presented by Roadside Attractions, Samuel Goldwyn Films, and Showtime Films, produced by M. Spurlock and The Con (New York: Hart Sharp Video, 2004).
5. An exception is a chapter on working conditions in Eric Schlosser's *Fast Food Nation*.
6. Mark Nord, Margaret Andrews, and Steven Carlson, *Measuring Food Security in the United States: Household Food Security in the United States, 2005* (Washington, D.C.: US Department of Agriculture, Economic Research Service, 2006).
7. At that time private organizations protested the League of Nations' decision, despite widespread hunger, to cut back on food production and destroy surpluses in its attempt to resolve the international economic crisis. See Michel Cepede, "The Fight against Hunger: Its History on the International Agenda," *Food Policy* 9, no.4 (1984): 282–290.

8. Anthony H. Chisholm and Rodney Tyers, "Food Security: An Introduction and Overview," in A. H. Chisholm and R. Tyers, *Food Security: Theory, Policy, and Perspectives from Asia and the Pacific Rim* (Lexington: Lexington Books, 1982).

9. For example, between 1989 and 1993 there was a 26 percent increase in the number of children living in families with incomes below 75 percent of the poverty line. See Cheryl A. Wehler, Richard Ira Scott, Jennifer J. Anderson, and Lynn Parker, *Community Childhood Hunger Identification Project: A Survey of Childhood Hunger in the United States.* (Washington, D.C.: Food Research and Action Center, 1995).

10. US House of Representatives. Food Security and Methods of Assessing Hunger in the United States, Serial 101–2 (Washington, D.C.: US Government Printing Office, 1989).

11. Kerstin Mechlem, "Food Security and the Right to Food in the Discourse of the United Nations," *European Law Journal* 10, no. 5 (2004): 631–648.

12. *First World Hunger: Food Security and Welfare Politics*, ed. Graham Riches (London: Macmillan, 1997).

13. Janet E. Poppendieck, "The USA: Hunger in the Land of Plenty," in Ibid.

14. In April 1992 four European-American Los Angeles Police Department officers were acquitted of charges of committing assault in the process of arresting African American motorist Rodney King. Within hours after the verdict was announced, a civil disturbance was in full swing.

15. Southern California Interfaith Hunger Coalition, *Seeds of Change: Strategies for Food Security in the Inner City* (Los Angeles: Southern California Interfaith Hunger Coalition, 1993).

16. Community Food Security Coalition, *A Community Food Security Act: A Proposal for New Food System Legislation as Part of the 1995 Farm Bill* (Hartford, CT: Hartford Food System, 1994).

17. US Congress, House of Representatives, *Review of the Administration's Proposals to Reform the Food Stamp and Commodity Distribution Programs. 1st session*, 8 June 1995, Serial No.104–16 (Washington, D.C.: US Government Printing Office, 1995).

18. Herb Reed, "The Problem Is Greater Than a Word" *The Washington Post,* 25 November 2006, A19.

19. Peter Eisinger, "Toward a National Hunger Count," *Social Service Review* 70, no. 2 (1996): 218.
20. Linda Neuhauser, Doris Disbrow, and Sheldon Margen, *Hunger and Food Insecurity in California.* (Berkeley: California Policy Research Center, 1995).
21. Mark Nord, Margaret Andrews, and Steven Carlson, *Measuring Food Security in the United States: Household Food Security in the United States,* 2005 (Washington, D.C.: US Department of Agriculture, Economic Research Service, 2006), 33.

Analyze

1. As a reader, what indication do you have that this is one of the more academic articles in this volume? What are the clues? Use examples from the text to back up your points.
2. Because the article was inspired by the USDA's elimination of the word "hunger" in favor of the term "very low food security," why might anti-hunger activists take umbrage at this decision? How does Allen articulate this difference in perspective?
3. What does Allen mean by a "discursive shift?" In the paragraph following this term, how does Allen anticipate the objections of her reader? What effect does this have?

Explore

1. Research ways in which governments or corporations have decided on other such "discursive shifts" in addition to the one Allen discusses. (Think of "corn sugar" instead of "high fructose corn syrup" as just one example.) What do you find? What do you believe are the reasons behind such discursive shifts?
2. Allen argues for the inclusion of "the voices and experiences of the hungry" as being crucial to these discussions and debates. Research some of these voices and experiences as a way to add perspectives that would suit Allen's article, were she to expand it.
3. When is it appropriate to shift language use from commonly held terms to others that may be seen as euphemistic—or, on the other hand, as obscuring? (Think "wardrobe malfunction," for instance.) Is there ever an appropriate time for this discursive shift? Why or why not?

Courtney E. Martin
"How to Address Obesity in a Fat-Phobic Society"

Author of "Perfect Girls, Starving Daughters: How the Quest for Perfection Is Harming Young Women" (2008), Courtney E. Martin has been called by Arianna Huffington a "hardcover punch in the gut." Actress Jane Fonda calls Martin's writing "varied, transformational, and necessary for us all." Martin is a founding partner of Valenti Martin Media, a communications consulting firm for social justice organizations. In this article, Martin calls on her readers to "do some soul-searching about our own attitudes about fat."

What does it mean to be "fat-phobic?"

A friend of mine—I'll call her Ellen—recently went to her regular medical clinic after realizing that she was newly suffering from an old family problem: acid reflux. Her doctor was out on maternity leave, so she met with a replacement. Without asking Ellen any questions about her relationship to her weight (she is overweight and well aware of it), he launched into a robotic exposition about dieting.

Ellen explained to him that she worked out regularly and also did her best to eat healthy, but had a philosophical problem with turning food into the enemy. He simply retorted: "The only way you're going to lose weight is to cut the carbs. So . . . cut the carbs."

"When he brought up my weight I wanted to have a real conversation with him, but instead he gave me his version of my 'problem,'" Ellen said. "It made me really angry."

My friend's experience is not an anomaly. In fact, it is representative of a still unchanged attitude among too many medical doctors and nutritionists that fat people are problems to be solved; if they can just come up with the perfect equation, they figure, BMIs can be lowered and the supposed obesity epidemic eradicated.

This attitude shows up in doctor's offices where overweight and obese   5 patients are often subjected to inquisition-like questioning. Yet they are rarely asked other, arguably more important questions: *What's your experience of your body? How is your quality of life? How do you feel about your weight?*

It also shows up in obesity intervention programs throughout the country, where a person's culture, class, education, or even genetics are overlooked in the dogged pursuit to motivate what too many clinicians see as "lazy Americans" to lose pounds.

It's not as if we don't have the evidence that these factors—culture, class, education, genetics—matter. Yet another study came out by University of Washington researchers who found gaping disparities in obesity rates among ZIP codes in the Seattle area. Every $100,000 in median home value for a ZIP code corresponded with a 2 percent drop in obesity.

Adam Drewnowski, director of the UW Center for Obesity Research, told the Seattle Post-Intelligencer, "If you have this mind-set that obesity has to do with the individual alone, then ZIP codes or areas really should not come into this. But they do, big-time."

This is not to say that individual behavior doesn't play a vital role in our country's obesity rate, but we too often neglect to think about the cultural and institutional influences on a person's behavior when it comes to eating and exercise.

10   You would never look at a working class, single mother driving a jalopy with three kids crawling around in the back and say, "Gees, what's her problem? Why can't she drive the Lexus hybrid like me?" You understand that she doesn't have the means, and furthermore, probably doesn't have the peer influence that would make it seem like a viable option.

Our judgmental, fat-phobic society seems even more ridiculous when you consider that there is a strong genetic component to weight. We now have ample scientific evidence suggesting that we are each born with a set point within which our metabolism will automatically adjust no matter how many calories we consume. It's like our working class mom could be dedicatedly saving up for that hybrid, but the money just keeps disappearing from her bank account.

Instead of vilifying fat people, this country needs to look long and hard at the roots of our obesity epidemic. While we can't change someone's genetics, we can work to change the institutional disparities that make maintaining a healthy weight difficult for people with less money. Encouraging supermarkets to open up in poor neighborhoods by adjusting zoning laws and creating tax-incentive programs is a start. More funding for public schools in low-income areas would translate into better quality food in the cafeterias and more nutrition and physical education.

In addition to addressing these classist systems, we need to do some soul searching about our own attitudes about fat. Until those of us who care about public health can truly separate the potential health risks of being overweight from our own internalized stigmas about fat, we won't be effective. We have to learn to distinguish between those who are satisfied with their current body size and those who want to lose weight, and then, learn to provide complex guidance that takes societal and genetic factors into account.

Those in the field of public health need to remember how motivation really works (hint: not by coercion or humiliation) and rethink how quality of life is measured when it comes to overweight patients. It is not the clinician's—often prejudiced, frequently rushed—point of view that matters most, but the individual's.

Dr. Janell Mensinger, the Director of the Clinical Research Unit at The   15
Reading Hospital & Medical Center, also recommends shifting the goals of obesity intervention programs: "Focusing on health indicators such as blood pressure, cholesterol, blood sugar would serve to de-stigmatize obese individuals and help them engage in better eating habits and physical activity for the purpose of healthier living as opposed to simply being thinner. Although I see some programs shifting in this direction, I don't think they have gone far enough."

Mensinger adds, "We have to avoid promoting the dieting mentality! Encourage acceptance of all shapes and sizes while promoting the importance of physical activity and eating well for the purpose of living and feeling better, mentally and physically. The people that most successfully achieve this goal are those with an expertise in eating disorders as well as obesity. They know best what can happen if the message is misconstrued."

Whether you are a primary care provider, a nurse practitioner, a nutritionist, or a community health advocate, I urge you to treat your next patient like a living, breathing human being with complicated feelings, economic concerns, and cultural affiliations. Weight loss isn't the ultimate goal; economic equality, cultural diversity, wellness and happiness are.

Analyze

1. How have the ways in which we treat and think of the obese become institutionalized—that is, an assumption, unchallenged, in everyday life? How does Martin provide evidence of these facts?

2. How do assumptions about class fit into the discussion about being "fat phobic?" To what effect? Do you believe Martin's evidence and conclusion?

3. Martin's audience might be said to be "complex," that is, she doesn't address just one group, but a number of groups concerned with this epidemic. Analyze the ways in which this argument is important for each group—and for others that Martin does not mention.

Explore

1. Identify visual representations of "fat phobia" (think about advertisements, commercials, magazine articles, billboards, etc.). Discuss these in the context of Martin's argument. To what conclusion do you come? Are there any contradictions to her arguments?

2. Explore further research about the sources of the obesity epidemic and fat phobia. Share this research with your classmates, and compare your findings. Is there general agreement with Martin? Are there any divergent opinions? Discuss.

3. How does one reconcile concern with the obesity epidemic in the United States with the desire to avoid any appearance of "fat phobia" or "fat shaming?"

John Seabrook
"Snacks for a Fat Planet"

John Seabrook has been a staff writer at *The New Yorker* magazine since 1993 and a contributor to various magazines and newspapers, including *The Village Voice, Harper's, Vanity Fair, The Nation*, and the *Christian Science Monitor*. His three books include *Nobrow: The Culture of Marketing, the Marketing of Culture* (2001). Seabrook has been described as an "incisive and amusing cultural critic." "Snacks for a Fat Planet" looks at PepsiCo as an example of how large food corporations are trying to meet the challenge set forth by the national crisis of obesity.

How might Seabrook characterize the relationship between large corporations and increasingly health-conscious consumers?

PepsiCo's headquarters sit on a broad, grassy hilltop in Purchase, New
York, the site of a former polo club, in rolling Westchester horse country. The office complex—seven identical white cubes joined at the corners,
designed in 1970 by Edward Durell Stone—looks more like a European
government ministry than the home of a business founded on sugary
drinks like Pepsi-Cola and Mountain Dew and salty snacks like Lay's
potato chips and Fritos corn chips. The entire hundred-and-sixty-eight-acre
campus is brand free, except for the PepsiCo flag, which floats next to the
Stars and Stripes over the main entrance and displays a globe encircled with
colored stripes that loosely correspond to PepsiCo's rainbow of brand
images. Scattered around the grounds, like giant boulders left behind by a
retreating glacier, is PepsiCo's collection of monumental sculptures, such as
Richard Erdman's "Passage," hewn from a four-hundred-and-fifty-ton block
of travertine, and Claes Oldenburg's thirty-seven-foot-high steel trowel,
which is embedded in the earth. Nearer the entrance, stands of exotic trees
and sunken Japanese gardens and stone walkways impart a monastic feel.

PepsiCo is the largest food-and-beverage company in the United States,
and the second-largest in the world, after Nestlé. If PepsiCo were a country,
the size of its economy—sixty billion dollars in revenues in 2010—would
put it sixty-sixth in gross national product, between Ecuador and Croatia.
Although the flagship brand, Pepsi-Cola, has always been second to
Coca-Cola, the Frito-Lay division is ten times larger than its largest com-
petitor, Diamond Foods, Inc., of San Francisco. Its products take up whole
aisles at Walmart. They are the first thing you see when you enter a deli or a
convenience store, and they're in pharmacies, office-supply stores, schools,
libraries, and the vending machines at work. PepsiCo's snacks are also
deeply embedded in our social rituals and national institutions. (At the
climactic moment of the national college-football championship game,
in January, when Auburn was about to kick the winning field goal, the
sportscaster Brent Musberger yelped, "This is for all the Tostitos!") If grazing on snacks throughout the day eventually comes to replace eating regular meals—a situation that already exists in some households—we'll have
PepsiCo to thank.

PepsiCo is also an empire of mind share. Pepsi is the second-most-
recognized beverage brand in the world, after Coke, and eighteen of

PepsiCo's other brands, which include Tropicana, Gatorade, and Quaker Oats, are billion-dollar businesses in their own right. In 2010, the company spent $3.4 billion marketing and advertising its brands. They represent a kind of promise to its customers—a guarantee that the drinks and snacks are safe, and that the taste of them, that irresistible combination of flavors, will be the same every time. But in another sense the brands are abstractions. The taste is the rootstock onto which PepsiCo grafts desires ("aspirations," as they say in the branding business) that have nothing to do with the products themselves. This duality in PepsiCo's products—part sensory, part aspirational—extends throughout the company's culture and its mission, as defined by Indra Nooyi, who has been its C.E.O. since October, 2006. It is not enough to make things that taste good, she says. PepsiCo must also be "the good company." It must aspire to higher values than the day-to-day business of making and selling soft drinks and snacks. Nooyi calls this "performance with purpose." The phrase is on the screen savers that pop up on idle computers around headquarters.

And yet, for all its riches, its vast reach, and its sense of high purpose, the PepsiCo empire is built on shifting sands. Over the course of the past half century, during which PepsiCo's revenues have increased more than a hundredfold, a public-health crisis has been steadily growing along with it. People are getting fatter. In the nineteen-eighties, rates of obesity started to rise sharply in the U.S. and around the world. By the nineteen-nineties, obesity reached epidemic proportions. One study cited by federal health officials estimates that, in 2008, obesity cost the U.S. a hundred and forty-seven billion dollars in health-care charges and resulted in about three hundred thousand deaths.

5   Many studies point to the ubiquity of high-calorie, low-cost processed foods and drinks as one of the major drivers of this condition. Snacks, in particular, play a role in childhood obesity, which is growing even faster than obesity in adults. Americans consume about fifty gallons of soda a year, more than four times the average per-capita consumption sixty years ago. Americans also ingest about thirty-four hundred milligrams of sodium per day, twice the recommended amount; sodium has long been linked to high blood pressure. And the oils and fats used in some fried potato and corn chips elevate cholesterol and can cause heart disease. In other words, that great taste promised by PepsiCo's brands, which relies heavily on sugar, salt, and fat, appears to be making some people sick, and its most devoted fans, the "heavy users," as they're known in the food industry, could be

among the worst afflicted. Cutting short the lives of your best customers isn't much of a strategy for long-term success.

Nooyi, who is fifty-five, is the first woman to lead the company, the first C.E.O. to come from outside the U.S. (she was born and raised in Madras), the first vegetarian, and the first Hindu. She has, on occasion, worn saris to work, and she keeps an image of Ganesh, the elephant-headed deity of good fortune, in her office. She has been known to hum aloud as she works (she says she has music running through her head all day) and to sing in the hallways—Beatles, Herman's Hermits, the Everly Brothers. Her sister, the singer Chandrika Tandon, was nominated for a 2011 Grammy Award in the Contemporary World Music category. Nooyi is tall, slim, poised, and looks well rested in spite of the fact that she says she works twenty hours a day, seven days a week. If she sleeps more than four hours, "I feel like I'm wasting time," she told me.

I met Nooyi in her office, which is in the corner of the executive wing of PepsiCo headquarters, on "4.3"—building four, floor three. She was dressed in stylish business clothes—black patent-leather high heels, a knee-length, copper-colored dress, and a short-waisted black jacket—and looked more like a media executive than a food-industry chieftain. The third story is cantilevered out over the two floors below it, so that it felt as if we were floating in space. Outside the window is a monumental steel sculpture by Arnaldo Pomodoro called "Triad," the tallest of the sculptures on the grounds: three steel columns, which look like ceremonial pillars from ancient Rome, appear to be bursting apart at the middle, revealing a mathematical grid inside, as though an empire were being destroyed from within by the forces of modernity. Inside, the air carried a slightly herbal aroma.

Nooyi has never run one of PepsiCo's divisions, and she hasn't managed any of its brands. She isn't a salesperson, like many of her predecessors. Since coming to PepsiCo, in 1994, at the age of thirty-eight, having worked for Motorola and the Swiss company Asea Brown Boveri, Nooyi has been in charge of PepsiCo's long-term corporate strategy. Unlike people in operations and sales, who have to worry solely about meeting quarterly-earnings targets and expanding existing markets, a corporate strategist must position the company for markets that don't yet exist, and may not for another twenty years. To do the job well requires vision, the communications skills to articulate that vision, and the ability to make people believe in the vision. Nooyi has a seer's light in her eyes when she talks about the company she wants PepsiCo to be: "the defining food and beverage company of the world."

Her long-term strategy is to make PepsiCo's "nutrition business" a much larger part of the company's portfolio than it is today. She wants to increase what she calls its "good for you" products—snacks and drinks made of grains, fruit, nuts, vegetables, and dairy—from the ten-billion-dollar business it is now into a thirty-billion-dollar business by 2020. "With the aging population," she said, "and with everyone's focus on health, products that are nutritiously good, or nutritionally better than anything else out there, are a huge opportunity. These categories are growing several times faster than anything else." She added, "Affordability and accessibility is something we know how to do very well. What if we were to add to this a third word that says 'authentic products'? 'Scientifically advantaged products'?"

10   Wait. Authentic? Or scientifically advantaged?

"Authentic. But these days, if they're authentic, you've got to have them be scientifically advantaged." She added, "I'm providing the same great taste—that's the common denominator—so you don't have to make a choice between health and taste. We can bring the best of our normal products, our life-style products, and make them affordable and available because of our scale, but then we bring you nutrition credentials as well."

PepsiCo's "good for you" products might not always be that good for you in a nutritional sense—many are loaded with sugar—but they are better for you than the "better for you" part of the portfolio, which is, in turn, healthier than the "fun for you" part of PepsiCo's business, which is by far the largest part—the soda and the chips. Just as PepsiCo creates its products out of whole foods, which are broken down into components and then, through processing, reassembled into drinks and snacks, so Nooyi has a tendency to lift words from their natural context and repurpose them to suit the needs of PepsiCo.

Although Nooyi stops short of accepting culpability for the obesity crisis—she thinks sedentary life styles, not energy-dense processed foods, are the main culprit—she agrees that PepsiCo has a responsibility to do something about the problem. "Large companies are powerful—they can play a big role—so we need to work with governments to provide solutions," she said. But she doesn't see the point in blaming food companies. "The real challenge is, instead of sitting down and figuring out who is responsible, specifically, why don't we say we need to be part of the solution?"

But isn't the problem that people eat too much? And wouldn't the best solution be to eat less? Since that would cut into the company's bottom line, it's hard to believe that PepsiCo is going to be leading the fight in the public-health realm.

"It's not a question of selling less," Nooyi responded. "It's a question of   15 selling the right stuff."

As a long-term business strategy, Nooyi's plan makes sense. One day, decades from now, people may look back on our reckless consumption of soft drinks and chips in the same way that we today look back at a three-pack-a-day smoking habit. In the U.S., the soft-drink and chip markets, while enormous, are no longer growing. And although almost half of PepsiCo's business is overseas (thirty per cent of it in developing countries), foreign markets eventually tend to follow U.S. trends. The markets of the future may well be in "packaged nutrition"—in enriched products like PepsiCo's SoBe Lifewater, which contains vitamins, and in its pricey Naked line of fruit juices and smoothies, which contain antioxidants. Another growing category is "functional" foods and beverages, like varieties of the sports drink Gatorade, which PepsiCo markets for specific physiological or metabolic attributes. (Thanks to Gatorade's new "fit series," you can drink G1 Prime before you work out, G2 Perform during your workout, and G3 Recover when you're cooling down.) Nooyi talks about making functional foods for different life stages—snacks for teens, snacks for pregnant women, snacks for seniors. (It sounds to me like specially formulated pet food for puppies and older dogs.) In the distant future—in the era of "personalized nutrition" that some of the scientists I met around PepsiCo foretold—snacks may evolve into delivery vehicles for a broad array of quasi-medical benefits. You can now go into a pharmacy and have your foot mapped by a Dr. Scholl's Custom Fit Orthotics machine, which will then recommend the right Dr. Scholl's products for you; in the future, you may be able to go into a convenience store, exhale into a machine that checks your metabolism, and find out which snacks you need to keep your Krebs cycle running smoothly.

For the present, however, and for some years to come, PepsiCo will be selling soft drinks and chips. Pepsi, Lay's, and Mountain Dew together accounted for more than thirty billion dollars in sales in 2010, and, because PepsiCo can make these products cheaply, its profit margins are huge.

Nooyi wanted me to see for myself how her company is going about scientifically advantaging its products, which is part of the "journey," as she likes to say, to the PepsiCo of the future. This involves reengineering the composition of its "fun for you" products—the sodas and the chips—to make them "better for you" by reducing the amount of sugar, salt, and saturated fat they contain. To do that, Nooyi has hired prominent scientists, built state-of-the-art laboratories, and significantly expanded the company's research-and-development capabilities.

My journey began in a potato-chip factory in Irving, Texas, outside Dallas, where PepsiCo is working on innovations in sodium reduction. As described to me by Mehmood Khan, an endocrinologist formerly with the Mayo Clinic, whom Nooyi brought in to lead the company's research efforts, the scientific challenge was to see whether the company could make a lower-sodium chip that tasted just as salty as a regular chip. "What we discovered is that people actually taste only about twenty to twenty-five per cent of the salt we put on our chips," Khan told me. "They swallow the rest of it without tasting it." But reducing the amount of salt changed what flavorists call "the taste curve"—that sudden spike of saltiness on the tongue, followed by a tingling around the sides of the mouth. "So we wondered, was there a different kind of salt crystal that would produce the same taste curve but with less salt?" Khan said. Their research was complicated by the fact that of the five primary taste sensations—salty, sweet, sour, bitter, and umami—the taste of salt is the least understood. "We don't know the molecular structure of the salt receptors, and we don't really understand the mechanism by which salt works," Khan went on. Nevertheless, collaborating with crystal technologists in Munich, PepsiCo was able to develop "15 micron salt," a new kind of salt that produces the same taste curve as the salt the company has been using—a pyramid-shaped crystal known as Alberger salt—but contains twenty-five to forty per cent less sodium. PepsiCo first used the new salt on its Walker brand of chips, which it sells in the U.K. By the end of 2012, 15 micron salt will be flavoring many of the Lay's plain chips made in the U.S.

20   Brian Schroeder, the manager of the Irving production facility, led me on a tour of the plant. We started outside, where the trucks with containers full of potatoes back up to the factory. Breeders for PepsiCo developed the potatoes, in Rhinelander, Wisconsin, to be the best for chipping—thin-skinned, round, and solid, with good color and flavor. An elevated conveyor carries the potatoes into the noisy and dimly lit plant, which smells of wet vegetables and cooking oil. They pass through peelers and hit the rotary slicers—metal cylinders with sharpened blades around the edges.

The spinning of the cylinders forces the chips to the sides, where the blades slice them one twentieth of an inch thick. The slices are washed and dried, and then plunged into the fryer, which is a big metal trough containing a briskly moving stream of boiling oil. The oil drives the water out of the slices and turns the starch in the potatoes crisp. The key to crunch is the rapid transfer of heat, and that's why most chips are fried, rather than baked. (Lay's does make baked potato chips, but not from actual potato slices. Baked chips are fabricated from potato flakes that are shaped into chips after baking; they lack the crispness of fried chips.) At Irving, the chips are fried in sunflower oil, which the company switched to in 2006, when it stopped using trans fats. PepsiCo contracts directly with the farmers who grow the sunflowers, thereby eliminating the middlemen. Through Agrofinanzas, a Mexican financial institution, it also offers the farmers micro-loans and other kinds of financial assistance.

After five seconds in the oil, the fried chips emerge onto a conveyor belt, where high-speed cameras inspect them. If a camera detects a blemish on a chip, it sends a signal to one of the airhoses under the conveyor, and a jet of air blows the chip off onto the floor. Salt is sprinkled onto the remaining chips from overhead receptacles. Because the new salt is lighter and finer than the old salt and tends to blow around, Schroeder said, shouting over the din, the engineers were in the process of changing the size of the apertures in the salt receptacles to insure a more even flow.

Schroeder invited me to taste the potato chips ("P.C.s") as they emerged from their salt shower. They were still warm, perfectly crunchy, and had a shimmer of oil on the surface. For some reason, the taste reminded me of the chips my mother sometimes packed in my lunchbox when I was a little kid.

Later that day, I got to try the new salt at Frito-Lay headquarters, in nearby Plano, Texas. First, I spoke to Dr. Greg Yep, an organic chemist and PepsiCo's senior vice-president of long-term research, who is in charge of the scientific work being done on the core ingredients. "In a lot of foods, you don't actually taste the salt," Yep said, pointing out that there's as much salt in one slice of white bread as there is in a small bag of Lay's—about two hundred milligrams. Pasta, cold cuts, prepared dinners, canned soups, bacon, cheese, and soy sauce all rank ahead of potato chips as sodium sources in our diets. (There are nearly a thousand milligrams of sodium in a tablespoon of soy sauce.) "But with our chips the salt is a big part of the taste, so we have to be very careful, when we're reformulating the recipe, not to change the taste," Yep said.

There were four white bags of plain Lay's chips on the table, each with a different kind of salt. The first bag had the Alberger salt, the second the new 15 micron salt, the third pretzel salt, and the fourth another new crystal that Pepsi has been working on. I tried the Alberger, felt the spike and the tingling, and tried to picture the taste curve in my mind. Then I kept that image in my head as I tasted the 15 micron salt. I tried to be scientific about it, but I kept thinking about those potato chips my mother put into my lunchbox.

25   A few days later, I met Greg Yep again, this time at PepsiCo's new research lab in Hawthorne, New York, to hear about the company's work in sugar reduction. He wanted me to see for myself PepsiCo's newest crusader—a robot that the company's scientists have fitted with human taste buds—in the quest for the holy grail, a natural, zero-calorie sweetener that tastes exactly like sugar. PepsiCo scientists grew cultured cells, injected the genetic sequences of the four known taste receptors (leaving out salt) into them, and then hardwired the cells to a computer.

The robot's job is to taste the samples that PepsiCo's network of "trekkers" collect from around the world. "Wherever a Pepsi can get to, our people can get to," Yep said excitedly. "We go into local villages, street markets, wherever, and we ask people, 'Hey, how'd you make this taste sweet? Did you put sugar in it, or something else?' We collect samples of everything— fruits, plants, roots, even bugs. Might be beetles—they have a nutty flavor. Might be bee larvae. Might be a certain variety of chili pepper which has a sweetness in the stem. Some samples are shipped back here to the lab, prepared as assays, and we feed everything to the robot." He added, "Before the robot, we had people tasting all those things, and it took forever, and some of the tastes were pretty unpleasant, as you can imagine, and sometimes dangerous. But now the robot tells us what we've got." When the robot tastes something humans might like, he explained, the computer scores it as a hit. "Out of a hundred thousand assays, we get maybe four hits."

The robot was encased inside a clear glass box, about fifteen feet square. It had a movable mechanical arm with a slender proboscis-like pipette at the tip. The arm would stop over a tray of assays, and the pipette would slide into a sample, "taste" it, and then the arm would move to the next tray. It can sample about forty thousand assays a day. We watched it work for several minutes, but it didn't turn up anything tasty.

The samples that are approved by the robot are further refined and analyzed and, eventually, incorporated into test batches of drinks and snacks that are presented to human tasters. But this is not merely a question of deciding what tastes good, or comparing one kind of taste with another; PepsiCo is also trying to understand how product descriptions like "healthy" or "good for you" might affect the way things taste. The company has conducted fMRI studies to test the hypothesis that calling a product "healthy" may lower taste expectations in the brain. In one study, a forty-calorie beverage was described as a "treat" to people just before they tasted it, and then the same beverage was called "healthy" and offered to the tasters again. The tests showed that people who scored high in reward sensitivity—i.e., those who are easily satisfied—found the beverage labelled "treat" to be more satisfying, while the people who scored low in reward sensitivity found the "healthy" beverage to be more satisfying. Since low-reward sensitivity is believed by some researchers to be a factor in obesity—low-reward people need to eat more than high-reward people to achieve the same level of satisfaction, or "bliss point"—PepsiCo's study suggests that the word "healthy" would appeal more to people with unhealthy eating habits. But that could be because unhealthy people only aspire to be healthy; they don't actually eat healthy food.

The taste tests at the Hawthorne lab take place both in small "sip and spit" rooms, which resemble the workstations in a dentist's office, and in a large conference room that has been fitted with a one-way mirror and concealed cameras. The reason for the cameras, Yep explained, is that "what people say about the way something tastes is a lot of times not what they really are thinking." The consumer may say he prefers the all-natural, lower-sodium, lower-calorie product, but in fact he really likes the one he's used to, the one made with artificial ingredients and loaded with sugar and salt. "So these cameras feed the video into facial-interpretation software," Yep said. "The software can tell if they are lying."

The overriding impression I carried away from my Hawthorne visit   30
was that, although it all comes back to taste at PepsiCo, the physical sensation of tasting has been so thoroughly mediated by advertising and packaging that no one knows anymore where the physiological experience ends and the aspirational experience begins. It's hard to guarantee the "same great taste" in a scientifically advantaged product when no one is sure just what that taste is.

As part of PepsiCo's commitment to being "the good company," the corporation wants to play a leading role in public-health issues, and particularly in the battle against obesity. Some people think this is ludicrous.

Marion Nestle, the author of "Food Politics" and a professor of food studies at N.Y.U., told me, "The best thing Pepsi could do for worldwide obesity would be to go out of business." Others, like Michele Simon, a public-health lawyer and the author of "Appetite for Profit," think PepsiCo is trying to coopt people who work on food issues in the public sector by sponsoring research and fellowships and by hiring former public officials as consultants and full-time employees. (David Kessler, the former head of the Food and Drug Administration, was a PepsiCo consultant, and George Mensah, who led efforts in addressing obesity at the Center for Disease Control and Prevention, now leads PepsiCo's research in obesity, nutrition, and health.) On the other hand, many people think that worldwide obesity is too large an issue for governments and public-health institutions like the World Health Organization to solve, and that big food companies have to help. In January, Michelle Obama, who founded the White House's Let's Move campaign, stood next to executives from Walmart to help promote public–private partnerships in fighting obesity. (Walmart pledged to eliminate trans fats from its products by 2015 and to pressure its suppliers to reduce the sugar, salt, and fat in processed foods across the industry.)

No one I met at PepsiCo better represents the complicated relationship between private food companies and public health than Derek Yach, the company's director of global-health policy. Yach, who is fifty-five, is an affable and smooth-talking South African epidemiologist whose specialty is non-communicable diseases. He made his name at the W.H.O., where, as the cabinet director under the director-general, Gro Harlem Brundtland, he was the architect of the Framework Convention on Tobacco Control, a landmark in public-health policy, which imposed strict limits on how tobacco companies sell their products around the world.

By the time the convention was adopted, in early 2003, Yach and Brundtland had turned their attention to the food industry. Some within the W.H.O. wanted to use the tobacco convention as a blueprint for dealing with Big Food—to represent the companies as moral pariahs and impose regulations on them, rather than try to negotiate. But others, Yach among them, thought the tactics that had worked with the tobacco companies would fail if tried on the food industry. "We were able to paint the tobacco companies as morally untouchable," he told me. "They sold one product, and it wasn't good for you—there's no way to make a healthy cigarette. But you can make healthy food."

Yach was on the W.H.O. committee that, in 2002, produced a draft of new dietary guidelines, which was circulated for comment among the United Nations' hundred and ninety-two member states. Among the recommendations were calls to limit added sugar to ten per cent of the total calorie intake and to limit daily salt intake to five grams per day. These were relatively modest proposals, but the food industry didn't like them. "The fact that the report talked about eating less and drinking less soda was seen as anti-business," Yach told me. During the debate over the draft, an industry executive told Yach, "The food industry is a trillion-dollar industry, and you better not mess with us." The sugar industry lobbied senators to write to Tommy Thompson, the Secretary of Health and Human Services under President George W. Bush, to remove the limit on sugar. In the final draft of the guidelines, approved in 2004, there were no target goals given for restrictions on sugar or salt intake.

The following year, Yach was removed from his stately office on the sixth floor of the W.H.O. headquarters, in Geneva, and installed in an obscure office on the ground floor. In an interview in 2004, he suggested that the food industry played a role in his demise. He left the organization that year, and joined the Yale School of Medicine, where he was the head of the global-health division. But he found the academic environment unsatisfying and moved on to the Rockefeller Foundation, where he was put in charge of crafting a global-health plan. It was there, in 2006, that he got a call from the office of Indra Nooyi, inviting him to lunch at PepsiCo headquarters in Purchase.

"We had salmon," he told me. "And it was very good salmon, too, and before I was halfway through it she had offered me a job."

What did she say?

"She said, 'I want you to do exactly what you were doing at the W.H.O., and do it here for us at PepsiCo.'" The guidelines on sugar and salt reduction that Yach had tried to push through at the W.H.O. would be a starting point, but Nooyi wanted to go beyond that. Yach would not have to go to member states for approval of these guidelines, and although there was a culture within PepsiCo that would resist change ("We make great-tasting treats that people love—what's wrong with that?" was how Yach characterized this attitude), there would be no need to build consensus within the organization, which was, after all, not a democratic institution but an autocracy. As George Mensah put it to me, "At the C.D.C., not only do you need a director to sign off on your proposals—you need congressional approval and a budget. Here, once you've convinced management that something is a smart business decision, they make the resources available to get something done."

Nooyi gave Yach a couple of days to think about her offer.

40   Did he consult with colleagues?

"I asked my mother what she thought." Yach paused. "She said, 'How could you possibly work for the company that sells that junk food?'"

Many in the world of public health were shocked when Yach took the job. *Public Health Nutrition*, a scientific journal, invited Yach to explain his motives, which he did in an editorial, stressing the need for collaboration between the public and private sectors in addressing food-related health issues. The journal also invited editorial commentary. Ricardo Uauy, of the International Union of Nutritional Sciences, was inclined to believe Yach's intentions, while Kaare R. Norum, a professor emeritus in the department of nutrition at the University of Oslo, was not. He wrote, "There is a basic conflict in working within the snack food sector, since branding snacks as 'healthy' only diverts attention from the real issues. In my view it is the culture of snacking—the consumption of superfluous calories between, or perhaps instead of healthy main meals—which is an unhealthy practice in itself."

But, at least from the point of view of setting dietary guidelines, Yach has been much more successful at PepsiCo than he was at the W.H.O. The company's proposals to cut the amount of salt and sugar in its products by twenty-five per cent by 2015 are comparable to the guidelines that Yach failed to get enacted at the W.H.O. Of course, they apply only to PepsiCo's products, and people who want the extra salt and sugar can find it elsewhere. Still, PepsiCo's consumer base is enormous—by some estimates, three billion people eat or drink one or another of its products in the course of a year.

Of all the challenges that PepsiCo faces on its journey to health and wellness, perhaps the greatest is how to bring the main brand along with it. Through its advertising, Pepsi-Cola has been associated with many aspirations over the years—most famously, in the nineteen-sixties it was the drink of the Pepsi Generation, the countercultural alternative to the establishmentarians who drank Coke—but a healthful diet isn't one of them. Caleb Bradham, the North Carolina pharmacist who invented the drink, in 1893, promoted it as a digestive aid—it supposedly stimulated the release of pepsin, an enzyme used in digestion—but, as with many other tonics, potions, and elixirs produced by the medicine men of that era, Pepsi's medicinal claims were pure hokum. Nevertheless, to bring the flagship brand more in line with PepsiCo's "performance with purpose" agenda, the drink has to do more than just taste good. And because Pepsi can't be described as good for you, even within Nooyi's generous definition of that phrase, the brand has to be good in some other way.

In 2010, the company launched the Pepsi Refresh Project, its main   45
marketing campaign for the brand. PepsiCo promised to give away twenty million dollars, in amounts ranging from five thousand to two hundred and fifty thousand dollars, to people with "refreshing ideas that change the world." The winning projects were those which received the most votes on the Pepsi Refresh Web site. In part, the strategy was to use social media to promote the image of PepsiCo as the good company, and, it was hoped, to colonize some part of the digital generation as the next Pepsi Generation. But PepsiCo also spent heavily on TV advertising, aiming the Pepsi Refresh Project at its traditional customer base.

In its first year, the Refresh campaign garnered more than eighty million votes, got three and a half million "likes" on Pepsi's Facebook page, and drew some sixty thousand Twitter followers. It was heartening to see so many worthy projects get funded—homeless shelters, school playgrounds, education programs for teen-age mothers—and maybe you thought better of PepsiCo for it. But the campaign didn't sell Pepsi. In 2010, the number of cases of blue-can Pepsi that were sold declined by 4.8 per cent from the previous year. During the same period, PepsiCo also lost 2.6 per cent of the over-all carbonated-drink market. More disastrous, on a symbolic level, regular Pepsi fell behind Diet Coke in sales—a Battle of Bosworth Field-like event in the war of the colas. It appears that hearing about all the good things PepsiCo is doing to help make the world a better place doesn't tempt you to down a Pepsi. (The *Wall Street Journal* reported that many of the voters and grant winners didn't buy soda at all.) John Sicher, the editor and publisher of *Beverage Digest*, told me, "What Pepsi didn't do with Refresh was sell the brand intrinsics—the things that make you want to drink it." There were no closeups of the caramel-colored liquid as it bubbled from the can, an image that somehow conveys the taste of the sugar coating the inside of your mouth as you take that first delicious sip. Coke's campaign, on the other hand, focussed heavily on intrinsics, presenting Coke as a pleasurable indulgence, and not as a means to any higher good.

The failure of the Refresh campaign is one of several setbacks that Nooyi has experienced lately. Rising energy and commodity prices have made many of PepsiCo's products more expensive to produce, shrinking the company's profit margins. Nooyi had to cut the 2011 earnings forecast from double-digit growth to seven or eight per cent, and when she was asked about this in a conference call with investment analysts, in February, she sounded testy in her replies. Some influential analysts have begun to question whether Nooyi's focus on nutrition is the best thing for the company. "They have to realize that at their core they are a sugary, fatty cola company, and people like that," Ali Dibadj, an analyst with Sanford Bernstein, told the *Financial Times* in March.

When I asked Nooyi about the notion that Pepsi should stick to what it does well, and not get distracted by the nutrition business, she said, "We want this company to be successful for decades going into the future. What we don't want is a Road Runner type of company—the coyote runs, falls into a ditch, picks himself up, goes splat again. Companies can't be that way. Companies have to be on a glide path that allows us to perform at a reasonable level for a long time. The only way you do it is you look around the bend constantly and say 'What's coming?' and then retool the company for the new reality."

She cited a comment that, she said, "haunts me forever," made by Charles Prince, the C.E.O. of CitiGroup, in July, 2007, on the eve of the financial crisis that his company helped bring about. "He said, 'As long as the music is playing, we have to keep dancing.' To me, that is symptomatic of what people want corporations to do, but it's also symptomatic of what C.E.O.s should not be doing. You don't dance like a dervish to the old music but think about different dances you have to learn for different genres of music." She added, "What I don't like is when people say, 'Give us even more top-tier performance, because we'd rather have that last couple of dollars, rather than you investing to make sure this company stays successful.'" In response to her critics, she said, "When we become C.E.O.s, they give us C.E.O. pills, and that allows us to remain strong in the face of all of this criticism."

50   My journey into the brave new PepsiCo ended on a cold but brilliantly sunny spring day when Nooyi invited me to the Purchase campus to taste some of the company's new products. Some were experimental colas, and others were a whole new category of "drinkified" snacks and "snackified" drinks, such as Tropolis, the squeezable juice packs that the company is currently testing in the Midwest. Before the formal tasting, we sat in the C.E.O.'s office and talked about some of the new products we were about to try.

"Let's say you give a kid a carrot," Nooyi explained. "And he says, 'I don't want to eat a carrot.' But you say, 'I tell you what, I'll give it to you in a wonderful drinkable form that's still as close to the carrot as possible.' All of a sudden, what have I done? I've drinkified the snack! Or I take a fruit juice and give it to you in a wonderful squeezable form, which is Tropolis. What have I done now? I've snackified the drink. So there's this new convergence area coming up, which is going to be a glorious area. If you don't want to eat oatmeal, tell you what—we'll give it to you in a drinkable form, with a little bit of fruit. We can even give you a little bit of crunch. You can drink it on the go, and it tastes great. And, guess what, we've just sneaked oatmeal into you."

We went down the hall to a conference room where Jonathan McIntyre, a biochemist who came to PepsiCo from DuPont, and several staff members had set up the tasting. The first phase was a "triangle tasting" of three experimental mid-calorie colas that PepsiCo has been tinkering with, which contain about half the sugar of blue-can Pepsi. In front of us were three trays, each bearing three small sampling cups filled with cola, and some salted crackers, a water glass, and a spit glass. The contest between Nooyi and me, on which we would be scored, was, in each round of tasting, to pick out the experimental cola from two regular Pepsis.

Nooyi is renowned for her Pepsi palate. She has said she knows the difference between Pepsi and Coke by smell alone. She beat me in the first round (I misunderstood the rules—long story) and we both guessed the experimental cola in the second round, so I still had a chance to tie going into the decisive third round.

The final experimental cola was the scientifically advantaged product that PepsiCo will begin selling within the next six months (its name is still secret)—a cola that is supposed to taste like regular Pepsi but that has sixty per cent less sugar. I heard it described around headquarters as "a very big deal." It uses "flavor enhancers"—biotech products that are not sweet themselves but increase the intensity of sweeteners, to re-create a full-sugar taste.

We tasted the colas one at a time, and when we finished McIntyre 55 asked me to guess first. I thought Cola 2 tasted different from the others. Nooyi said she thought Colas 2 and 3 tasted exactly the same; Cola 1 was different.

We were both wrong. Cola 3 was the cola that has sixty per cent less sugar. Nooyi professed amazement—"Colas 2 and 3 tasted identical to me!" she exclaimed. "Identical!" But I suspected that she may have lost on purpose, in order to let the product win. Where was that facial-interpretation software when you needed it?

We moved on to the snackified and drinkified items. First was a "drinkable oats" beverage, which will launch in Mexico and Brazil this fall, under the Quaker Oats brand, and is expected to make its way to the States in the near future. It contains eight grams of oats per serving, eight grams of protein from skim milk, fruit juice, and sugar. I couldn't taste the oatmeal that Nooyi was sneaking into me, but maybe that was the slightly chalky texture I didn't like. Next were chilled vegetable soups, which PepsiCo currently markets in Europe under its Alvalle brand. There were several different kinds of gazpacho, all of which tasted delicious to me, like soup smoothies. "Talk about convenience," Nooyi said. "You don't have to worry about heating it or microwaving it. And what if we gave this to you in a very aspirational container, with a spoon made out of whole grain to eat it with?" She opened her eyes very wide, and the seer light came out of them.

"I've seen her light up on that one," McIntyre said.

"I don't light up—I'll kick your ass on that one," Nooyi said, with a laugh.

60   "I'm just saying it excites you!" McIntyre replied, a little nervously.

"Why aren't these soups available in the States?" I asked.

"The American consumer has to be trained," Nooyi said. "We have to train Americans that gazpacho is a great, close-to-nature soup."

"Cold soups are a difficult concept for many Americans," McIntyre said. "We'll put them on a journey. We'll stretch them a little bit, and before you know it they'll go to the gazpacho. But we may have to start them with something a little bit closer and move them along as we go."

"And make it aspirational," Nooyi said. "We have to find spokespeople for these products who are aspirational, like what Britney Spears or Michael Jackson did for Pepsi, or like a Michael Jordan for Gatorade, except they would say, 'But I started my day with *this*.'"

65   Finally, we sampled the coconut water that PepsiCo began selling last year in the U.S., under its Naked brand, made from Brazilian green coconuts. It was sweet, but not as sweet as Naked's Mighty Mango, which I have come to crave in the morning.

"It's not in my local deli yet," I said.

"It will be tomorrow," one of the staff members said.

And, sure enough, there it was.

Analyze

1. In reading this article before we decided to include it in this volume, we were struck by its balance—that is, its appreciation of both sides of a fiery debate. Do you agree? Cite evidence from the article to discuss your view of the piece's "balanced" perspective regarding points of view.

2. How would you analyze Seabrook's description of Indra Nooyi, the CEO of PepsiCo? How do you feel about Nooyi, based on Seabrook's description? Why? What about Seabrook's choice of language, or other factors, leads you to have these impressions?

3. Using examples from the article, analyze the ways in which PepsiCo represents a challenge faced by many corporations in the United States. How would you summarize these challenges? What is Seabrook's perspective on Pepsi's ability to meet these challenges? Do you agree? Why or why not?

Explore

1. Reflect on the products you have encountered in the changing land-scape of grocery stores over the past several years. What changes seem to be a direct reaction to the global health crisis, the drive to eat healthy foods, and the near-mandate to eschew those perceived to be unhealthy?

2. Seabrook mentions that "many studies point to the ubiquity of high-calorie, low-cost processed foods and drinks" as a primary reason for declining health. With some research, find one or more studies that prove this connection and that support Seabrook's mentioning this as a known fact.

3. Have a debate or discussion in class wherein you explore the relation-ship between the marketing of unhealthy foods and the attempt by marketers to assuage concerns on the part of increasingly health-conscious consumers. How do marketers do what they do? With what level of success? Why?

Marion Nestle
"School Food, Public Policy, and Strategies for Change"

Longtime scholar, professor, and academic administrator, Marion Nestle has served as senior nutrition policy advisor in the Department of Health and Human Services and was managing editor of the 1988 Surgeon General's Report on Nutrition and Health. In addition to other government posts, Nestle has written extensively about food policy and nutrition, including *Food Politics: How the Food Industry Influences Nutrition and Health* (2002) and *What to Eat* (2006). Nestle also writes regularly for *The Atlantic* and writes a regular "Food Matters" column for the San Francisco *Chronicle*. This article examines the implications of food corporations marketing to and for children.

How would you describe Nestle's call to action?

School food is a "hot button" issue, and it well deserves to be. It lies right at the heart of issues related to equality in our society. Americans live in a pluralistic society. For democracy to work, the interests of constituencies must be appropriately balanced. School food is about the balance between corporate interests and those of advocates for children's health.

The nutritional health of American children has changed during this century, improving dramatically in some ways, but not in others. In the early 1900s, the principal health problems among children were infectious diseases made worse by diets limited in calories and nutrients. As the economy improved, and as more was learned about nutritional needs, manufacturers fortified foods with key nutrients, the government started school feeding programs, and the results were a decline in nutrient deficiency conditions. That severe undernutrition has now virtually disappeared among American children can be counted as one of the great public health achievements of the twentieth century. For the great majority of American children, the problem of not having enough food has been solved. Whether children are eating the right food is another matter.

Indeed, the most important nutritional problem among children today is obesity—a consequence of eating too much food, rather than too little. Obesity rates are rising rapidly among children and adolescents, especially those who are African-American or Hispanic. The health consequences also are rising: high levels of serum cholesterol, blood pressure, and "adult-onset" diabetes. This increase has occurred in response to complex societal, economic, demographic, and environmental changes that have reduced physical activity and promoted greater intake of foods high in calories but not necessarily high in nutrients.

This shift—from too little to too much food—has created a dilemma   5
for the United States Department of Agriculture (USDA), other federal agencies, and many of my fellow nutritionists. Since its inception, the USDA has had two missions: to promote American agricultural products and to advise the public about how best to use those products. The school lunch program derived precisely from the congruence of the two missions. The government could use up surplus food commodities by passing them along to low-income children. As long as dietary advice was to eat more, the advice caused no conflict.

Once the problems shifted to chronic diseases, however, the congruence ended. Eat less means eating less of fat, saturated fat, cholesterol, sugar, and salt, which in turn means eating less of the principal food sources of those nutrients—meat, dairy, fried foods, soft drinks, and potato chips. USDA was then faced with the problem of continuing to promote use of such foods while asking the public to eat less of them—a dilemma that continues to the present day.

For the federal government to suggest that anyone eat less of any food does not play well in our political environment; such suggestions hurt sales. This matters, because we vastly overproduce food in this country—a secret seemingly known only to analysts in the Economic Research Service. The average per capita supply of calories available from food produced in the U. S.—plus imports, less exports—is 3,900 per day for every man, woman, and child, more than twice what is needed on average. These are food availability figures and they cover food wasted, fed to pets, and fats used for frying, but they have gone up by 600 calories since 1970 and are more than sufficient to account for rising rates of obesity among adults and children. The point here is that overproduction makes for a highly competitive food supply. People can only eat so much. So to sell more, companies must get us to eat their foods rather than those of competitors, or to eat more, thereby encouraging us to become obese.

The stakes are very high. Food is a $1.3 trillion annual business, with the vast percentage of profits going to added-value products rather than basic commodities. It pays to turn wheat into sugared breakfast cereals, or potatoes into chips. Farmers get only a small share—18% or so—of the consumer's food dollar, less for vegetables, fruits, and grains than for meat and dairy. So there is a big incentive to marketers to make food products with cheap raw ingredients like fat and sugar. And they do—to the tune of 12,000 or so new products every year. There are now 320,000 foods on the market (not all in the same place); the average large supermarket contains 40,000 to 60,000 food products, more than anyone could possibly need or want.

This level of overproduction has kept growth in the food industry stagnating for years at about a 1% growth rate, far lower than in comparable industries. Corporations need better growth rates than that to satisfy shareholders. To expand sales, food companies can try to sell products overseas, or they can try to increase market share at home. With this understood, it is evident why marketers so relentlessly pursue children as potential sales targets: children 7 to 12 years of age spend billions of their own money on snacks and beverages, and teenagers have billions more to spend on candy, soft drinks, ice cream, and fast food—precisely the types of foods that promote high caloric intakes. The influence of children on adult spending is even greater. Kids are said to influence one-third of total sales of candy and gum, and 20% to 30% of cold cereals, pizza, salty snacks, and soft drinks.

10   Food companies say they are not responsible for the changes in society that make kids demand their products. They point to decreasing family size, older parents, working parents, and single parents all predisposing to greater indulgence of kids. Kids are more spoiled; coupled with other changes in society, they are also less independent. From the age of eight on, my friends and I could and did take New York subways by ourselves, a level of independence utterly inconceivable today. Parents want their kids to make independent choices whenever they can, and foods are perfect opportunities for such decision-making, which is just what marketers want.

Of course, what kids are doing instead of taking subways is watching food commercials on TV or on the Internet. Advertisers quite unapologetically direct marketing efforts to kids as young as six. They consider this targeting quite sensible. And they know how to do it. The research available to help advertisers target children is awe-inspiring in its comprehensiveness, level of detail, and thoroughly undisguised cynicism. Not only have marketers identified precisely the kinds of packages and messages most likely to attract boys, girls, or kids of varying ages, but they justify advertising to children as a public service.

The USDA is a complex agency with multiple constituencies. Because of internal conflicts of interest, the agency cannot protect the integrity of the school meals program on its own. It is already clear, for example, that Congress believes that more competition is good for schools. If USDA wants to help children prevent obesity through healthier school lunches, it needs to be working with a much broader set of allies. USDA cannot tell children to eat less of any food, and the school meal programs still reflect the dual goals of their origin. My recommendation would be to enter into partnership with the Department of Health and Human Services and the Department of Education to develop an interagency alliance for a national school health campaign focused on obesity prevention using the Healthy People 2010 goals as a starting point.

What particularly disturbs me about commercial intrusions into school meals is that they are so unnecessary. Schools are perfectly capable of producing nutritionally sound foods that taste good and are enthusiastically consumed by students as well as teachers. From my own observations, a healthy school meals program (in every sense of the word) requires just three elements: a committed food service director, a supportive principal, and devoted parents. It just seems so obvious that the future of our nation demands each of these elements to be in place in every one of the 95,000 schools in the country. These are, after all, our children.

There needs to be one place in society where children feel that their needs come first—not their future as consumers. In American society today, schools are the only option. That's why every aspect of school food matters so much and is worth every minute spent to promote and protect its integrity.

Analyze

1. Analyze Nestle's contention that school food, as an issue and in practice, "lies right at the heart of issues related to equality in our society." What do you discover? What evidence supports this argument?

2. This article is clearly a type of "call to action" on the part of the author towards the reader. Who seems to be the target audience here? How can you tell? Why would Nestle choose a particular audience for her argument?

3. "Food companies say they are not responsible for the changes in society that make kids demand their products." What do you think of this statement? Does Nestle's evidence help argue against this statement? Why or why not? What other arguments for or against the statement might be appropriate?

Explore

1. Write an essay calling on other resources that further explores the ways in which the food industries' overproduction has influenced the content of school lunches. What are the connections? What other factors—school districts, budgets, etc.—might be involved?

2. Research other critiques of food lunch programs. What do you find? Do these replicate Nestle's arguments, or do they enhance (or refute) them? How so?

3. Explore information about free and reduced-price school lunch programs, considering the relationship between socioeconomic status and access to healthy foods. Use those sources to create a presentation where you argue a point of view based on evidence from these sources.

Forging Connections

1. Analyze the intersection of food policy, corporate interest, and public good, using examples from several of the articles in this chapter and others in this volume. What can you argue as your point of view after reviewing three of these articles? What evidence can you use from them to back up your argument?

2. In what ways do our choices about language—whether about controversial subjects or in everyday conversation—reveal ways in which language influences both our attitudes and our actions? Discuss how various articles in this chapter connect to this conversation with very different approaches to language use and style. (For instance, consider the articles by Allen, Martin, and others.)

Looking Further

1. Find two additional articles or essays about obesity, extending your search beyond the United States. Prepare a presentation for your class, giving classmates the two articles you've found in advance of your discussion. Summarize the articles, and explore how they expand our understanding of obesity, now as a global problem. Lead your classmates in a discussion about the relative merits of the articles you've chosen, using specific examples from these articles and others you've read in this chapter.

2. Consider a paradox of this chapter: that we seem to read about either too much food or too little food. How does the culture created by this paradox—of access or excess—show itself and influence the decision making of corporations? Consider the ways in which food is branded, marketed, and the like.

Food and American Culture

In the earlier chapters of this anthology, we have read about how food itself can be viewed as a critical aspect of identity formation: Our feelings about food are shaped by our cultural contexts, our families, our histories, our traditions—and the places in which we grow up.

The articles in this chapter, on the other hand, are informed by broader aspects of American culture and social conditions. That is, as Americans, what do we eat? Why? To what traditions do we adhere? How are the results of politics, gender, and social need part of culture? How do politics and culture begin to be part of social fabric? As you read the selections in this chapter, consider how various dimensions related to food (production, distribution, consumption, disposal) play a role in the shaping of American culture and values—and vice versa.

Brett Martin
"Good Food Everywhere" An Excerpt

Brett Martin is a correspondent for *Gentleman's Quarterly* and a frequent contributor to other publications such as *Bon Appetit, Food and Wine,* and *Vanity Fair.* His latest book, *Difficult Men: From* The Sopranos *and* The Wire *to* Mad Men *and* Breaking Bad, focuses on the new "golden age" of television drama and affirms Martin's wide-ranging interests and versatility as a writer. More relevant to this volume, Martin is a 2013 recipient of the James Beard Award for Journalism. The excerpt that follows introduces Martin's culinary road trip through the United States.

What is Martin really exploring in this food trip?

And so here we are, under the arc lights, under the Southern California stars, on a picture-perfect summer evening in America. The kids are arriving, headlights swinging slowly down La Brea, down Beverly. They're cruising, looking for parking, checking out the scene at the car wash and gas station on the corner.

I myself am driving a brand-new bright red Ford F-150 pickup truck. This feels important. If you've never been in one of these monsters, it's hard to describe how mighty and right it makes you feel. You understand why men who drive trucks drive like assholes: *(a)* There's a good chance that, despite mirrors the size of a normal human car's hubcaps, they simply don't see other vehicles. *(b)* In some larger, existential sense, all other vehicles have ceased to exist. Driving an F-150 makes you want to run over smaller, lesser cars. It makes you want to invade smaller, lesser countries.

So, with all this fine American muscle rumbling underneath me, I roll up to The Truck Stop. Except, for all its *American Graffiti* trappings, this is no temple to car culture. The pumps are covered. A handwritten sign reads no gas. The shiny, souped-up vehicles everybody's lining up to see aren't here for a drag race. And those beautiful kids may have youthful hunger in their eyes, but not, it would seem, for young love. A couple, he in black-on-black Yankees cap, she in Snooki sweats and flip-flops, wander arm in arm between the idling trucks. "Ohmigod," she squeals as they approach one. "Those homemade pierogies are uh-mazing." They kiss.

Elsewhere, they're lining up for lobster rolls at the Lobsta Truck; for artisanal Pittsburgh-style "Sammies" at Steel City Sandwich; for salad, of all things, at the Flatiron Truck: butter lettuce and heirloom carrots sliced mandoline thin, tossed with mustard vinaigrette, and topped with pieces of steak marinated in star anise, cooked *sous vide*, finished on the grill, and sent off with a puff of shiitake-mushroom dust. If there's a muse here, an avatar presiding over all this transmutation of energy to young America's stomach from organs slightly farther south, it's the mud-flap girl emblazoned on the most popular truck in the lot. She's a classic: in recline, chest thrust forward, dewy lips lifted and parted to receive—yes, ah yes—a Gruyère and double-cream-Brie grilled cheese sandwich.

But you know this. You've been there, or some version of there. Food   5 trucks have become to food scenes what porcupines are said to be to a forest: a sign that you've got a healthy, vibrant ecosystem at work. And by the time I stood before The Grilled Cheese Truck, midway through a monthlong journey from sea to shining sea, I could already state without equivocation that the nation's food ecosystem was thriving. I'd had magnificent meals in an airport and in a hospital. My coastal urban bigotry had been undermined by amazing eating in small out-of-the-way cities. Just that morning, on a seedy stretch of the Venice Beach boardwalk, where the air hangs heavy with the smell of medical marijuana and white-man's dreads, I had breakfasted on artisanal bread pudding and Blue Bottle coffee from a closet-sized counter squirreled amid the henna-tattoo and cheap-sunglass shops.

It had long since become clear that the fortuitous collision of political, philosophical, health, and fashion movements that together form the Food Revolution had, over the past decade, penetrated nearly every corner of American life. We are now a nation with so many farmers' markets that *The New York Times* has reported that *farmers* are getting a little worried. A nation in which phrases like "Kosher in Fargo?" or "Filipino in Detroit?"—which once would have been failed pitches for fish-out-of-water sitcoms—are now perfectly reasonable queries on foodie boards. We the people have come to rely on, indeed feel entitled to, good food *everywhere*.

Given the generally blah economic climate, what, it's fair to ask, exactly the hell is going on? How to square the seemingly unstoppable upward trajectory of our eating lives with the supposed downward trajectory of nearly everything else?

> How to square the seemingly unstoppable upward trajectory of our eating lives with the supposed downward trajectory of nearly everything else?

Analyze

1. The author takes considerable time in the introductory paragraphs of this article to set a certain tone and to present himself and his attitude in a certain way. Looking at the language, his description of himself (and of others who drive the same vehicle he does), how does he set this tone? Why, and to what effect?

2. How does Martin draw upon aspects of popular culture to make his points about food? How do these references help to define the context in which this "food revolution" is taking place?

3. In what ways does Martin's physical journey—the road trip—serve as a metaphor for a more complex, intellectual project?

Explore

1. "Indeed, there is no place left—geographic or institutional—where good food would be noteworthy simply for being unlikely." How might we reconcile the increased likelihood of finding great food in unlikely places with noticeable absences in certain areas, for instance— urban ones? Look beyond Martin's essay to find one unlikely place where good food prevails and compare it with another where access to any food is problematic.

2. Discuss what the author means when he writes, "How to square the seemingly unstoppable upward trajectory of our eating lives with the supposed downward trajectory of nearly everything else?"

3. Martin's journey takes him to good food in unlikely places (a hospital, a truck stop, etc.). Research a similarly unusual or unlikely food phenomenon in your own community, whether it's at home, at your college, or where you work. What do you find? Interview several of your colleagues or family members (or friends) and determine how these first-hand accounts reveal (or not) the effect of these "food surprises" on the atmosphere of that place and the people who work or live there.

Beverly Cox and Clara Sue Kidwell
"A Native American Thanksgiving"

The food editor of *Native People's Magazine* and the former editor and director of styling for *Cook's Magazine*, Cox is a prolific cookbook writer. Clara Sue Kidwell is a professor of Native American Studies at the University of California, Berkeley. She also is assistant director of cultural resources for the National Museum of the American Indian at the Smithsonian Institution. "A Native American Thanksgiving" was published the week of Thanksgiving in 1991.

How much do you think you know about Thanksgiving?

The actual site of the first Thanksgiving feast shared by English settlers and Native Americans in the New World has not been determined.

We know that John Smith and his group of Jamestown settlers in Virginia probably would not have survived the winter of 1608 without the help of Pocahontas and her father, Powhatan, the powerful chief of the Powhatan Confederacy.

It is also recorded that the Pilgrims, landing farther north at Plymouth in 1620, might well have perished without the generosity and advice of Squanto of the Pautuxet tribe and Chief Massasoit of the neighboring Wampanoughs.

Wherever the first celebration took place, one thing is certain: Early English settlers in both colonies had reason to thank the Indians for their survival.

The Algonquian-speaking tribes who greeted the settlers in Virginia 5 and Massachusetts were skilled hunters, gatherers and farmers who treated the newcomers with the hospitality traditionally extended to guests, sharing with them both food and knowledge of how to survive in the wilderness.

The diet of the Algonquian- and Iroquoian-speaking peoples of the Northeast included a wide variety of nuts, berries, seeds, roots, wild game and seafood. Lobsters, clams and mussels abounded in coastal areas, although lobster—such a delicacy now—was used mainly as bait when Indian men fished for bass and cod. Deer filled the woods.

If turkey was served at the first Pilgrim Thanksgiving, it was probably a small, tough, wild bird, likely seized by hand as it gobbled up the kitchen leavings around an Indian village. An abundance of ducks flew overhead and paddled in the lakes and marshes.

Farming was an important part of life. The Iroquois people planted large crops of corn, beans and squash, which they called the Three Sisters (an Iroquois myth tells of three beautiful maidens who were often seen walking by moonlight around the fields).

Farming was largely women's work. Mohawk women poked holes into the ground with digging sticks and sowed their seeds. When corn plants first sprouted, the women piled dirt up around their bases to support them and protect them from insects.

10   Later they planted beans—the second of the Three Sisters—near the corn so the bean runners could climb the corn stalks. Squashes were also planted around the base of the corn so that their broad leaves would keep the soil moist and cool.

We may not know the date on which the "first Thanksgiving" took place, but the date on which Americans celebrate Thanksgiving today was originally proclaimed by Abraham Lincoln in 1863 and set as an official federal holiday by a resolution of Congress in 1941.

And, while Americans set aside a single day to give thanks, Native Americans gave thanks at various times throughout the year in different parts of the country. Northwest Coast people, for instance, celebrated the first salmon run of the season by preparing a ceremonial feast of the first salmon caught.

On the Great Plains, the Sioux, the Cheyenne and other tribes held a feast whenever a young boy killed his first animal. Even the smallest bird or mouse was the main course. The feast recognized the boy's new skill and his promise as a successful hunter.

The Chippewa in the Great Lakes region had feasts of wild rice in mid-September after a successful harvest. The Chippewa Indian community in Minneapolis and St. Paul still has an annual Mahnomin (the Chippewa word for wild rice) festival in the fall to give thanks.

15   The Iroquois people began a cycle of ceremonies with a maple festival in early spring and ended with the harvest festival in the fall, as the work of planting and gathering ended.

Thanksgiving feasts and ceremonies of various kinds go on today in many Indian communities throughout the country. Giving thanks is also an ongoing part of life. If Native Americans were skilled hunters and planters, they were also aware that they had to maintain proper relationships with the spirits of nature who were the source of their bounty. They thanked the spirits with the hope that they would be generous in the coming hunting or planting season.

The Thanksgiving menu given below (from the book, *Spirit of the Harvest: North American Indian Cooking*, by Beverly Cox and Martin Jacobs (Stewart, Tabori & Chang, 1991: $35)) includes a variety of dishes made from ingredients typical of the Native American cooking. Traditionally, food was not served in courses as we would serve it today. At an Indian feast, sweet and savory dishes were served together.

If one followed Indian custom, everything would be eaten out of the cooking pot, using one's fingers or perhaps slabs of bread made from beech nut or cornmeal mixed with water and baked on hot stones.

Some of the cooking techniques and ingredients in the recipes were introduced into Indian diets by Europeans. The menu represents, then, the mixing of two cultures that took place because of that first Thanksgiving, wherever and whenever it was.

 ## PUMPKIN SOUP

1 small (12-inch) pumpkin or 1 (29-ounce) can solid-pack pumpkin
1 to 2 tablespoons peanut or sunflower oil (if using fresh pumpkin)
Salt, pepper
1 to 3 tablespoons maple syrup or honey
¼ to ½ teaspoon ground dried spicebush berries or allspice
3 to 4 cups chicken or beef stock

Thinly sliced green onion tops, chopped hazelnuts and roasted pumpkin and hulled sunflower seeds for garnish

If using fresh pumpkin, place pumpkin in baking dish and roast at 350 degrees until easily pierced with knife, about 1 hour. Allow pumpkin to cool. Slice off top and scoop out seeds. Clean pumpkin fibers from seeds and discard fibers.

Toss seeds with oil and season to taste with salt. Spread out on baking sheet and return to oven 15 to 20 minutes or until crisp and golden. Reserve for garnish (or for snacks). Scrape pumpkin flesh from shell and mash or puree in food processor if smoother texture is desired.

Place fresh or canned pumpkin in large saucepan. Season to taste with salt, pepper, maple syrup and spicebush berries. Gradually stir in enough stock to give soup consistency desired. Simmer over medium heat about 5 minutes or until hot. Serve soup in small pumpkin or squash shells. Garnish with green onions, hazelnuts and pumpkin and sunflower seeds. Makes 4 to 6 servings.

Each serving contains about:
260 calories; 659 mg sodium; 1 mg cholesterol; 16 grams fat; 25 grams carbohydrates; 9 grams protein; 3.08 grams fiber; 56% calories from fat.

CRAB APPLES HELD *a special place at Northwest Coast tribal feasts. Steamed, then mashed and sometimes combined with berries, the crab apples were always served with eulachon (candlefish) oil to important guests. Traders and missionaries introduced both brown and white sugar. Brown sugar was made into cakes and later boiled down to a syrup. Lumps of brown sugar were served at feasts. In this recipe, brown sugar syrup is used to glaze a Canada goose, which traditionally would have been spit-roasted on a green alder- or apple-wood branch held over a wood fire. Since this is impractical for most modern cooks, we suggest using a standard covered grill. We've also provided instructions for that most modern device: the oven.*

GRILLED CANADA GOOSE

5 to 7 pounds charcoal
1 (8-pound) wild Canada or domestic goose, dressed
2 teaspoons ground ginger
Salt, pepper
2 cups chopped dried crab apples or other dried apples
1 cup dried cranberries, optional
½ cup dried currants
1 ½ cups alder or apple- wood chips, soaked in water, optional
Brown Sugar Sauce

Prepare charcoal grill, with cover, using about 5 pounds charcoal. Rinse goose and pat dry. Remove any excess fat from body cavity.

If using domestic goose, pierce skin along base of breast and thighs so fat will drain off. Rub goose with 1 teaspoon ginger and sprinkle lightly with salt and pepper.

Combine dried crab apples, cranberries, currants and remaining ginger in mixing bowl. Stuff body cavity with mixture. Truss goose.

Arrange red-hot coals around large drip pan. Sprinkle damp wood chips over coals. Place goose on grill, over drip pan. Cover grill leaving all vents open. Cook, allowing 15 to 25 minutes per pound, until juices run clear with no hint of pink when thickest part of thigh is pierced. Baste with Brown Sugar Sauce during last hour of cooking time. During grilling, check coals every hour, and add few more if necessary to maintain heat. Allow goose to sit about 15 minutes before carving. Makes 6 servings.

Note: Goose may also be oven-cooked. Prepare bird as instructed in recipe. Roast goose at 400 degrees 45 minutes to 1 hour, then lower oven to 325 degrees and roast 1 1/4 to 1 1/2 hours, until juices run clear with no hint of pink when thickest part of thigh is pierced. Baste with Brown Sugar Sauce during last 1/2 hour of cooking.

BROWN SUGAR SAUCE

¾ cup brown sugar, packed
2 tablespoons water

Combine brown sugar and water in small saucepan. Cook over medium-high heat until mixture comes to boil. Continue stirring and cooking 2 minutes, then remove from heat.

Each serving contains about:
516 calories; 136 mg sodium; 114 mg cholesterol; 28 grams fat; 35 grams carbohydrates; 32 grams protein; 0.58 grams fiber; 48% calories from fat.

WATERCRESS, *a member of the mustard family, grows wild in brooks throughout the United States. Native Americans gathered a variety*

of wild greens, including watercress, and ate them raw in salads. Northeastern Indian tribes made vinegar from the sap of the sugar maple tree. The sap was combined with buds and twigs and left in a sunny spot to ferment, then strained through a cloth. An Indian salad dressing might combine a vinegar made from fermented maple sap with a sweetener, such as maple syrup, honey, or sugar and oil.

WILD WATERCRESS SALAD

2 to 3 bunches wild or cultivated watercress
3 tablespoons cider vinegar
2 tablespoons maple syrup
¼ cup sunflower oil
1 green onion, thinly sliced
Salt, pepper

Rinse watercress in 2 to 3 changes cold water. Remove and discard tough stems. Combine vinegar and maple syrup in salad bowl. Gradually whisk in sunflower oil. Add watercress and green onion. Toss lightly. Season to taste with salt and pepper. Serve immediately. Makes 6 servings.

Each serving contains about:
100 calories; 56 mg sodium; 0 mg cholesterol; 9 grams fat; 5 grams carbohydrates; 0 grams protein; 0.11 grams fiber; 82% calories from fat.

EARLY EUROPEAN SETTLERS *in North America learned from the Indians to make large unleavened loaves of corn bread. The dough was spread on a board and placed beside the fire to bake. When cooked on one side, it was turned over and baked on the other side. Often the blade of a hoe was used both to prop up the board beside the fire for baking and as an improvised cooling rack on which the baked loaves would lean.*

HOE CAKES (ALGONQUIAN NOKAKE)

2 cups water
2 cups cornmeal
1 teaspoon salt
2 tablespoons butter
1 tablespoon chopped fresh dill, optional

Bring water to boil in saucepan. Stir in cornmeal, salt, butter and dill. Place in buttered 8-inch square pan and bake at 375 degrees 25 minutes. Cut into squares and serve. Makes 6 servings.

Each serving contains about:
204 calories; 434 mg sodium; 10 mg cholesterol; 5 grams fat; 36 grams carbohydrates; 4 grams protein; 0.35 grams fiber; 20% calories from fat.

THOUGH NATIVE AMERICAN *pie making on the Great Plains dates back only to the 1800s (when reservations were established), mincemeat is closely related to pemmican, one of the most traditional Indian foods. In fish-eating areas, such as the Pacific Northwest, dried fish is used as the base. In the Great Plains, venison or buffalo jerky is pounded and mixed with dried berries and melted tallow. This recipe for Venison Mincemeat Pie comes from Margaret Ketchum Walker of Cheyenne, Wyoming, whose late husband, George Walker, was a member of the Sac and Fox tribe.*

VENISON MINCEMEAT PIE

1 quart apple cider
2 cups seedless raisins
½ cup dried currants
½ cup dried tart or sweet cherries (if not available, substitute currants)
3 apples, peeled, seeded and chopped
1 cup chopped suet

½ pound ground venison
2 teaspoons salt
2 teaspoons ground cinnamon
2 teaspoons ground ginger
2 teaspoons ground cloves
1 teaspoon grated nutmeg
½ teaspoon ground allspice
1 unbaked (9-inch) double crust Traditional Pie Crust
½ egg, beaten with 1 tablespoon milk or water

Combine cider, raisins, currants and cherries in large saucepan. Cover and simmer over low heat 1 1/2 to 2 hours. Add apples, suet, venison, salt, cinnamon, ginger, cloves, nutmeg and allspice. Simmer 2 hours longer (mixture will be about 4 cups). If making more than few days ahead, divide mixture in half and freeze.

Fill chilled pie crust with mincemeat. Arrange strips of top crust over filling and brush lightly with egg wash. Fold overhanging edges of crust over strips and flute edges. Place in lower third of 400-degree oven and bake 15 minutes. Reduce oven temperature to 350 degrees and bake 40 to 50 minutes until crust is golden brown and filling is bubbling. Makes 1 (9-inch) pie, or 12 servings.

  ## TRADITIONAL PIE CRUST

1 ½ cups unbleached flour
½ teaspoon salt
6 tablespoons lard or vegetable shortening, chilled
¼ cup plus 1 tablespoon cold water

Combine flour and salt in mixing bowl. Cut in lard until mixture resembles coarse meal. Gradually stir in cold water until dough comes together. Turn dough onto lightly floured surface. Divide into 2 rounds, 1/3 portion for top crust and 2/3 portion for bottom crust. Wrap in wax paper or plastic wrap. Refrigerate at least 30 minutes before rolling out, or freeze if making several days in advance.

Roll out larger round at least 10 inches in diameter and 1/4-inch thick. Line 9-inch pie plate. Cut remaining crust into strips for top, using serrated cutter, if desired. Chill crusts at least 1/2 hour.

Each serving contains about:
380 calories; 521 mg sodium; 32 mg cholesterol; 15 grams fat; 57 grams carbohydrates; 8 grams protein; 1.04 grams fiber; 35% calories from fat.

CRANBERRIES HAVE LONG *been used by Eastern Woodland tribes as a vitamin-rich addition to fall and winter dishes. As we researched cranberry recipes, we became intrigued by the combination of ingredients and cooking methods used in a recipe for cranberry pudding included in "Indian Cooking" by Herb Walker. The recipe adaptation given below produces a fluffy marshmallow-like concoction that will both please and mystify those who consume it.*

FLUFFY CRANBERRY PUDDING

3 cups cranberry juice
½ cup maple syrup
½ cup uncooked cream of wheat
1 cup Cranberry-Maple Sauce

Place cranberry juice and syrup in medium saucepan and bring to boil over medium heat. Gradually add cream of wheat, stirring constantly. Reduce heat to low and cook, stirring constantly, 10 minutes longer.

Transfer to large mixing bowl and beat 10 minutes, until pudding is almost tripled in volume. Serve warm or chilled. Top with Cranberry-Maple Sauce. Makes 6 servings.

CRANBERRY–MAPLE SAUCE

2 cups fresh cranberries
1 cup maple syrup

1 cup water
¼ teaspoon ground dried spicebush berries or allspice, optional

Combine cranberries, maple syrup and water in saucepan. Bring to boil over medium-high heat. Reduce heat to medium-low and cook, stirring often, about 15 minutes, until berries have burst and sauce has thickened. Stir in spicebush berries. Cool and serve at room temperature. Sauce is best made several hours in advance so that flavors blend. Makes 2 cups.

Each serving contains about:
340 calories; 13 mg sodium; 0 mg cholesterol; 0 grams fat; 85 grams carbohydrates; 2 grams protein; 0.38 grams fiber; 1% calories from fat.

Analyze

1. Clearly, the article is written to be highly informative. It is also meant to counter our fairly narrow view as Americans of what this holiday is about. Looking at their use of language—and their fairly short paragraphs—analyze the tone constructed by the authors. How would you characterize that tone? What effect does it have?

2. What can we learn by looking at the recipes provided by the authors? Describe the recipes, the ingredients used, and the methods of preparation. Look at these through the lens of a historian or an anthropologist: how would you describe what you notice, and what conclusions do you draw from this information?

3. How is Thanksgiving a "hybrid" tradition?

Explore

1. Cox and Kidwell note that "If one followed Indian custom, everything would be eaten out of the cooking pot, using one's fingers..." Are there customs you follow that are equally reflective of your family, your culture, or both? What are these? How do they shape the Thanksgiving holiday for you?

2. The authors write that "Farming was an important part of life" for Native Americans at the time of the first Thanksgiving. Cox and Kidwell make a very global statement here with little information.

Research the importance of farming at the time of the first Thanksgiving. Why was farming important? What evidence have you found to support its importance?

3. Cox and Kidwell also mention that "Farming was largely women's work," and presumably, other chores related to the meal were women's work as well. What has changed, and what is similar, from that snapshot of Thanksgivings past to Thanksgivings present, meals with which you are familiar?

Josephine Beoku-Betts
"We Got Our Way of Cooking Things: Women, Food, and Preservation of Cultural Identity among the Gullah"

Josephine Beoku-Betts is a professor of sociology and women's studies at the University of Wisconsin, Madison. Her primary research is on feminist and postcolonial discourses on science, particularly the experiences of African scientists. This essay explores issues of food preparation and gender inequality.

How is gender inequality manifested in this particular culture?

This article examines the significance of cultural practices related to food and women's role in the formation and continuance of these practices in Gullah communities in the Sea Islands of Georgia and South Carolina. I argue that although food preparation, under pressure of dominant cultural practices, may be viewed as a measure of gender inequality and women's subordination in the household, analysis of the relationship between women and food preparation practices can broaden understanding of the construction and maintenance of tradition in marginalized cultural groups, a neglected aspect of the study of social organization within sociology. The study uses ethnographic data based on field observations and semistructured interviews with 22 women over several visits made between 1989 and 1992.

Food preparation and dietary practices have rarely been studied by sociologists, although they hold great potential for an understanding of gendered social relations, knowledge construction, and cultural identity in communities. Because this area of work and cultural activity traditionally has been viewed as a "natural role" for women, its value has not been acknowledged seriously or appreciated in the production of cultural knowledge systems (Smith 1987, 18–9). Analysis of the relationship between women and food preparation practices, however, can broaden our understanding of the construction and maintenance of tradition in culturally defined systems, a neglected aspect of the study of social organization within the discipline of sociology. Feminist studies show that examination of this aspect of women's work clarifies the character and significance of women's household activities (DeVault 1991; Oakley 1974). Even though food preparation perpetuates relations of gender inequality in the household, under given circumstances it can provide a valued identity, a source of empowerment for women, and a means to perpetuate group survival (DeVault 1991, 232).

This article illuminates how women, as primary actors responsible for managing and preparing food in the household and the community, contribute to our understanding of the formation and continuance of food-related cultural practices in Gullah communities. I argue that although food preparation, under pressure of dominant cultural practices, may be viewed as a measure of gender inequality and of women's subordination in the household, it also can promote resistance and strengthen cultural identity in marginalized cultural groups.

By drawing on the analytical constructs of an Afrocentric value system (self-reliance, women-centered networks, the use of dialogue and connectedness with community, spirituality, and extended family), Black feminist studies provide a framework for conceptualizing knowledge construction and cultural identity from the perspective of Black women's lives (Gilkes 1988; Gray White 1985; Collins 1990; Reagon 1986; Steady 1981; Terborg-Penn 1987). These studies show that cultural beliefs, values, and traditions are transmitted largely in women-dominated contexts such as the home, the church, and other community settings.

5   The work of scholars such as Angela Davis (1971, 7) illuminates how African American women have contributed to the formation and continuance of African American cultural institutions. Davis argues that under slavery, cultural beliefs and practices were transmitted largely by the

performance of nurturing and caregiving roles, which enslaved women provided primarily in the family and the community. Although caregiving activities may have reinforced women's oppression in the household, these roles were significant in that they provided women with the only meaningful opportunity to influence their families in ways not immediately subject to control by their oppressors.

In discussing women's role in more recent struggles affecting African Americans, Johnson Reagon (1986, 79) argues that African American women have helped to create and maintain a cultural identity in their communities that is independent of the dominant culture. For example, she contends that if women did not teach these traditions to younger members of their communities, the youths would never know how far African Americans had come, or the depth of that struggle. Hill Collins also stresses the importance of viewing the Black woman as "the something within that shape[s] the culture of resistance and patterns of consciousness and self-expression in the Black community" (1990, 142). She postulates that Black women may seem to conform to institutional rules of the dominant culture, but closer examination reveals that historically they have resisted such structures by promoting their own self-definitions and self-valuations in safe spaces that they create among other Black women.

This article contributes to this discourse by examining the significance of cultural practices related to food and the role of women in forming and continuing these practices in Gullah communities in the coastal region of Georgia and South Carolina. I give particular attention to the significance of the natural environment as a primary food source in the culture, the centrality of particular foods such as rice, the rituals and norms of food preparation, and efforts to preserve these practices under pressure of social change and intrusion by the dominant culture.

Historically in Gullah communities, both men and women have played a vital role in procuring and preparing the food necessary for their families' survival. Studies, however, reveal very few examples of men's activities in domestic food preparation. Food preparation in Gullah households tends to be gender-specific and organized around particular tasks; each successive task is more highly gender-stratified. Although men are more likely to engage in activities such as hunting, fishing, gardening, and preparing meat and seafood for cooking and barbecues, women also participate in these activities when they choose to do so. Although most men are knowledgeable about cooking, and most mothers seem to teach both their sons and daughters how to cook, men rarely cook regularly in the household. Women more often take responsibility for cooking and feeding, and they appear to be the custodians of food rituals and practices that perpetuate the group's survival.

Data Sources and Analysis

This study uses ethnographic data based on my field observations and semi-structured interviews with 22 Gullah women in the Sea Islands and neighboring mainland communities in South Carolina (Wadmalow, St. Helena, John's, Edisto, and Coosaw Islands) and Georgia (Sapelo and St. Simon's Islands, and Harris Neck community) over several visits made between 1989 and 1992. My research interest in this region stems from my background as an African scholar who was raised in a West African rice-cultivating society; later I conducted research on rural households and rice cultivation in that society. As a result, I felt that I was uniquely prepared to examine historical and cultural connections in the food practices of West African and Gullah rice cultures. To collect naturalistic observational data on the significance of Gullah food practices, I arranged to stay with selected families in two of the communities I studied. I also kept a journal of my daily experiences and observations while living with my host families.

10   Women participating in the study were drawn from each of the communities mentioned above. The criteria for selection were that they were descendants of formerly enslaved African Americans from these islands and that they had been raised there. I found participants through key individuals and community organizations. Through snowballing and by a process of proving my credibility as an African woman researcher interested in making cultural connections between the rice culture of West Africa and the rice culture of the Gullah, I selected a number of women willing to work with me as study participants.

Semistructured interviews were designed to give the participants an opportunity to voice their opinions and experiences in their own terms. Although the interviews followed guidelines, they allowed ample opportunity for women to elaborate or to introduce issues they considered relevant. Interviews with each participant usually were completed in one and a half to two hours, although in some cases subsequent interviews were necessary. Interviews focused on participants' knowledge of Gullah food practices and rituals, management of food practices in the home and community, and their role in preserving and transmitting these practices to later generations. About two thirds of the interviews were tape recorded; the others, with women unwilling to be taped, were written down verbatim.

The strategies I used to gain access and establish trust among the participants varied according to the situation of each community. In communities where local residents seemed to be better informed about their African heritage, I worked under the auspices of key individuals and community groups. Sometimes they sent a representative to accompany me to interviews and extended invitations to social events to which I might not have had access otherwise. In other communities, where local residents seemed more reluctant to talk to outside researchers because of negative experiences in the past, it worked to my advantage to distance myself from my university affiliation and to engage myself in the life of these communities. In one community, regular attendance at church services and midday meals at a local community center helped me develop a kinlike relationship with two respected senior women. They taught me the importance of being associated as the guest, relative, or friend of a respected person to gain acceptance among community residents.

Study participants range in age from 35 to 75. They include nine widows living alone or with their children or grandchildren, two single parents, and eleven married women living with their families. Most of the younger women are employed in service or public-sector jobs; the older women are more likely to be homemakers or retired from wage employment. Although the youngest respondent has two years of college education and the oldest has no formal schooling, education for the majority ranges from completion of the third to the twelfth grade. All names used in the study are pseudonyms.

Eight other women whom I asked to interview declined to participate in the study. Most of these women came from one particular community and were the daughters of older women who were participating. They were more ambivalent about my presence than were their mothers because they felt that past experiences with university researchers or journalists had proved to be exploitative. Time constraints from family responsibilities and wage employment also contributed to these women's reluctance to participate.

In analyzing the interviews with study participants, I regarded their narratives both as individual accounts of daily experiences in managing food practices and as a form of custodianship and conveyance of oral traditions about the significance of the Gullah food system. I took this approach because many of the interviews contained an element of reflection about the past as a backdrop for commentary on the present. Although some of this reflection was deliberate because of my interest in establishing historical and cultural connections, the participants and the other community members to whom I spoke also tended to organize their talk so as to provide a background to contextualize their meaning.

The data analysis strategies used in this study are qualitative and inductive. As described by Anselm Strauss, qualitative research is a form of data analysis that "occurs at various levels of explicitness, abstraction, and systematization" (1990, 4–6). It involves extensive use of field observations and intensive use of interviews as data collection techniques, and emphasizes "the necessity for grasping the actors' viewpoints for understanding interaction, process, and social change" (pp. 4–6).

The data were transcribed almost verbatim, although I did some light editing (such as inserting explanatory or connecting words in a bracket) or excluded small sections of an interview when the material seemed somewhat peripheral to the issue under discussion. After transcribing the taped data, I searched for themes repeated in both taped and untaped interviews, focusing on the rituals and management of food preparation over several stages of the process. My aim was to develop a detailed understanding of these ritual practices in the Gullah household. By looking for detailed, perhaps even mundane, information about each stage of food preparation, styles of cooking, flavors of food, eating practices, and (if possible) the meanings attached to these practices, I hoped to show any variety occurring among households and to establish connections for historical and sociological analysis. I also used my daily journal entries to provide context when analyzing the data.

The Significance of the Gullah

Gullah communities in the Sea Islands and neighboring mainland regions in Georgia and South Carolina provide a unique opportunity to study some of the distinctive elements of African cultural influences on African American culture in the United States. Despite variations in the demographic structures and economic practices of communities on or near these islands, strong similarities exist in proximity of location and in historical and cultural background. One significant characteristic of these communities, for example, is that most residents are descendants of enslaved Africans who worked on these islands as early as the seventeenth century. Beginning in that period, Africans were captured and transported as slaves from various regions in Africa, extending from Angola to the Upper Guinea Coast region of West Africa. Between 1670 and 1800, however, Africans from rice-cultivating regions in West Africa, such as Liberia, Sierra Leone, Senegal, Gambia, and Guinea, were sought because of their knowledge of cultivation of rice, which was then a lucrative crop in Georgia and South Carolina (Holloway 1990, 4; Littlefield 1981; Wood 1974). Rice planters were particularly interested in enslaving Africans from the "Rice Coast" of West Africa because the planters themselves lacked knowledge about rice cultivation in tropical conditions. The system of rice cultivation adopted in these coastal regions of Georgia and South Carolina drew on the labor patterns and technical knowledge of the enslaved West Africans (Littlefield 1981; Opala 1987; Wood 1974).

Because of the geographical isolation of these islands, cohesive communities evolved and preserved African cultural traditions more fully than in any other group of African Americans in the United States. These traditions are represented in the Gullah language spoken among Sea Islanders, in birth and naming practices, in folktales, in handicrafts such as grass-basket weaving, carved walking sticks, and fishing nets, in religious beliefs and practices, and in a food culture based on rice (Creel 1990; Georgia Writers' Project [1940] 1986; Jones-Jackson 1987; Opala 1987; Turner 1949).

Today the sources of livelihood in these Sea Island communities vary 20 according to available economic opportunities. In communities such as John's, Wadmalow, Edisto, St. Helena, Ladies, and Hilton Head Islands, many inhabitants are engaged in the vegetable truck industry; others are involved in fishing, crabbing, and marketing of crafts. Most of the young and the old in these communities garden, fish, hunt, and sell crafts and other services to supplement their incomes (Jones-Jackson 1987, 17). As a result of development of the tourist industry, such as on Hilton Head and St. Simon's Islands, many inhabitants (particularly women) work in minimum wage service positions. Limited employment opportunities on islands still inaccessible by bridge, such as Sapelo Island in Georgia and Daufuskie Island in South Carolina, have led many of the younger or more highly educated community members to seek work elsewhere, causing an imbalance in the age structure of their populations. Sapelo Island, for example, has a population of just 67 people; a disproportionate number are in the economically dependent years, over 60 and under 18.

Connections between the Natural Environment and Gullah Food Practices

The value of self-sufficiency in food supply is an integral aspect of the Gullah food system. Men and women of all ages are conversant with hunting, fishing, and gardening as ways to provide food. From an early age, both men and women are socialized into the concept and the practice of self-sufficiency as a primary goal of the food system and are encouraged to participate in the outdoor food-procuring activities of parents and other kin or community members. Velma Moore, a woman in her mid-40s and a key participant in my study, became sensitive to environmental causes when, as a child, she accompanied both parents on daily walks in the woods. This experience taught her a variety of survival skills involving the use of the island's natural resources for subsistence and medicine. She learned how and where to collect medicinal herbs, and when and for what purpose they should be used. She also learned various folk remedies that had been passed down in her family for generations, such as life everlasting tea for colds or leaves of the mullien plant for fever. Velma recollected that when she was a child, her mother kept these herbs on hand in the kitchen and stood over a reluctant patient to make sure every sip of the tea was consumed. Now married and the mother of five children, Velma pointed out that she encourages the practice of these traditions among her sons and daughters. She even performs regionally as a storyteller and writes local newspaper articles about the significance of these traditions in her culture.

Grandparents also play an important role in developing children's skills in food self-sufficiency. A typical example was Maisie Gables, a lively and active woman about 70 years of age. When I interviewed Miss Maisie, as she was called, I did not know that our scheduled appointments conflicted with her plans to go fishing with her five-year-old granddaughter, whom she was teaching to fish. Miss Maisie explained later that her granddaughter liked fishing from an early age, so she had decided to cultivate this interest by teaching her the necessary skills, as she had once been taught by her mother. By transmitting these skills, which are part of collective memory, the senior generation of Gullah women fosters and sustains cultural identity intergenerationally, thus broadening the base of cultural knowledge in the community.

While the Gullah depend on their natural surroundings as a reliable source of food, they also have a deep understanding of their coexistence with other living things and believe that the use of these resources should be moderate and nonexploitative. This sense of shared membership in the natural environment stems from Gullah belief systems, which emphasize harmony and social exchange between the human and the natural world. Such a view is influenced by African spiritual beliefs, which are community centered and involve a set of relationships involving God, the ancestors, other human beings (including those yet unborn), and other living and nonliving things. In this complex system of relationships, the well-being of the whole is paramount; individual existence is woven into the whole.[1]

Some aspects of this worldview are reflected in my interview with Velma Moore. She describes herself as a self-taught woman, although "self-taught" does not adequately describe her intelligence, strong will, and vast knowledge of Gullah history and culture. During one interview, she revealed that she, like many Gullah women, had been taught to hunt and would do so if necessary. Even so, she considered herself a keen environmentalist, with concern for the protection of nature, and would not engage in such activities for recreation because "it is not sporting to go up and kill animals that can't shoot you back." In other words, although she would rely on these resources for survival, anything beyond that purpose would threaten the harmony with nature.

Velma also expressed concern about the threat of environmental destruction in the region, a result of increasing tourism and economic development. She conceptualized this problem in connection with the struggle to preserve her own endangered cultural heritage: 25

> I always felt that if you don't deal with one and the other, if you just strictly deal with one, then you're losing the rest of it. Because you cannot have stabilization in a minority community in this area here unless you recognize the culture and the environment. And if you mess up the environment, and you move the people away because the environment is not right, then you are taking away their culture at the same time. So if you take away their land, you are also taking away the culture when you move the people, and so forth. (Velma Moore, 1991)

In making this connection between the threat of environmental destruction and the survival of her own cultural heritage, Velma reveals an awareness of her relationship, represented by culture, with other living beings, both human and nonhuman. She does not distinguish between the two because she perceives them as natural allies in a struggle to protect tradition from the intrusion of dominant cultural practices. Because both are woven into her existence, the survival of one depends on that of the other and must be defined and challenged from this standpoint.

Interviews with Gullah women suggest that engagement in fishing, gardening, hunting, and other outdoor activities is not based strictly on gender role divisions. Although many of the outdoor activities related to food procurement are men's domain, women are more likely to be associated with these activities than men are with activities regarded as women's domain. In other words, it seems that at each successive stage of food preparation (which can overlap somewhat), work activities become more gender-specific. This is true, for example, of role expectations in some fishing activities, such as men's use of the cast-net method and women's use of the reel and rod method.

I observed, however, that women make judgments about what is appropriate for them, which give them some flexibility in choosing activities they wish to pursue. In the Moore family, for instance, Velma's husband and son were responsible for planting vegetable crops for their garden, while Velma took responsibility for weeding and maintaining the garden. Velma, however, also expected their help in weeding because she did not want to be burdened with an activity that is monotonous and unpopular among men. Similar attitudes were revealed in my discussions with these women:

INTERVIEWER: Do you both do the same type of fishing?

VELMA MOORE: Well, yes and no. We both fish with the reel rod and he fishes with the cast net more than I do, although occasionally I go fishing with the cast net, too. But he basically does that.

INTERVIEWER: But you do cast-net fishing, too?

VELMA: Oh yeah. Most of us women here can. Most—I retract that—most of the older womens here can.

INTERVIEWER: You mean you still go hunting?

WILLIETTA DAVIES: Um hum. Like we [self and husband] go hunting for coon and thing in the night. We goes with the truck. We usually go at night anywhere around the island. I use an A-22 gun and a flashlight. I like to take the light and blind their eyes. I catch the eyes of that raccoon, and I stop and shoot.

INTERVIEWER: What do you catch?

WILLIETTA: Raccoon, possum.

INTERVIEWER: I can't believe that (laugh).

WILLIETTA: That's the only two sport I like now. I don't go dancing and I don't drink. I like to go [hunting] and fishing, and that's the truth. I love it.

The Centrality of Rice in Gullah Culture

Dependence on rice as a staple food is the most significant way the Gullah express cultural identity through food practices. Rice is the main food that links Gullah dietary traditions with the food traditions of West African rice cultures; women play a primary role in fostering the continuance of these practices. In such cultures a person is not considered to have eaten a full meal unless rice is included.

Although most Gullah families no longer cultivate rice regularly, people   30 are still conscious of its significance. Rice was described as the central part of the main family meal by at least 90 percent of the women I interviewed. Typical were responses like

> It's the one that makes us fat because we go to sleep on it. . . . My father used to say, "Eat something that sticks to your rib." (Velma Moore, 1991)
>
> Many people feel if rice isn't cooked, they haven't eaten. Take my grandson, for instance. No matter what you cook, whether it's potatoes or macaroni, you have to prepare a separate portion of rice for him. Otherwise he'll feel like he hasn't eaten. (Carla Bates, 1989)
>
> Rice is security. If you have some rice, you'll never starve. It is a bellyful. You should never find a cupboard without it. (Precious Edwards, 1992)
>
> Well, they have to have that rice 'cause, see, they be working hard at the farm and they have to have something to give them strength. They don't hardly bother with too much grits. They eat that grits in the morning now. But when dinnertime come they have to have that rice. They always say that Black people like too much rice. They don't eat like the white people. I don't know why they always say so. (Wilma Davies, 1991)

Because of Gullah women's daily involvement in food preparation in the home, they are very conversant with the stories and traditions passed down in their families about the significance of rice to their culture. On the occasions when I stayed as a guest in study participants' homes and helped prepare evening meals, women often shared stories and folktales with me, as well as songs and dances connected with their rice culture. On Sapelo Island I learned about formerly enslaved women who prepared special rice cakes made with honey for their families on particular days and months of the year, in observance of Muslim religious festivals.[2] Women also told me about folk traditions such as a song called "Blow Tony Blow." This accompanied a traditional dance still performed by Gullah women at cultural festivals to demonstrate how rice grain was removed from its husk with a flat, round, woven grass-basket called a fanner.

Several elderly women also recalled a time when rice held such a special place in their communities that children were not permitted to eat it except on Sundays or special occasions:

> They have folklore on rice down here. One of the things we grew up with, for instance, after the birth of a child you wasn't given rice—no rice. Because rice is supposed to been too starchy for the newborn baby to digest through the mother's milk, and so you wasn't given rice to eat at all. (Velma Moore, 1991)
>
> Some of the old folks believe that rice was also a cure for sick chickens, believe it or not. If your chicken were looking like they were kind of sick, you was to feed them raw rice, and it supposed to make them feel better. So they will take raw rice and toss them in the chicken yard. (Velma Moore, 1991)
>
> I've known people to parch rice and make their coffee. Put it in the frying pan or something, and you toss it lightly and keep shaking it lightly until it brown—you mix it and you can drink it, and you put water and you make [it] like coffee. (Velma Moore, 1991)

These accounts are distinctive because of choice of words and expressions used to communicate custodianship of these traditions. For example, the use of terms such as "security," "strength," "bellyful," "makes us fat" helps us to understand the role of this food not only as a means of survival when families are on the brink of economic disaster but also in times of plenty. Recollections of folklore traditions similarly enable us to explore the versatility of the culture, as expressed in the ability to transform rice into a form of coffee or a cure for animal ailments.

It is also significant that these recollections are narrated by women, because through such stories we learn how marginalized cultural groups construct a familiar and identifiable world for themselves in a dominant cultural setting. This point is addressed in Orsi's (1985) study of the role of popular religion in an Italian Catholic community in Harlem between 1880 and 1950. Orsi contends that identity is often constructed through a people's ability to discover who they are through memory. Although pressure from a dominant culture may weaken their ability to reproduce their knowledge and perceptions of themselves and of their world, the ability to remember and to create a communion of memory in the group provides the foundation for establishing membership and continuity of that group (p. 153). A parallel can be drawn in the role of Gullah women in maintaining a sense of shared tradition through food practices. Through their recollections of stories and songs and in their performance of dances and enactments of past traditions, they create a frame of reference alternative to those promoted in the dominant culture, while at the same time transmitting collective memory to the next generation.

One way of promoting an alternative frame of value reference through food practices is in the daily observance of strict rituals of rice preparation. In Gullah and West African rice cultures, for example, it is typical to commence the preparation of rice by picking out any dirt or dark looking grains from the rice before washing it. Then the rice is washed vigorously between the hands a number of times before it is considered clean enough for cooking. As a girl growing up in Sierra Leone, I was taught to cook rice in this way. I still follow this practice faithfully, even though most of the rice available for sale today in the United States is labeled as prewashed.

Whenever Gullah women speak of cooking rice, they distinguish between the various types of grains before explaining which cooking method will be most appropriate for a particular grain. They also take pride in describing the proper texture and consistency of a well-cooked pot of rice, although the suggestion that food must have a particular appearance to be satisfying is as culturally specific to the Gullah as to other ethnic groups.[3] Indeed, the belief that well-cooked rice must be heavy to be filling to the stomach is a cultural trait that the Gullah share with many African societies that eat heavy staple foods (Bascom 1977, 83; Friedman 1990, 83).

Gullah women also control the interaction of their food practices with those of the dominant culture by emphasizing the preferred place of rice in the main meal. For example, even though foods associated with other ethnic groups are generally eaten in Gullah families (e.g., lasagna, pizza, hamburgers), the women I interviewed tend to categorize such foods as snacks, not meals. To illustrate this point, the following discussion took place between me and one participant.

BETTY: Well, occasionally there is, you know, maybe lasagna. That is an occasional thing. Um, pizza is something that the kids love. And we have that like—that is never a meal. That's like if you have a bunch of guys dropping over and you are going to have pizza and pop, or tea, and a salad, you know, something like that. But it is never a meal, never.

INTERVIEWER: For you it is like a snack.

BETTY: Yeah, it is more like a snack. Yeah, definitely. It's like a snack. . . . need to have some type of rice. (Betty Smith, 1992)

In the following accounts of how various women cook a pot of white rice, we see how Gullah women establish cultural boundaries by situating rice at the center of their food system:

INTERVIEWER: How do you like to prepare your rice?

MAISIE: Well, I scrub it real good with water. With my hands scrub all that dirt off it.

INTERVIEWER: Yes, that's how we do it too back home.

MAISIE: I know, I'd say most Black people [do that]. Some Black people don't wash it you know, they try to take the vitamins from it. How can you eat all them germs? [If] I can't wash it [then] I don't want it. Then I put [the rice] in my pot and just put enough water, you know, to steam it without draining it off. I don't drain my rice. That's it. (Maisie Gables, 1991)

Two others commented

> Well, I don't like it real dry and I don't like it real soft. Just medium. Some people, they cook their rice so that all the grain just fall apart, but I don't like it real dry. I wash all that stuff off. Pick those strings and things out of it 'cause you have to take all that out. So we wash it good. Now the one that you plant and beat yourself has more

starch on it than the one you buy at the store. And you have to wash it real good. [Then] I average the water, put a little soda in it. I don't use so much salt now. And if it have too much water on it, I pour it off. Then I let it boil according to what kind of heat—now that you have electric or gas stove, now you see you turn it down medium until it soak down. I don't wait until it get real moist. Even up [turn the heat] on it to steam it down. (Willietta Davies, 1991)

and   40

Gosh, some of that depends on the rice too because you got short grain rice, you got long grain rice. And sometime you tend to fix one a little different from the other. I basically starts mine in cold water, I wash it in the same pot. I will just pour it in the pot. We don't measure it. So I just pour it in the pot what I think the amount I need. I go to the sink and I'll wash it . . . twice to clean it off. Pour the necessary water back on it and salt it and put it on the fire, and let it come to a full boil. The heat is usually reduced about three times, 'cause it's high until it starts boiling, then the middle, you let it cook a little normally for a while, then once all the water has evaporated or boiled into the rice, then you turn it real low so that it stay back there and soak and get just right. (Velma Moore, 1991)

Each of these examples reflects a sense of continuity of tradition as each stage of the process is described. For example, measurements are not discussed. This means that such recipes have been handed down by word of mouth and depend to some extent on one's particular taste. Also, each person emphasizes that the rice has to be washed well and that it must be cooked in just enough water to allow it to steam on its own, without the interference of draining or stirring. All of these descriptions might be said to follow a common tradition handed down from the period of slavery and still practiced in present-day West African rice cultures.[4]

These examples also reveal that the task of cooking rice is laborious and time-consuming. The Gullah, however, are fairly conservative in accepting innovations that might alter some of their existing practices. For example, labor-saving devices such as rice cookers, now in common use, do not seem to be used in the Gullah households I visited. One possible example of this cultural conservatism can be demonstrated in the story of a rice cooker

I gave to a family with whom I often stay and with whom I had shared the joys of a rice cooker when they visited my home. Although they appreciated the gift and showed it off to neighbors and family members, on two subsequent visits I noticed that it was still in its box and that rice was cooked in the familiar way. The family's reluctance to use the cooker more regularly might imply a lack of respect for custom, as well as fear of jeopardizing the survival of a tradition that is already endangered.

Such a line of reasoning is developed in Williams's (1985) analysis of the role of tamales in the food practices of Tejano migrant families. Williams suggests that in the wider context of Tejano culture, the preparation of tamales symbolizes the Tejanos' sense of who they are in an alien cultural setting and is a means of strengthening interpersonal bonds within the community. Tejano women play a key role in this process by monopolizing the traditional skills and knowledge necessary to enhance understanding of the significance of this food in their group identity (Williams 1985, 122–23). In the case of the Gullah, one could argue that by conforming to the traditional rice-cooking practices, women serve as a medium to control the limits of interaction between their food practices and those of the wider dominant culture. As shown by their covert reluctance to use my gift, which is a major time-saving device for those who prepare rice daily, my friends may interpret a change in their way of cooking to mean the eventual loss of skills and practices they are striving to keep alive for future generations of their people.

Rituals and Norms of Meal Preparation

Gullah culture is influenced strongly by rules and norms of West African food preparation. Many women who cook perpetuate these practices daily. One of these practices involves the selection, the amounts, and the combination of seasonings for food. These elements differentiate Gullah cooking practices from those of other cultures, according to many women I interviewed. Although the Gullah identify certain foods as their own, such as Hoppin' John (rice cooked with peas and smoked meat), red rice, rice served with a plate of shrimp and okra stew, and collard greens and cornbread, the interaction between European American, Native American, and African American food systems in the South has carried these popular southern dishes across ethnic lines. One way in which Gullah women try to control cultural boundaries in their way of cooking these foods, as distinct from other southern practices, is to assert that although similar foods are eaten by others in the South, their style of preparation and the type of seasonings they use are different. Just as West African cooking is characteristically well seasoned with salt, pepper, onions, garlic, and smoked meat and fish, Gullah food is flavored with a combination of seasonings such as onions, salt, and pepper, as well as fresh and smoked meats such as bacon, pigs' feet, salt pork, and (increasingly) smoked turkey wings (to reduce fat content). The Gullah women's views are expressed clearly in the following statements:

INTERVIEWER: As an African American living in this area, what do you think makes the food you eat different?

Culture and what's available to you. I call it a "make do" society on Sapelo because you can't run to the supermarket to get things. We are plain cooking. We use salt, pepper, and onion as basic additives. Our flavoring comes from the type of meat we put in it. Bacon is white folks' food, pig tails, neck bones, and ham hock is what we use. Soul food is what other Americans call it, but we consider these to be foods we always ate. We never label ourselves or our food. (Velma Moore, 1991)

On Sapelo you got things like red peas and rice. You know, they cook the same things on that side over there too, but we assume that we have the monopoly on it, that nobody cooks it the way we cook it . . . although they call it the same thing, the ingredients may be a little different than they use, or the taste is definitely different. So it's considered Sapelo food. I mean very few places you go [where] they cook oysters and rice or they cook clam and gravy the way we do, and stuff like that. So we got our way of cooking things. So we pretty proud of calling it Sapelo food. Yes. (Vanessa Buck, 1989)

By claiming these features of the food system as their own through daily cooking practices, and by situating this knowledge in the community through the use of such words as "we" and "strictly ours," the Gullah women maintain the credibility and validity of a familiar and recognizable tradition in resistance to pressure to conform to dominant cultural practices.

A strong preference for food produced and prepared from natural ingre- 45 dients is another norm of Gullah food practice. In many of my interviews, women stated that much of the food they prepare for their families is grown locally and naturally. When asked to comment on what makes Gullah food distinctive, Betty Smith, who is married, in her mid-40s, and an active community and church member, explains:

> A lot of what we eat is locally grown. Not the rice, but everything else. We dabble in other things that are imported, but . . . I guess the type of food we eat is indigenous to this area. It's what we have kind of grown up on. Most of my food is still prepared traditionally. My rice is usually boiled. I don't buy parboiled rice. I don't buy too many processed foods.

Annie Willis, who is in her 70s and also is active in church and community activities, lamented the demise of locally grown foods and expressed concern about the quality, taste, and health implications of store-bought foods:

> When I was a child coming up, we never used to put fertilizer in our crop to rush up the food. Food used to taste much better then than now. The old folks didn't have as many health problem as we are having and they ate all those forbidden foods. I think it's the fertilizers and chemicals they put in the food now. Seem to me that children were more healthy in those days than they are now. (Annie Willis, 1989)

The suggestion that the younger generation of Gullah may no longer prepare food strictly from naturally produced sources implies that the Gullah way of producing and preparing food is symbolically significant and a mark of their difference from other cultures. These statements also reflect a concern for the customs and traditions threatened by the influence of urban development in the region. By recalling a past that their foremothers and forefathers created, these women set a context in which the values of their community can be understood and reclaimed for future generations of Gullah.

The women's statements also reveal concern about the expectations of custom and tradition and how these can be accommodated to the demands of present-day family life and employment. Certainly many of the traditional foods eaten by the Gullah must be time-consuming to prepare, and one cannot always prepare them regularly if one has a full-time job or other commitments. How do women cope in these circumstances? Several women employed outside the home admitted that they had made some adjustments. Pat Forest, a 43-year-old woman who is employed full time as a nursing aide in a local health clinic, lives with her husband and four children, who range from 10 to 22 years of age. Because of the demands of her job and her role as primary caregiver in the family, I was not surprised to learn that she prepares red rice by using a precooked tomato-based sauce rather than cooking from scratch. Traditionalists in the community would frown on this type of cooking, however. Some women told me that they often save time by preparing part of the meal the night before serving it or that they might prepare traditional meals only on specific days of the week such as Saturday and Sunday. Some women even said that they simply do not set a time for the main evening meal until it is prepared to their satisfaction. Several also mentioned that they had taught their sons and daughters to take on some of the basic responsibilities of cooking, especially the daily pot of rice.

The ways in which these women manipulate time constraints to accommodate the customary demands of their food practices suggest efforts to uphold the central role of these food practices in the home, but also to exercise the flexibility needed for modern living. Although the women show respect for the culture and even express some guilt about failure to conform fully, their actions suggest that they are walking a fine line (albeit rationalized by time pressures): They are maintaining tradition while adjusting to modern influences that potentially might endanger that tradition.

In common with West African cultures, the Gullah tend to prepare 50 excess amounts of food for a meal in case someone should pay a visit. In West Africa, in fact, it would be embarrassing for a host to prepare or send out for food for unexpected guests (Bascom 1951, 52; Finnegan 1965, 67). Even under the economic constraints facing many West African societies today, such a tradition is upheld as strongly as possible because it is still viewed as a mark of prestige for both the head of the household and the cook. Although the Gullah do not necessarily view this tradition as a symbol of prestige, some of its elements are common in many of the homes I visited while conducting this study. As Velma Moore explained to me:

> I'm always able to feed another person in my home. People [here] will automatically cook something more just in case a stranger drops in.

As my study proceeded, I knew that the local residents were beginning to open up to me when, after several visits, I was offered food, whether or not it was mealtime.

Efforts to Transmit Traditional Food Practices

Much effort is being made to keep these traditions alive through oral tradition and everyday practice. Observers are pessimistic about what the future holds for a people who now consider themselves an endangered species (Singleton 1982, 38). One of the leading concerns expressed by residents of these communities is that the survival of this coastal culture is threatened by the rapid economic growth and development of tourist centers in the region. According to Emory Campbell, director of the Penn Center on St. Helena Island, South Carolina:

> The Black native population of these islands is now endangered, and we don't have too much time to protect oysters, fish, and crab. Developers just come in and roll over whoever is there, move them out or roll over them and change their culture, change their way of life, destroy the environment, and therefore the culture has to be changed. (Singleton, 1982, 38)

The lack of stable employment opportunities on these islands is also cause for concern, because it has created an imbalance in the age structure; a high percentage of young adults leave for employment elsewhere. Also, it is felt that the drive toward a more materialistic way of life in the region will lead, in the long term, to an array of social problems such as alcoholism, marital conflicts, and youth delinquency (Singleton 1982, 38). The task of transmitting cultural traditions to a rapidly declining younger generation of Gullah poses a challenge to those committed to preserving this way of life. Such transmission will be difficult unless the living context of the culture can be preserved according to Charles Joyner, a folklorist and scholar of Gullah history and culture (Nixon 1993, 56). The women I interviewed also expressed this attitude:

> You've got to have culture in order to make your community stable and stay in one place. And so how else can white people come in and say, "Oh, these people down here speak Gullah or Geechee," and

want to learn more about your culture, but at the same time they want to buy your land and push you out. How can you come down and visit me in my area, but I'm hanging on by a thread because you want my area. What do you suppose they'll show their friends and talk about? You know, they'll say, "This used to be a Gullah community, a Geechee community, but now they all live there in the heart of Atlanta or someplace else." It's not going to work. You can't move papa from [here], sit him in the middle of Atlanta, and say, "Make your cast net." Who's he going to sell cast net to in the middle of Atlanta? ... all of a sudden he'll die. So you can't move the culture and tradition from one area and just plant it in another area. . . . You've got to nurture it here, pass it down, teach children, and so forth. It's a slow process. You've got to know how to do it and you can teach other people how to do it. (Velma Moore, 1991)

In view of these concerns, how does the analysis of women's role as carriers of food preparation practices inform us about cultural survival strategies among the Gullah? How do women transmit knowledge of these practices to the younger generation? How do their strategies relate to emerging themes in the study of Black women?

Perhaps the most relevant context for understanding knowledge trans- 55 mission among Gullah women may be African-derived cultural practices that stress motherhood, self-reliance and autonomy, extended family, and community-centered networks (Collins 1990; Steady 1981). Each practice is centered in either the home or the community, and the two spheres of activity are mutually reinforcing. Within these domains an alternative framework of identity is constructed and women serve as transmitters of cultural knowledge.

The concept of motherhood illustrates how women use their spheres of activity to transmit cultural traditions. Motherhood among the Gullah is not limited to a biological relationship, but also can embrace other relationships with women termed "othermothers" (women who assist bloodmothers by sharing mothering responsibilities) (Collins 1990, 119). Othermothers may include grandmothers, sisters, aunts, or cousins who take on child care, emotional support, and even long-term responsibilities for rearing each other's children. According to Jones-Jackson (1987), "It is not unusual for a child [in the Sea Islands] to reach adulthood living not more than a block from the natural parent but residing with another relative who is perhaps childless or more financially secure" (p. 24). It is also common to see a neighbor helping to prepare a meal next door or being offered a meal without concern that parental permission would be required.

The concept of family extends beyond the nuclear family to include extended and even fictive family ties. Responsibilities and obligations within the family are defined in this context; they facilitate the development of family communities where relatives live close to each other, and promote cooperative values through shared roles and socialization practices. Women of all generations, as mothers and as extended-family members, play a critical role in fostering self-reliance and a sense of collective memory in their children of both genders. They do so through the daily preparation and eating of traditional foods and by using informal conversation to teach family history and cultural traditions.

I learned about the use of informal conversation when I attended a funeral at the home of a Gullah family. In the evening, after the funeral ceremonies were finished and most people had left, all the women of the family sat together in the living room with their children at their feet, eating and telling each other family stories. Someone asked about the people in a family photograph. My hostess described the context in which the photo was taken (which happened to be a family meal) and recalled each family member present, including the wife and mother, who was in the kitchen cooking when the photo was taken. Because children are expected to eventually manage their own lives, both sons and daughters are taught the skills of self-reliance through cooking. Parents believe that their children must know these things to survive in the wider culture.

Much of this socialization takes place around the mother or in the family, but much is also learned from trial and error. Velma Moore recalls:

> I learned to cook by trial and error and mama. Nobody teaches you how to cook, not over here. They allow you to play cook in the kitchen and watch them. Tradition always leaned towards girls cooking, but that boy, if he was hungry, he was expected to go in there and fix something for himself. Not that he had to sit there and starve all week until somebody's sister come home. So he learned how to cook, just like his sisters did. If a parent was home and he was home, they'd come up and ask him, "Hey, you was home all day. How come you didn't put on the rice?" or "How come you didn't

boil the beans or something?" And so they would ask him the question that they would ask girls. At least I know mama did (laugh).

Strong bonds between women are also established through women- 60
centered networks, which promote cooperative values in child care and informal economic activities (such as grass-basket weaving and quilting), in the opportunity to share experiences and ideas and in fostering the development of positive self-images, self-affirming roles, and self-reliance as women (Bush 1986, 120; Collins 1990, 119; Steady 1981, 6). The social exchange of goods and services and the flow of information and ideas that emanate from this type of networking encourage the development of positive self-images and community awareness in the children in these communities. While staying with Gullah families, I often observed exchanging and giving of food and other goods and services among women and their families, although many people commented that this practice was declining. Often when people went fishing or gathered vegetables and pecans, the women sent these foods to neighbors and friends, especially elderly individuals or couples who could no longer move around easily.

Finally, as Jones (1986) points out, preparation and serving of food by Black women in a secular communion of fellowship "symbolize[s] the spiritual component of collective survival" (p. 230). Women who prepare food for church activities play a vital role in helping these community-centered institutions to become sites of cultural preservation and spiritual fellowship, because food is an integral part of the ritual activities associated with spiritual fellowship. During the planning of church functions such as church anniversaries, weddings, and funerals, women who are known for their skills in preparing particular dishes are usually asked to prepare foods such as collard greens, red rice, peas and rice, cornbread, and chicken.

> When we go on a church picnic, we have a little cook-out like hot dogs and hamburgers, stuff like that. When we have the anniversary of the church, we cook soul food. And we have collard greens, and string beans, butter beans, fried chicken, some kind of roasts, macaroni and cheese, cornbread, and red rice. (Bernice Brown, 1989)
>
> We eat our food every day on St. Helena Island, and we also eat it at church anniversaries, weddings, and funerals. When we raise money to help the church, like women's day, the pastor's anniversary, the choir anniversary, we cook our food. (Queenie Moore, 1989)

Some women, including a study participant from Wadmalow Island, also raise funds for their church by preparing meals for sale in their homes.[5] Organizing such a party often involved considerable work in preparing traditional dishes such as red rice, fried fish, barbecued pigs' feet, collard greens, and shrimps and okra served with rice. Usually, my informant's friends and relatives helped her to prepare the food. Members of the church congregation and other community members then were expected to show their support by attending the party and paying for the food, as they would in a restaurant.

By extending food preparation to embrace the church family, the actions of women, who usually do this work, promote a sense of shared tradition and spiritual identity among church members, especially among youths and those who lack the time or talent to practice these traditions. This activity also reinforces community-centered networks by providing a context for dialogue, mutual mentoring, and spiritual development, especially among women in the community (Young 1992, 16).[6]

Conclusion

Although women in most societies serve as primary preparers of food for the household, this aspect of their daily lives has not received much analytical attention. Not only have women been largely excluded from the process of knowledge construction and validation, the work of food preparation has also been devalued and rendered invisible because of a dominant culture that views it as a "natural role" for women (Collins 1990; Smith 1987). Even in feminist scholarship there is an underlying tension when this issue is discussed because of the dual nature of food preparation as a valued work activity and as "women's work." On the one hand, it provides women with a source of valued identity and empowerment; on the other, it is a means of perpetuating relations of gender inequality and women's subordination in the household (DeVault 1991, 232). Feminists who advocate changes in this sphere usually recommend equitable distribution of housework among household members, cutting back on housework, and creating new family roles for men (Chodorow 1978; Hochschild and Machung 1989; Oakley 1974). DeVault (1991), however, argues that in changing the organization of food preparation in the home, one must be careful not to trivialize its value and its symbolic meaning in the expression of shared group membership. In other words, DeVault advocates preserving the essence of caring that is built into this activity, although in a way that would not maintain relations of inequality for those who perform it (DeVault 1991, 233–35).

I have argued here that through regular food preparation and manage-   65 ment of feeding in the family and the wider community, African American women in Gullah communities perpetuate cultural identity and group survival. Cultural preservation through food preparation and feeding is a highly conscious act on the part of these women; it is tied closely to their judgments about when to accept, and when to resist, change. Gullah women, therefore, are willing to take shortcuts in cooking when time pressures demand it, but they seem less willing to compromise their feelings about nature and environmental protection or to tamper with the "unique" seasonings they say are a component of true Gullah cooking.

Gullah women devise and transmit alternative ways of understanding their culture by relying on African-derived systems of knowledge, which promote motherhood, women-centered networks, self-reliance, extended family, and community-centeredness. Reliance on these values has enabled Gullah women to resist negative images of their past; they use common but resourceful strategies such as everyday practice, teaching by example, and providing constant recollections of their past through storytelling and other oral traditions. Although present attempts to define and preserve the unique cultural tradition of these communities are threatened seriously by the pace of economic development in the region, Gullah women have learned from their mothers and grandmothers that the observance and practice of the underlying principles of their traditions are vital to the survival and preservation of their culture.

Notes

1. See Margaret Washington Creel (1990) and Patricia Jones-Jackson (1987, especially 24–28). A good background to African spiritual philosophy is John Mbiti (1969).

2. Former slaves Katie Brown and Shad Hall from Sapelo Island, Georgia, when interviewed by the Federal Writers' Project in the 1930s, vividly described a special rice cake made with honey that their African Muslim grandmother prepared for the family on particular Muslim fast days (Georgia Writers' Project [1940] 1986, 162, 167). Thomas Winterbottom ([1803] 1969), a British physician who worked in Sierra

Leone at the end of the eighteenth century, also reported that the Muslims he encountered liked to make cakes of rice and honey.

3. One may find that even when a meal displays the qualities they claim it must have to be satisfying or filling, it still might not be acceptable to a given people if that food is not their preferred staple.

4. See Charles Joyner (1984, 96) for a description of how rice was cooked on some slave plantations in South Carolina, given by Goliah, who was enslaved on the plantation of Robert F.W. Allston.

5. Interview with May Taylor, Wadmalow Island, 1989.

6. Although I recognize the important contributions of Gullah women in the development of the Black church and in its spiritual leadership and community development activities, they have made this contribution at the expense of holding leadership positions. In the formal authority structure of African American churches, men generally control these positions. Women lack due recognition and status, and they continue to fight to attain a measure of power and influence in many Black churches. At the same time, they have shown different patterns of leadership within the church community by fostering a sense of collective autonomy and "woman consciousness" (Gilkes 1988, 228). Like the activities of women who organize voluntary missionary societies, teach Sunday school, raise funds, and become prayer band leaders and church mothers, the activities of women who prepare food for church functions show that women use this sphere of influence in the church to foster a sense of shared tradition and spiritual identity in their communities.

References

Bascom, W. 1951. Yoruba food. *Africa* 21:41–53.

Bascom, W. 1977. Some Yoruba ways with yams. In *The anthropologist's cookbook*, edited by J. Kuper. New York: Universe Books.

Bush, B. 1986. "The family tree is not cut": Women and cultural resistance in slave family life in the British Caribbean. In *In resistance: Studies in African, Caribbean, and Afro-American history*, edited by G. Y Okihiro. Amherst: University of Massachusetts Press.

Chodorow, N. 1978. *The reproduction of mothering.* Berkeley: University of California Press.

Collins, P. Hill. 1990. *Black feminist thought: Knowledge, consciousness, and the politics of empowerment.* Boston: Unwin Hyman.

Creel, M. Washington. 1990. Gullah attitudes toward life and death. *Africanisms in African-American culture*, edited by Joseph E. Holloway. Bloomington: Indiana University Press.

Davis, A. 1971. Reflections on the Black woman's role in the community of slaves. *Black Scholar* (December):3–15.

DeVault, M. L. 1991. *Feeding the family: The social organization of caring as gendered work*. Chicago: University of Chicago Press.

Finnegan, R. S. 1965. *Survey of the Limba people of northern Sierra Leone*. London: Her Majesty's Stationery Office.

Friedman, C. G. 1990. Africans and African-Americans: An ethnohistorical view and symbolic analysis of food habits. In *Encounters with American ethnic cultures*, edited by P. Kilbride, J. C. Goodale, and E. R. Ameisen. Tuscaloosa: University of Alabama Press.

Georgia Writers' Project. [1940] 1986. *Drums and shadows: Survival studies among the Georgia coastal Negroes*. Athens: University of Georgia Press.

Gilkes, C. 1988. "Together and in harness": Women's traditions in the Sanctified Church. In *Black women in America: Social science perspectives*, edited by M. R. Malson, E. Mudimbe-Boyi, Jean F. O'Barr, and M. Wyer. Chicago: University of Chicago Press.

Gray White, D. 1985. *Ar'n't I a woman? Female slaves in the plantation South*. New York: W. W. Norton.

Hill Collins, P. 1990. *Black feminist thought: Knowledge, consciousness, and the politics of empowerment*. Boston and London: Unwin Hyman.

Hochschild, A. R., and A. Machung. 1989. *The second shift: Working parents and the revolution at home*. New York: Viking.

Holloway, J. 1990. *Africanisms in American culture*. Bloomington: Indiana University Press.

Jones, J. 1986. *Labor of love, labor of sorrow: Black women, work, and the family from slavery to the present*. New York: Vintage Books.

Jones-Jackson, P. 1987. *When roots die: Endangered traditions on the Sea Islands*. Athens: University of Georgia Press.

Joyner, C. 1984. *Down by the riverside: A South Carolina slave community*. Urbana: University of Illinois Press.

Littlefield, D. 1981. *Rice and slaves: Ethnicity and the slave trade in colonial South Carolina*. Baton Rouge: Louisiana State University Press.

Mbiti, J. 1969. *African religions and philosophy*. New York: Praeger.

Nixon, R. 1993. Cultures in conflict: Sea Island communities are fighting for their survival, stirring new hopes along the coast of South Carolina. *Southern Exposure* (Fall):53–56.

Oakley, A. 1974. *The sociology of housework.* New York: Pantheon.

Opala, J. 1987. *The Sierra Leone–Gullah connection.* Freetown: USIS.

Orsi, R. A. 1985. *The Madonna of 115th street: Faith and community in Italian Harlem, 1880–1950.* New Haven, Conn: Yale University Press.

Reagon, B. Johnson. 1986. African diaspora women: The making of cultural workers. *Feminist Studies* 12:77–90.

Singleton, V. 1982. We are an endangered species: An interview with Emory Campbell. *Southern Exposure* 10:37–39.

Smith, D. E. 1987. *The everyday world as problematic: A feminist sociology.* Boston: Northeastern University Press.

Steady, F. 1981. *The Black woman cross-culturally.* Cambridge, Mass: Schenkman.

Strauss, A. L. 1990. *Qualitative analysis for social scientists.* Cambridge: Cambridge University Press.

Terborg-Penn, R. 1987. *Women in Africa and the African diaspora.* Washington, D.C.: Howard University Press.

Turner, L. 1949. *Africanisms in the Gullah dialect.* Chicago: University of Chicago Press.

Williams, B. 1985. Why migrant women feed their husbands tamales: Foodways as a basis for a revisionist view of Tejano family life. In *Ethnic and regional foodways in the United States: The performance of group identity,* edited by L. Keller Brown and K. Mussell. Knoxville: University of Tennessee Press.

Winterbottom, T. [1803] 1969. *An account of the Native Africans in the neighbourhood of Sierra Leone.* London: Frank Cass.

Wood, P. 1974. *Black majority: Negroes in colonial South Carolina from 1670 through the Stono Rebellion.* New York: Alfred A. Knopf.

Young, K. Porter. 1992. *Notes on sisterhood, kinship, and marriage in an African-American South Carolina Sea Island community.* Memphis, Tenn.: Memphis State University, Center for Research on Women.

Analyze

1. How does Beoku-Betts describe her methodology for making her argument? What is that methodology?

2. Although there are sexist motivations for women becoming food nurturers and providers, how do these practices also make women the

"torch bearers" for cultural preservation? Why is this important? Analyze the author's evidence for making her claims.

3. Analyze and discuss the author's description of Gullah culture and the place it serves in larger American (mostly Southern) coastal culture.

Explore

1. "On the one hand, [food preparation] provides women with a source of valued identity and empowerment; on the other, it is a means of perpetuating relations of gender inequality and women's subordination in the household." Use this quote as a framework for exploring another subculture and determining the effect to which this is the case for that subculture. (You might also explore whether there are instances of gender roles being reversed in a particular subculture.)

2. Discuss with your classmates and then write an essay about a "torch bearer" you know, whether the torch is kept regarding family food, lore, or other cultural tradition, and whether that person is male or female.

3. Construct an oral history, interviewing a chief food preparer you know. How does this person see him- or herself? How do you see this person? Are the narratives consistent? To what effect?

Jack Hitt
"A Confederacy of Sauces"

Jack Hitt contributes regularly to *The New Yorker* and to *This American Life*. He has won prestigious Peabody and Pope Awards, and he is currently touring in a one-man show called "Making Up the Truth." The show explores the intersection of his own biography and contemporary brain science. "A Confederacy of Sauces" investigates what happens when two brothers disagree about food and politics.

 How is buying a barbecue sandwich a "political act?"

While I was back home last spring in Charleston, S.C., doing some work with my nephew, we decided to drive over to a barbecue joint one afternoon for some pulled pork and sauce. The place I like is called Melvin's, famous both for its good barbecue and its fine pedigree. Melvin is a Bessinger, a clan whose name in South Carolina has the same kind of power that barbecue legends like Gates or Bryant do out in Kansas City.

But my nephew warned me that lately there had been a feud. Barbecue had somehow gotten mixed up with issues of race and heritage. Ugly fighting words had been exchanged, leaving a residue of aggrieved feelings. The quarrel had finally touched the third rail of contemporary Carolina anger, the only topic more sensitive than sauce recipes, Strom Thurmond jokes and Charleston genealogy combined: the meaning of the Civil War. And once again, the war had re-enacted its old bitterness, setting brother against brother. Only not at Gettysburg this time, but in a hickory pit redolent with crackling.

"Buying a barbecue sandwich is now a political act," my nephew explained to me. "You have to declare which side you're on." On a culinary level, barbecue is one of those democratic dishes that have an inexplicable power to start fights, like pizza. People defend their favorite pit as passionately as a homeland (ask any Gates fiend about Bryant's), and chefs guard their secret recipes (which tend to involve strangely commonplace ingredients like A.1. Steak Sauce or red-wine vinegar or margarine) with a paranoia worthy of Coca-Cola or K.F.C. But in South Carolina, barbecue has also become an occasion to vent what should be declared the state's official emotion: aggrievement. See, ours is different from yours.

If you were to draw a line north from Charleston to Columbia and shade in most of the low country to the east, you would form the Devil's Triangle of barbecue. There, the sauce is based on mustard, not tomatoes, and vinegar, not brown sugar, is the dominant back-taste. I have a friend these days from Kansas City. I brought up the subject of mustard-based sauce at his dinner table the other day and was hooted down for daring to speak about such a hideous abomination when a bottle of Gates's finest was actually present at the table. Of course, I wasn't comparing anything, I was just—all I was saying was that mustard, that sauce. . . . I went home that night feeling, well, aggrieved.

5   The first shot of South Carolina's modern barbecue war occurred the day the State Legislature lowered the Confederate flag from the Capitol dome in Columbia on July 1, 2000. The flag had been flying there since

1962, and last year the N.A.A.C.P. initiated a boycott of the state to force it down. The lowering of the flag, at high noon, was covered live on television with an O.J.-like camera shot of the flag being carried down the dark internal steps of the dome. The tone of the TV broadcast was lugubrious, funereal and, of course, aggrieved.

That afternoon, Maurice Bessinger, who has nine restaurants in and around the capital, hoisted the Confederate flag over each one.

"I surrounded the city of Columbia with Confederate flags," Maurice explained when I went to visit him at his headquarters. "I didn't even tell my wife. I had it all planned." As a character, Maurice is not unknown around the state. (He once owned a plantation-size piece of land and named it Tara.) He looks like a cross between Colonel Sanders and the rich guy on the Community Chest cards in Monopoly: a bantam rooster of a man with snowy hair and mustache. In addition to his Maurices Bar-B-Q restaurants, he sells his trademark yellow sauce, dubbed Carolina Gold, in stores, with his own image smiling down from every bottle. He built a big bottling plant in 1993 that supplied 3,000 grocery stores from Tampa to New York with his stuff. His hickory fires burned 24 hours a day and consumed so much wood that Maurice bought an entire plantation near Columbia merely to supply himself with the 60 cords he needed each week. By 1999, Maurice had created the largest commercial barbecue operation in the country.

Just inside the door of his main restaurant is a set of tables that form a kind of shrine to Maurice's ancestors and his beliefs. There are pictures of his parents and grandparents, as well as framed letters from his heroes, George Wallace and Pat Buchanan. (Maurice's main pit doubled as the state's Buchanan for President headquarters in 1996.) The tables hold pamphlets on a range of subjects, one titled "McCarthyism and Lincolnism" and another that traces the symbology of the Confederate flag back to "4,000-years-old hieroglyphics," when the flag was "used by Jehovah-God in prehistoric times to fight battles for liberty and freedom."

"The whole thing wouldn't have happened if it wasn't for John Monk," Maurice told me. Last August, Monk, a local newspaper columnist, quoted one of the pamphlets explaining the relationship between the Bible and slavery. "Many of those African slaves blessed the Lord for allowing them to be enslaved and sent to America," it said. (In my experience, I have found that blacks can get grouchy when Southern whites talk knowingly on the issue of slave gratitude.)

10   Alarmed by Monk's column and fresh from their victory on the flag issue at the Capitol, black leaders felt aggrieved by Maurice's flag-raising, and they held a news conference to express their views. At the time, Maurice was close to inking a deal to take his sauce national, expanding beyond his East Coast base. But last Sept. 11, faced with growing public pressure, Sam's Club pulled his sauce from its shelves. The next day, Wal-Mart, too, banned Carolina Gold and was followed by Food Lion, Harris Teeter, Bi-Lo, Kroger and Publix. But the venerable Southern chain Piggly Wiggly (aka "the Pig") held out. A spokesman announced that the Pig would defend its customers' right to choose.

Enter a North Charleston minister, James Johnson, who met with the director of the Pig as the official representative of the Southern Christian Leadership Conference in the South Carolina low country.

"I told him we had the buses from the churches and that we'd have them parked next to each of his stores to bus every customer to Harris Teeter if we had to," he recalled. The Pig caved quickly.

"I lost about 98 percent of my bottled-sauce business," Maurice said. He wouldn't divulge precisely how much his overall sales (both restaurant and retail store) had fallen. But he estimates that he has lost $20 million from the boycott. Today, his bottling plant, which cost him millions to build, is largely idle.

Not long after the boycott began, a yellow sauce quite similar to Maurice's began to fill up the empty shelves of the Piggly Wigglys around Charleston. In the wake of Maurice's fall, a market niche had appeared, and right away an entrepreneur seized the advantage.

15   "He opened the door because of his flag views, see, and we took the chance—why shouldn't we?" said the new kid on the block: Melvin Bessinger, Maurice's older brother. Still sporting some blond hair and piercing blue eyes at age 78, Melvin, the owner of Melvin's Southern BBQ and Ribs in Charleston, considers himself an old-line egalitarian: "I don't say anything about black people, as long as they're educated and do right. I don't hold myself up as better than nobody."

Melvin's son David, who works with Melvin, said that right after they got into the Pig they secured Maurice's old shelf space at the Bi-Lo. Maurice was enraged. He went public with a nasty sound bite that he recited several times for me as well: "I taught Melvin everything he knows about barbecue sauce—but I didn't teach him everything I know."

Then an unlikely avenging angel appeared to smite Maurice's enemies: enter Johnson, once again. The minister says he got a call from a local television station that fed him a tip about all Bessinger sauce being the same. So Johnson called for yet another boycott.

"What happened was that black people saw our sauce in the Piggly Wiggly downtown on Meeting Street," Melvin told me. "They thought Maurice was putting his sauce in our bottles and calling it Melvin's." This confusion forced Melvin to speak publicly. He issued a press release through his attorney, officially denying his brother. "Melvin and his brother do not share political or social views," it said. "Despite their being brothers, they do not speak to each other. Melvin's views on the Confederate flag, slavery and race relations are not those of his brother."

Stories appeared on the wire services about the dispute, saying that the only conversation that had passed between the two brothers in years was an aggrieved grunt of "Hi" at their sister's funeral last October. In Charleston, Melvin's son David said they had taken "Bessinger" off their bottle entirely.

"I'm ashamed to use my last name," he told *The Charleston Post-Courier.* 20

Soon thereafter, Johnson held a news conference at Melvin's. He said he had been shown convincing evidence that Melvin's bottling operation was different from Maurice's, and he publicly endorsed Melvin's sauce.

When I later asked him, out of the glare of the TV lights, for his true feelings about the sauces, Johnson confessed: "I've never tasted Maurice's, to be honest. The truth is, I don't even eat barbecue. I try to avoid pork and the red meats."

Johnson explained that he had always avoided Maurice's restaurants. He knew about Maurice long before the flag controversy, he said. Maurice had been an outspoken Wallace supporter during the civil rights movement. Maurice maintained segregated dining facilities and separate entrances for blacks and whites until a 1968 Supreme Court decision (*Newman v. Piggie Park Enterprises*) forced him to change his policy.

On a hot and humid day in Columbia, I walked to the front steps of South Carolina's Capitol. Maurice had invited me to attend a rally to condemn the lowering of the Confederate flag, with a big Bessinger barbecue afterward. Turnout was pretty high. I'd guess 500 people, mostly wearing dour expressions. The mission was to express aggrievement, especially for the politicians who voted to take down the flag—aka the "turncoats." Flags flew everywhere—tiny ones for the kiddies, large swaying flags cocked in flag holsters for the real zealots. I was mildly afraid, as if someone might suddenly point at me and start ululating.

25   The politicians speaking that day, including the state's lieutenant governor and attorney general, knew their crowd well. There was no pig-biting demagoguery, only laurels for the nobility of dying for states' rights and the repeated assertion that the flag and the war never involved slavery, just high-minded constitutional theory. All of this got wrapped up in honey-tongued rhetoric and tied with a bow called "heritage"—reminding me once again how little contemporary Confederate history has to do with the past.

What neo-Confederates really want, paradoxical as it may seem, is not to be thought of as racists. The people in the crowd were tired and agitated over having to answer for Lester Maddox and Bull Connor 40 years later. In an age of identity politics, when every group can boast of some noble and brave past, neo-Confederates want one too. To effect this, they look at the multiple and confusing causes and interests that erupted into the Civil War and remove from that historical tapestry the threads of slavery, racism and hatred. What's left is honor in battle, the cause of states' rights and heritage. That is the truth they want the Confederate flag to stand for today.

All of which partly accounted for one of the minor celebrities meandering through the crowd—Stanley Lott. He was the very picture of wartime suffering. Clothed in rags, he carried a huge Confederate flag while a necklace of large porcelain battle flags jangled against his chest. But what really distinguished Lott at the rally was that he's black. Wearing a grim face, he was hunched over, it seemed, from the weight of all the heavy metaphor he bore. A white woman beside me, dressed in antebellum widow's weeds and matching bonnet, stepped up to him hesitantly.

"Yes, ma'am," Lott said in greeting. "Nice day for a rally. Nice day." The woman tugged at her elbow-length lace glove until her pale hand was free. She stretched it across the radius of her hoop skirt.

"I just want to shake your hand," she said. Her voice cracked, and she began to cry. "For knowing the truth."

30   "Yes, ma'am," Lott said, comforting her hand and confirming her truth. "Yes, ma'am."

Maybe 200 people turned out at the post-rally barbecue at Maurice's bottling plant. He had set up a giant shed to seat 500, so the gathering looked like a failure. The machines were walled off by pallets of Maurice's boxes, each stamped with the word "Kosher." Maurice, a lay preacher, began the long afternoon of speeches.

"This is our only hope," Maurice explained, pointing to the giant Confederate flag behind him. "As the government gets more and more tyrannical, they will hand over more power to a world government. And then the Antichrist will just come in and say, 'Thank you very much.'"

Maurice is comfortable weaving religion with barbecue: there is a weekly Bible-study session at each of his pits. Later on, in the privacy of his office, he let slip a secret of his sauce. "The recipe," he said, "is in the Bible."

"Does it start with Jesus' parable of the mustard seed?" I joked. Maurice's eyes flared, as if I had correctly guessed that his middle name was Rumpelstiltskin, and he refused to discuss it further.

"You can just say that my Carolina Gold is a heavenly sauce," he said. 35 "I believe that after the rapture there will be a big barbecue, and I hope the Lord will let me cook."

Bessinger sauce has always had mythic qualities, even in its origins. Like Jack of Beanstalk fame, the Bessingers' father, Joe James, took a desperate risk during the Depression in order to feed his 11 children: he sold the family's only working assets, a cow named Betsy and a mule, and used the proceeds to open a restaurant. His gamble paid off. Joe's Grill, halfway between Charleston and Columbia on the old highway, was soon jammed with visitors. What people seemed to really go for was Joe's tangy mustard sauce.

During World War II, 11-year-old Maurice worked in the restaurant while Melvin, seven years older, fought the Germans. Melvin landed at Normandy, was captured in battle, escaped from a P.O.W. camp and was hidden from the Nazis in a Munich attic by a German woman. When Melvin returned to South Carolina with a Purple Heart and a Bronze Star, his father proudly brought his war-hero son into the restaurant—the same restaurant where Maurice had been working every day. Maurice was not happy.

"Daddy said he had put in the will that I would get the restaurant," Maurice said. "But after he died in 1949, the will couldn't be found. Momma gave the restaurant to Melvin. She always preferred him because his looks sort of favor her people, you know. Melvin was always Momma's pet." Maurice ran off and joined the Army, eventually serving in Korea.

"Maurice never has liked me," Melvin said. "I don't know why. I think he's jealous. I think in his heart he loves me, though, because I love him."

40   Melvin might want to read Maurice's new book. Titled *Defending My Heritage*, it's due to be published this month. Maurice describes Melvin as a vicious and sadistic older brother who stole food from him during the Depression. One violent beating by Melvin left an 8-year-old Maurice with "bloody stripes up and down my back." The book is bound to attract attention outside the family as well. In it, Maurice defends segregation because "blacks prefer the company of blacks while whites prefer the company of whites" and describes his earliest Jewish customers as "quite stingy and difficult to serve."

Given the volatile family dynamic, it's not surprising that in the decades after the war, Bessinger brothers opened and closed barbecue pits all over the low country of South Carolina. Upon returning from Korea, Maurice and another brother, Joe Jr., opened Piggie Park in Charleston. The place no longer exists except in legend. You ordered from your car on scratchy metal intercoms, and young girls came out to snap a tray onto your open car window. I remember that the onion rings were as big around as cup saucers and fried in a smooth, thick dough. I also remember that all the whites parked under a central tin roof and the blacks parked against the wall.

On this trip, I decided to taste all the Bessinger sauces fresh from their respective fires, all in a single day. I ate at Maurice's in Columbia and then drove to Charleston. There, Melvin's two pits occupy James Island and Mount Pleasant. Another brother, Thomas, has a place on the Savannah highway. Yet another, Robert, has two pits in North Charleston. None of the brothers compete side by side with the others. They have spread out and covered the low country. I grew up being told that yellow sauce was my cultural heritage. But it's clear that without the siblings' anxieties and their nomadic habits, Joe Sr.'s recipe would have died out after Joe's Grill closed. South Carolina would have remained just another outpost in the national camp of red barbecue sauce.

In the meantime, the brothers' interpretations of Dad's original sauce have created subtle but noticeable distinctions. Maurice's is definitely sweetened (probably for mass-market consumption) and tastes yummy at first. Melvin's has a strong, good burned flavor, but my guess is that some of that derives from liquid smoke. Robert's is serviceable. And then there's Thomas's. Thomas avoided me strenuously when I tried to discuss the family brouhaha, getting his secretary to lie and say he wasn't in as I called him from my car phone and stared at him through the window. Still, in my opinion, his was the best, terrifically balancing the tangs of mustard and vinegar with a wood fire's charry flavor.

"They have an ego problem," Robert said when I caught up with him. "Melvin wants to be the chief, and Maurice wants to be the major chief." Robert admits that he doesn't have quite the ambition of his brothers. He doesn't bottle his sauce or even trick out his store with barbecuey décor like old scythes or yokes. There's a picture of Arnold Palmer near the cash register. Robert checks the books every morning and plays golf every afternoon. He makes a living and can't understand how it all came to this.

"If we make politics out of barbecue, then what's next?" he said. "Political 45 hamburgers? Political French fries?"

Probably. Maurice said that even though the grocery store chains have banned his sauce, some stores sell his sauce out of the manager's office in brown paper bags and others just stock it out in the open. Johnson confirms that he occasionally gets reports of Maurice's sauce being slipped back onto the shelf, and he has to revive his threats to get it taken off. According to Maurice, heritage groups like the Sons of Confederate Veterans have started coming into his shops, and they have made up for the loss in black business. Of course, blacks now avoid Maurice's altogether. The old segregation of the Piggie Park days has reconstituted itself for a new age.

In the heyday of the civil rights movement, many Southerners resented the federal government for singling out the Southern states for special remedies on the argument that segregation imposed by law was different from de facto separation of the races. The reaction back home, naturally, was to feel picked on, and then aggrieved. Now, Southerners can be proud that their racial divide is strictly voluntary, just as it is everywhere else.

Analyze

1. How does the dispute between Maurice and Melvin illustrate that barbecue has become mixed up with "issues of race and heritage?"
2. It is no secret that this is a fairly amusing article. Analyze the ways in which Hitt uses language and story to make his points. What effect do his techniques have on the reader? Are they useful in making Hitt's points?
3. What are the main ideas of the essay? Describe the serious arguments that Hitt seems to be making, despite the humor.

Explore

1. Explore other aspects of American culture that you've witnessed that seem to reveal divisions between types of food and cultural preferences.

2. At one point, a speaker within the article asks the following: "If we make politics out of barbecue, then what's next? Political hamburgers? Political French fries?" Research a product or dish that has somehow become controversial or political. How are these symbols or metaphors for more serious attitudes or political positions?

3. Explore Hitt's use of understatement as a way to make a point—think about his characterization of Maurice, for instance. How do devices such as understatement reveal Hitt's own attitudes? Research other such devices in writing and see whether Hitt employs them as a way to advance his narrative.

Jason Sheehan
"There's No Such Thing as Too Much Barbecue"

Jason Sheehan is currently the food editor of *Philadelphia Magazine.* A James Beard Award winner for food criticism, he also has been a chef, a dishwasher, a grill cook, and a fry-cook. His first book, called *Cooking Dirty,* was named one of the ten best nonfiction books of the year (2010) by *Time* magazine. As you will see, Jason Sheehan "believes in barbecue."

Why does Jason Sheehan believe that "there is no such thing as too much barbecue?"

After listening to the results of this project for several weeks, I knew I could do three minutes, too. Certainly not on world peace or the search for meaning in an increasingly distracted world or anything as grave and serious as all that, but on a belief just as true.

I believe in barbecue. As soul food and comfort food and health food, as a cuisine of both solace and celebration. When I'm feeling good, I want barbecue. And when I'm feeling bad, I just want barbecue more. I believe in barbecue in all its regional derivations, in its ethnic translations, in forms that range from white-tablecloth presentations of cunningly sauced costillas, to Chinese take-out spareribs that stain your fingers red, to the most authentic product of the tarpaper rib shacks of the Deep South. I believe that like sunshine and great sex, no day is bad that has barbecue in it.

I believe in the art of generations of pit men working in relative obscurity to keep alive the craft of slow smoking as it's been practiced for as long as there's been fire. A barbecue cook must have an intimate understanding of his work: the physics of fire and convection, the hard science of meat and heat and smoke—and then forget it all to achieve a sort of gut-level, Zen instinct for the process.

I believe that barbecue drives culture, not the other way around. Some of the first blows struck for equality and civil rights in the Deep South were made not in the courtrooms or schools or on buses, but in the barbecue shacks. There were dining rooms, backyards and roadhouse juke joints in the South that were integrated long before any other public places.

I believe that good barbecue requires no decor, and that the best 5 barbecue exists despite its trappings. Paper plates are okay in a barbecue joint. And paper napkins. And plastic silverware. And I believe that any place with a menu longer than can fit on a single page—or better yet, just a chalkboard—is coming dangerously close to putting on airs.

I believe that good barbecue needs sides the way good blues need rhythm, and that there is only one rule: Serve whatever you like, but whatever you serve, make it fresh. Have someone's mama in the back doing the "taters" and hush puppies and sweet tea, because Mama will know what she's doing—or at least know better than some assembly-line worker bagging up powdered mashed potatoes by the ton.

I believe that proper barbecue ought to come in significant portions. Skinny people can eat barbecue, and do, but the kitchen should cook for a fat man who hasn't eaten since breakfast. My leftovers should last for days.

I believe that if you don't get sauce under your nails when you're eating, you're doing it wrong. I believe that if you don't ruin your shirt, you're not trying hard enough.

I believe—*I know*—there is no such thing as too much barbecue. Good, bad or in-between, old-fashioned pit-smoked or high-tech and modern; it doesn't matter. Existing without gimmickry, without the infernal swindles and capering of so much of contemporary cuisine, barbecue is truth; it is history and home, and the only thing I don't believe is that I'll ever get enough.

Analyze

1. This piece appeared as an Opinion Essay as part of "This I Believe" on National Public Radio. Sheehan is quick to acknowledge that his belief is not tantamount to a belief in the importance of world peace or the "search for meaning." How effectively does Sheehan make the case, then, for his belief in barbecue? Through what means?

2. "I believe that barbecue drives culture, not the other way around." How does Sheehan defend this statement? Are you convinced? What arguments could be made for the opposite—that culture drives barbecue?

3. Sheehan says that barbecue is "truth" and that it is "history" and "home." What details would you include to expand his fairly brief discussion—and from his point of view?

Explore

1. Research the role that barbecue shacks—or other food destinations— played in the civil rights movement. What else do you find that expands Sheehan's arguments? Discuss with your classmates why food establishments might become fertile ground for significant cultural or political movements.

2. How do barbecue and other foods become associated with all that is cheap, excessive, and messy? Discuss why this is desirable, from Sheehan's point of view and your own. Do you disagree? Why or why not?

3. Research other American dining traditions about which you could write a similar essay. Summarize its characteristics and make a presentation to your class in a similar "This I Believe" vein.

Food Stamps—Two Perspectives

Bill Turque is a Montgomery County reporter whose work appears regularly in the Washington *Post*. **Jim Geraghty** is a regular contributor to the *National Review* online.

Consider the perspectives of both articles, especially given their contradictions of one another.

Bill Turque
"Montgomery Officials Try Eating for $5 a Day"

Joshua P. Starr, superintendent of Montgomery County Public Schools, peered at the shelves of coffee Monday morning at the Rockville Giant supermarket. He grabbed a can of Nature's Promise for $4.69. Then he saw the Cafe Bustello at $3.09 and swapped.

"What's the least expensive bread?" he asked a clerk, who guided him to the Arnold Whole Wheat, on special this week, two loaves for $3. Still, Starr took just one.

Over in the produce section, County Council member Craig Rice placed a $3.50 bag of potatoes in his basket, next to the two oranges and three apples. "You can make french fries and hash browns in the morning," said Rice (D-Upcounty). "Gotta have good starch."

Starr, Rice, other county officials and community leaders agreed to spend just $25 on food for the next five days, an attempt to simulate the everyday fact of life for residents enrolled in the federal Supplemental Nutrition Assistance Program, once known as food stamps. Americans are receiving SNAP benefits in record numbers: 46.2 million people in 22 million households last spring, according to the Congressional Research Service, at a cost of more than $70 Billion.

Hunger receives scant mention in Montgomery, where the median   5
household income is $92,000 and growth, transportation and education

dominate the policy discussion. "What most people know about the county is how well it does," said Council President Nancy Navarro (D-Mid-County).

But amid the wealth there are pockets of urgent need. Almost 27,000 low-income Montgomery households received SNAP assistance last year, a 138 percent increase from 2007, according to county figures. A family of four earning less than $2,400 a month is eligible for help.

The region's other prosperous counties have similar under-the-radar populations that struggle for enough food. In Fairfax County and Falls Church, for example, about 23,000 households (54,300 people) rely on SNAP, according to a 2011 report by the county's Department of Neighborhood and Community Services.

Elected officials across the country—including the District's congressional delegate, Eleanor Holmes Norton (D); Newark Mayor Cory Booker (D); and Colorado Gov. John Hickenlooper (D)—have taken on the "SNAP/Food Stamp Challenge," a creation of the nonprofit Food Research and Action Center, as a way of highlighting hunger issues and helping them understand what economically pressed constituents face.

"This isn't about us," Rice said. "It's about making sure people understand how tough it is."

10   The initiative has received some dings from commentators, who call it a new fad diet for the political class. It is, at best, a brief duck of the head into the world inhabited by the hungry and poor.

While the Montgomery officials who shopped at Giant on Monday will likely get hunger pangs, they'll still sleep in warm beds, free from worry about paying the next utility bill. Starr, the schools superintendent, makes $250,000 annually. Rice and the other council members earn more than $100,000.

None of them had to stand in the cold waiting for a bus to bring them to the market. Nor will hunger be a household experience; most officials said family members, such as Starr's children (ages 5, 9 and 11) and Rice's (7 and 10), will not participate.

"The idea of doing it has the merit of at least partially experiencing what low-income people experience," said Timothy Smeeding, director of the Institute for Research on Poverty at the University of Wisconsin at Madison. "But if your kids are going to eat different, that's probably not legit."

Smeeding added that officials would do well this week to walk into a food pantry or soup kitchen, something many SNAP recipients do to supplement their diets.

Still, many said Monday's shopping experience was an eye-opener. 15 Program rules exclude pet food, soap, vitamins, paper products or household supplies. Council member Nancy Floreen (D-At Large), a breast cancer survivor, said it was difficult to devise a healthful diet on $25. Board of Education President Christopher Barclay, who has Type II diabetes and bought spinach, oranges, granola and soy milk, also was surprised by the difficulty of eating healthfully but cheaply, especially with the prices at Giant.

"With all due respect to our hosts, I would be shopping where I could get food for less," he said.

At the checkout counter, Council member Valerie Ervin (D-Silver Spring), who organized the Montgomery challenge, discovered that she'd busted her threadbare budget, running up $28.96.

"Take the canned salmon off," Ervin said. She also had to put back a bag of Goya black beans to push her bill down to $24.80. That sum bought ramen noodles, a loaf of bread, an eight-pack of eggs, two bags of frozen vegetables, a small chicken, two boxes of onion soup mix, four apples, an orange, a box of yellow rice and two cans of tuna.

Officials taking the challenge have been asked to keep track of the food they eat each day and to write journal entries describing how they feel.

They are scheduled to reconvene Friday evening at the Civic Building 20 in Silver Spring to talk about the experience. And there will be food, Ervin said, a bit longingly, as she contemplated the week ahead.

Jim Geraghty
"Lawmakers' Headline-Grabbing Food Stamp Diet"

Over in the *Washington Post* today, they do a flattering article on Montgomery County officials who are spending just $25 on food for the next five days, "an attempt to simulate the everyday fact of life for residents enrolled in the federal Supplemental Nutrition Assistance Program, once known as food stamps." They're only the latest lawmakers to announce to the world they'll be doing this; District's congressional delegate, Eleanor Holmes Norton, Newark Mayor Cory Booker and Colorado Gov. John Hickenlooper have also done the same, garnering quite a bit of press attention in the process.

According to the U.S. Department of Agriculture, the program served over 46 million people in an average month last year, with that amounting to 75 percent of those eligible and 65 percent of those classified "working poor." The average monthly payment is $133.48. You can find the income eligibility tables here; for a family of four it's about $29,976, a level I think that a broad consensus would agree is indeed low-income (presuming recipients are accurately reporting all of their income). (Before you gasp, "and that's before taxes!" note that about 62 percent of those making $30,000 or less pay no income tax.)

Of course, it's extremely difficult to feed yourself, much less a family, on $25 for five days. But the title of the program itself makes clear that it's not meant to be the sole source of your ability to afford food; it is specifically labeled *supplemental*. As CNN reporter Christine Romans noted, "The government designs it so this is on top of what little money you might have, food pantries, soup kitchens. Some people are getting meals quite frankly in schools and the like, like kids are getting, you know, two meals a day in schools." When asked about this, Booker complained that the media spends too much time discussing "the pregnancy of a princess" and not enough time discussing poverty. Fine, but let's be clear that these politicians aren't really "simulating the everyday fact of life" for SNAP recipients, they're simulating a slightly worse situation.

The lawmakers, giving the media detailed lists of their food purchases to let us know just how compassionate they are, are actually attempting to get by by spending less than most recipients, who can afford to spend more than $5 per day. With low incomes, it may not be much more than that, but at least they have the option. If the argument is that the amount of assistance offered to each individual and household receiving SNAP ought to be increased, then fine, let's have that argument. Americans are a kind and generous people. But we could do with fewer lawmakers rushing to tell the press just how virtuous they are because they've decided to eat very little for five days.

Analyze

1. Analyze the argument of each article. What is the overall perspective of each? What is the relationship of one to the other?
2. Compare and contrast the ways in which the reporters present their information. Which is more effective? Less so? Why?
3. What was the motivation for officials to eat on a "food stamp diet?" What fault does Geraghty find with their intentions? Why might some consider this initiative "a new fad diet for the political class?" How might you defend this "fad?"

Explore

1. Despite Geraghty's clear disapproval of "food stamp" diets and of politicians' attempts to follow them, both articles seem to acknowledge that there is a hunger crisis in the United States. Turque says these initiatives are "a brief duck of the head into the world inhabited by the hungry and poor." Research other newspaper articles about this topic—or about similar initiatives, such as homelessness. Debate with your classmates the effectiveness or desirability of such "initiatives."
2. Research food stamp legislation in your own state and explore the issue through the lens of a taxpayer, a politician, and a family in need. Discuss with your classmates. What differences do you find? What is your conclusion?
3. Find two additional articles in newspapers about food stamps. Although we know that newspaper reporters should be neutral regarding their subjects, this is not always the case. What seem to be the positions of the reporters who have written the articles? Neutral? Critical? Sympathetic? Analyze the language to support your assessment.

Forging Connections

1. The pieces in this chapter are wide ranging in subject and style. Select two very different articles and find ways to connect them in terms of audience, subject, or style.
2. How do various regions in the United States seem to have food identities or conflicts that might also reveal something about politics? Consider the two essays in this chapter about barbecue as a basis for your research and discussion.

Looking Further

1. Choose a region of the United States—preferably not the South because that is treated in this chapter—and prepare a multimodal presentation about the particular culinary traditions of that region. Research the history of that culinary tradition within that region.

2. Whereas some of the essays and articles in this chapter glorify culinary traditions, others (such as the articles about food stamps) shed light on aspects of America's food culture about which some are less proud. Do some research to determine what other aspects of American food culture are not necessarily positive in their origin, preparing an expository essay in which you explain this circumstance while arguing your point of view about it.

Food,
6 Travel, and
Worldviews

Travel and views of the world are inextricably linked. The pieces in this chapter are wide ranging, each asking readers to step out of their own contexts and approach the worldviews of others. The authors in this chapter ask us to think of travel and food not only as literal journeys, but also as metaphorical and gastronomic journeys.

Our relationships with food begin close to us—likely at home—and the essays that follow may, in fact, tie together the various perspectives, topics, and approaches you have read throughout this volume in ways that are both similar and different. As you read through these essays carefully, consider, too, not only where your relationships with food started, but also how food has led you to a particular worldview—and also to a wider set of perspectives.

Lisa Heldke
"Let's Eat Chinese! Reflections on Cultural Food Colonialism"

A professor of philosophy at Gustavus Adolphus College in St. Peter, Minnesota, Lisa Heldke writes extensively about the intersection of food and her major academic interest. Heldke is particularly interested in agricultural ethics, localism, and sustainability, and a recent book is called *Exotic Appetites: Ruminations of a Food Adventurer* (2003). Her forthcoming book, *Philosophers at Table*, reflects her hybrid interests, as does the subject of the following essay.

 What is "cultural food colonialism?"

> In my home town, meat-potatoes-and-vegetable meals predominated in most homes, and an "ethnic" meal most likely meant spaghetti with red sauce . . .

When I went away to graduate school, I entered a world of experimental cooking and eating, a world heavily populated by academics and people with disposable incomes who like to travel. It's a world where entire cuisines go in and out of vogue in a calendar year. Where lists of "in" cuisines, ingredients, techniques, and restaurants are published in glamorous magazines featuring pictures of gorgeous food on their covers and articles inside about how saffron is harvested. It's a world in which people whisper conspiratorially about the great little place serving Ethiopian food—well, Eritrean, actually—that just opened up. The world of food adventuring was a wonderful world, full of tastes, textures, and smells I had never, ever encountered growing up in Rice Lake, Wisconsin. In my home town, meat-potatoes-and-vegetable meals predominated in most homes, and an "ethnic" meal most likely meant spaghetti with red sauce at the Bona Casa in Cumberland, fifteen miles away. As a 4-H-er, my favorite project was cooking, and my favorite year the one during which I was enrolled in a cooking project called "International Foods." There I learned how to make Swedish Christmas cookies and chili with V-8 juice.

Moving to Evanston right next to Chicago for graduate school was like moving to a culinary Disneyland. Within the first few months, I'd jettisoned the boxes of instant mashed potatoes and cans of Campbell's soup I'd brought with me and started stocking my cupboard with bulgur and tree ear fungus purchased at small neighborhood groceries that looked nothing like Duke's Family Grocery on Rice Lake's Main Street. Each week, I scoured the *Chicago Reader* for two-for-one restaurant coupons for interesting ethnic restaurants I could get to on the "El." Even a graduate student could afford to eat in those places.

In the mid-1980s, Thai restaurants were opening in large numbers in Chicago, and I still remember my first visit to one. My roommate's parents were in town, and they took us to dinner at the Thai Star Cafe on State Street. I tasted *Kai Thom Kha*—a chicken soup made with coconut milk, lemon grass, and *kha* or galangal, a spice related to ginger—and realized that I'd never tasted anything like it before. The food I experienced that evening probably contained at least six spices with which I'd never come in contact. After the meal, the four of us sat around marveling at how wonderful the food had been—and my, how very inexpensive, too! (Now, I marvel at the fact that I can buy a shiny foil packet of powdered *Kai Thom Kha* mix in my local food co-op.)

After eating my way through the inexpensive ethnic restaurants of Chicago and Evanston during graduate school (the weekend I defended my dissertation, I celebrated with meals at both an Indian and a Peruvian restaurant), I moved to a small town in Minnesota, and then to another small town in Minnesota. There, I found my food adventuring severely curtailed; the few restaurants tended toward pizza, burgers, and the occasional steak, and in the grocery stores food from major American conglomerates dominated the shelves. Of course, some of my colleagues who were not products of the upper Midwest did find the foods of the area exotic—and often unrecognizable. They did feel like food adventurers when they found Jello with peas in it at the restaurant salad bar, or when they went to a lutefisk dinner sponsored by the local Lutheran church. But for me, Jello salad and lutefisk were very old, as well as very unappetizing, news.

Despite the dearth of opportunities for food adventuring in my new   5 hometown, I found ways to scrape by. On weekend visits to Minneapolis and St. Paul, trips to professional conventions, sabbaticals in other towns, and summer vacations, I managed to collect dining experiences in restaurants serving all sorts of ethnic cuisines, ranging from the relatively routine (Vietnamese food in St. Paul) to the more unusual (Tibetan food at "America's Second Only Tibetan Restaurant" in Bloomington, Indiana), to the really-pretty-darn-rare (dinner at a short-lived Hmong restaurant in Minneapolis). By scouring the "Restaurants by Ethnicity" section of the Manhattan Yellow Pages, I found a place serving Burmese food within walking distance of the hotel where I was staying for the American Philosophical Association convention. Following a friend—a newspaper food critic and self-described food adventurer on an "eat your way around the world" tour for his paper—through the streets of Cochin, India, late one night, I landed at a neighborhood family restaurant featuring Moghul food. And when I had dinner in Minneapolis with another friend, we would eat at her idea of a comfort-food restaurant: an Ethiopian place right near her office at the university.

"Experiment" was my middle name; I'd try (nearly) anything once, and I actively sought any and all opportunities to increase the number and range of eating adventures I had. Experimentation had its risks and dangers of course—the dangers of ordering a dish that was too spicy, too full of "weird" foods—but that risk was just part of the adventure. I was not alone on my quests; wherever I adventured, I could always be sure of company. No matter what crowd I was in, there was always someone else like me, eager to eat things she'd never heard of before. I was becoming a food adventurer, and I (mostly) didn't look back.

Over time, though, I started to have some suspicions about my food adventuring. For one thing, various experiences made me feel uncomfortable about the easy acquisitiveness with which I approached a new kind of food, the tenacity with which I collected adventures. Was such collecting really just a benign recreation, like collecting Pogs or Pez containers or, God forbid, Hummel figurines? Or was it more like collecting cultural artifacts—Hopi ceremonial masks, say—a kind of collecting that many Hopi regard as a particularly invasive form of appropriation? It seemed to me that foods were often intertwined in their cultures in ways that many ritual objects are. Did that mean that my easy, breezy sampling of them also counted as appropriation? Was I stealing their bones—roasted, braised, or boiled, perhaps—but stealing nonetheless?

Other experiences made me reflect on the circumstances that conspired to bring these cuisines into my world in the first place. On my first visit to an Eritrean restaurant, for example, I found myself thinking about how disturbing and complicated it was to be tasting the food of people who were in the middle of a calamitous famine—and also thinking about the fact that not eating in the restaurant wouldn't exactly solve anything either (whatever the anything was that needed solving). If it's exploitative of me to eat the foods of marginalized Others in casual ignorance, with no regard for the cultural context of those foods, then what is it to refuse to eat the food of the Other (especially when this very concrete Other is attempting to make a living by selling it to me and people like me)?

An offhand remark in a murder mystery started me thinking about the reasons there were so many Vietnamese restaurants in Minneapolis/ St. Paul, reasons directly connected to the U.S. war in Vietnam, and the resultant dislocation of Vietnamese, Laotian, and Hmong people. (So, since the Other didn't want to move to Minneapolis, and since they probably only started a restaurant out of necessity, am I acting in solidarity with them, or am I just taking advantage of their disadvantage? And don't try to tell me that "this is just dinner, so lighten up.")

Eventually, I put a name to my strange penchant for cooking and eating   10 ethnic foods—most frequently and most notably the foods of third-world cultures. (And yes, that's a term I worry about.) The unflattering name I chose for my activities was "cultural food colonialism," which made me your basic colonizer. As I saw it, my adventure eating was motivated by an attitude that bore an uncomfortable resemblance to the various ideologies of western colonialism. When I began to examine my culture-hopping in the kitchen and in restaurants, I found echoes of nineteenth-and early twentieth-century European painters and explorers, who set out in search of ever "newer," ever more "remote" cultures which they could co-opt, borrow from freely and out of context, and use as the raw materials for their own efforts at creation and discovery. Richard Burton and Henry School-craft, for example, reported that they had "discovered" the headwaters of the Nile and the Mississippi, respectively—but only after local folks had led them to the spots they sought. Later, Paul Gauguin went to Tahiti to "immerse [himself] in virgin nature, see no one but savages, live their life . . ." in order that he might make "simple, very simple art"—using their lives and art as his raw material.[1]

Of course I knew that it was much too simplistic to label my adventuring unregenerately colonialist and reject it out of hand, which is at least one of the reasons I didn't stop eating out. After all, weren't my eating and cooking also efforts to play, and to learn about other cultures in ways I genuinely intended to be respectful? Surely such noble intentions deserve some credit! Perhaps. But though the picture grew more complicated, I could not ignore the fact that underneath, or alongside, or over and above all these other reasons for my adventuring, I was motivated by a deep desire to have contact with and somehow to own an experience of an Exotic Other to make myself more interesting. Food adventuring, as I was coming to think about it, made me a participant in cultural colonialism, just as surely as eating Mexican strawberries in January made me a participant in economic colonialism.

Move ahead fifteen years from my first adventure in that Chicago Thai restaurant, to a Thai restaurant in Dublin. In fifteen years, I'd had countless adventures, as well as countless opportunities to experience misgivings about my adventuring ways. I'd also tried to develop ways to resist my colonizing tendencies, to disrupt the colonizing scripts that present themselves so readily when I set foot in an ethnic restaurant or grocery store or open an ethnic cookbook.

While vacationing in Ireland, my partner and I found ourselves ravenously hungry very early one evening in Dublin. Five thirty is an inconvenient time to be hungry in Ireland; most restaurants don't open for dinner until a much more fashionable hour, so unless you can satisfy yourself with pub food, your only options are to tough it out or wander the streets in hopes of finding someplace open. Luck, however, was with us that evening; we stumbled upon an open Thai restaurant.

Sounds odd, I know, but finding a Thai restaurant in Ireland felt strangely reassuring. When we're at home in Minnesota, we eat Thai food whenever we get the chance—which means whenever we can manage to be in Minneapolis or St. Paul around dinner time. I'm always shopping around for another Thai restaurant to visit, and once inside, I tend to try lots of dishes on the menu (surprise). Peg, on the other hand, prefers familiar foods; she sticks to her favorite dish, *pad thai* (the Thai national dish, restaurant menus inform me). She's become something of a *pad thai* connoisseur in the last few years. She knows which places use too much *nam pla* (fish sauce) or ketchup in the sauce, the ones that pile on the scallions (also a no-no), and the ones where the peanuts dusting the noodles are fresh and generous. *Pad thai* has become comfort food for her, the way grilled cheese sandwiches and ginger ale were when she was a kid.

15   So, here we were in a Thai restaurant in Ireland, feeling surreally confident after days of moving tentatively (and somewhat squeamishly) through an unfamiliar world of pub lunches and full Irish breakfasts. (Do you know what black pudding is? Have you ever confronted it at the breakfast table?)

I remember walking into the restaurant thinking, "Well, at least I'll know how to behave here; I know how to behave in Thai restaurants." Armed with this sense of belonging, of being in the know, I immediately began deciding which features of the restaurant's decor were genuinely Thai, and which were of obvious Irish origin—this despite my never having been in Thailand in my life, and having spent a grand total of six days in Ireland so far. I found myself chuckling at the sight of the red-haired, freckled Irish teenager dressed in traditional Thai shirt and trousers who filled our water glasses. What in the world did those wacky Irish think they were trying to prove by dressing up in traditional Thai costumes? Surely they didn't think they were passing for Thai—with that hair?!

In the midst of my complacency, however, I also found myself confused and a bit ill at ease. Here I was, staring in the face of a cross-cultural entrepreneurial enterprise that did not in any (apparent or necessary) way involve the United States, or a U.S. influence. Some Thai people apparently just moved to Ireland and opened a restaurant—and it looked like they didn't even pass Go (a.k.a. the United States) to do it. How could this be? (And, more to the point, what would their *pad thai* taste like?)

Then our server came. I'd already decided, upon seeing her, that she had to be Thai, given her facial features and hair. Imagine my surprise and confusion when I said, in my best American-Thai-restaurant language, *"Pad thai*, please," and she responded, "Excuse me?" I tried it again. No luck. After the third time, I resorted to ostensive definition, and she said "Ohhhh," followed by something I didn't understand, then went off to place our order. I decided, in that instant, that she must not be Thai, must be from some other Southeast Asian nation, and didn't in fact even speak Thai. (Note to self: ethnicity of servers doesn't "match" cuisine, appearances to the contrary. Authentic anyway?) What other possible explanation could there be for the fact that she didn't understand my request for *pad thai*? Surely it couldn't be that my rendition of the term *pad thai* was unintelligible to a native speaker of the language—could it? And surely if she were Thai, she would speak Thai—wouldn't she? Unbelievably, it bothered me that I was not understood when I uttered a single phrase in a language I don't speak, to a person who may or may not have spoken that language either.

All the while that I assessed the restaurant and its staff, another part of me (the cynical bystander part) watched myself in operation and wryly noted my eagerness to separate the authentically Thai elements from the "Irish Thai" ones. I was surprised—and embarrassed—to realize how willingly and easily I slipped into my food adventurer ways, with all the presumptions and ideological underpinnings essential to that role:

1. Novel and exotic is always better. Thai food in Minneapolis? Not bad. Thai food in Ireland? Even better.
2. Slavish devotion to authenticity is a must. Is that the pot They would use to make a dish? Do the Thai really use ketchup in *pad thai*? (And aren't I, the white girl, just the person to make that assessment?)
3. The ethnic Other (the server, in this case) is a resource I may use to meet my own expectations, fill my own desires, and thereby embellish my own identity. Wouldn't my server always understand me? Wouldn't she be happy to tell me some insider anecdotes about her "native land" (never mind that she's actually from Co. Kerry and not Bangkok)?
4. The United States is culinary central, the place through which any "foreign" culture must pass before relocating to another "foreign" locale. And American culture is a plain white plate, ideal for setting off the features of an ethnic cuisine without imparting any flavors of its own. Why wouldn't I be knowledgeable about the difference between "authentic" Thai and Irish-influenced Thai restaurants? I'm American for God's sake—the perfect person to judge true authenticity!

Are you still with me? Okay, I know: you want to hear about the *pad thai*. Fine. It was really pretty good. A little too sweet for my taste (could Irish ketchup be even sweeter than American?), but really very tasty. And no evidence of black pudding anywhere.

20   Fifteen years of food adventuring and billions of calories later, I'm no more settled about my actions, no clearer about my choices than I was before. If anything, I've come to feel that my actions, and their context, are much more complicated than my categories of analysis can possibly reveal.

So what have I learned? Well, I've learned to stop trying to satisfy my philosopher's desire for clarity, and my Good Girl's desire to have clean hands in all of this. And I've learned that despite my valiant efforts to take all the fun out of food, I won't destroy or save the world at the dinner table. And I've learned that at the end of the day, around dinner time to be precise, I still love food, especially something that is new and different to me. But I've also admitted that just by eating "ethnic" we adventurers don't have a claim on another culture. Neither can we pretend to understand it because we think we know how the natives eat. Good intentions aside, that is simply impossible.

Try looking at it this way: diving into all the squid, olives, dolmades, and baklava in the world just isn't going to teach me all that much about Athenian culture or Peloponnesian traditions. At the end of the day, it's all Greek to me.

Now would you please pass the lemon soup?

Note

1. Quoted in Daniel Guerin, *The Writings of a Savage: Paul Gauguin*, p. 48.

Further Reading

Churchill, Ward. "Spiritual Hucksterism." *Z Magazine*. December 1990: 94–98.

Guerin, Daniel, ed. *The Writings of a Savage: Paul Gauguin*. trans. Eleanor Levieux. New York: Viking, 1978.

hooks, bell. *Black Looks: Race and Representation*. Boston: South End, 1992.

Kadi, Joanna. *Thinking Class*. Boston: South End, 1996.

Lutz, Catherine A,. and Jane L. Collins. *Reading National Geographic*. Chicago: University of Chicago Press, 1993.

Messenger, Phyllis Mauch, ed. *The Ethics of Collecting Cultural Property: Whose Culture? Whose Property?* Albuquerque: University of New Mexico Press, 1989.

Pratt, Mary Louise. *Imperial Eyes: Travel Writing and Transculturation*. New York: Routledge, 1992.

Said, Edward. *Orientalism*. New York: Vintage, 1979.

Trinh T. Minh-ha. *Woman Native Other: Writing Postcoloniality and Feminism*. Bloomington: Indiana University Press, 1989.

Vizenor, Gerald. *The People Named the Chippewa*. Minneapolis: University of Minnesota Press, 1984.

Analyze

1. Although this article begins with a personal story, it has a rather academic tone overall. Analyze the language and other qualities that make it so. What is the effect of the writer's style in achieving the author's purpose—and what is that purpose?

2. Heldke writes, "As I saw it, my adventure eating was motivated by an attitude that bore an uncomfortable resemblance to the various ideologies of western colonialism." What does this mean? What evidence does Heldke provide? (You may need to find a working definition of "colonialism" as a start.)

3. What do Heldke's experiences seem to indicate about our shared experiences, assumptions, and stereotypes about other cultures? What does she conclude about her own experiences and analyses of those experiences?

Explore

1. Heldke equates her food colonialism with the experiences of explorers and others. For instance, she mentions Richard Burton, Henry Schoolcraft, and Paul Gauguin. Research information about these people and argue their relevance to this discussion using the resources that you discover.

2. Organize a discussion among your peers in which you look at yourselves and your experiences in "ethnic restaurants" and the extent to which you are "colonial" in your outlook. What do you discover? Why? Be sure to develop specific examples and argue a point of view, using this article as your model.

3. Heldke's position in this article is that of someone from the outside of a culture looking into it through food. Explore your sense of the perspectives of those in the opposite situation: that is, those who bring their culture through food "to the table." How do examples in Heldke's article give you a sense of that experience? How might you expand your sense of that experience?

Pico Iyer
"Daily Bread"

Pico Iyer is the author of many books about travel and culture, including *Video Night in Katmandu* (1989), *The Lady and the Monk* (1992), and *The Global Soul* (2001). He has also contributed to *Time* magazine since the 1980s. His most recent book is *The Man within My Head* (2013), his second novel, which centers on crossing cultures and journeys both literal and metaphorical. In "Daily Bread," Iver recounts his experience at a monastery.

What does "the daily bread" represent to the author?

The quiche is as soft as hope itself, and the long spears of asparagus are so elegant on the plate that to pick one up feels like messing with the symmetry of a Klee. There are bowls of lettuce in our midst, and the chunky vegetable soup alone would make for a hearty meal. Bottles of salad dressing crowd the blond-wood table, large enough for six of us, while early-spring sunlight streams into the window-filled refectory, so that it feels as if we're tasting radiance and taking a long draught of the sun.

The man next to me, his white hood down, springs up to cut the fluffy long fingers of quiche for an older neighbour, who lives now with Parkinson's. Then he comes back and tells me about the nine-hour drive he just took to an ashram in southern India, and the forest fire that wiped out a colleague's place in the hills of Santa Barbara. I ask him if he saw the movie about the monks of the Grande Chartreuse and we talk about the Dalai Lama, Tanzania, how best to die. One of the men who's just left this place—for Jerusalem, to work for peace—used to zealously keep the Sabbath in the midst of all these Catholics.

"I suppose monks are the only ones who don't keep the Sabbath," I say to my friend Raniero.

"The inner Sabbath only," he says, his cheek dimpling as if he were not the prior.

In the corner there are two large tubs of green-tea ice cream and Italian   5
spumoni dessert; next to them, two plates of peach pie with fruit so fresh I wonder if it's been airlifted over from the Garden. In another corner is a thermos of hot water and all the teas, fancy and a little less so, that modern California can devise. We talk of common friends—Berkeley, Shanghai,

LA—and I hear from a beaming monk how all the miles collected on the monastery credit card are sending him this summer—first class!—to Rio.

Then Raniero gets up and rings a little bell. "Dear God," he says, quickly, without fuss, "thank you for this food and the friendship around these tables. Special blessings to Benedict, for preparing this excellent meal. As we go forth from this room and back to our duties, may we always see that light that shines in others and in ourselves."

"You free for some washing-up, Pico?" the man next to me, in an apron, says. Seconds later, I am standing next to the former prior, in his eighties, and the current one, working briskly, as we chat, to make all the plates shine again.

What in the world am I doing here, you might ask? I sometimes ask myself. I'm not a Catholic, and nine years of enforced chapel twice a day at British boarding school (with Latin hymns on Sunday nights) seemed to satisfy more than a lifetime's quota of religion. I respect those people who have the groundedness and selflessness that faith often brings—the alertness to compassion and a larger view of things—but I'm not quick to call those virtues mine.

Yet what I am is a traveller, whose life is about trying to occupy shoes—and lives and hearts—very different from my own; and a human being, who cannot fail to be washed clean and opened up by silence. So I come to this Benedictine hermitage, tucked into the central coast of California, and sit in a little cell looking out on the great blue plate of the Pacific, 1300 feet below, scintillant in the sunshine, blue–green waters pooling around rocks, filling the horizon from one end of my deck to the other, and think about what travel really means, and why these men in hoods seem like the most fearless and spirited adventurers I've ever met.

10   A monk wants to be clear and undistracted in his journey, so he doesn't have too much to eat (in theory), or too little; there's nothing uncomfortable about this place, and sometimes I feel almost embarrassed at how well treated we visitors are. In my little trailer—"Hesychia," it's called, meaning "spirit of stillness"—there's a large pot of Extra-Crunchy Skippy peanut butter ("Fuel the Fun!") above the stove, next to a bag of Swiss Miss Milk Chocolate. In the communal kitchen, the ten or twelve people staying here on retreat can help themselves to "Very Cherry" yoghurt and extra-virgin olive oil, Colombian coffee and kosher salt. Someone has contributed pineapple salsa from Trader Joe's to the communal refrigerator, and one large bottle is always filled with oatmeal raisin cookies.

Every day, at 12.30, bells ring—as they do for Mass—and a monk drives down in a cracked blue hatchback, no licence plate on it, dust swirling up behind him as he accelerates out of the Monastic Enclosure, and brings us a tureen of hot soup, a main dish, some vegetables and often extras, from which each of us collects a lunch to eat in silence in our rooms. One day it is carrot soup, flecks of Bugs Bunny's favourite floating on the surface so it looks like strawberry yoghurt. Another day there are egg rolls, and pasta shells with salmon in them (fish the only ingredient to disrupt the monks' vegetarianism). One year every dish came with a sprig of mint, or some basil, courtesy of a chef from a four-star restaurant in San Francisco who was spending a year here on retreat, getting himself in order. *"Buon appetito!"* the monk always says as he leaves the glass trays on the counter, to come and collect them again an hour later.

If I wanted mere food, I realised some years ago—steaks and sorbets and spicy panang curry with strong chillies—I could find them almost anywhere these days, ten minutes from my home or across the world in some fairy-tale palace; if I wanted a meal to remember, I could go back to Aleppo or Buenos Aires or Hanoi. But after seventeen years of criss-crossing the globe, I came to think that it was only the food I couldn't see that really sustained me and only inner nutrition that made me happy, deep down. A meal I grabbed in a Paris McDonald's, to keep me walking through the streets of the 6th *arrondissement*, left me hungry ten minutes after I'd finished it; a richer, fancier lunch left me so replete that all energy for exploration was gone for the day.

Here I just get into a car and drive up a winding mountain road along the sea, three hours from my mother's house, and find that I am perpetually full and hungry for more with every breath—the way, in love, you thirst for the other's company, yet know that even years together will never be enough.

Now, as the bells ring and ring—time is so slowed down here that I explore every moment as I would the crevices and soft spots in a new lover or a simple honey-flavoured candy exploding in my mouth like caviar—I can reach in my little trailer for the rice and bean chips (with adzuki beans) I've brought up or (as I've smuggled in here on more than fifty retreats now over nineteen years) the jumbo bag of chocolate chip cookies. In the monastery bookstore they're selling Chocolate Fudge Royale and Special Gourmet Mocha Mix in hazelnut flavour. Pieces of the hermitage's celebrated moist fruitcake are available, free of charge, by the cash register, and

15

bottles of Monastery Creamed Honey sit among the Tibetan prayer bowls and rosaries.

But mostly what I do here is think about daily bread, and what communion means in the context of the traveller's daily lifelong companions: restlessness and solitude. In silence the day stretches out and out till sometimes it feels as if yesterday were an eternity ago. I wake up as the first light begins to show above the hills, and make toast and two cups of tea for myself in my little kitchen. I take long walks along the monastery road, stopping at the benches set around every turn to watch the sun sparkle on the water and the coastline to the south slough off its coat of early-morning fog. I read and read—Patti Smith, Marcus Aurelius, Werner Herzog, Thomas Merton— and attention becomes so sharpened that every snatch of perfume, scuffling rabbit or echo hits me like a shock.

The day itself becomes my fuel. I reach for some "simply cashew, almond and cranberry" trail mix from my suitcase. I stop by the kitchen to pick up an apple. I handwrite letters to friends far away, make plans for the summer, watch the colours turn above the ocean as the darkness falls.

Not having anywhere to go or anything I have to do—no telephone or laptop or television—makes each hour feel as nutritious as a Christmas feast. And spending so many hours in silence, all emptied out, gives new meaning to community when the monks invite us to share in their lunch after Sunday Mass (I go to lunch though I skip the Mass).

Sometimes, when I don't intend to, or am just walking down the road, or reading a biography of the incorrigibly licentious Lord Rochester, I think about what I seek at mealtime. It's not the tastes I savour (I was born and grew up in England, so my taste buds were surgically removed at birth); it's the setting, the circumstances, the company. I would rather, as Thoreau might have muttered, eat a hunk of bread with a friend over good conversation, in a place of beauty such as this, than suffer through a multicourse opera at El Bulli. The food is a means to happiness, a sense of peace; and the true meaning of happiness, as Socrates told me yesterday morning, is not to have more things but to need less. I've never been in a restaurant where people seem so much themselves—which is to say at home—as at the Sunday lunches with the monks.

20　　It's really just a story of love and attention, I come to think—and not even caring which is which, or where one ends and the other begins. I've been lucky enough to eat *injera* bread at Lalibela on New Year's Eve, and to step down into a basement kitchen in Lhasa, where red-cheeked Tibetan girls were cooking up a feast. I've had $300 French kaiseki meals along the red-lanterned lane of the Pontocho district, near my home in Kyoto, looking out on the Kamo River and the eastern hills of the old capital beyond, a moon above the temple spires. I've relished vegetarian meals in a blue restaurant painted over with the lines of Neruda in Easter Island on the first day of the millennium.

But I don't think any place has taught me what a meal is—not just food and not just fuel—so much as here. "Get up and eat, else the journey will be long for you!" was the topic of the week's sermon at St Anthony's church, in the middle of modern Istanbul, when I looked in on it seven months ago. Now I reach into my bag of Reduced Guilt white corn tortilla chips, and pull out of a drawer one of the "sweet–hot soft ginger-candies" a friend gave me on the way up here. The journey doesn't seem long at all. At the very best restaurants I've visited, my body changes a little when I'm through, and my mood lifts a bit too. Here, when I'm finished with my lunch, I feel as if my life has been transformed.

Analyze

1. This article is at once a narrative about experience in a monastery and explorations in the world, especially explorations through food. What are the differences in these two types of experiences? How does Iyer draw connections between the two?

2. "Not having anywhere to go or anything I have to do—no telephone or laptop or television—makes each hour feel as nutritious as a Christmas feast." How can this be? Explain, using examples throughout the article, what the author might mean by this statement.

3. How would you articulate Iyer's philosophy on both travel and food, using specific examples from the text? For instance, he writes, "what I am is a traveller, whose life is about trying to occupy shoes—and lives and hearts—very different from my own." In what other ways does Iyer reveal what you might call his philosophical goals?

Explore

1. Reflect differently on the quote cited above ("Not having anywhere to go") and, referring to examples from the text, comment on your

own experience as it might be were you to experience this solitude and deliberate "unconnectedness."

2. Iyer writes about the people he "reads and reads," specifically mentioning Patti Smith, Marcus Aurelius, Werner Herzog, and Thomas Merton. Who are these people? Why might they be important in the author's journey? Select at least two and work with your peers to prepare a presentation for class.

3. Iyer has also written an essay called "Why We Travel," which has been widely published and is very popular and easily available. Find this article, read it, and then write an essay in which you use both "Why We Travel" and "Daily Bread" to explore the larger, more philosophical connections between travel and food.

Tim Cahill
"The Rooster's Head in the Soup"

Tim Cahill is a travel writer living in Montana; he is a regular contributor to *National Geographic Adventure Magazine*. Cahill is also founding editor and editor at large for *Outside Magazine*. He has written several books about travel, including *A Wolverine Is Eating My Leg* (1989), *Pass the Butterworms: Remote Journeys Oddly Rendered* (1998), and *Lost in My Own Backyard: A Walk in Yellowstone National Park* (2004). Cahill was also an editor of *Best American Travel Writing* in 2006. This piece explores our attitudes toward new and strange foods.

How does Cahill's article influence the way that we confront the unknown?

Do you eat the thing or what? It's a rooster's head and it's floating in the soup. You are in a dirt-floored hut, a two-room adobe family home up in what is called the Eyebrow of the Jungle, the Ceja de Selva, in the cloud forests of Peru. The Peruvian family has allowed you to camp on their little farm and now they've invited you to dinner. Out comes the first dish. It's a yellow soup. And there's a rooster's head floating in it. Skeletal thing: no skin or eyeballs. Nothing inside the cranial cavity at all.

That was the first time I asked myself the Question most avid travellers are presented with at one time or another. Are they making fun of me, or is the rooster's head really given to the honoured guest? Back then, I spent some moments wrestling with the implications. Ruminating, so to speak. Assumption #1: they are, in fact, making fun of me. Okay. What's the worst that can happen? I chomp down on the fragile bones of the skull and everyone bursts out laughing. Well, it wouldn't be the first time I was the object of hilarity. I can generally salvage that situation by simply laughing right along with everyone else. They might think I'm an imbecile, but no-one is going to be insulted.

Now assume that the rooster's head is, in fact, a local delicacy. If you treat it as a joke, there is a good chance you will alienate your hosts. You absolutely do not want to alienate your hosts. Not up here in the Eyebrow of the Jungle where the trails are steep and sometimes lead to a crumbling precipice over a 5000-foot drop. You don't want to alienate your hosts if you need them to tell you where the pre-Columbian ruins are. You don't want to alienate your hosts if you are going to camp in their vicinity for several days because you are, in fact, genuinely interested in the local culture. Finally, you don't want to alienate them because refusing a delicacy might be a mortal insult, to be avenged with machetes. Probably not, but why take the chance? Let them laugh instead.

So the Answer to the Question is simple enough: you eat what's put in front of you. It's a no-brainer. Just like that white avian skull, floating in the soup.

The fowl tale I've recounted happened in Peru over three decades ago, but I've spent a lot of the intervening time travelling in the hinterlands of various countries, and something similar has happened to me on every continent, save Antarctica. Out in the back country, in those remote places where folks do not have much contact with the outside world, people tend to be generous with their food. Some kind family is always offering me something that, at first glance, does not seem to be 100 per cent palatable. Baked turtle lung. Sheep's eyeballs.

Smile and choke it down. That's my policy. If they have something vaguely alcoholic to drink—palm wine, corn beer—all the better. In central Africa, under the Virunga volcanoes, people make a kind of banana beer they call *pombe* that is served in one-litre brown glass bottles that once contained beer. *Pombe* simply means beer in Swahili, but I was cautioned about this banana variety: don't pour it into a glass, said the brewer himself;

you don't want to actually see it. The *pombe* is best drunk with a wooden straw. This is because the fermenting bananas leave a thick layer of black sludge on the glass. I've since learned that, in the final brewing process, the beer can be filtered through a fine cloth. I'm thinking that my brewer may have found that process superfluous.

Banana *pombe* was the after-work libation for a couple of African guides who were taking me out to see a group of mountain gorillas. The animals lived low on the volcanoes, in the visually limited world of the bamboo forests, and care had to be taken not to blunder onto the gorillas and startle them. They could run away. Or charge. Neither situation was ideal.

So it was thirsty work, crawling through the bamboo along a gorilla path, trying not to make any noise. When we walked home in the evening, the guides always checked a certain home built of sturdy wooden slats. If there were flowers in a vase on the porch, it meant that the brewer who lived there had *pombe*. We were obliged to stop and help this gentleman dispose of the beer, which has about a 48-hour shelf life. It was our duty. Should the brewer have unsold bottles on his shelf he could, the guides informed me solemnly, simply stop making *pombe*.

The stuff was a titch sweet and seemed to contain as much alcohol, drop for drop, as anything brewed by Anheuser-Busch. It was fine to sip beer through a straw after a sweaty day of crawling after primates. The way I saw it, I was helping the brewer and the community's beer drinkers, and learning all kinds of things about gorillas I might never have found out entirely sober.

10   While my policy is to eat what is put in front of me, I have tried, over the years, to reciprocate when I can. Usually I just have camp food, and if I have learned one thing, it is this: no-one on earth likes freeze-dried scrambled eggs.

I do recall a memorable meal I once cooked in Indonesia. I was visiting the Karowai, a clan of Papuans who live in tree houses. Some Karowai groups, especially those who live away from the river, are unaware of the outside world. The group I trekked through the swamp to meet had been contacted only the previous year. My travelling companions and I came upon this group in their tree house and we negotiated with them, standing in clouds of mosquitoes and shouting fifty feet up through the branches.

Eventually we were welcomed. The house was a large wooden platform, shaded by the tree itself. There were few mosquitoes and the wind was fresh.

We met three men, two older, one younger. There were three women. The men, one couldn't help but notice, wrapped their penises with leaves. The women wore straw skirts.

There was a wooden wall and on it was the skeleton of a fish about the size of a trout. The remains of a fine meal? Just offset from the one wall were dozens of hardball-sized rocks arranged as a fire pit and the women placed something white and doughy-looking on the coals. It was, I was told, a staple starchy food made from powdered sago palm. After a short time, the women broke off a piece of the bread-like substance and handed it to me. It felt like a lighter version of Silly Putty and was so bland as to be almost tasteless. But, no, there was an unpleasant sour aftertaste.

I smiled brightly and nodded vigorously, a suggestion that this was a delicious treat. The Karowai stared at me in glum suspicion. They knew perfectly what it was. They ate it every day. Why did I climb fifty feet up a rickety ladder just to lie to them?

We stayed with the Karowai for several days and one night we asked if   15 we might make the dinner. Rice was what we had. We doctored it with oil and bottled lemon juice and garlic salt. As the younger man ate, moisture formed in the corners of his eyes. He took another mouthful, eating with his fingers while tears coursed down his cheeks. Now what had I done?

Translating took a while, but in the fullness of time I learned that the man was crying because this rice was the best thing he'd ever eaten in his life. The other Karowai nodded in agreement. Never, I believe, has a chef been so complimented.

The next morning, overcome with an unwarranted confidence, I fixed freeze-dried scrambled eggs for everyone. The Karowai ate sparingly and stared at me, wan smiles on their faces. I recognised the expression. It was one I'd felt on my own face many times over the years. They were smiling the smile you smile when you've just eaten the rooster's head.

Analyze

1. What is the tone and writing style of the essay, particularly the first paragraph? For instance, why do you think Cahill uses the pronoun "you?" To what effect?

2. Cahill writes, "you eat what's put in front of you. It's a no-brainer." According to the text, what are the larger cultural implications of either eating or rejecting what's put in front of you?

3. The author seems to be commenting on the attitudes of Western, likely (mostly) American travelers as they encounter far more exotic eating experiences and cuisines than their own. What are these attitudes? In what fashion does Cahill describe them? Is he fair? Judgmental? How would you describe the position he takes? Why?

Explore

1. Cahill's initial reaction to the rooster head was to wonder this: "Are they making fun of me, or is the rooster's head really given to the honoured guest?" Research customs related to hospitality and food for a particular culture that is not your own. What do you find? Prepare a presentation—multimedia, if possible, using written as well as visual texts—for your peers.

2. One might say that there are larger, important questions and discussions raised by this article, issues related to cultural difference and one's acceptance of those practices different from one's own. A related, ethical question, however, is this: Are there cultural practices that you research that break ethical boundaries of your own traditions, cultural practices, or ways of negotiating the world? Research one such very different practice, and be prepared to argue why we should *not* negotiate or accept it as legitimate.

3. Draw upon your own experiences as you have encountered foods, for instance, that are tremendously different from what you are used to. Using this article as a touchstone, compare and contrast these differences and how you chose to negotiate them. To what extent did this experience/set of experiences help you appreciate the cultural differences between you and someone else? Why or why not?

Coleman Andrews
"Everything Comes from the Sea"

Called a "gastronomic globetrotter," Coleman Andrews is known for his cookbooks and is something of a legend in the food world. Founder and editor of *Saveur* magazine until 2006, Andrews then became a restaurant

critic for *Gourmet*. Andrews has won awards from the James Beard Foundation and the International Association of Culinary Professionals. The following piece evokes the food of Venice, particularly the importance of fishing
industries.

Why would the author choose this title?

I t's lunchtime in Venice, and my friend Bepi and I are sitting under a red
umbrella in front of a restaurant called Busa Alla Torre on the tourist-
clogged glassblowing island of Murano. There are tourists here too, but
Bepi, a retired bank auditor and part-time glass merchant from neighboring Burano, takes his eating seriously ("The best moment of the day," he
says, "is when your knees are under the table"). Plus, he's an old friend of the
establishment's proprietor, Lele Masiol, so I'm pretty sure our meal is going
to be something special.

Big, red-haired, red-faced and gregarious, Masiol looks like he should be
running a pub in County Tipperary, not a trattoria on the Venetian lagoon.
But he's a local boy too, and when Bepi says "Today we want to eat *alla
Buranese*"—Burano-style—Masiol knows exactly what he means and
heads for the kitchen.

Five minutes later, he returns with a couple of plates covered in shrimp
barely an inch long, lightly floured and fried and still in their edible shells.
They are accompanied by a big spoonful of *baccalà mantecato*, a creamy
purée of stockfish (the air-dried brother of salt cod), a dish so important to
the local cuisine that there is a *confraternità*, or brotherhood, dedicated to
its appreciation. It also comes with a small slab of grilled white polenta,
which is about the most delicious bit of cornmeal mush I think I've ever
tasted.

We've barely finished when the next course arrives: slightly larger
shrimp, peeled and quickly boiled, then dressed with olive oil and parsley
and served with fried baby artichokes from the garden island of Sant'Erasmo
alongside a pool of soft white polenta. Polenta is the defining starch in traditional Venetian cooking (pasta and risotto were rare in working-class
homes here until the mid-20th century), and there's more of it with the
next dish. This time it comes with *moleche*, softshell shore crabs about the
size of silver dollars, *in saor*, which means marinated in vinegar with sweet
onions, pine nuts and raisins. "Okay," says Masiol, "now I'll give you *risotto
di gô*." This is a dish found nowhere else but Venice, though rarely on the

ten-language tourist menus. *Gô* ("goby" in English) is a small fish that's too bony to eat by itself but is used to flavor rice—which many cooks manage by putting poached *gô* in a linen bag and squeezing the juices into the pot. Because the flavor of *gô* is mild, Masiol has upped the ante by adding two varieties of minuscule clams, known locally as *bevarasse* and *malgarotte*, neither any bigger than a baby's fingernail.

5   Finally, just to make sure we've had enough to eat, Masiol brings a gorgeous fritto misto. He has prepared it with *moleche* and lots of scampi, the emblematic Adriatic crayfish—actually a tiny lobster (and nothing to do, incidentally, with the garlicky shrimp dish that's popular in Italian-American restaurants)—as well as thin bits of zucchini, onion, eggplant, sweet pepper and carrot. "Lele buys at least half of his seafood from retired fishermen who bring back just a little of this and a little of that," says Bepi as we finish. "That's why he has some of the best in Venice."

I didn't know it at the time, but as we were enjoying this excellent repast, the Giudecca canal, in the heart of Venice, was clogged with fishing boats (an estimated 200 of them) protesting the Italian government's implementation of new European Union fishing rules. These would, among other things, mandate the use of nets with mesh large enough to let most of what Bepi and I ate at Busa Alla Torre slip through.

It's not much of an exaggeration to say that in Venetian cuisine, everything comes from the sea. In this case, "sea" means the Mediterranean in general and the Adriatic in particular, but especially the salty expanses of the Venetian lagoon—a vast wetland, one of the largest in the Mediterranean basin, covering about 136,000 acres of mudflats, salt marshes and open water. Several of the islands in this lagoon yield vegetables of extraordinary quality, and its tidal fringes harbor wild ducks and other game birds that are an important part of traditional Venetian cooking. But the real bounty is the breathtaking array of top-quality fish, shellfish and cephalopods (squid, octopus and the like), some of them found only here.

Seafood comes to the city primarily through the Mercato Ittico all'ingrosso del Tronchetto, the big wholesale fish market near the Piazzale Roma (where the city's bus depot and parking garage complexes are located). Fluorescent-lit, with aisles of wet floors lined with crates and Styrofoam boxes full of fish and shellfish of every description, it isn't a very romantic place. Seafood of the highest quality is sold there, but because local waters produce nowhere near enough to supply the city's needs, much of what's on offer is frozen, and a lot of it comes not from the Mediterranean but from the Atlantic and the Pacific. A few years ago, in fact, the market issued a statement estimating that only around 20 percent of the seafood sold there was local. I've heard estimates that it's probably closer to 10 percent.

Because the Tronchetto facility feeds the more famous and infinitely more picturesque Venice fish market near the Rialto Bridge—officially the Mercato del Pesce al Minuto, or Retail Fish Market—a fair amount of what's sold there is frozen and/or foreign, too. Strolling through the market's open-sided, Gothic-style pavilions (open Tuesday through Saturday) early last summer, I thought it looked like maybe 35 or 40 percent of the seafood was local—at least gauging by the proudly displayed labels marked *Nostrani*, meaning "Ours."

Here is some of what I saw, in addition to the Sicilian swordfish and tuna 10 and Scottish salmon: *moleche*, scampi, *calamaretti* (small squid), *mazzancolle* (tiger prawns), *canestrelli* (bay scallops), *peoci* (little thick-bearded mussels), *bovoletti* (tiny sea snails that are boiled, then dressed with olive oil, garlic and parsley), and three types of octopus—tiny *folpetti*, larger *moscardini* (with bodies about the size of golf balls) and *piovre*, which are three or four times larger still. There was also *seppie grosse* (large cuttlefish), *seppie tenerissime* ("very tender" smaller cuttlefish), *orata* (gilthead bream), *coda di rospo* (monkfish tail), *razza* (ray), *San Pietro* (John Dory), *triglia* (red mullet), *solioglia* (sole) and *passerini* (literally "little sparrows," but a kind of small lagoon sole that is typically dredged in flour and fried).

At least some of this, I realized, might not be here the next time I visit. "When I read about the new fishing regulations," says Luca di Vita, "I saw five of my best-selling dishes disappear." Di Vita and chef Bruno Gavagnin run Alle Testiere, a 22-seat urban *osteria* near the lively Campo Santa Maria Formosa that happens to serve some of the best seafood in Venice and not much else. Restaurants often bring you the menu plus a "fresh sheet," listing the fish brought in that day. At Alle Testiere, the fresh sheet *is* the menu. On the day I visit, the small selection of dishes includes a shrimp and raw asparagus salad, spaghetti with *bevarasse* clams and four or five kinds of simple grilled fish. I order three of Alle Testiere's classics: bay scallops on the half shell with wisps of orange and onion; remarkable *gnocchetti* (small gnocchi) with *zotoeti*, the tiniest squid you can imagine, in a sauce improbably but deliciously accented with cinnamon; and salty-fresh prawns *alla busara*, in a slightly spicy sweet-and-sour tomato sauce.

After lunch, di Vita sits down to talk about Venetian seafood and the new fishing regulations. "Look," he says, "the Adriatic isn't deep—maybe

35 meters [115 feet] at most—and shallower water means smaller fish and shellfish. The things we fish aren't babies; they're actually full-grown. They don't get any bigger. The new laws are perfect for the southern Mediterranean, but not for here. These little creatures are our treasure, the base of our cuisine." Alle Testiere gets a lot of its fish not from Tronchetto or the Rialto market but from Chioggia, the fishermen's port at the southern end of the lagoon. "A lot of restaurants here have survived the financial crisis by buying cheaper fish—frozen and imported," says di Vita. "For us, this isn't an option. Either you choose to work with fresh fish every day or you don't. We do."

Another restaurant that does is Al Covo, whose proprietor, Cesare Benelli, has been known to post his daily bills in the window so anyone can see when and where he bought the local seafood he's serving. A warm, charming place off the Riva degli Schiavoni near the Arsenale, Venice's medieval shipyard and armory, Al Covo serves traditional Venetian dishes with subtle modern touches. The marinated fresh anchovies with eggplant and the black spaghetti (colored with cuttlefish ink) with scampi, confit cherry tomatoes and wild fennel are irresistible. The *bigoli* (thick whole-wheat spaghetti) in a sauce of anchovies and onions is about as perfect an interpretation of this Venetian standby as you'll find anywhere. To me, though, Benelli's greatest triumph is his fried seafood. In late spring and autumn, he prepares *moleche* with strings of red onion and matchstick potatoes—fish-and-chips as I suspect must be served in heaven. And year-round he produces a simple classic fritto misto, which at the very least will include scampi, calamari and bay scallops along with zucchini, onions and usually another vegetable or two, but will often contain whatever other little fish or crustacean Benelli has bought that day. Whatever's in it, it will be fresh, crisp and perfect.

15   Venetian seafood, particularly the small stuff, lends itself very nicely to *cicchetti* (sometimes spelled *cichetti*), the bar snacks that are often called Venetian tapas. These are served mostly in small, lively establishments called *bacari*, though the line between a *bacaro* and an *osteria* is not very well defined. The oldest *bacaro/osteria* in Venice is Do Spade (Two Swords), dating back to 1488. One of the newer places, where Bepi and I end up one evening, is Ostaria al Garanghelo, opened in 2003 (and not to be confused with Osteria al Garanghelo, on Via Garibaldi). The paper placemats on the tables in this long, wood-paneled room—which includes, unusually for Venice, a high communal table with 18 stools around it—are printed with

Venetian sayings. One is *In ostaria no vago ma co ghe so ghestago* (I don't go to the osteria, but when I do go, I stay), an easy sentiment to understand at a place like this. My Venetian-Italian dictionary defines *garanghelo* as *baldoria*, which means revelry or merrymaking. Bepi says the word also implies a casual meeting with friends.

Chef Renato Osto, also a co-owner of al Garanghelo, doesn't tamper with tradition. His food is simply, unapologetically Venetian, which is not to say it lacks inspiration. His *baccalà mantecato* is very creamy and almost elegant—so smoothly beaten, cracks Bepi, that "it's made with more elbow grease than olive oil"—while his sardines *in saor* seem especially pure, the onions soft but still white instead of caramelized brown, with no sign of pine nuts or raisins. The tomato sauce in which his octopus swims, on the other hand, is dense and intensely flavored. Osto also has a long menu of risotto and spaghetti dishes, many of them piscatorial in nature. His risotto with scampi and porcini—"a kind of surf and turf," Bepi calls it—is positively decadent. If you order his *spaghetti alla busara* with scampi and jumbo shrimp, the waiter will bring you a bib; you'll need it as you slurp up every last bite.

Of course, there are a number of places in Venice where you can have first-rate seafood in grander settings, if that's what you're after. Do Forni (Two Ovens), just off the Piazza San Marco, for one, is a handsome, old-fashioned *ristorante* with tuxedo-clad captains, serving carts, hotel silver and dressed-up Venetians out for a night on the town, all under the watchful eye of Eligio Paties, an old-school professional who's been in charge since 1973. More than half the menu here is seafood, and the specialty of the house is a gloriously simple dish of lightly poached scampi and large scallops on a bed of arugula and a sauce made of nothing more than olive oil, lemon juice, salt and pepper. I sample two varieties of fritto misto, one with little croquettes of *baccalà mantecato*, miniature sardines, squares of mozzarella and thin wedges of eggplant, and the other with *moleche* and oversize scampi. Next comes a particularly fine-grained version of the classic risotto *nero*, full of cuttlefish and its ink, followed by an attractively straightforward grilled Adriatic sole with lemon butter. It is all immensely satisfying, and it occurs to me as I finish that if I lived in Venice, I might never eat meat again.

The next morning I'm awakened by a chorus of dissonant horns. Looking out my window, down to the canals, I see the fishing boats are back for another day of protests, zigzagging among the vaporetti and water taxis and gondolas. I'm as much of a conservationist as any sensible person in the 21st century, and I'm sure the EU regulations weren't imposed without good reason. At the same time I feel sympathy for the fishermen, whom I suspect fear losing not only their livelihoods but their very identities. There's a possibility that the Italian government will be able to negotiate some exceptions for traditional fishing practices; there's also a possibility that Venetians won't pay any more attention to the new rules than Parisians do to the smoking ban in cafés.

I hope something works out. Catching and selling and cooking and eating the abundance of the lagoon has shaped Venetian life for as long as there have been Venetians. Here, in this city built on and defined by water, far more than lunch and dinner comes from the sea.

Analyze

1. Look carefully at the opening paragraphs of this essay, noting in particular the author's use of language and his way of unfolding the scene. How would you describe what Andrews is doing? What effect does this have on your reading of this piece? Why?

2. Andrews notes that "at least some of this [what he sees and eats] . . . might not be here the next time I visit." Why is this the case? How does Andrews reconcile his travel through Venice and his appreciation of its food with the realities of politics and sustainability? Be sure to point to specific examples in the text.

3. What is the overall message of this article? How does the beauty of the scene, the use of Italian language to name the dishes, and the like contrast with the overall point the author wants to make? Is this contrast effective? Why or why not?

Explore

1. Although much attention has been paid to the environmental effects of overfishing in the United States, use this article as a start toward researching similar concerns elsewhere in the world. What are some of the economic and environmental ramifications of the collapse of fishing industries worldwide? What examples support your argument?

2. "Catching and selling and cooking and eating the abundance of the lagoon have shaped Venetian life for as long as there have been

Venetians." How do these environmental issues ultimately have an impact on culture? What potentially is lost, for instance, when environment affects cultural practice? Why?

3. Andrews uses this meal as a vehicle toward understanding cultural, linguistic, historical, and economic histories and implications. Think of a meal that you have had while traveling—near or far—and research what might be the historical, economic, or cultural contexts of that meal, using this essay as your model.

Anthony Bourdain
"Dead Heads"

Controversial and popular commentator, writer, and television personality, Anthony Bourdain is known for being both cynical and adventurous, which, along with his extensive knowledge as a chef, has legitimately certified his expertise. He became well known in the culinary world with the publication of his book, *Kitchen Confidential: Adventures in the Culinary Underbelly* (2000). Now, Bourdain is primarily known for television shows chronicling his experiences traveling and eating around the world. The following article documents one such adventure in Asia.

 Why, according to Bourdain, is this a "story that SHOULD be true"?

At a *kopi tiam* in Geylang one night, while happily tearing the flesh, fat, and cartilage out of a shark head, a Singaporean friend told me a story. He felt his were the Chosen People, the Enlightened Ones, and that this story was particularly illustrative of exactly why. It was probably apocryphal, maybe not true at all, possibly utter bullshit. I don't care. It's a story I want to be true. It's a story that SHOULD be true. As my friend told it:

Back in the day, when wealthy merchants used to travel across China in caravans, they were, from time to time, set upon by organized gangs of bandits and highwaymen. These enterprising free-market enthusiasts would ambush columns suddenly and without mercy, quickly slaughtering guards and escorts, then stripping the members of the party of any valuables before killing them. The head man, however, they always saved for last.

Dragged kicking and screaming and begging for his life from his litter, forced to kneel on ground still soaked with the blood of his bearers and entourage, he would find himself at the feet of the chief bandit. The chief bandit, inevitably a fearsome-looking fellow, would offer the trembling merchant a whole cooked fish. Steamed, grilled—it didn't matter. But it was always whole.

"Eat!" The chief bandit would command, pushing the fish in the direction of his prisoner. There would be a hush as the other bandits took a break from looting, disemboweling, postmortem violation, or any totemic preservation of remains they might be engaged in to move close to the action for what was clearly a Very Important Moment.

5   If the terrified merchant's fingers or chopsticks moved straight to the fish's head, tunneling into the cheek, perhaps, or tearing off a piece of jowl, there would be much appreciative murmuring among the Chief Bandit and his colleagues.

By choosing the multitextured, endlessly interesting mosaic of flesh buried in the fish's head, their captive proved himself a man of wealth and taste. Clearly a man such as this possessed more wealth than what he and his caravan were currently carrying. This man would no doubt be missed by his family and his many wealthy friends, at least some of whom would likely pay a hefty ransom. The bandits would spare his life in the reasonable expectation of future gain.

If, however, the merchant chose instead to peel off a meaty hunk of boneless fillet, the bandits would jerk a cutlass across his neck immediately. This nouveau riche yuppie scum would be worth only as much as he carried in his, pockets. Not worth keeping alive—much less feeding. Nobody would miss this asshole. The minute he chose fillet over head he proved himself worthless.

This tale is a fairly lurid example of a widely held principle throughout Asia and Europe—the older, smarter food world—that the head is the best part. Put a pile of shrimp or crayfish in front of a Spaniard, a Chinese, or any self-respecting Cajun for that matter, and they sure as shit will know what to do with it: suck the brains and juice and all that good stuff right outta those heads!

Chefs know, too. They know that no matter how hard they try, no matter what they do, they will NEVER create a sauce better than the hot goo that comes squirting out of a prawn's head after a short time on a griddle. In Japan, whole restaurants are dedicated to the enjoyment of carefully grilled fish heads and collars. Fish-head curry is enjoyed and cherished by millions of Indians both within India and without. In many Portuguese restaurants, the limited number of *merluzza* heads are reserved in advance for VIP customers. The rest must suffer with steaks and fillets.

So what's our problem with heads? Sure, cheeks are well-known to most 10 urban American diners these days. Tongue has been enjoying something of a comeback. But for as long as I can remember, the appearance of a whole animal head on the plate or in film has rarely been a welcome sight.

Upon our first encounter with John Huston as Noah Cross in *China-town*, we identify him immediately as a bad guy teeming with incestuous, pederastic, murderous evil. How do we know this? Two reasons. He keeps mispronouncing Jake's name—referring to him not as "Mr. Gittes" but as "Mr. Gitz"—and worse, FAR worse, he's devouring a whole, sinister-looking fish.

"I hope you don't mind. I believe they should be served with the head," Cross says.

"Fine," says Jake (played by Jack Nicholson), "as long as you don't serve chicken that way."

The thing is just lying there the whole scene, dead eyes looking up at us. The underlying message is simple: only a monster would eat a fish with the head still on—and only an entity of previously unimagined cruelty would insist that his guest do so as well.

"You may think you know what you're dealing with," warns Cross, "but 15 believe me, you don't." He's talking about a massive conspiracy involving political corruption, theft of natural resources, real-estate fraud, and murder, but he could just as well be talking about that fish head. It's scary. It's big. It's "ugly." It's the unknown.

"It's what the DA used to tell me about Chinatown," replies Jake, our hero and, as it turns out, the only guy in the film who doesn't know what's going on.

Captain Willard sits at a lavishly appointed dining table in an air-conditioned trailer somewhere in South Vietnam. He is about to receive his orders from what appears to be a superior in military intelligence and two officers of the CIA. A uniformed waiter serves lunch, and the camera lingers over a platter of head-on shrimp.

"I don't know how you feel about this shrimp," says the commanding officer in this early scene from *Apocalypse Now*, "but if you'll eat it, you never have to prove your courage in any other way." We know now that these men Willard is sitting with are some bad bastards, untrustworthy without a doubt, and whatever they're asking him to do will be fundamentally dishonest and awful.

But the shrimp heads, like *Chinatown*'s whole fish, also imply something more. Their black, beady, unseeing eyes, sitting at this incongruously luxurious table, are full of warning. They hint at the Great Unknown, warning that no matter what Captain Willard might have seen in the past, whatever he thinks he might know, he in fact knows nothing about what awaits him upriver, beyond the Do Lung Bridge.

20   Of course the portentousness of sea beasts is not limited to American films. Think of the end of *La Dolce Vita*. Our hero, Marcello (played by Marcello Mastroianni), has just emerged from an almost-orgy that turned into a bitter, drunken humiliation of a woman. He and his fellow partygoers stumble onto the beach in the early morning, where they happen upon a giant sea creature, dragged up by fishermen's nets. Marcello notes the staring eyes. Moments later, a young waitress who earlier in the film served as a possible muse/angel figure calls out to him from across a narrow channel of water. Marcello can't hear her. They attempt to communicate for a few seconds, but their words are lost in the noise of the wind and the surf. He gives up, shrugs, and returns to his shallow, pleasure-seeking entourage, none of whom really care about him. Here, the fish head is not a signifier of evil at all, but a cruel reminder of everything Marcello has turned his back on: love, self-knowledge, any kind of spiritual life.

(During the initial release of the movie, the fish was widely interpreted as a classic symbol of Christian [and pre-Christian] belief. Its appearance, dead—along with many other "anti-religious" images in the film—was seen by some as the director's way of suggesting that God was dead, too.)

Certainly the mysterious fish and its wide-open, lifeless eyes are a reminder and a rebuke, once again, of the Great Unknown. But in this case, they remind Marcello not only of what he doesn't know but of what he has chosen not to know.

Perhaps the vilest calumny against head eating appeared in the wildly popular 1979 short film *Fish Heads*, directed by actor Bill Paxton.

Debuting as a comedy interstitial featuring Barnes and Barnes on *Saturday Night Live*, it quickly became a stand-alone sensation, and its message of hate and barely concealed racism only reinforced then-prevalent attitudes of cultural imperialism and craniophobia.

Under an Alvin and the Chipmunks–inspired vocal track of "Fish heads, fish heads/Roly-poly fish heads/Fish heads, fish heads/Eat them up, yum," the action exploits homeless and Asian stereotypes, finding much to laugh at in poverty and the indigenous foodways of ethnic minorities. Soon after the video hit heavy rotation on MTV, the streets were filled with would-be skinheads chanting its infectious chorus. Worse, the song was eventually covered by Duran Duran. Perhaps no single representation in the twentieth century did so much to set gastronomy back.

By the time a horse's head famously appeared in the bed of film director   25 Jack Woltz in *The Godfather*, horse meat had long since been rejected by mainstream diners in America. Granted, during the time period in which the action takes place, horse tartare was still quite popular in Europe, but it is unlikely that Don Corleone's emissaries delivered the head as a gift for the kitchen, so much as a straightforward and gruesome warning.

In fact, in the annals of animal heads on film, I can find only one happy appearance of this most delicious and delightful body part. Only one time when the head of a creature—in this case a duck—brings enlightenment, laughter, pleasure, or joy, as it should:

In *A Christmas Story*, Bob Clark's classic film of the short stories of Jean Shepherd, our adorable child protagonist Ralphie and his family have had their Christmas turkey destroyed by a pack of feral dogs owned by their unseen neighbor and archenemy Krampus. (Is it a coincidence that the name echoes the evil Santa doppelgänger of Eastern European legend?)

Their original meal cruelly demolished, the family resorts to visiting an empty Chinese restaurant where they order Peking duck as a surrogate turkey. The waiter delivers the bird whole, then brings his cleaver down, loudly separating head from body. Ralphie and family shriek with delight. It is the happiest moment in the story. The family is at its most joyful, together and functional, inspired by the severed head of a humble waterfowl—a duck epiphany, if you will. An all-too-rare example.

What is it about the topmost part of what is presumably food that elicits in us such fear, loathing, and derision? Is it the eyes that we abhor? Is it the unknown we see reflected in those unmoving, unseeing lenses—symbols of all we don't know, or can't know?

30   Or is the blank stare of the fish or game bird to be avoided lest we be reminded of our complicity in the death of another living thing? Perhaps it is death itself that we seek to avoid. The eyes of our victims beckon us, mock us, suggest that we will be joining them soon.

Analyze

1. Bourdain has a distinctive voice as a writer, and his critics often condemn his arrogance, crassness, and sarcasm. How would you characterize the tone Bourdain creates in this reading? And how might that tone influence the way an audience responds to Bourdain's argument?

2. The story about the bandits and the fish head, which begins this reading, takes the shape of a parable. That is, readers should glean a lesson—a moral, of sorts—from the narrative. What lesson, then, should readers learn from the introductory story? In what way does this "tale" influence your understanding of the rest of Bourdain's article?

3. What does Bourdain mean when he writes, "Perhaps it is death itself that we seek to avoid"? Explain the argument Bourdain is making, using specific examples from the text.

Explore

1. Bourdain writes that "This tale is a fairly lurid example of a widely held principle throughout Asia and Europe—the older, smarter food world—that the head is the best part." How, according to Bourdain, are Asia and Europe "older" and "smarter" in their approaches to food? Use outside resources to further explore Bourdain's statement, researching additional ways that either Asian or European cultures take an "older, smarter" approach to eating.

2. As Bourdain indicates in this article, eating a fish head is akin to a rite of passage in some cultures. Are there similar rites of passage within your own culture, family, or community? Are those rites used as a way to mark a coming of age—or, perhaps, as in this reading, a way to separate "insiders" from "outsiders?" Craft a narrative essay in which you explore a particular rite of passage—one that you may or may not have participated in yourself. What does the rite signify, both to the individual and to the larger community?

3. Bourdain uses many pop-culture references (*La Dolce Vita, The Godfather,* Bill Paxton, *SNL,* etc.) to substantiate his argument that "the appearance of a whole animal head on the plate or in film has rarely been a welcome sight." With a small group of your peers, work to find additional examples of America's "problem with heads"—or other unfamiliar food behaviors—and prepare a presentation in which you compare and contrast the way Bourdain's points echo other, similar discussions in this chapter, using specific examples to make your arguments.

Peter Menzel and Faith D'Aluisio
"Hungry Planet: What the World Eats"

Peter Menzel and Faith D'Aluisio are life partners as well as co-authors. Menzel is a freelance photojournalist who has received a number of awards for his work, which has appeared in such publications as *National Geographic, The New York Times Magazine,* and *Time Magazine.* D'Aluisio is a former television news producer, and she is now the editor of the publishing imprint, Material World Books. The photographic essay that follows explores "what the world eats."

How does the visual image present "what the world eats" in a particular way?

Introduction

Peter Menzel and I invited ourselves to dinner with 30 families in 24 countries to explore humankind's oldest social activity, eating. Anyone who remembers grocery shopping 20 years ago knows that the U.S. diet has changed rapidly but fewer people realize that this transformation is worldwide. Some dietary changes are due to globalization as large-scale capitalism reaches new places. Others are due to rising affluence, as people in formerly impoverished places gain the means to vary their diet, first eating more meat and fish, then pizza and burgers. And some changes are due to the tides of migration, as travelers, immigrants and refugees bring their own foods to new lands and acquire new tastes in return. To learn more, we watched typical families the world over as they farmed, shopped, cooked and ate. At the end of each visit, we created a portrait of the family surrounded by a week's worth of their groceries. The sum, we hope, is a culinary atlas of the planet at a time of extraordinary change.

This book began with a single mouthful of noodles. In the mid-1990s, Peter and I found ourselves in a small covered motorboat off the southern coast of the island of New Guinea, speeding through the Arafura Sea. It was early spring—typhoon season was approaching. At this time of year, storms can come up so quickly that the local charter planes suspend operations at the slightest hint of bad weather, and even the illegal fishing trawlers plundering the tropical seas around the island are extra careful. Because our assignment schedule was tight, we couldn't wait for a less stormy day. Instead, we hunted for an experienced boat captain willing to make the seven-hour journey to the Asmat—a heavily forested section of the Indonesian province of Papua—one of the most remote places on earth.

Peter is a photojournalist and I am a writer, and we have worked together in almost 50 countries over the last 12 years. We generally focus on international stories, and that day eight years ago we were headed to the Asmat to document the lives of its hunting and gathering inhabitants.

From the Asmat's ramshackle capital, Agats, we took a 40-foot longboat three hours up the Pomats River to the village of Sawa. It was a small, poor place deep in the rain forest, a collection of wooden huts without running water, electricity, telephones, or roads of any kind. Its people live hand to mouth, felling towering sago palm trees and mashing the pulp to make their staple food, a kind of bread. When they can get them, they eat sago grubs. Occasionally, they get fish from the river. It was the steamiest, swampiest place I'd ever been. And it was there, an hour or two after our arrival, that this book began.

Peter and I were (respectively) photographing and talking with a tall skinny man and his two sons, all three of whom showed the marks of hard living. Like many in the village, the man was blind in one eye from vitamin deficiencies; the children had skin diseases and looked seriously undernourished. As we were talking, the older boy pulled a dry brick of instant ramen noodles out of its wrapper and munched it down. His naked, pot-bellied little brother tipped the ramen's flavoring packet into his own mouth and worked the powder around with his tongue until it dissolved. I was mesmerized. I saw this scene play out again and again during our time in Sawa, a place with next to no connection to the rest of the world—children eating an uncooked convenience food intended to simplify the busy lives of people very far away.

I asked a Catholic priest, a longtime resident missionary, about the   5 noodles. He said that logging money had begun to trickle into the villages of these hunters and gatherers. Accompanying the cash came the first merchant to Sawa, a Sulawesian who sold dried food and snacks. Now there's nothing intrinsically wrong with the occasional quick snack of ramen noodles in processed broth, but you don't have to be a food activist to wonder if it is a good idea for the Asmattans, already struggling to find basic nourishment, to dose themselves with jolts of sugar, salt, and artificial flavors.

Since that visit to the Asmat we've seen similar scenes worldwide, and have noticed that something odd—even revolutionary—is going on in the world of food. Producing and consuming food is one of humankind's oldest and most basic activities, but the signs of change are everywhere. Riding in taxis through Beijing, we'd see scads of Kentucky Fried Chicken outlets springing up. A grandfather in rural China who remembers the pain of hunger railed against the young Chinese he sees now, wasting food. Here at home, on assignment in the Midwest, we saw endless rows of corn and soy, and learned that much of it is now genetically modified. (For better or worse, we Americans don't know when we are eating GM foods—and when we aren't.) In the suburbs of Paris, we met French teenagers whose favorite meals were Pad Thai and sushi. A young mother living in Mexico told me that she had no idea what were the ingredients of soft drinks. Her sedentary family of five was drinking six gallons of Coca-Cola a week, to the exclusion of most other beverages, even as she worried about the family's growing weight and dental problems.

The global marketplace has changed the way people are eating. Societies that are becoming less physically active are also increasing their consumption of energy-dense foods. Even without the academic studies, it's easy to spot—just look around. Many affluent countries are overfed. And unfortunately, it seems that in the developing world, even before people attain a level of affluence that helps ensure their adequate nutrition, they are eating in ways almost guaranteed to make them less healthy. As charitable organizations continue their desperately important campaigns against world hunger, others begin equally important campaigns against world obesity. Meanwhile, activists left, right, and center denounce food corporations, food scientists, food conservationists, and food regulators.

To try to make sense of this fascinating, baffling, important muddle, we worked our way around the world and looked at the everyday food of everyday people everywhere—the heaping plates at middle-class mealtimes, the meager communal bowls shared by families crushed by poverty, the sacks of grain served up by overworked aid organizations, the clamorous aisles in hypermarkets, the jam-packed shelves in mom-and-pops, the foods prescribed by religious doctrine, the foods of celebration, subsidized foods. We met people along the way who helped us illustrate the bewildering diversity of what humankind eats in the 21st century: global food, snack food, fast food, junk food, health food, functional food, complimentary food, fortified food, organic food, processed food.

The result—the book in your hands—is not a diet book. Nor is it a jeremiad about supposedly evil corporations, or the supposed enemies of progress, or any of the other sides in the debate about the politics of food. Rather, it is an attempt at a global portrait at a time of momentous change— a freeze-frame snapshot of a fast-moving target.

Process

10   Gathering information for any project that spans multiple countries is dauntingly difficult, but this one was particularly hard, not least because I often had to introduce concepts that are taken for granted in the developed world. Take, for instance, the idea of a recipe. At Breidjing Refugee Camp in eastern Chad, I asked our translator, Hassane, about the recipe for *aiysh*, the thick porridge that is the staple food of the Sudanese families in the camp. Hassane looked completely blank. I explained that we wanted to write down the method by which D'jimia, the woman we were speaking with, cooked *aiysh*. "How can we get such a thing?" Hassane asked. "There is no such plan for cooking. She learned it from her mother." "I realize that," I replied, "but I must write down how *aiysh* is made, so that the people who read this book can make sense of the food and the process that D'jimia uses to make it." "They only make it, they don't talk about it," he argued. "I realize that, Hassane," I tried again, "but D'jimia will talk about it if we ask her. Please tell her that I have watched many, many women

make *aiysh*, and now I want to ask about the method she uses, so I can write it down for the book."

Peter had exited this conversation, understandably enough, and was photographing at the next tent block, where a group of men were slaughtering a goat for the celebration of the end of Ramadan. D'jimia and the chief of her tent block—who was translating Hassane's Arabic into D'jimia's native Massalit—watched our exchange with interest.

"This is much too difficult," Hassane repeated, shaking his head, as we began anew—from English to Arabic, Arabic to Massalit, and back again. Within a short time, D'jimia had outlined the instructions for making *aiysh*, and we had moved on to talking about the life she and her five children used to lead, and the plentiful food they'd had in Sudan, before being forced into Chad by the Janjawiid. (p. 56).

But the flow of information was not just one-way. Sometimes the project taught our subjects as much as it taught us. After our visit to the British village of Collingbourne Ducis in Wiltshire and the subsequent family food portrait, Deb Bainton e-mailed: "I can't believe that I was honest enough to let you photograph the amount of Mars bars I ate in a week—the average British family will be pleased to see that! I eat hardly any these days, so I suppose I've moved on to something equally unhealthy—scary thought, if I've started to get remotely healthy!" (p. 140).

As the message from Deb Bainton and my cross-cultural exchange in Chad suggest, assembling this book was a long, arduous, fascinating, and occasionally charming experience. (For details on the methodology, please see page 278.) Along the way, we asked for additional input from Marion Nestle, Carl Safina, Alfred W. Crosby, Corby Kummer, Francine R. Kaufman, and Charles C. Mann. (Contributors' profiles can be found on page 284.)

As I write this Peter is outside in our garden shoveling compost into a 15 wheelbarrow and getting ready for the spring growing season in Northern California. I've placed my weekly food order with Planet Organics in San Francisco and filled the coffeepot with good clean water from our 250-foot machine-drilled well. All the while, I'm thinking about Amna Mustapha, the winsome 12-year-old girl we got to know in Chad, hauling cooking water out of a temporary hand-dug well in a dry riverbed every day (p. 68). And I'm thinking about D'jimia, the widowed mother of five, on the Chad–Sudan border, thankful for the food rations from the world community, and the United Nations tent over her family's head, but wanting fervently to go back home to Sudan and her mango trees. She's worried about affording the cost of a single handful of dried okra (p. 56).

I'm also reminded of a story told to me by our friend Charles Mann, who is occasionally our editor. More than a decade ago, he says, Peter and he went to Chetumal, on the Mexico–Belize border. "It was a real hole," he explained, "at least back then. The only restaurant open late at night was completely empty except for us. The menu was, shall we say, limited; the service, none too enthusiastic. But we are upbeat and adventurous folks, right? On the menu is *pulpo y hígado*—octopus and liver. I figure it's like *paglia e fieno*, the Italian dish, which isn't actually a platter of straw and hay, but green and yellow pasta. This too must be, you know, a metaphor. So I order it. It comes. It's chunks of octopus in pureed beef liver. Now, I am ordinarily a member of the Clean Plate Club. This is the first time in years that I not only can't finish a dish, I can't start it. Years later, I see a cartoon of a waiter in a tux bellying up to a table with this smoking, charred mass on a platter. "It's a fried telephone book," he tells the horrified customer. "We put it in French, and you ordered it." That was me," said Charles. Actually, from time to time, that's all of us.

The Mustapha Family of Dar es Salaam Village—Fatna, 3, Amna Ishakh, 9, Rawda, 5, Amna, 12, Khadidja Baradine, 42, Halima, 1,

Figure 6.1

Nafissa, 6, Mustapha Abdallah Ishakh, 46, and Abdel Kerim, 14, with one week's food in November.

Chad, the Mustapha Family of Dar es Salaam Village

ONE WEEK'S FOOD IN NOVEMBER

Food Expenditure for This Week: 10,200 CFA francs (Communauté Financiére Africaine)/$18.33 USD

Source—Hungry Planet: What the World Eats, 2005.

Grains & other starchy foods: **

Millet,* 4 coro—a "coro" is a Chadian unit of volume approximately equal to 2.1 qt; millet flour,* 3 coro; sorghum,* 3 coro.

Dairy: **

Milk,* 7 coro, from family cows.

Meat, fish & eggs: $2.16**

Chickens,* 8.8 lb meat, after cleaning; goat meat, dried on the bone, 6.6 lb.

Fruits, vegetables & nuts: $7.19**

Watermelons, 22 lb; harar (squash), 17.6 lb; dates, 1 coro; okra,* dried, 1 coro; red onions,* 1 coro; garlic,* 0.5 coro; tomatoes,* dried and milled, 0.5 coro; red peppers,* dried and milled, 0.3 coro; peanuts,* 3 coro.

Condiments: $8.54

Peanut oil, 1.1 gal; sugar, 0.5 coro; salt, 0.5 coro.

Beverages: $0.44

Tea, 3.5 oz; water, hand or animal carried half a mile from the wadi, for both drinking and cooking.

*Homegrown

**Market value of homegrown foods, if purchased locally: $25.44

The Ayme Family of Tingo—Livia, 15, Natalie, 8, Moises, 11, Alvarito, 4, Jessica, 10, Orlando, 35, Ermelinda, 37, Orlando Junior, 0, and Mauricio, 2, with one week's food in September.

Ecuador

The Ayme Family of Tingo

ONE WEEK'S FOOD IN SEPTEMBER

Food Expenditure for This Week: $31.55

Source—Hungry Planet: What the World Eats, 2005.

Grains & other starchy foods: $17.40**

White potatoes, 100 lb; white rice, broken, 50 lb, cheaper than whole rice; ground wheat,* 15 lb; corn flour, 10 lb; white flour, fine,

Figure 6.2

10 lb; green pea flour, 8 lb; white flour, coarse, 6 lb. Note: The Aymes normally grow their own potatoes and corn, but have none to harvest at this time of year. They have eaten the last of their homegrown barley.

Dairy: **

Milk, 1.8 gal, from family cows; only part of the week's supply is shown in the photograph.

Meat, fish & eggs: none.

Fruits, vegetables & nuts: $11.25

Plantains, 13.4 lb; yellow bananas, 6.2 lb, purchased over-ripe as they are cheaper that way; oranges, 3.6 lb; lemons, 2.5 lb; Andean blackberries, 1 lb; lentils, 10 lb; carrots, 3.6 lb; red onions, 3 lb; leeks, 2 lb; lettuce, 1 head.

Condiments: $2.90

Brown sugar, 11 lb, purchased as a cake, used for sweetening coffee and eaten as candy; salt, 1.5 lb; vegetable oil, 16.9 fl oz; cilantro, 1 bunch.

Beverages: **

Stinging nettle, 1 small bunch, gathered wild for tea; corn silk, 1 handful, boiled in water for both tea and medicine; water from a nearby spring, carried by hand, for drinking and cooking.

* Homegrown

Figure 6.3

**Market value of homegrown foods, if purchased: $3.20

The Le Moine Family of Montreuil—Laetitia, 16, Delphine, 20, Eve, 50, and Michel, 50, with one week's food in November.

France

The Le Moine Family of Montreuil

ONE WEEK'S FOOD IN NOVEMBER

Food Expenditure for This Week: 315.17 euros/$419.95

Source—Hungry Planet: What the World Eats, 2005.

Grains & other starchy foods: $23.41

Bread, 3.9 lb; English white bread, 1.8 lb; Barilla spaghetti, 1.1 lb; country bread, 1.1 lb; potatoes, 1.1 lb; croissants, with chocolate, 8.8 oz; Kellogg's corn flakes, 7.9 oz; croissants, 3.5 oz.

Dairy: $24.45

Auchan (store brand) milk, 2.1 qt; Danone fruit yogurt, 2.2 lb; Yoplait Perle de Lait natural (plain) yogurt, 2.2 lb; chocolate yogurt, 1.3 lb; Yoplait Perle de Lait coconut yogurt, 1.1 lb; butter, 8.8 oz; Saint Nectaire cheese, 8.1 oz; goat cheese, 4.9 oz; Auchan Swiss cheese, grated, 2.5 oz.

Meat, fish & eggs: $92.29

Beef, frozen, 2.2 lb; grenadier fish 1.7 lb; salmon, 1.3 lb; eggs, 8; beef carpaccio, 1.2 lb; shrimp, 14.5 oz; chicken, 14.3 oz; Auchan sausage, 14.1 oz; Auchan ham, 12.7 oz; lamb, 12.3 oz; duck, 10.6 oz; rib eye steak, 7.4 oz; Auchan ham, sliced, 7.1 oz; tuna, 4.6 oz.

Fruits, vegetables & nuts: $54.96

Pineapple, 2.9 lb; yellow bananas, 2.2 lb; persimmons, 2 lb; Royal Gala apples, 1.8 lb; pears, 1.1 lb; kiwis, 14.1 oz; oranges, 9.6 oz; prunes, 8.8 oz; green grapes, 7 oz; tangerines, 6.4 oz; mixed vegetables, fresh, 5.3 lb; mixed vegetables, frozen, 4.4 lb; tomatoes, 3.5 lb; pumpkin, 1.9 lb; hearts of palm, 1.8 lb; green beans, 15.5 oz; beetroot, 9.4 oz; cabbage, 8.8 oz; avocado, 1; artichokes, 6.9 oz; soy germ, 6.4 oz; scallions, 3.2 oz; Auchan chives, 1 bunch; garlic, 0.4 oz; walnuts, 1.1 lb.

Condiments: $32.22

Maille vinegar, 1.3 qt; black currant jam, 10.6 oz; olive oil,‡ 10.2 fl oz; sunflower oil, 10.2 fl oz; honey, 7.1 oz; Nutella chocolate spread, 7.1 oz; ketchup, 6.2 oz; sugar 5.3 oz; cornichons (small tart pickles), 3.5 oz; mayonnaise, 1.8 oz; mustard, 1.8 oz; parsley, 1 small bunch; basil,* 1 bunch; salt, 0.7 oz; celery salt, 0.5 oz; black basil, dried, 0.4 oz; black pepper, 0.1 oz.

Snacks & desserts: $17.10

Apple compote, 1.7 lb, a dessert of stewed or baked fruit; Nestlé chocolate mousse, 12.7 oz; Gerblé orange soya biscuits, 9.9 oz; Nestlé raisin, hazelnut, almond dark chocolate, 8.8 oz; Balisto cereal bars, 7.1 oz; biscuits, 5.3 oz; Lindt dark chocolate, 3.5 oz; Nestlé caramel dark chocolate, 3.5 oz.

Prepared food: $85.66

Tomato tabouleh, 1.2 lb; ham and mozzarella pizza, 15.9 oz; stuffed vine leaves, 14.1 oz; Auchan salad, 11.5 oz; surimi (Japanese frozen minced fish mixed with sugar and other additives), 7.1 oz; cafeteria food, 10 meals, with meat, vegetables, fruit, and bread. On a scale of one to ten, the parents rate the several-course cafeteria meals as an eight or nine in both nutrition and taste.

Fast food: $32.51

Shanghai Express: sushi, 1 order; Chinese food, 1 order; McDonald's: 1 McChicken sandwich, French fries, Evian water.

Beverages: $44.76

Wattwiller mineral water, 2 gal; Verniere mineral water, 2 gal; Volvic mineral water, 3.2 qt; orange juice, 2 1.1-qt cartons; Sojasun soy milk, 2 1.1-qt cartons; Auchan tomato juice, 1.1 qt; Joker carrot juice, 1.1 qt; Tropicana fruit juice, 1.1 qt; cider, 25.4 fl oz; red wine,

Figure 6.4

25.4 fl oz; William Grant's whiskey, 5 fl oz; Auchan coffee, 2.5 oz; Twinings of London Earl Grey tea, 25 teabags.

Miscellaneous: $12.59

Auchan assorted cat food, 3.5 lb; Friskies cat food, 15.9 oz.

*Homegrown (small bunch of herbs); ‡Not in photo

The Patkar Family of Ujjain—Neha, 19, Akshay, 15, Jayant, 48, and Sangeeta, 42, with one week's food in April.

India

The Patkar Family of Ujjain

ONE WEEK'S FOOD IN APRIL

Food Expenditure for This Week: 1,636.25 rupees/$39.27 USD

Source—Hungry Planet: What the World Eats, 2005.

Grains & other starchy foods: $5.35

Chapatis (flat bread), 13.2 lb; wheat flour, 8.8 lb; potatoes, 3.3 lb; white rice, 3.3 lb; poha (flattened white rice), 2.2 lb; Modern Special white bread, sliced, 1 loaf; porridge, 1.1 lb; chickpea flour, 1.1 lb.

Dairy: $9.70

Milk,‡ 1.9 gal; yogurt curds, 4.4 lb; Nestlé Everyday Dairy Whitener milk powder, 1.1 lb; ice cream, assorted flavors, 15.9 oz; ghee (clarified butter), 8.8 oz.

Meat, fish & eggs: The family is of the Brahmin caste, and does not eat either meat or fish.

Fruits, vegetables & nuts: $7.73

Watermelon, 6.6 lb; oranges, 4.4 lb; green grapes, 2.2 lb; limes, 12.8 oz; coconut, one-half; red onions, 5.5 lb; gourd, 3.3 lb; bitter gourd, 2.2 lb; cabbage, 2 heads; cauliflower, 1 head; tomatoes, 2.2 lb; yellow lentils, 2.2 lb; eggplant, 1.7 lb; chickpeas, 1.1 lb; cucumber, 1.1 lb; green lentils, 1.1 lb; okra (also called lady fingers), 1.1 lb; red beans, 1.1 lb; black-eyed beans, 8.8 oz; coriander, 8.8 oz; green bell pepper, 8.8 oz; green chili peppers, 3.5 oz; ground nuts, 1.1 lb.

Condiments: $4.47

Soybean oil, 1.1 qt; salt, 1.1 lb; Nilon's pickles, 8.8 oz; white sugar, 8.8 oz; Maggi tomato ketchup, 7.1 oz; cumin seed, 3.5 oz; fenugreek seeds, 3.5 oz; mint, 3.5 oz; mustard seed, 3.5 oz; black pepper, 1.8 oz; garlic chutney, 1.8 oz; mango, dried and powdered, 1.8 oz; parsley, 1.8 oz; red chili powder, 1.8 oz; aniseed, 0.9 oz; turmeric powder, 0.9 oz; asafetida (powdered gum resin), 0.4 oz; cloves, 0.4 oz.

Snacks & desserts: $2.33

Gulab jamoon (deep-fried dumplings), 1.1 lb, served soaked in cardamom-flavored syrup; upma rawa (savory semolina dish), 1.1 lb; papad (thin, crisp, sun-dried wafers of dal flour) 8.8 oz, eaten as a snack or served sprinkled on soup; biscuits, 3.5 oz; corn-flour crackers, 3.5 oz; extruded noodle, 3.5 oz; rice-flour crackers, 1.8 oz; wheat-starch crackers, 1.8 oz.

Prepared food: $1.94

Khaman (sweet, steam-baked chickpea cakes), 1.1 lb; Maggi 2-minute noodles, 7 oz; Everest chhole masala (chickpea masala), 3.3 oz; poori (fried wheat-flour flat breads), 3 pieces.

Street food: $3.07

Chhole bhature (spicy chickpea curry with flat bread); idli (steamed rice cakes); pav bhaji (bread rolls with spicy mashed vegetables); pizza, 1 small; uttapam (thick and crispy flat bread made with coconut milk), served with spicy vegetables; dosa, (crispy savory pancake), 5, served with chutney or other spicy relishes; bhel poori (savory puffed rice with chutney); tomato, cucumber, and onion sandwich, 1 small.

Restaurants: $2.88

Figure 6.5

Shree Ganga Restaurant: dinner for four, including Malai kofta (mashed potato dumplings in vegetable gravy); navratan korma (fruits and vegetables cooked in a creamy sauce and flavored with herbs, spices, and cashews); jeera fried rice (fried with cumin seeds); tandoori roti (flat bread), cooked in a tandoor, or clay oven; fried dahl (lentil-flour flat bread); papad; green salad; pickles; dessert.

Beverages: $1.80

Thumbs Up cola, 2.1 qt; Godrej chai house tea, 5.3 oz; Nescafe Sunrise instant coffee, 0.5 oz; well water, for drinking and cooking.

‡Not in photo

The Casales Family of Cuernavaca—Bryan, 5, Emmanuel, 7, Alma Casales Gutierrez, 30, Arath, 1, and Marco Antonio, 29, with one week's food in May.

Mexico

The Casales Family of Cuernavaca

ONE WEEK'S FOOD IN MAY

Food Expenditure for This Week: 1,862.78 Mexican pesos/$189.09

Source—Hungry Planet: What the World Eats, 2005.

Grains & other starchy foods: $15.76

Corn tortillas, 22.1 lb; bread rolls, 3.1 lb; Morelos white rice, 2.2 lb; potatoes, 2.2 lb; Bimbo white bread, sliced, 1 loaf; Kellogg's Special K cereal, 1.1 lb; Morelos pasta, 1.1 lb; La Moderna pasta, 14.1 oz; pan dulces (sweet bread), assorted, 8.8 oz; bread sticks,‡ 3.5 oz.

Dairy: $26.81

Alpura 2000 whole milk, 1.9 gal; Alpura sour cream, 2.1 qt; Muecas ice cream pops, 1.1 qt; Yoplait yogurt, 1.1 qt; cheese, hand-made, 1.1 lb; La Lechera condensed milk, canned, 14 oz; cottage cheese, 13.6 oz; Carnation evaporated milk, 12 oz; Manchego cheese, 8.8 oz; cream cheese, 6.7 oz; butter, 3.5 oz.

Meat, fish & eggs: $42.81

Chicken, pieces, 15.4 lb; crab, 2.7 lb; eggs, 18; tilapia (fish), 2.3 lb; catfish, 2.2 lb; sausage, 6.6 oz, one month's worth shown in photo; FUD ham, 5.6 oz.

Fruits, vegetables & nuts: $44.21

Mangos, 13.2 lb; pineapples, 6.6 lb; watermelon, 6.6 lb; oranges, 5.5 lb; cantaloupe, 4.4 lb; guavas, 2.2 lb; quinces, 2.2 lb; yellow bananas, 2.2 lb; roma tomatoes, 6.6 lb; tomatillos, 6.6 lb; corn,‡ 4 ears; avocados, 7; chayote squash, 2.2 lb; Morelos beans, 2.2 lb; white onions, 2.2 lb; zucchini, 2.2 lb; La Costeña pickled jalapeño peppers, canned, 1.6 lb; green beans, 1.1 lb; jalapeño peppers, fresh, 1.1 lb; broccoli, 12.8 oz; garlic, 8.8 oz; chipotle peppers (smoked jalapeños), 7.1 oz.

Condiments: $9.37

Capullo canola oil 2.1 qt; margarine, 15.9 oz; McCormack mayonnaise 13.8 oz; salt 8.8 oz; garlic salt 3.2 oz; McCormack black pepper 3.2 oz; cumin , 0.7 oz; bay leaves, dried, 0.5 oz.

Snacks & desserts: $6.27

Rockaleta chili lollipops, 1.2 lb; Ricolino pasitas chocolate candy, 1.1 lb; Gamesa crackers, 15.9 oz; Drums marshmallows, 12 oz; Rockaleta chili candy, 5.7 oz.

Prepared food: $4.79

Doña Maria mole (savory sauce made from chocolate and chili), 2.1 lb; Knorr chicken bouillon, 3.2 oz.

Beverages: $39.07

Coca-Cola, 12 2.1-qt bottles; water, bottled, 5 gal; Victoria beer, 20 11.8-fl -oz bottles; Jumex juice, 1.3 qt; Gatorade Fierce Black Hurricane drink, 1.1 qt; Gatorade lime drink, 1.1 qt; Nescafe, instant, decaf, 7.1 oz; tap water, for cooking.

Figure 6.6

‡Not in photo

Note: Grocery expenditure for one week, before the Casales family closed their shop and Marco Antonio moved to the US to find work.

The Çelik Family of Istanbul—Aykut, 8, Semra, 15, Mêtin, 16, Mehalat, 33, Mêhmêt, 40, and Habibe Fatma Kose, 51, with one week's food in January.

Turkey

The Çelik Family of Istanbul

ONE WEEK'S FOOD IN JANUARY

Food Expenditure for This Week: 198.48 New Turkish liras/ $145.88 USD

Source—Hungry Planet: What the World Eats, 2005.

Grains & other starchy foods: $10.46

Bread, 32 loaves, 49.4 lb, 2 loaves missing—the family ate them while waiting for the photograph to be taken; potatoes, 11 lb; rice, 6.6 lb; yufka (thin pastry sheets), 2.2 lb, purchased from a street vendor; Filiz pasta, 1.1 lb.

Dairy: $12.16

Yogurt, 2.1 qt; feta cheese, in water, 2.2 lb; Dost milk, 1.1 qt; drinkable yogurt (Bandirma style), 1.1 qt; Sana butter, 8.8 oz.

Meat, fish & eggs: $11.50

Eggs, 24; hamsi (anchovy-like fish), 1.1 lb, generally eaten twice a month; beef, 13.2 oz, eaten one or two times a month only. The meat shown in the picture is enough for one month.

Fruits, vegetables & nuts: $56.53

Oranges, 6.6 lb; tangerines, 6.6 lb; dates,‡ 2.2 lb; yellow bananas, 2.2 lb; pomegranates, 2.1 lb; zucchini, 7.9 lb; tomatoes, 4.4 lb; black olives, 3.3 lb; chickpeas, dried, 3.3 lb; cabbage, 1 head; carrots, 2.2 lb; eggplant, 2.2 lb; leeks, 2.2 lb; lentils 2.2 lb; lettuce, 2 heads; peppers, ‡ 2.2 lb; spinach, 2.2 lb; yellow onions, 2.2 lb; cucumber, 1.7 lb; arugula, 1 lb; Avsarlar nuts, mixed, 2.2 lb.

Condiments: $9.60

Sunflower oil,‡ 1.1 qt; Bal Küpü white sugar, cubed, 1.1 lb; jam, 10.6 oz; honey, 10.1 fl oz; mint, dried, 8.8 oz; salt, 8 oz; cinnamon, 7.1 oz; pepper, 7.1 oz.

Snacks & desserts: $0.51

Seyidoglu helva (sesame seed paste cookie), 1.1 lb.

Prepared food: $1.36

Knorr Gunun Corbasa dry soup, powdered, 11.2 oz.

Homemade food:

Stuffed pastries, approx. 4.4 lb, sheets of yufka (unleavened pastry dough) formed then filled with arugula and feta, listed above; dolmas, approx. 2.2 lb, grape leaves stuffed with spices, rice, vegetables, and meat, listed above.

Beverages: $29.66

Efes beer, 8 17-fl -oz bottles; Coca-Cola, 8 12-fl-oz cans; Fanta orange soda, 2.1 qt; Hediyelik tea, 3.3 lb; Pepsi, 3 12-fl-oz cans; Coca-Cola light, 12 fl oz; Nescafe VIP instant coffee, 3.5 oz; bottled water, purchased for cooking and drinking.

Miscellaneous: $14.10

Tekel cigarettes, 7 pks; Simarik bird food, 20 oz.

The Revis Family of North Carolina—Brandon Demery, 16, Tyrone Demery, 14, Rosemary, 40, and Ronald, 39, with one week's food in March.

United States

The Revis Family of North Carolina

ONE WEEK'S FOOD IN MARCH

Food Expenditure for This Week: $341.98

Figure 6.7

Source—Hungry Planet: What the World Eats, 2005.

Grains & other starchy foods: $17.92

Red potatoes, 2.3 lb; Nature's Own bread, sliced, 1 loaf; Trix cereal, 1.5 lb; Mueller fettuccini, 1 lb; Mueller spaghetti, 1 lb; Uncle Ben's Original white rice, 1 lb; Flatout flatbread wraps, 14 oz; New York Original Texas garlic toast, 11.3 oz; Harris Teeter (store brand) Flaky Brown-n-Serve dinner rolls, 11 oz.

Dairy: $14.51

Harris Teeter milk, 1 gal; Kraft cheese, shredded, 8 oz; Kraft sharp cheddar cheese, sliced, 8 oz; Kraft Swiss cheese, sliced, 8 oz; Kraft Cheese Singles, 6 oz; Kraft Parmesan cheese, grated, 3 oz; Harris Teeter butter, 2 oz.

Meat, fish & eggs: $54.92

Harris Teeter beef, pot roast, 2.5 lb; Harris Teeter pork chops, 1.9 lb; Harris Teeter chicken drumsticks, 1.7 lb; eggs, 12; Harris Teeter chicken wings, 1.5 lb; Armour Italian-style meat balls, 1 lb; Gwaltney bacon, Virginia-cured with brown sugar, 1 lb; Harris Teeter ground turkey, 1 lb; shrimp,‡ 1 lb; StarKist tuna, canned, 12 oz; honey-baked ham, sliced, 9 oz; smoked turkey, sliced, 7.8 oz.

Fruits, vegetables & nuts: $41.07

Dole yellow bananas, 2.9 lb; red seedless grapes, 2.4 lb; green seedless grapes, 2.2 lb; Birds Eye baby broccoli, frozen, 4 lb; yellow onions, 3 lb; Green Giant corn, canned, 1.9 lb; Green Giant green beans, canned, 1.8 lb; Bush's vegetarian baked beans, canned, 1.8 lb; cucumbers, 1.4 lb; Harris Teeter tomatoes, vine-ripened, 1.2 lb; Del Monte whole leaf spinach, canned, 13.5 oz; garden salad, packaged, 10 oz; Italian salad mix, packaged, 8.8 oz; pickled mushrooms, 7.3 oz; Harris Teeter peanuts, 1 lb.

Condiments: $12.51

White sugar, 1.6 lb; Ruffles ranch dip, 11 oz; Crisco vegetable oil, 6 fl oz; Nestle Coffee-Mate, French vanilla, nonfat, 6 fl oz; Food Lion garlic salt, 5.3 oz; Hellmann's mayonnaise, 4 oz; Newman's Own salad dressing, 4 oz; Jiffy peanut butter,‡ 3 oz; black pepper, 2 oz; Harris Teeter Original yellow mustard, 2 oz; Heinz ketchup, 2 oz; salt, 2 oz; Colonial Kitchen meat tenderizer, 1 oz; Durkee celery seed, 1 oz; Encore garlic powder, 1 oz.

Snacks & desserts: $21.27

Mott's apple sauce, 1.5 lb; Munchies Classic mix, 15.5 oz; Kellogg's yogurt-flavored pop tarts,‡ 14.7 oz; Orville Redenbacher's popcorn, 9 oz; Harris Teeter sunflower seeds, 7.3 oz; Lays Classic potato chips, 5.5 oz; Lays Wavy potato chips, 5.5 oz; Del Monte fruit in cherry gel, 4.5 oz; Extra chewing gum, 3 pks; Snickers candy bar, 2.1 oz; M&M's peanut candy, 1.7 oz.

Prepared food: $24.27

Bertolli portobello alfredo sauce, 1 lb; Ragu spaghetti sauce, chunky mushroom and bell peppers, 1 lb; Maruchan shrimp flavored ramen, 15 oz; California sushi rolls, 14 oz; Campbell's cream of celery soup, 10.8 oz; Hot Pockets, jalapeño, steak & cheese, 9 oz; shrimp sushi rolls, 7 oz.

Fast food: $71.61

McDonald's: 10-pc chicken McNuggets, large fries, large Coca-Cola, Filet-o-Fish meal; Taco Bell: 4 nachos Bell Grande, 2 soft tacos, taco supreme, taco pizza, taco, bean burrito, large lemonade; Burger King: double cheeseburger, onion rings, large Coca-Cola; KFC: 2-pc chicken with mashed potatoes, large Coca-Cola; Subway: 6-inch wheat veggie sub, 6-inch wheat seafood crab sub; Milano's Pizzeria: large sausage pizza, large pepperoni pizza; I Love NY Pizza: 4 pizza slices.

Restaurants: $6.15

China Market: shrimp fried rice, 2 orders; large fruit punch.

Beverages: $77.75

Budweiser, 24 12-fl-oz cans; bottled water, 2 gal; Harris Teeter cranberry–apple juice cocktail, 4 2-qt bottles; diet Coca-Cola, 12 12-fl-oz cans; A&W cream soda, 2 2.1-qt bottles; 7UP, 6 16.9-fl-oz bottles; Harris Teeter cranberry–raspberry juice cocktail, 2 2-qt bottles; Harris Teeter ruby grapefruit juice cocktail, 2 2-qt bottles; Capri Sun, 10 6.8-fl-oz pkgs; soda,‡ 5 12-fl-oz cans, purchased daily by Brandon at school; Arbor Mist strawberry wine blenders, 1.1 qt; Gatorade,‡ 16 fl oz; Powerade,‡ 16 fl oz; Snapple, Go Bananas juice drink, 16 fl oz; Maxwell House instant coffee, 1.5 oz; Kool-Aid, black cherry, 0.5 oz; breakfast tea, 5 teabags; tap water for drinking and cooking.

‡ Not in photo

Analyze

1. As you have noticed, this particular reading takes the shape of some alphabetic text (the introduction), a photo essay, and charts describing the costs of food in various countries. How do particular images seem to argue a certain point of view?

2. Select one of the charts that indicates the cost of food and discuss how this information complements the visual image associated with it.

3. Some of this book's overall argument is made in the form of implied contrasts. Analyze two seemingly contrasting images—for instance, the Mustaphas family from Chad and the Revis family from the United States—and, moving beyond simplistic, obvious comparisons, come to a well-argued conclusion about the differences between the two images and what they say about food, lifestyle, and cultures.

Explore

1. Review all of the charts describing the cost of food in various places. Create a food expenditure chart for your own family, living group, or any other group with whom you spend a week eating. What do you find? Are there any surprises regarding the types of food you eat, your assumptions about food, and the costs? Explain.

2. Consider creating a photo essay of your own for the previous question. (Just use your or a friend's smart phone if you do not own a camera.) How do your images explain or further enhance your food chart? What, if anything, did you do—or wish you could do—to better contextualize, or even manipulate, the images? Why? To what effect?

3. How do the various images you see here contextualize, reinforce, or defy your preconceived notions about particular cultures? Why is this the case? Explain, using details from the introduction and the images themselves.

Jane Kramer
"The Food at Our Feet"

Jane Kramer, European correspondent for *The New Yorker,* has written several books and received the 1981 National Book Award for Nonfiction for her book, *The Last Cowboy.* Her most recent book is *Lone Patriot: The Short Career of an American Militiaman* (2002). Kramer's column, "Letter from Europe," has been a regular feature in *The New Yorker* for the past twenty years. This piece focuses on the popularity of foraging around the world.

As the author asks, "Why is foraging all the rage?"

I spent the summer foraging, like an early hominid with clothes. It didn't matter that the first thing I learned about that daunting pastime of hunter-gatherers and visionary chefs was that nature's bounty is a thorny gift. Thorny, or, if you prefer, spiny, prickly, buggy, sticky, slimy, muddy, and, occasionally, so toxic that one of the books I consulted for my summer forays carried a disclaimer absolving the publisher of responsibility should I happen to end up in the hospital or, worse, in the ground, moldering next to the Amanita phalloides that I'd mistaken for a porcini. I was not deterred. I had foraged as a child, although it has to be said that children don't think "forage" when they are out stripping raspberry bushes and blackberry brambles; they think about getting away before the ogre whose land they're plundering catches them and turns them into toads. I could even claim to have foraged as an adult, if you count a mild interest in plucking berries from the caper bushes that cling to the walls of an old hill town near the farmhouse in Umbria where my husband and I go, in the summertime, to write. Caper berries are like blackberries; they amount to forage only in that they are not *your* berries.

I wasn't the first throwback on the block. The pursuit of wild food has become so fashionable a subject in the past few years that one eater.com blogger called this the era of the "I Foraged with René Redzepi Piece." Redzepi is the chef of Noma, in Copenhagen (otherwise known as the best restaurant in the world). More to the point, he is the acknowledged master scavenger of the Nordic coast. I'll admit it. I wanted to forage with Redzepi, too.

June

I began working my way toward Denmark as soon as I arrived in Italy. I unpacked a carton of books with titles like "Nature's Garden" and "The Wild Table." I bought new mud boots—six euros at my local hardware store—and enlisted a mentor in the person of John Paterson, an exuberant Cumbria-to-Umbria transplant of forty-seven, who looked at my boots and said, "What's wrong with sneakers?" Paterson is a countryman, or, as he says, "not a reader." He is the kind of spontaneous forager who carries knives and old shopping bags and plastic buckets in the trunk of his car. (I carry epinephrine and bug repellent.) Being lanky and very tall, he can also leap over scraggly brush, which I, being small, cannot. Cumbrians are passionate about foraging—perhaps because, like their Scottish neighbors, they have learned to plumb the surface of a northern landscape not normally known for its largesse. What's more, they share their enthusiasm and their secret places, something the old farmers in my neighborhood, most of them crafty foragers, rarely do. The peasants of Southern Europe do not easily admit to foraging—at least not to strangers. For centuries, foraged food was a sign of poverty, and they called it "famine food," or "animal food." The exception was truffles and porcini, which today command enough money for a good forager to be able to wait in line at the supermarket, buying stale food with the bourgeoisie. Some of my neighbors have truffle hounds penned in front of their chicken coops, ostensibly keeping foxes at bay. But they never ask to truffle in the woods by my pond when I'm around and, by local etiquette, they would have to offer some of the precious tubers they unearth to me. They wait until September, when I'm back in New York, and keep all my truffles for themselves.

Paterson got his start foraging—"Well, not actually foraging, more like scrumping"—as a schoolboy, combing the farms near his uncle's Cockermouth sawmill for the giant rutabagas, or swedes, as the English call them, that children in Northern Europe carve into jack-o'-lanterns at Halloween. He worked in his first kitchen at the age of twelve ("I washed the plates," he says. "I was too shy to wait on tables") and twenty-five years later arrived in Umbria, a chef. Today, he has a Romanian wife, two children, and a thriving restaurant of his own—the Antica Osteria della Valle—in Todi, a town where people used to reserve their accolades for the meals that Grandmother made and, until they tasted his, had already driven away two "foreign" chefs, a Neapolitan and a Sicilian. In early June, I was finishing a plate of Paterson's excellent tagliarini with porcini when he emerged from the kitchen, pulled up a chair, and started talking about the mushrooms he had discovered, foraging as a boy, in a patch of woods near a bridge over the River Cocker. "All those beautiful mushrooms!" he kept saying. He told me about green, orange, and red parrot mushrooms and parasol mushrooms and big cèpes called penny buns and bright, polka-dotted fly agarics "so huge they could fill a room" and mushrooms "like white fennels that grow from the shape of saucers into gilled cups." He ate judiciously, but admired them all. In Italy, he started foraging for porcini to cook at home. At the Osteria, where he has to use farmed porcini, he roasts the mushrooms in pigeon juice, fills them with spinach, and wraps them in pancetta. He said that foraging had inspired his "bacon-and-eggs philosophy of little things that work together."

5   A week later, we set out for some of his favorite foraging spots. We stopped at the best roadside for gathering the tiny leaves of wild mint known in Italy as *mentuccia* ("Fantastic with lamb") and passed the supermarket at the edge of town, where only the day before he'd been cutting wild asparagus from a jumble of weeds and bushes behind the parking lot ("Great in risotto, but it looks like I took it all"). Then we headed for the country. We tried the field where he usually gets his wild fennel ("The flowers are lovely with ham and pork") and found so much of that delicious weed that the fronds, rippling across the field in a warm breeze, looked like nature's copy of Christo's "Running Fence." I was hoping to find *strioli*, too. *Strioli* is a spicy wild herb that looks like long leaves of tarragon. It grows in fields and pastures in late spring and early summer and makes a delicious

spaghetti sauce—you take a few big handfuls of the herb, toss it into a sauté pan with olive oil, garlic, and *peperoncini*, and in a minute it's ready. But there was none in sight, so we turned onto a quiet road that wound through fields of alfalfa and wheat and soon-to-be-blooming sunflowers, and parked next to a shuttered and, by all evidence, long-abandoned farmhouse that I had passed so often over the years that I thought of it as *my* house and dreamed of rescuing it.

Foraging places are like houses. Some speak to you, others you ignore. I wasn't surprised that the land around that tumbledown house spoke to Paterson. He jumped out of the car, peered over a thicket of roadside bush and sloe trees, and disappeared down a steep, very wet slope before I had even unbuckled my seat belt—after which he emerged, upright and waving, in an overgrown copse enclosed by a circle of trees. Cleared, the copse would have provided a shady garden for a farmer's family. To a forager, it was perfect: a natural rain trap, sheltered against the harsh sun, and virtually hidden from the road. Everywhere we turned, there were plants to gather. Even the wild asparagus, which usually hides from the sun in a profusion of other plants' leaves and stalks, was so plentiful that you couldn't miss it. We filled a shopping bag.

Wild asparagus has a tart, ravishing taste—what foragers call a wilderness taste—and a season so short as to be practically nonexistent. It's as different from farmed asparagus as a morel is from the boxed mushrooms at your corner store. I was ready to head back and start planning my risotto, but Paterson had spotted a patch of leafy scrub and pulled me toward it. He called it *crespina*. I had never heard of *crespina*, nor, after months of searching, have I found it in any Italian dictionary. It's the local word for spiny sow thistle—a peppery wild vegetable whose leaves taste a little like spinach and a lot like sorrel and, as I soon discovered, come with a spiky center rib sharp enough to etch a fine line down the palm of your hand if you've never handled them before. (I regard the small scar that I got that day as a forager's mark of initiation.) We added a respectable bunch of leaves to the shopping bag, and carried the overflow up to the car in our arms. An hour later, we were separating and trimming the morning's spoils in the tiny restaurant kitchen where, six days a week, Paterson cooks alone for fifty people ("Where would I put a sous-chef?" he said, stepping on my foot) and comparing recipes for wild-asparagus risotto. Here is his "most beautiful way" to make it: Snap off the fibrous ends of the asparagus spears and crush them with the blade of a knife. Simmer them in water or a mild stock until the stock takes flavor. Strain the stock. Pour a cupful of white wine into rice that's been turned for a minute or two in hot olive oil and some minced onion. As soon as the wine boils down, start ladling in the stock. Keep ladling and stirring until the rice is practically al dente and the last ladle of stock is in the pan. Now fold in the asparagus heads. In no time, all you will need to do is grate the Parmesan and serve.

I made Paterson's risotto for dinner that night, along with a roast chicken and the *crespina* leaves, sautéed for a minute, like baby spinach, in olive oil and a sprinkling of red-pepper flakes; the spines wilted into a tasty crunch. The next night, I chopped my fronds of wild fennel and used them to stuff a pork roast. When I called Paterson to say how good everything was, he told me, "Free food! There's nothing like it. It always tastes better."

July

I went to Oxford to give a talk, and got to forage in Pinsley Wood, an ancient forest near a village called Church Hanborough. You can find the original wood in the Domesday Book—the "unalterable" tax survey of English and Welsh land holdings compiled for William the Conqueror in 1086—and, indeed, the only altered thing about that venerable preserve is that now it's a lot smaller, and everyone can enjoy it. In spring, when the ground is covered with bluebells, foragers complain about having to contend with lovers, nestled in sheets of sweet-smelling flowers, watching the clouds go by. By July, the bluebells are gone and there are no distractions.

10   My friends Paul Levy and Elisabeth Luard—writers, foragers, and distinguished foodies (a word that, for better or for worse, Levy is said to have coined)—walked me through Pinsley Wood, armed with bags and baskets. Our plan was to make a big lunch with everything edible we found. Levy, a polymath whose books range from a biography of G. E. Moore during his Cambridge Apostle years to a whirlwind sampler of culinary erudition called "Out to Lunch," has been the food and wine editor of the *Observer*, an arts correspondent of the *Wall Street Journal*, and, for the past eight years, the co-chair of the Oxford Symposium on Food and Cookery. Luard, who began foraging as a botanical illustrator and traveller and whose many cookbooks include the estimable "European Peasant Cookery"—a virtual travelogue of foraged and home-grown food—is the symposium's executive director.

My husband and I were staying with Levy and his wife (and self-described "arts wallah"), Penelope Marcus, at their Oxfordshire farmhouse, a rambling place, almost as old as Pinsley Wood, with a kitchen garden so vast and various in its offerings that I was tempted to ditch my mud boots, which had turned out to be plastic-coated cardboard (six euros do not a Welly make), and do my foraging there, in flip-flops, with a pair of gardening shears and a glass of iced tea waiting on the kitchen table. In fact, we began our foraging at the Levys' barn wall, in a small overgrown patch of wild plants where fresh stinging nettles were sprouting like weeds (which is what they are) among the blackberry brambles and the dandelion greens and the malva, a purple flower often used in *melokhia*, a delectable Egyptian soup that I once ate in London but, alas, have never been able to replicate. We were going to use the nettles for an English broad-bean-and-vegetable soup that afternoon.

We drove to the wood in Luard's old Mazda—past a village allotment with wild oats growing outside the fence and, inside, what looked to be a bumper crop of opium poppies—and listened to Luard and Levy talk about forest plants. Don't bother with "dead nettles"—stingless flowering perennials that had no relation to *our* nettles and, to Luard's mind, were not worth eating. Don't overdo the elderberry unless you need a laxative. Beware of plants with pretty berries or pretty names, and, especially, of plants with both—which in the Hanboroughs means to remember that the flowering plant called lords and ladies, with its juicy scarlet berries and sultry, folded hood, was more accurately known to generations of poisoners as the deadly Arum "kill your neighbor." "A stinky plant," Levy said. I wrote it all down.

Levy considers himself a "basic local forager," which is to say that he doesn't drive three or four hours to the sea for his samphire and sea aster; he buys them at Waitrose. He loves wild garlic, and knows that sheets of bluebells in Pinsley Wood mean that wild garlic is growing near them. He "scrabbles" for the food he likes at home. "I can identify Jack-by-the-hedge for salad," he told me. "And I can do sloes, brambles, elderberries. Anyone who lives in the countryside here can. Elisabeth is the more advanced forager, but I do know a little about truffles and wild mushrooms. Three of us once identified more than twenty mushroom species near here in Blenheim Park, and I'm quite good at chanterelles and porcini." Levy thinks of Pinsley Wood as his neighborhood mushroom habitat. It has an old canopy of oak and ash, but it also has birch trees (chanterelles grow in their shade), and most of the interior is beech (porcini and truffles). Summer truffles are pretty much what you find in England. They are black outside and pale, grayish brown inside, and you have to dig twice as many as you think you'll need to match anything like the deep flavor of France's black winter truffles in a *sauce périgueux*.

Levy and my husband, who had been planning to spend a quiet day at the Ashmolean but was shamed out of it, immediately started following a network of burrowed tunnels—a "sett"—that led them into the wood near clusters of beech trees with small, circular swells of dark, moist earth beneath them. Swells like those are a sign of truffles, pushing up the ground. Setts mean that badgers probably got to the truffles first. A good truffle dog, like a hungry badger, can sniff its way to a truffle by following the scent of the spores left in its own feces from as long as a year before. The difference between a truffle dog and a badger—or, for that matter, the boar that trample my sage and rosemary bushes in their rush to my pond to root and drink—is that your dog doesn't go truffling without you, and when it digs a truffle, as many Italian truffle dogs are trained to do, it mouths it gently and gives it to you intact. Or relatively intact. A few weeks later, when Paterson and I went truffling with an obliging local carabiniere named Bruno Craba and his two truffle terrier mutts, one of the dogs surrendered so helplessly to the intoxicating smell of semen that the tubers emit—known to foodies as the truffle umami—that she swallowed half a truffle the size of a tennis ball before presenting the rest of it to her master.

15   Being without benefit of a truffle dog, let alone a small spade or even a soup spoon for loosening the soil, Luard and I abandoned the men, who by then were up to their wrists in dirt, hoping to find a truffle that the badgers had missed. They didn't. With lunch on our minds, we went in search of more accessible food. "Pea plants—plants of the Leguminosae family—are mostly what you get here," Luard told me. You have to look for seed-bearing pods and single flowers with four "free" petals (which "The New Oxford Book of Food Plants" describes as "a large upper standard, 2 lateral wings, and a boat-shaped keel"). I left the identifying to her. Luard, who has foraged in twenty countries, has been called a walking encyclopedia of wild food. She was.

While we gathered pea plants, I learned that British countrywomen thicken their jellies with rose hips, crab apples, and the red fruit clusters of rowan bushes, which people in Wales, where Luard lives, plant by their doors to keep witches away. (There's a recipe for "hedgerow jelly" in her new book, "A Cook's Year in a Welsh Farmhouse.") Passing what looked to be the remains of a wild ground orchid, I was instructed in the virtues of "saloop," a drink made from the powder of crushed orchid roots which, for centuries, was the pick-me-up of London's chimney sweeps—"The Ovaltine and Horlicks of its time, with more protein than a *filet de boeuf*," Luard said. (You can read about saloop in Charles Lamb, who hated it.) We walked past silverweed plants ("Edible but not tasty") and meadowsweet ("The underscent of vanilla in the flowers makes a nice tea") and the leaf shoots of young, wild carrots ("Skinny as can be means good in soup") and teasel ("Not for eating; for combing wool") and butterwort, which, like fig-tree sap in Italy, is a vegetable rennet, "good for making cheese." Along the way, I discovered that farm children in southern Spain, where Luard lived with her family in the seventies, ate wild-fennel fronds and "sucked on the lemony stalks" of wood sorrel on their way to school, by way of a second breakfast. "Children are a huge source of information about wild food," she told me. "In Spain, I would ask the village women to tell me what they foraged and how they cooked it, and they wouldn't answer—they were embarrassed by foraging, like your Italian neighbors—but their children knew. My children would walk to school with them, eating the leaves and berries that their friends plucked from the roadside verges. They learned from their friends, and I learned from them. I've lived in a lot of places, and I've discovered that a basic knowledge of food runs all the way through Europe. The people I lived with cooked, of necessity, what they grew, and the wild food they added—the changing taste of leaves and nuts, for instance—was what gave interest to those few things. It taught me that when you grow enough to eat you begin to make it taste good. That's not a frippery, it's a need."

Luard, as senior forager, was in charge of lunch. Levy was in charge of fetching claret from the cellar and coaxing heat from an unpredictable Aga. Marcus was in charge of setting the garden table, while my husband, who had volunteered for the washing up, wandered around, keeping up the conversation. And I was stationed at the sink, sorting and cleaning a good deal of Pinsley Wood. It was an unfortunate assignment, since I tend to daydream at kitchen sinks, and the better the dream the slower my pace. Sorting our forage took me half an hour. Cleaning it took twice as long, given the number of bugs clinging to every leaf and flower, not to mention Luard's instructions, among them separating the yarrow leaves we'd collected from any lingering trace of petals, and scraping the hairy calyxes from the bottom of borage flowers. We sat down to lunch at four-thirty. The soup was a vegetarian feast of flageolets with (among other good, wild things) nettles, yarrow leaves, and dandelions, and the salad a spicy mix of wild sorrel, dandelions, onion flowers, and borage flowers. But my favorite dish was the scrambled eggs that Luard made with an unseemly amount of farm butter and double cream and a mountain of fresh sorrel. The sorrel for that came from the Levys' kitchen garden, a few feet from the back door.

August

I wasn't really ready for René Redzepi. I had tried to prepare. I downloaded the stories that appeared last spring, when a jury of chefs and food writers, convened by the British magazine *Restaurant*, named Noma the world's best restaurant for the second year. I studied the photographs in Redzepi's cookbook, memorized the names in his glossary of plants and seaweeds, and even tried to improvise on some of his simpler recipes with my local produce—impossible in a part of Italy where the collective culinary imagination is so literally "local" that broccoli is considered a foreign food and oregano is dismissed as "something the Tuscans eat." But I flew to Denmark anyway, planning to make a trial foraging run in western Zealand with my Danish friend (and fellow-journalist) Merete Baird, who spends her summers in a farmhouse overlooking Nexelo Bay—a trove of wilderness food—and likes to eat at Lammerfjordens Spisehus, a restaurant run by one of Redzepi's disciples. My foraging trial ended before it began, in a freezing downpour, and, as for the restaurant, the storm had left me so hungry that, at dinner that night, I passed up the young chef's lovely deconstructed tomato-and-wild-herb soup and his leafy Noma-inspired offerings and ordered two fat Danish sausages and a bowl of warm potato salad.

I met Redzepi at Noma early the following afternoon. He arrived on an old bike, chained it outside the restaurant—a converted warehouse on a quay where trading ships once unloaded fish and skins from Iceland, Greenland, and the Faroe Islands—and tried to ignore the tourists who were milling about, their cameras ready, hoping for a shot of arguably the most famous Dane since Hamlet. In fact, most of them barely glanced at the small young man with floppy brown hair, in jeans, battered sneakers, and an untucked wrinkled shirt, locking up his bike. Redzepi is thirty-three, with a wife and two small children, but he can look like a student who slept in his clothes and is now running late for an exam. The most flamboyant thing about him may be the short beard he frequently grows—and just as frequently sheds. It is hard to imagine him in a white toque or a bloody apron or, à la Mario Batali, in baggy Bermudas and orange crocs. When I left for my hotel that day, one of the tourists stopped me: "That kid you were with earlier? His bike's still here."

Redzepi opened Noma in 2003, at the age of twenty-five, backed by the gastronomical entrepreneur of a successful catering service and bakery chain (whose bread he doesn't serve) and a "new Danish" furniture designer (whose advice he routinely rejects). He was nine years out of culinary school, during which time he had apprenticed at one of Copenhagen's best restaurants, endured a long *stage* in the unhappy kitchen of a testy three-star Montpelier chef, and made molecular magic in Catalonia with Ferran Adrià. "I ate a meal at elBulli," as he tells the story, "and as soon as I finished I went up to Adrià and asked for a job. He said, 'Write me a letter.' So I did. A few weeks later, I found a job offer, complete with contract, in the mail." He stayed at elBulli for a season, and, in the course of it, landed his next job—at Thomas Keller's French Laundry, in Napa Valley, where he was much taken with the emphasis on local food. He was back in Copenhagen, cooking "Scandinavian French" at the restaurant Kong Hans Kælder, when the call came asking if he'd like a restaurant of his own.

"We had the idea: let's use local products here," he told me the next morning. We were at a diner, making a caffeine stop on the way to a beach at Dragør—a town on the Øresund Sea, about twenty minutes from the outskirts of Copenhagen—where he likes to forage. "But I was very unhappy at first. Why? Because we were taking recipes from other cultures, serving essentially the same 'Scandinavian French' food, and just because you're using local produce to make that food doesn't mean you're making a food of your own culture. I started asking myself, What is a region? What is the sum of the people we are, the culture we are? What does it taste like? What does it look like on a plate? It was a very complex thing for us—the idea of finding a new flavor that was 'ours.'"

Five years later, having raised the money for a research foundation called the Nordic Food Lab, he hired an American chef named Lars Williams—who arrived with a degree in English literature, a passion for food chemistry, and fifteen lines of the first book of "Paradise Lost" tattooed on his right arm—to preside over a test kitchen on a houseboat across the quay from Noma and begin to "release the umami of Nordic cuisine." At the moment, they were looking for some in a liquid concentrate of dried peas,

20

which I had sampled on the houseboat the day before. (It was quite good, with the rich bite of a soy concentrate and, at the same time, a kind of pea-plant sweetness.) And they planned to look for more in a brew of buckwheat and fatty fish, starting with herring or mackerel. They were also "looking into" Nordic insects, Redzepi said. (On a trip to Australia last year, he had eaten white larvae that he swore tasted "exactly like fresh almonds.") "The question for us is how to keep that free-sprouting spirit here," he told me. "In gastronomical terms, we're not at the finish line, but we know what it could be."

A Nordic cuisine, for Redzepi, begins with harvesting the vast resources of a particular north—running west from Finland through Scandinavia and across the North Atlantic to the Faroes, Iceland, and Greenland—and using them to evoke and, in the end, re-imagine and refine a common culture of rye grains, fish, fermentation, salt, and smoke, inherited from farmers and fishermen with hardscrabble lives and a dour Protestant certainty that those lives wouldn't be getting easier. Redzepi's mother, who worked as a cleaner in Copenhagen and loves to eat at Noma, comes from that Protestant Danish stock. But the cook in the family was his father, a mosque-going Muslim from Macedonia who drove a taxi. "When I was growing up, we'd leave the city for long periods in the summer and stay in the village where my father was born," Redzepi told me. "It was a two-car village, and cooking, for him, was kill the chicken, milk the cow. When he eats at Noma, he says, 'Well, it's not exactly up my alley.' His alley is homey stews, homey peasant flavors, and lots of beans." When I told Redzepi about a blog I'd read, calling him a Nordic supremacist, he laughed and said, "Look at my family. My father's a Muslim immigrant. My wife, Nadine, is Jewish. She was born in Portugal and has family in France and England. She studied languages. If the supremacists took over, we'd be out of here."

Redzepi remembers foraging for berries as a boy in Macedonia. He loves berries. Gooseberries, blueberries, blackberries, lingonberries—any berries in season, at hand, and edible. He carries a bowl of berries around Noma's kitchens, popping them into his mouth while he checks a prep station or talks to a chef or even stands at the front stove, finishing a sauce. He also loves mushrooms. There are some two hundred edible varieties in Denmark's woods, and he is working his way through them all. But, at the moment, the food he cherishes is cabbage—from the big, pale cabbages that he slices and steams, at home, in a knob of butter and a half inch of his wife's leftover tea, to the tiny, vividly green-leaved wild cabbages that sit in pots, basking

in ultraviolet light, on a steel counter in the middle of one of Noma's upstairs kitchens, waiting for the day they're ready to be wrapped with their
stems around a sliver of pike perch and served to customers on a beautiful
stoneware plate, between a green verbena sauce and a butter-and-fish-bone
foam. One of the first things he told me, the day we met, was that, for him,
the great surprise of foraging in Nordic Europe was to see cabbages sprouting from rotting seaweed on a beach, and to realize how much food value
the sea, the sand, and the nutrients released in the rotting process could
produce.

It's an experience that he wants the people on his staff to share before   25
they so much as plate a salad or get near a stove. Seventy people work at
Noma. They come from as many as sixteen countries—English is their
lingua franca—and it's safe to say that every one of them has made a foraging trip to the sea or the woods (or both) with Redzepi. "There's a new guy
from the Bronx working here," he told me, when he was introducing the
kitchen staff. "I want to take him to the forest. I want to see the first time
he gets down on his knees and tastes something. The transformation begins
there."

The beach near Dragør was bleak, but it was bursting with plants I had
never dreamed of eating, and I was ready for transformation. "Foraging is
treasure hunting," Redzepi said; you'll find the treasure if you believe it's
there. It's also homework. When he began foraging in Denmark, he stayed
up nights reading. He bought botany books and field guides—the most
useful being an old Swedish Army survival book that had taught soldiers
how to live for a year in the wilderness on the food they found. At first,
he foraged with the Army manual in his pocket. Then he began consulting
other foragers. Now he forages with his iPhone. "I know a great professional forager in Sweden," he told me. "If I see something I can't identify,
I call her up, point my iPhone, send her a picture of what I'm seeing, and ask
her what it is. At the beginning, I had a little problem with beach thistles—
my throat started to close from those weird flowers—but that was the worst
time. I got connected to the sea and soil, and now they're an integral part of
me. I experience the world through food."

We started out in a thicket of rose-hip bushes at the edge of the beach,
where wild grass was just beginning to give way to sand and seaweed. The
berries looked like tiny cherry tomatoes, and there were so many of them
that, after a few minutes, we left Redzepi's "scavenger sous-chef," who had
driven us out that morning—Redzepi hates driving—with the job of

locating a couple of large garbage bags and filling them. (I ate some of the berries that night, at dinner, in a warm salad of lovage, zucchini, wild herbs, and an egg fried at the table in a hot skillet.) Redzepi pickles his rose-hip flowers in apple vinegar, and preserves the berries as a thick purée, for winter dishes. The picking season is short in Denmark, and he has to start gathering in mid-spring in order to dry, smoke, pickle, or otherwise preserve—and, in the process, concentrate the flavor of—a lot of the vegetables and fruits that his customers will be eating in December. He told me about beach dandelions with nippy little bouquets of flowers and tiny roots that taste "like a mix of fresh hazelnuts and roasted almonds," and about the vanilla taste of wild parsnip flowers, and about pink beach-pea flowers that taste like mushrooms. By the time we got to the water, we were sampling most of what we found. We ate a handful of short beach grass that tasted like oysters, and a cluster of spicy lilac beach-mustard flowers that made the mustard in jars seem tame. We snacked on enormous leaves of sea lettuce that came floating by. They tasted, to me, like mild, salty cabbage that had just been scooped out of a pot-au-feu. Redzepi serves a lot of sea lettuce at Noma. He breaks it down in a *saporoso* of white-wine vinegar (to make it "easier to eat," he says, and also to bring out its "ocean flavor") and wraps it around cod roe or oysters, or folds it into a poached-egg-and-radish stew.

The weather in Denmark begins to turn in August. It was too late in the summer for sea goosefoot, or for the bladder wrack that bobs near the shore like bloated peas and, according to Redzepi, is just as sweet. The scurvy grass we discovered was too old to eat. But the beach horseradish that day was perfect. It had the "big hint of wasabi taste" that Redzepi likes so much that he serves the leaves folded over sea urchin. By late morning, with the wind cutting through our sweaters, we were still roaming the beach and tasting. "It's amazing, all these foods in the sand," Redzepi said. "One of my most important moments foraging—important in the history of Noma—was on a windblown beach like this one. I saw this blade of grass, this chive-looking thing, growing out of some rotting seaweed. I put it in my mouth. It had a nice snap, with the saltiness of samphire. And a familiar taste. A taste from somewhere else. I thought, Wait a minute, it's cilantro! This isn't Mexico, it's Denmark, and I've found cilantro in the sand." That night, his customers ate beach cilantro, which turned out to be sea arrow grass. "We put it in everything that was savory."

There are never fewer than five or six foraged foods on Noma's menu, and usually many more. By now, Redzepi depends on professional foragers to supply most of them, but he and his staff still provide the rest. Earlier this year, they gathered two hundred and twenty pounds of wild roses for pickling, and a hundred and fifty pounds of wild ramps. By November, there were thirty-three hundred pounds of foraged fruits and vegetables stored at Noma, ready for winter. Redzepi told me that ninety per cent of everything he serves is farmed, fished, raised, or foraged within sixty miles of the restaurant, and while most chefs with serious reputations to maintain will occasionally cheat on "local," even the Jacobins of the sustainable-food world acknowledge that Redzepi never does. Early this fall, a food critic from the *Guardian* noted that the millionaires flying their private jets to eat at restaurants like Noma leave a carbon footprint far more damaging than the one Redzepi is trying to erase at home. Redzepi thinks about that, too, but not much. He says that the point of Noma isn't to feed the rich—that in his best-possible-world Noma would be free, because "there is nothing worse than charging people for conviviality." The point is to demonstrate how good cooking with regional food, anywhere in the world, can be. His mission is to spread the word.

On an average Saturday night, Noma's waiting list runs to a thousand people. The restaurant seats forty-four, and Redzepi has no real desire to expand. His partners keep asking, "When will the money begin to flow?" He ignores them. For now, at least, whatever profit Noma makes (last year, three per cent) goes right back into the business of sourcing and preparing the kinds of food that people who *do* get reservations come to the restaurant to eat. Most of the cultivated crops he uses (including his favorite carrots, which are left in the ground for a year after they mature, and develop a dense texture and an almost meaty taste) are grown for him on a polycultural farm, an hour away in northwest Zealand, that he helped transform. His butter and milk (including the buttermilk with which he turns a warm, seaweed-oil vegetable salad dressing into an instantly addictive sauce) come from a nearby Zealand biodynamic farm. Everything else he serves is "Nordic" by anyone's definition. His sea urchin comes from a transplanted Scot who dives for it off the Norwegian coast. The buckwheat in Noma's bread comes from a small island off the coast of Sweden; I downed a loaf of it, watching Redzepi cook lunch. The red seaweed I ate that night at dinner—in a mysteriously satisfying dish involving dried scallops, toasted grains, watercress purée, beech nuts, mussel juice, and squid ink—came from a forager in Iceland. The langoustine that was served on a black rock (next to three tiny but eminently edible "rocks" made from

30

an emulsion of oysters and kelp, dusted with crisped rye and seaweed crumbs) came from a fisherman in the Faroe Islands. Even Redzepi's wine list, which used to be largely French, now includes wines from a vineyard that Noma owns on Lilleø, a small island off Denmark's North Sea coast. I tried an unfiltered, moss-colored white from the vineyard that night. It looked murky in the glass, but I wish I had ordered more.

Redzepi was fifteen, and finishing the ninth grade, when his homeroom teacher pronounced him "ineligible" for secondary school and said that he would be streamed out of the academic system and into trade school and an apprenticeship. He chose a culinary school only because a classmate named Michael Skotbo was going there. Their first assignment was to find a recipe, cook it, and make it look appetizing on a plate. "You were supposed to dig into your memories of food, of taste, and my most vivid was from Macedonia," Redzepi told me. "It was my father's barnyard chicken—the drippings over the rice, the spices, the cashew sauce. I think that my first adult moment was cooking that spicy chicken. My second was when we found a wonderful cup and put the rice in it—with the chicken, sliced, next to it on the plate. I had an idea. I said to Michael, 'No, don't put the sauce on the meat. Put the sauce *between* the chicken and the rice. We came in second in flavor and first in presentation." I asked him who won first in flavor. "A butcher," he said. "He made ham salad. It was terrific."

The boy who couldn't get into high school now speaks four or five languages, publishes in the *Guardian* and the New York *Times*, speaks at Yale, and last year disarmed an audience of literati at the New York Public Library with a philosophical riff on the beauty of aged-in-the-ground carrots, not to mention a biochemical acumen that many scientists, and most other chefs, would envy. To call Redzepi an autodidact is beside the point. His friends say he was born bored. "Wherever I go, I read, I look, I taste, I discover, I learn," he told me. "I'm cooking with mosses now. They were a whole new discovery for me. I tasted them for the first time foraging in Iceland. Some mosses are hideous, but those were so lush and green I had to try them. I took some back to Reykjavík, where a guy I'd met ground it for me and put it into cookies. Then I went to Greenland. For years, in Greenland, it looked like the reindeer were eating snow. Now we know they were eating moss. We call it reindeer moss. The moss on trees and bushes has a mushroomy taste—we deep-fry it, like potato chips—but the ones growing from the ground, up near caves, they have the taste and texture of noodles."

I ate reindeer moss at Noma, deep-fried, spiced with cèpes, and deliciously crisp. It was the third of twenty-three appetizers and tasting dishes I ate that night, the first being a hay parfait—a long infusion of cream and toasted hay, into which yarrow, nasturtium, camomile jelly, egg, and sorrel and camomile juice were then blended. The second arrived in a flower pot, filled with malted, roasted rye crumbs and holding shoots of raw wild vegetables, a tiny poached mousse of snail nestling in a flower, and a flatbread "branch" that was spiced with powdered oak shoots, birch, and juniper. I wish I could describe the taste of those eloquent, complex combinations, but the truth is that, like most of the dishes I tried at Noma, they tasted like everything in them and, at the same time, like nothing I had ever eaten. Four hours later, I had filled a notebook with the names of wild foods. Redzepi collected me at my table, and we sat for a while outside, on a bench near the houseboat, looking at the water and talking. I didn't tell him that I'd passed on the little live shrimp, wriggling alone on a bed of crushed ice in a Mason jar, that had been presented to me between the rose-hip berries and the caramelized sweetbreads, plated with chanterelles and a grilled salad purée composed of spinach, wild herbs (pre-wilted in butter and herb tea), Swiss chard, celery, ground elder, Spanish chervil, chickweed, and goosefoot, and served with a morel-and-juniper-wood broth. I told him that it was the best meal I had ever eaten, and it was.

September

I came home to New York, checked my mail, and discovered that I had missed the Vassar Club's "foraging tour" of Central Park. It was quite a relief. I ordered a steak from Citarella (by phone, for delivery), walked to the Friday greenmarket on Ninety-seventh Street for corn and tomatoes, and was home in fifteen minutes. I spun some salad from my corner store, unpacked my suitcase, plugged in my laptop, uncorked the wine, and cooked dinner. It seemed too easy. Surveying my kitchen, I wondered where I would put a Thermomix or a foam siphon with backup cartridges or a Pacojet or a vacuum-pack machine or even a No. 40 ice-cream scoop—all of which I would need just to produce the carrot sorbet and buttermilk-foam dessert that I'd been eying in Redzepi's cookbook. Where would Redzepi put them in his own kitchen? Then I remembered the sliced cabbage, steamed with a knob of butter in a half inch of leftover tea.

35   Noma isn't about home cooking or even foraging. The restaurant is a showcase, a virtuoso reminder that only a small fraction of the planet's bounty gets to anyone's dinner table, and that most of it is just as good as what does get there—even better, if it's cooked with patience, imagination, and a little hot-cold chemistry. It seems to me now that if you take John Paterson's enthusiasm for little wild things that work together and Elisabeth Luard's conviction that those things express the timeless "taste-good" ingenuity of peasant cooking, the message is not so different from Redzepi's. Most of us eat only what we know. It's time to put on our boots (or our sneakers) and look around.

Analyze

1. Kramer's language is very sophisticated and is so from the very start of the article. Look up any words that seem especially exotic, and then analyze why their use is important—and why Kramer doesn't define them for you. What purpose do these language choices serve, and what does it say about Kramer's assumed audience?

2. How is this essay about "exploring" in the literal sense as Kramer goes around the world to forage—and as she prepares diligently for each phase of the trip? How does foraging itself become a metaphor for exploration, and for what purpose is that the case in this article?

3. Analyze the other methods by which Kramer advances the wonderful nature of foraging. Consider, for instance, her embedded recipes and her use of such words as "ravishing" to describe the taste of asparagus. What effect do these techniques have on your reading?

Explore

1. Kramer writes, "Most of us only eat what we know. It's time to put on our boots (or our sneakers) and look around." Do some exploring on your own—whether literally (outside) or through other types of research. How does what you find challenge "what you know?" Discuss the ways in which these insights potentially reshape your worldview about food and the ways you acquire and prepare it.

2. The author acknowledges that "the pursuit of wild food has become so fashionable." Look up other articles or sources about the practices of foraging (for instance, some must do it out of necessity and not

fashion), and create a presentation that looks at the act of foraging in ways that are very different from Kramer's. How do these two types of foraging compare, both in process and in the "cultural" contexts surrounding them?

3. Explore your reaction to Kramer as a speaker—as writer of this article, that is—and as traveler. What do you notice, basing your view on her "voice" and the examples she uses in her narrative?

Anya Von Bremzen
"The Last Days of the Czars," Excerpt from *Mastering the Art of Soviet Cooking*

A global citizen, Anya Von Bremzen divides her time between New York City and Istanbul, Turkey. She is a contributing editor at *Travel and Leisure* magazine, and she is the winner of three James Beard awards. Von Bremzen has written articles for *Saveur, Gourmet, Food and Wine,* and other publications devoted to food and travel. The following is an excerpt from *Mastering the Art of Soviet Cooking: A Memoir of Food and Longing* (2013).

How do politics, food, place, and worldview intertwine?

My mother is expecting guests.

In just a few hours in this sweltering July heat wave, eight people will show up for an extravagant czarist-era dinner at her small Queens apartment. But her kitchen resembles a building site. Pots tower and teeter in the sink; the food processor and blender drone on in unison. In a shiny bowl on Mom's green faux-granite counter, a porous blob of yeast dough seems weirdly alive. I'm pretty sure it's breathing. Unfazed, Mother simultaneously blends, sautés, keeps an eye on Chris Matthews on MSNBC, and chatters away on her cordless phone. At this moment she suggests a plump modern-day elf, multitasking away in her orange Indian housedress.

Ever since I can remember, my mother has cooked like this, phone tucked under her chin. Of course, back in Brezhnev's Moscow in the seventies when I was a kid, the idea of an "extravagant czarist dinner" would have provoked sardonic laughter. And the cord of our antediluvian black Soviet *telefon* was so traitorously twisted, I once tripped on it while carrying a platter of Mom's lamb pilaf to the low three-legged table in the cluttered space where my parents did their living, sleeping, and entertaining.

Right now, as one of Mom's ancient émigré friends fills her ear with cultural gossip, that pilaf episode returns to me in cinematic slow motion. Masses of yellow rice cascade onto our Armenian carpet. Biddy, my two-month-old puppy, greedily laps up every grain, her eyes and tongue swelling shockingly in an instant allergic reaction to lamb fat. I howl, fearing for Biddy's life. My father berates Mom for her phone habits.

Mom managed to rescue the disaster with her usual flair, dotty and determined. By the time guests arrived—with an extra four non-sober comrades—she'd conjured up a tasty fantasia from two pounds of the proletarian wurst called *sosiski*. These she'd cut into petal-like shapes, splayed in a skillet, and fried up with eggs. Her creation landed at table under provocative blood-red squiggles of ketchup, that decadent capitalist condiment. For dessert: Mom's equally spontaneous apple cake. "Guest-at-the-doorstep apple charlotte," she dubbed it.

5   Guests! They never stopped crowding Mom's doorstep, whether at our apartment in the center of Moscow or at the boxy immigrant dwelling in Philadelphia where she and I landed in 1974. Guests overrun her current home in New York, squatting for weeks, eating her out of the house, borrowing money and books. Every so often I Google "compulsive hospitality syndrome." But there's no cure. Not for Mom the old Russian adage "An uninvited guest is worse than an invading Tatar." *Her* parents' house was just like this, her sister's even more so.

Tonight's dinner, however, is different. It will mark our archival adieu to classic Russian cuisine. For such an important occasion Mom has agreed to keep the invitees to just eight after I slyly quoted a line from a Roman scholar and satirist: "The number of dinner guests should be more than the Graces and less than the Muses." Mom's quasi-religious respect for culture trumps even her passion for guests. Who is she to disagree with the ancients?

And so, on this diabolically torrid late afternoon in Queens, the two of us are sweating over a decadent feast set in the imagined 1910s—Russia's Silver Age, artistically speaking. The evening will mark our hail and farewell to a grandiose decade of Moscow gastronomy. To a food culture that flourished at the start of the twentieth century and disappeared abruptly when the 1917 revolution transformed Russian cuisine and culture into *Soviet* cuisine and culture—the only version we knew.

Mom and I have not taken the occasion lightly.

The horseradish and lemon vodkas that I've been steeping for days are chilling in their cut-crystal carafes. The caviar glistens. We've even gone to the absurd trouble of brewing our own kvass, a folkloric beverage from fermented black bread that's these days mostly just mass-produced fizz. Who knows? Besides communing with our ancestral stomachs, this might be our last chance on this culinary journey to eat *really well*.

"The burbot liver—*what* to do about the burbot liver?" Mom laments,   10 finally off the phone.

Noticing how poignantly scratched her knuckles are from assorted gratings, I reply, for the umpteenth time, that burbot, noble member of the freshwater cod family so fetishized by pre-revolutionary Russian gourmands, is nowhere to be had in Jackson Heights, Queens. Frustrated sighing. As always, my pragmatism interferes with Mom's dreaming and scheming. And let's not even mention *viziga*, the desiccated dorsal cord of a sturgeon. Burbot liver was the czarist foie gras, *viziga* its shark's fin. Chances of finding either in any zip code hereabouts? Not slim—none.

But still, we've made progress.

Several test runs for crispy brains in brown butter have yielded smashing results. And despite the state of Mom's kitchen, and the homey, crepuscular clutter of her book-laden apartment, her dining table is a thing of great beauty. Crystal goblets preen on the floral, antique-looking tablecloth. Pale blue hydrangeas in an art nouveau pitcher I found at a flea market in Buenos Aires bestow a subtle fin-de-siècle opulence.

I unpack the cargo of plastic containers and bottles I've lugged over from my house two blocks away. Since Mom's galley kitchen is far too small for two cooks, much smaller than an aristocrat's broom closet, I've already brewed the kvass and prepared the trimmings for an anachronistic chilled fish and greens soup called *botvinya*. I was also designated steeper of vodkas and executer of Guriev kasha, a dessert loaded with deep historical meaning and a whole pound of home-candied nuts. Mom has taken charge of the main course and the array of *zakuski*, or appetizers.

A look at the clock and she gasps. "The *kulebiaka* dough! Check it!"   15

I check it. Still rising, still bubbling. I give it a bang to deflate—and the tang of fermenting yeast tickles my nostrils, evoking a fleeting collective memory. Or a memory of a received memory. I pinch off a piece of dough and hand it to Mom to assess. She gives me a shrug as if to say, *"You're* the cookbook writer."

But I'm glad I let her take charge of the kulebiaka. This extravagant Russian fish pie, this history lesson in a pastry case, will be the pièce de résistance of our banquet tonight.

"The kulebiaka must make your mouth water, it must lie before you, naked, shameless, a temptation. You wink at it, you cut off a sizeable slice, and you let your fingers just play over it. . . . You eat it, the butter drips from it like tears, and the filling is fat, juicy, rich with eggs, giblets, onions. . . ."

So waxed Anton Pavlovich Chekhov in his little fiction "The Siren," which Mom and I have been salivating over during our preparations, just as we first did back in our unglorious socialist pasts. It wasn't only us Soviet-born who fixated on food. Chekhov's satiric encomium to outsize Slavic appetite is a lover's rapturous fantasy. Sometimes it seems that for nineteenth-century Russian writers, food was what landscape (or maybe class?) was for the English. Or war for the Germans, love for the French—a subject encompassing the great themes of comedy, tragedy, ecstasy, and doom. Or perhaps, as the contemporary author Tatyana Tolstaya suggests, the "orgiastic gorging" of Russian authors was a compensation for literary taboos on eroticism. One must note, too, alas, Russian writers' peculiarly *Russian* propensity for moralizing. Rosy hams, amber fish broths, blini as plump as "the shoulder of a merchant's daughter" (Chekhov again), such literary deliciousness often serves an ulterior agenda of exposing gluttons as spiritually bankrupt philistines—or lethargic losers such as the alpha glutton Oblomov. Is this a moral trap? I keep asking myself. Are we enticed to salivate at these lines so we'll end up feeling guilty?

20   But it's hard not to salivate. Chekhov, Pushkin, Tolstoy—they all devote some of their most fetching pages to the gastronomical. As for Mom's beloved Nikolai Gogol, the author of *Dead Souls* anointed the stomach the body's "most noble" organ. Besotted with eating both on and off the page—sour cherry dumplings from his Ukrainian childhood, pastas from his sojourns in Rome—scrawny Gogol could polish off a gargantuan dinner and start right in again. While traveling he sometimes even churned his own butter. "The belly is the belle of his stories, the nose is their beau," declared Nabokov. In 1852, just short of his forty-third birthday, in the throes of religious mania and gastrointestinal torments, Nikolai Vasilievich committed a slow suicide rich in Gogolian irony: *he refused to eat.* Yes, a

complicated, even tortured, relationship with food has long been a hall-mark of our national character.

According to one scholarly count, no less than eighty-six kinds of edibles appear in *Dead Souls*, Gogol's chronicle of a grifter's circuit from dinner to dinner in the vast Russian countryside. Despairing over not being able to scale the heights of the novel's first volume, poor wretched Gogol burned most of the second. What survives includes the most famous liter-ary ode to kulebiaka—replete with a virtual recipe.

"Make a four-cornered kulebiaka," instructs Petukh, a spiritually bank-rupt glutton who made it through the flames. And then:

> In one corner put the cheeks and dried spine of a sturgeon, in an-other put some buckwheat, and some mushrooms and onion, and some soft fish roe, and brains, and something else as well. . . . As for the underneath . . . see that it's baked so that it's quite . . . well not done to the point of crumbling but so that it will melt in the mouth like snow and not make any crunching sound.
>
> Petukh smacked his lips as he spoke.

Generations of Russians have smacked their own lips at this passage. Historians, though, suspect that this chimerical "four-cornered" kulebiaka might have been a Gogolian fiction. So what then of the genuine article, which is normally oblong and layered?

To telescope quickly: kulebiaka descends from the archaic Slavic *pirog* 25 (filled pie). Humbly born, they say, in the 1600s, it had by its turn-of-the-twentieth-century heyday evolved into a regal golden–brown case fanci-fully decorated with cut-out designs. Concealed within: aromatic layers of fish and *viziga*, a cornucopia of forest-picked mushrooms, and butter-splashed buckwheat or rice, all the tiers separated by thin crepes called *blinchiki*—to soak up the juices.

Mom and I argued over every other dish on our menu. But on this we agreed: without kulebiaka, there could be no proper Silver Age Moscow repast.

When my mother, Larisa (Lara, Larochka) Frumkina—Frumkin in English—was growing up in the 1930s high Stalinist Moscow, the idea of a decadent czarist-era banquet constituted exactly what it would in the Brezhnevian seventies: laughable blue cheese from the moon. Sosiski were Mom's favorite food. I was hooked on them too, though Mom claims that the sosiski of my childhood couldn't hold a candle to the juicy Stalinist article. Why do these proletarian franks remain the madeleine of every *Homo sovieticus?* Because besides sosiski with canned peas and *kotleti* (minced meat patties) with kasha, cabbage-intensive soups, mayo-laden salads, and watery fruit *kompot* for dessert—there wasn't all that much to eat in the Land of the Soviets.

Unless, of course, you were privileged. In our joyous classless society, this all-important matter of privilege has nagged at me since my early childhood.

I first glimpsed—or rather *heard*—the world of privileged food consumption during my first three years of life, at the grotesque communal Moscow apartment into which I was born in 1963. The apartment sat so close to the Kremlin, we could practically hear the midnight chimes of the giant clock on the Spassky Tower. There was another sound too, keeping us up: the roaring *BLARGHHH* of our neighbor Misha puking his guts out. Misha, you see, was a food store manager with a proprietary attitude toward the socialist food supply, likely a black market millionaire who shared our communal lair only for fear that flaunting his wealth would attract the unwanted attention of the anti-embezzlement authorities. Misha and Musya, his blond, big-bosomed wife, lived out a Mature Socialist version of bygone decadence. Night after night they dined out at Moscow's few proper restaurants (accessible to party bigwigs, foreigners, and comrades with illegal rubles), dropping the equivalent of Mom's monthly salary on meals that Misha couldn't even keep in his stomach.

30   When the pair stayed home, they ate unspeakable delicacies—batter-fried chicken tenders, for instance—prepared for them by the loving hands of Musya's mom, Baba Mila, she a blubbery former peasant with one eye, four—or was it six?—gold front teeth, and a healthy contempt for the nonprivileged.

"So, making kotleti today," Mila would say in the kitchen we all shared, fixing her monocular gaze on the misshapen patties in Mom's chipped aluminum skillet. "Muuuuusya!" she'd holler to her daughter. "Larisa's making kotleti!"

"Good appetite, Larochka!" (Musya was fond of my mom.)

"Muuusya! Would *you* eat kotleti?"

"Me? Never!"

35   "Aha! You see?" And Mila would wag a swollen finger at Mom.

One day my tiny underfed mom couldn't restrain herself. Back from work, tired and ravenous, she pilfered a chicken nugget from a tray Mila had left in the kitchen. The next day I watched as, red-faced and teary-eyed, she knocked on Misha's door to confess her theft.

"The chicken?" cackled Mila, and I still recall being struck by how her twenty-four-karat mouth glinted in the dim hall light. "Help yourself anytime—*we dump that shit anyway.*"

And so it was that about once a week we got to eat shit destined for the economic criminal's garbage. To us, it tasted pretty ambrosial.

In 1970, into the eleventh year of their on-and-off marriage, my parents got back together after a four-year separation and we moved to an apartment in the Arbat. And kulebiaka entered my life. Here, in Moscow's most aristocratic old neighborhood, I was shooed out of the house to buy the pie in its Soviet incarnation at the take-out store attached to Praga, a restaurant famed "before historical materialism" (that's ironic Sovietese for "distant past") for its plate-size *rasstegai* pies with two fillings: sturgeon and sterlet.

Even in the dog days of Brezhnev, Praga was fairly dripping with *klass*—a fancy *restoran* where Misha types groped peroxide blondes while a band blasted, and third-world diplomats hosted receptions in a series of ornate private rooms.

"Car of Angola's ambassador to the door!"

40

This was music to my seven-year-old ears.

If I loitered outside Praga intently enough, if my young smile and *"Khello, khau yoo laik Moskou?"* were sufficiently charming, a friendly diplomat might toss me a five-pack of Juicy Fruit. The next day, in the girls' bathroom, aided by ruler and penknife, I would sell off the gum, millimeter by millimeter, to favored classmates. Even a chewed-up blob of Juicy Fruit had some value, say a kopek or two, as long as you didn't masticate more than five times, leaving some of that floral Wrigley magic for the next masticator to savor. Our teacher's grave warnings that sharing capitalist gum causes syphilis only added to the illegal thrill of it all.

I loved everything about shopping at Praga. Loved skipping over the surges of brown melted snow and sawdust that comrade janitors gleefully swept right over the customers' feet. Loved inhaling the signature scent of stale pork fat, *peregar* (hangover breath), and the sickly sweet top notes of Red Moscow perfume. Loved Tyotya Grusha (Aunt Pear), Praga's potato-nosed saleslady, clacking away on her abacus with savage force. Once, guided by some profound late socialist instinct, I shared with Grusha a five-pack of Juicy Fruit. She snatched it without even a thank-you, but from then on she always made sure to reserve a kulebiaka for me. "Here, you loudmouthed infection," she'd say, also slipping me a slab of raisin-studded poundcake under the counter.

And this is how I came to appreciate the importance of black marketeering, *blat* (connections), and bribery. I was now inching my own way toward privilege.

45   Wearing shiny black rubber galoshes over my *valenki* (felt boots) and a coat made of "mouse fur" (in the words of my dad), I toted the *Pravda*-wrapped kulebiaka back to our family table, usually taking the long way home—past onion-domed churches now serving as warehouses, past gracious cream and green neoclassical facades scrawled with the unprintable slang that Russians call *mat*. I felt like Moscow belonged to me on those walks; along its frozen streetscape I was a flaneur flush with illicit cash. On Kalinin Prospect, the modernist grand boulevard that dissected the old neighborhood, I'd pull off my mittens in the unbearable cold to count out twenty icy kopeks for the blue-coated lady with her frosty zinc ice cream box. It was almost violent, the shock of pain on my teeth as I sank them into the waffle cup of vanilla *plombir* with a cream rosette, its concrete-like hardness defying the flat wooden scooping spoon. Left of Praga, the Arbatskaya metro station rose, star-shaped and maroon and art deco, harboring its squad of clunky gray *gazirovka* (soda) machines. One kopek for unflavored; three kopeks for a squirt of aromatic thick yellow syrup. Scoring the soda: a matter of anxious uncertainty. Not because soda or syrup ran out, but because *alkogoliks* were forever stealing the twelve-sided beveled drinking glass—that Soviet domestic icon. If, miraculously, the drunks had left the glass behind, I thrilled in pressing it hard upside down on the machine's slatted tray to watch the powerful water jet rinse the glass of alcoholic saliva. Who even needed the soda?

Deeper into Old Arbat, at the Konservi store with its friezes of socialist fruit cornucopias, I'd pause for my ritual twelve-kopek glass of sugary birch-tree juice dispensed from conical vintage glass vats with spigots. Then, sucking on a dirty icicle, I'd just wander off on a whim, lost in a delta of narrow side streets that weaved and twisted like braids, each bearing a name of the trade it once supported: Tablecloth Lane, Bread Alley. Back then, before capitalism disfigured Moscow's old center with billboards and neons and antihistorical historicist mansions, some Arbat streets did retain a certain nineteenth-century purity.

At home I usually found Mom in the kitchen, big black receiver under her chin, cooking while discussing a new play or a book with a girlfriend. Dad struck a languid Oblomovian pose on the couch, playing cards with himself, sipping cold tea from his orange cup with white polka-dots.

"And how was your walk?" Mother always wanted to know. "Did you remember to stop by the house on Povarskaya Street where Natasha from *War and Peace* lived?" At the mention of Tolstoy, the Juicy Fruit in my pocket would congeal into a guilty yellow lump on my conscience. Natasha Rostova and my mom—they were so poetic, so gullible. And I? What was I but a crass mini-Misha? Dad usually came to the rescue: "So, let's have the kulebiaka. Or did Praga run out?" For *me*, I wanted to reply, Praga never runs out! But it seemed wise not to boast of my special *blat* with Aunt Grusha, the saleslady, in the presence of my sweet innocent mother.

Eating kulebiaka on Sundays was our nod to a family ritual—even if the pie I'd deposit on the kitchen table of our five-hundred-square-foot two-room apartment shared only the name with the horn of plenty orgiastically celebrated by Gogol and Chekhov. More *bulka* (white breadroll) than *pirog*, late-socialist kulebiaka was a modest rectangle of yeast dough, true to Soviet form concealing a barely there layer of boiled ground meat or cabbage. It now occurs to me that our Sunday kulebiaka from Praga expressed the frugality of our lives as neatly as the grandiose version captured czarist excess. We liked our version just fine. The yeast dough was tasty, especially with Mom's thin vegetarian borscht, and somehow the whole package was just suggestive enough to inspire feverish fantasies about pre-revolutionary Russian cuisine, so intimately familiar to us from books, and so unattainable.

Dreaming about food, I already knew, was just as rewarding as eating.   50

For my tenth birthday my parents gave me *Moscow and Muscovites*, a book by Vladimir Giliarovsky, darling of fin-de-siècle Moscow, who covered city affairs for several local newspapers. Combining a Dickensian eye with the racy style of a tabloid journalist, plus a dash of Zola-esque naturalism, Giliarovsky offered in *Moscow and Muscovites* an entertaining, if exhausting, panorama of our city at the turn of the century.

As a kid, I cut straight to the porn—the dining-out parts.

During the twentieth century's opening decade, Moscow's restaurant scene approached a kind of Slavophilic ideal. Unlike the then-capital

St. Petersburg—regarded as pompous, bureaucratic, and quintessentially foreign—Moscow worked hard to live up to its moniker "bread-and-salty" (hospitable)—a merchant city at heart, uncorrupted by the phony veneer of European manners and foods. In St. Petersburg you dressed up to nibble tiny portions of foie gras and oysters at a French restaurant. In Moscow you gorged, unabashedly, obliviously, orgiastically at a *traktir*, a vernacular Russian tavern. Originally of working-class origins, Moscow's best *traktirs* in Giliarovsky's days welcomed everyone: posh nobles and meek provincial landowners, loud-voiced actors from Moscow Art Theater, and merchants clinching the million-ruble deals that fueled this whole Slavophilic restaurant boom. You'd never see such a social cocktail in cold, classist St. Petersburg.

Stomach growling, I stayed up nights devouring Giliarovsky. From him I learned that the airiest blini were served at Egorov's *traktir*, baked in a special stove that stood in the middle of the dining room. That at Lopashov *traktir*, run by a bearded, gruff Old Believer, the city's plumpest *pelmeni*— dumplings filled with meat, fish, or fruit in a bubbly rosé champagne sauce—were lapped up with folkloric wooden spoons by Siberian gold-mining merchants. That grand dukes from St. Petersburg endured the four-hundred-mile train journey southeast just to eat at Testov, Moscow's most celebrated *traktir*. Testov was famed for its suckling pigs that the owner reared at his dacha ("like his own children," except for the restraints around their trotters to prevent them from resisting being force-fed for plumpness); its three-hundred-pound sturgeons and sterlets transported live from the Volga; and Guriev kasha, a fanciful baked semolina sweet layered with candied nuts and slightly burnt cream skins, served in individual skillets.

And kulebiaka. The most obscenely decadent kulebiaka in town.

Offered under the special name of Baidakov's Pie (nobody really knew who this Baidakov was) and ordered days in advance, Testov's golden cased tour de force was the creation of its 350-pound chef named Lyonechka. Among other things, Lyonechka was notorious for his habit of drinking *shchi* (cabbage soup) mixed with frozen champagne as a hangover remedy. His kulebiaka was a twelve-tiered skyscraper, starting with the ground floor of burbot liver and topped with layers of fish, meat, game, mushrooms, and rice, all wrapped in dough, up, up, up to a penthouse of calf's brains in brown butter.

And then it all came crashing down.

In just a bony fistful of years, classical Russian food culture vanished, almost without a trace. The country's nationalistic euphoria on entering World War I in 1914 collapsed under nonstop disasters presided over by the "last of the Romanovs": clueless, autocratic czar Nicholas II and Alexandra, his reactionary, hysterical German-born wife. Imperial Russia went lurching toward breakdown and starvation. Golden pies, suckling pigs? In 1917 the insurgent Bolsheviks' banners demanded simply the most basic of staples—*khleb* (bread)—along with land (beleaguered peasants were 80 percent of Russia's population) and an end to the ruinous war. On the evening of October 25, hours before the coup by Lenin and his tiny cadre, ministers of Kerensky's foundering provisional government, which replaced the czar after the popular revolution of February 1917, dined finely at the Winter Palace: soup, artichokes, and fish. A doomed meal all around.

With rationing already in force, the Bolsheviks quickly introduced a harsher system of class-based food allotments. Heavy manual laborers became the new privileged; Testov's fancy diners plunged down the totem pole. Grigory Zinoviev, the head of local government in Petrograd (ex–St. Petersburg), announced rations for the bourgeoisie thusly: "We shall give them one ounce a day so they won't forget the smell of bread." He added with relish: "But if we must go over to milled straw, then we shall put the bourgeoisie on it first of all."

The country, engulfed now by civil war, was rushed toward a full-blown, and catastrophic, centralized communist model. War Communism (it was given that temporary-sounding tag *after* the fact) ran from mid-1918 through early 1921, when Lenin abandoned it for a more mixed economic approach. But from that time until the Soviet Union's very end, food was to be not just a matter of chronic uncertainty but a stark tool of political and social control. To use a Russian phrase, *knut i prianik*: whip and gingerbread.

There was scarce gingerbread at this point.

Strikes in Petrograd in 1919 protested the taste (or lack thereof) of the new Soviet diet. Even revolutionary bigwigs at the city's Smolny canteen subsisted on vile herring soup and gluey millet. At the Kremlin in Moscow, the new seat of government, the situation was so awful that the famously ascetic Lenin—Mr. Stale Bread and Weak Tea, who ate mostly at home— ordered several investigations into why the Kremlyovka (Kremlin canteen) served such inedible stuff. Here's what the investigation found: the cooks couldn't actually cook. Most pre-revolutionary chefs, waiters, and other food types had been fired as part of the massive reorganization of labor, and the new ones had been hired from other professions to avoid using "czarist cadres." "Iron Felix" Dzerzhinsky, the dread founding maestro of Soviet terror, was besieged by requests from Kremlin staffers for towels for the Kremlyovka kitchens. Also aprons and jackets for cooks. Mrs. Trotsky kept asking for tea strainers. In vain.

Part of the Kremlyovka's troubles sprang from another of War Communism's policies: having declared itself the sole purveyor and marketer of food, and setter of food prices, the Kremlin was not supposed to procure from private sources. And yet. The black market that immediately sprang up became—and remained—a defining and permanent fixture of Soviet life. Lenin might have railed against petty speculators called *meshochniki* (bagmen), the private individuals who braved Dzerzhinsky's Cheka (secret police) roving patrols to bring back foodstuffs from the countryside, often for their own starving families. But in fact most of the calories consumed in Russia's cities during this dire period were supplied by such illegal operators. In the winter of 1919–20, they supplied as much as 75 percent of the food consumed, maybe more. By War Communism's end, an estimated 200,000 bagmen were riding the rails in the breadbasket of the Ukraine.

War Communism showed an especially harsh face to the peasantry. An emphatically urban party, the Bolsheviks had little grasp of peasant realities, despite all the hammer-and-sickle imagery and early nods toward land distribution. To combat drastic grain shortages—blamed on speculative withholding—Lenin called down a "food dictatorship" and a "crusade for bread." Armed detachments stalked the countryside, confiscating "surpluses" to feed the Red Army and the hungry, traumatically shrunken cities. This was the hated *prodrazverstka* (grain requisitioning)—a preview of the greater horrors to come under Stalin. There was more. To incite Marxist class warfare in villages, the poorest peasants were stirred up against their better-off kind, the so-called kulaks ("tight-fisted ones")—vile bourgeois-like objects of Bolshevik venom. "Hang (hang without fail, so the people see) no fewer than one hundred known kulaks, rich men, bloodsuckers," Lenin instructed provincial leaders in 1918. Though as Zinoviev later noted: "We are fond of describing any peasant who has enough to eat as a kulak."

65   And so was launched a swelling, unevenly matched war by the radicalized, industrialized cities—the minority—to bring to heel the conservative,

religion-saturated, profoundly mistrustful countryside—the vast majority. Who were never truly fervent Bolshevik supporters.

Agriculture under War Communism plummeted. By 1920, grain output was down to only 60 percent of pre–World War I levels, when Russia had been a significant exporter.

It goes without saying that the concept of cuisine went out the window in those ferocious times. The very notion of pleasure from flavor-some food was reviled as capitalist degeneracy. Mayakovsky, brazen poet of the revolution, sicced his jeering muses on gourmet fancies:

> *Eat your pineapples, gobble your grouse*
> *Your last day is coming, you bourgeois louse!*

Food was fuel for survival and socialist labor. Food was a weapon of class struggle. Anything that smacked of Testov's brand of lipsmacking—kulebiaka would be a buttery bull's-eye—constituted a reactionary attack on the world being born. Some czarist *traktirs* and restaurants were shuttered and looted; others were nationalized and turned into public canteens with the utopian goal of serving new kinds of foods, supposedly futuristic and rational, to the newly *Soviet* masses.

Not until two decades later, following the abolition of yet another wave   70 of rationing policies, did the state support efforts to seek out old professional chefs and revive some traditional recipes, at least in print. It was part of a whole new Soviet Cuisine project courtesy of Stalin's food-supply commissariat. A few czarist dishes came peeping back, tricked out in Soviet duds, right then and later.

But the bona fide, layered fish kulebiaka, darling of yore, resurfaced only in Putin's Moscow, at resurrect-the-Romanovs restaurants, ordered up by oligarch types clinching oil deals.

Mom and I have our own later history with kulebiaka.

After we emigrated to America in 1974, refugees arriving in Philadelphia with two tiny suitcases, Mom supported us by cleaning houses. Miraculously, she managed to save up for our first frugal visit to Paris two years later. The French capital I found haughty and underwhelming. Mom, on the other hand, was euphoric. Her decades-long Soviet dream had finally been realized, never mind the stale *saucissons* we fed on all week. On our last night she decided to splurge at a candlelit smoky bistro in the sixteenth arrondissement. And there it was! The most expensive dish on the menu—our fish-filled kulebiaka! That is, in its French incarnation, coulibiac—one of the handful of à la russe dishes to have made the journey from Russia in the mainly one-way nineteenth-century gastronomic traffic. Nervously counting our handful of tourist francs, we bit into this coulibiac with tongue-tingled anticipation and were instantly rewarded by the buttery puff pastry that shattered so pleasingly at the touch of the fork. The lovely coral pink of the salmon seemed to wink at us—scornfully?—from the opened pie on the plate as if to suggest France's gastronomic noblesse oblige. The Gauls, they just couldn't help being smug. We took a second bite, expecting total surrender. But something—wait, wait—was wrong. *Messieurs-dames!* Where did you hide the dusky wild mushrooms, the dilled rice, the *blinchinki* to soak up all those Slavic juices? What of the magically controlled blend of tastes? This French coulibiac, we concluded, was a fraud: saumon en croute masquerading as Russian. We paid the bill to the sneering garçon, unexpectedly wistful for our kulebiaka from Praga and the still-unfulfilled yearnings it had inspired.

It was back in Philadelphia that we finally found that elusive holy grail of Russian high cuisine—courtesy of some White Russian émigrés who'd escaped just before and after the revolution. These gray-haired folk had arrived via Paris or Berlin or Shanghai with noble Russian names out of novels—Golitsyn, Volkonsky. They grew black currants and Nabokovian lilacs in the gardens of their small houses outside Philadelphia or New York. Occasionally they'd attend balls—balls! To them, we escapees from the barbaric Imperium were a mild curiosity. Their conversations with Mother went something like this:

75   "Where did you weather the revolution?"

Mom: "I was born in 1934."

"What do the Soviets think about Kerensky?"

Mom: "They don't think of him much."

"I heard there've been major changes in Russia since 1917."

80   Mom: "Er . . . that's right."

"Is it really true that at the races you now can't bet on more than one horse?"

The Russian we spoke seemed from a different planet. Here we were, with our self-consciously ironic appropriations of Sovietese, our twenty-seven shades of sarcasm injected into one simple word—*comrade*, say, or *homeland*. Talking to people who addressed us as *dushechka* (little soul) in pure, lilting, innocent Russian. Despite this cultural abyss, we cherished every moment at these people's generous tables. Boy, they could cook! Suckling pig stuffed with kasha, wickedly rich Easter molds redolent of vanilla, the Chekhovian blini plumper than "the shoulder of a merchant's daughter"—we tasted it all. Mom approached our dining sessions with an ethnographer's zeal and a notebook. Examining the recipes later, she'd practically weep.

"Flour, milk, yeast, we had all those in Moscow. Why, why, couldn't I ever make blini like this?"

One day, an old lady, a Smolianka—a graduate of the prestigious St. Petersburg Smolny Institute for Young Women, where culinary skills were de rigueur—invited us over for kulebiaka. This was the moment we had been waiting for. As the pie baked, we chatted with an old countess with a name too grand to even pronounce. The countess recounted how hard she cried, back in 1914, when she received a diamond necklace as a birthday gift from her father. Apparently she had really wanted a puppy. The kulebiaka arrived. Our hearts raced. Here it was, the true, genuine kulebiaka—"naked, shameless, a temptation." The mushrooms, the *blinchiki*, even *viziga*, that gelatinous dried sturgeon spine our hostess had unearthed somewhere in deepest Chinatown—all were drenched in splashes of butter inside a beautifully decorated yeast pastry mantle.

As I ate, Tolstoy's *Anna Karenina* flashed into my mind. Because after some three hundred pages describing Vronsky's passion for Anna, his endless pursuits, all her tortured denials, the consummation of their affair is allotted only one sentence. And so it was for us and the consummate kulebiaka. We ate; the pie was more than delicious; we were satisfied. Happily, nobody leapt under a train. And yet . . . assessing the kulebiaka and studying our hostess's recipe later at home, Mom started scribbling over it furiously, crossing things out, shaking her head, muttering. *"Ne nashe"*— not ours. I'm pretty sure I know what she meant. Dried sturgeon spine? Who were we kidding? Whether we liked it or not, we were Soviets, not Russians. In place of the sturgeon, defrosted cod would do just fine.

It took us another three decades to develop a kulebiaka recipe to call our own—one that hinted at Russia's turn-of-the-century excess, with a soupçon of that snooty French elegance, while staying true to our frugal past.

But that recipe just wouldn't do for our 1910s feast tonight.

We needed to conjure up the real deal, the classic.

My mother is finally rolling out her kulebiaka dough, maneuvering intently on a dime-size oasis of kitchen counter. I inhale the sweetish tang of fermented yeast once again and try to plumb my unconscious for some collective historical taste memory. No dice. There's no yeast in my DNA. No heirloom pie recipes passed down by generations of women in the yellowing pages of family notebooks, scribbled in pre-revolutionary Russian orthography. My two grandmothers were emancipated New Soviet women, meaning they barely baked, wouldn't be caught dead cooking "czarist." Curious and passionate about food all her life, Mom herself only became serious about baking after we emigrated. In the USSR she relied on a dough called *na skoruyu ruku* ("flick of a hand"), a version involving little kneading and no rising. It was a recipe she'd had to teach *her* mother. My paternal babushka, Alla, simply wasn't interested. She was a war widow and Soviet career woman whose idea of dinner was a box of frozen dumplings. "Why should I *bake*," she told Mother indignantly, "when I can be reading a book?" "What, a *detektiv*," Mom snorted. It was a pointed snort. Russia's top spy thriller writer, the Soviet version of John le Carré, was Grandma's secret lover.

90   Peering into the kitchen, I prod Mom for any scraps of pre-revolutionary-style baking memories she might retain. She pauses, then nods. *"Da*, listen!" There were these old ladies when she was a child. They were strikingly different from the usual blob-like proletarian babushkas. "I remember their hair," says Mom, almost dreamily. "Aristocratically simple. And the resentment and resignation on their ghostly faces. Something so sad and tragic. Perhaps they had grown up in mansions with servants. Now they were ending their days as kitchen slaves for their own Stalin-loving families."

My mom talks like that.

"And their *food?*" I keep prodding. She ponders again. "Their blini, their pirozhki (filled pastries), their *pirogs* . . . somehow they seemed airier, fluffier . . ." She shrugs. More she can't really articulate. Flour, yeast, butter. Much like their counterparts who had fled Bolshevik Russia, Mom's Moscow old ladies possessed the magic of yeast. And that magic was lost to us.

And that was the rub of tonight's project. Of the flavor of the layered Silver Age kulebiaka we had at least an inkling. But the botvinya and the Guriev kasha dessert, my responsibilities—they were total conundrums. Neither I nor Mom had a clue how they were meant to taste.

There was a further problem: the stress and time required to prepare a czarist table extravaganza.

Over an entire day and most of the night preceding our guests' arrival, 95
I sweated—and sweated—over my share of the meal. Have you ever tried
making Guriev kasha during one of the worst New York heat waves in
memory?

Thank you, Count Dmitry Guriev, you gourmandizing early-nineteenth-
century Russian minister of finance, for the labor-intensive dessert bearing
your name. Though actually by most accounts it was a serf chef named
Zakhar Kuzmin who first concocted this particular kasha (*kasha* being the
Russian word for almost any grain preparation both dry and porridgy).
Guriev tasted the sweet at somebody's palace, summoned Kuzmin to the
table, and gave him a kiss. Then he bought said serf-chef and his family.

Here is how Kuzmin's infernal inspiration is realized. Make a sweetened
farina-like semolina kasha, called manna kasha in Russian. Then in a pan or
skillet layer this manna with homemade candied nuts, and berries, and
with plenty of *penki*, the rich, faintly burnished skins that form on cream
when it's baked. Getting a hint of the labor required? For one panful of
kasha, you need at least fifteen *penki*.

So for hour after hour I opened and closed the door of a 450-degree oven
to skim off the cream skins. By two a.m. my kitchen throbbed like a furnace. Chained to the oven door, drenched in sweat, I was ready to assault
palaces, smash Fabergé eggs. I cursed the Romanovs! I cheered the Russian
Revolution!

"Send your maid to the cellar." That charming instruction kicked off
many of the recipes in the best surviving (and Rabelaisian) source of
pre-revolutionary Russian recipes, *A Gift to Young Housewives* by Elena
Molokhovets. How my heart went out to that suffering maid! Serfdom
might have been abolished in Russia in 1861, but under the Romanovs the
peasants—and, later, the industrial workers—continued to live like subhu-
mans. Haute bourgeois housewives gorged on amber fish broths, rosy
ham, and live sterlets, while their domestics had to make do with *tyuria*
(a porridgy soup made with stale bread and water), kvass, and bowlfuls of
buckwheat groats. Yes, the revolution was necessary. But why, I pondered in
my furnace kitchen, why did things have to go so terribly wrong? Woozy
from the heat, I brooded on alternative histories:

Suppose Kerensky's provisional government had managed to stay in 100
power?

Or suppose instead of Stalin, Trotsky had taken over from Lenin?

Or suppose—

Suddenly I realized I'd forgotten to skim off new *penki*. I wrenched open the oven. The cream had transformed into cascades of white sputtering lava covering every inside inch with scorched white goo. I'd need a whole cadre of serfs to clean it all off. I screamed in despair.

Somehow, at last, at five a.m., I was done. A version of Guriev kasha, no doubt ersatz, sat cooling in my fridge under a layer of foil. Falling asleep, I recalled how at the storming of the Winter Palace thirsty, violent mobs ransacked the Romanovs' wine cellar, reportedly the largest and the best-stocked in the world. I congratulated them across the century, from the bottom of my heart.

105   I blink blearily. Ah, the mysteries of the czarist stomach. "Maybe excess is the point?" I suggest meekly.

Mom shrugs. She goes ahead and arranges the filling and its anti-mush *blinchiki* into a majestic bulk. Not quite a Testov-style skyscraper, but a fine structure indeed. We decorate the pie together with fanciful cut-out designs before popping it into the oven. I'm proud of Mom. As we fan ourselves, our hearts race in anticipation, much like they did for our encounter decades ago with that true kulebiaka chez White Russian émigrés.

But the botvinya still hangs over me like a sword of doom.

A huge summer hit at Giliarovsky's Moscow *traktirs*, this chilled kvass and fish potage—a weird hybrid of soup, beverage, fish dish, and salad—confounded most foreigners who encountered it. "Horrible mélange! Chaos of indigestion!" pronounced *All the Year Round*, Charles Dickens's Victorian periodical. Me, I'm a foreigner to botvinya myself. On the evening's table I set out a soup tureen filled with my homemade kvass and cooked greens (*botva* means vegetable tops), spiked with a horseradish sauce. Beside it, serving bowls of diced cucumbers, scallions, and dill. In the middle: a festive platter with poached salmon and shrimp (my stand-in for Slavic crayfish tails). You eat the botvinya by mixing all the elements in your soup bowl—to which you add, please, ice. *A Gift to Young Housewives* also recommends a splash of chilled champagne. Ah yes, booze! To drown out the promised "chaos of indigestion," I'll pour my horseradish vodka.

"Fish and kvass?" says my mother. *"Foo."* (Russian for *eek*.)

110   *"Aga* (Yeah)," I agree.

"Foo," she insists. "'Cause you know how I hate poached salmon."

Mom harbors a competitive streak in the kitchen. I get the feeling she secretly wants my botvinya to fail.

"You've made what? A real botvinya? Homemade kvass?"
Our first guests, Sasha and Ira Genis, eyeball Mom's table, incredulous. Mom hands them the welcome *kalach*, a traditional bread shaped like a purse. Their eyes grow wider.

Analyze

1. How is this excerpt from Von Bremzen's book something of a "hybrid" memoir—that is, how does it interweave past and present? What is the effect?
2. How would you describe the tone of this excerpt? Why? Use specific examples from the piece to back up your point.
3. In an interview, Von Bremzen says that it is both "ironic and fitting" that she "dedicated myself to food as my career because in Russia, it was such an object of longing and desire and attention because of . . . constant shortages." In contrast to many of the authors in this book, the author's relationship to memories of food is not always positive. Use specific information from the text to analyze this author's relationship to food. To what conclusion do you arrive?

Explore

1. At one point in the narrative, the author says, "Suppose Kerensky's provisional government had managed to stay in power? Or suppose instead of Stalin, Trotsky had taken over from Lenin?" Clearly, this story is about more than food. Research these people; why does Von Bremzen connect them with the process of cooking *penki?*
2. Elsewhere in the interview we mentioned earlier, Von Bremzen says, "I'm probably the only American food writer who's grown up in a communal apartment where a kitchen was shared by eighteen other families." Using research tools, create a presentation for your class that fully contextualizes the history that prompts this quote.
3. Explore the ways in which Von Bremzen evokes types of character, that is, what people are like and how they behave, whether it's her own persona, the character of her mother, or others. Write an essay about a person or people in your own social circle or family using the author's style of evoking character. Then, present to your peer group or your class what you believe their characteristics are.

Forging Connections

1. Many of the readings in this chapter ask us to look closely at differing views of the world, the ways in which we approach different cultures and different cuisines. Using two or three readings, lead a discussion in which you and your classmates determine the ways in which one needs to be mindful as we approach that which is "different."

2. Select two or three of the readings in this chapter and determine, specifically, the ways in which each might be seen as representing "gastronomic globetrotting."

Looking Further

1. Research the "travelogue" as a genre—whether it's a form of travel writing or a travel-related short film. What do you find? How do several of the pieces in this chapter—and elsewhere in the book—suit the notion of "travelogue?" Taking this one step further, propose a travel experience of your own, one that likely will take you to a new place within your existing community (think about neighborhoods with which you are unfamiliar, less familiar, nearby towns, etc.). After you have studied the genre of the travelogue, use it to guide your explorations into that new neighborhood, and write or produce a travelogue of your own.

2. The Von Bremzen excerpt clearly evokes historical and political contexts as she writes about food, character, and cultures. Research, discuss, and craft a paper on historical context(s) for another of the articles in this chapter or the book, even if the author him or herself doesn't especially invoke (but seems to imply) such contexts.

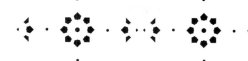

Epilogue: Cooking and Culture

Although food writing may be new to you, the concept of the recipe likely is not. You may have recipes that have been told to you by friends and relatives, whereas others might be scribbled on the backs of envelopes, preserved on index cards, or stored in ring binders designed especially for that purpose. You've likely seen print cookbooks of various types, too. More likely, you share recipes on social media—whether Facebook, with a tweet, or by researching the many food recipe websites that are available.

We selected the three sample recipes that follow because each represents a different time, place, and meaning for the ritual and importance of food. All three connect in various ways to the subjects of the chapters in this book, and we encourage you to make additional connections.

Michael Berenbaum; Cara DeSilva, Ed.
In Memory's Kitchen: A Legacy of the Women of Terezin, Excerpts of the Introduction and Recipes

This recipe and others in *In Memory's Kitchen* were handwritten by women in the concentration camp, Terezin, during World War II. These recipes served as the memoir, so to speak, for these women, who were starved, and most of them did not survive the harsh, brutal conditions. Why would people who are starving not only talk about food—which seems to make sense—but also write about it? What function might these handwritten cookbooks serve?

Building on the context you've read from the forward and the introduction to *In Memory's Kitchen*, research the historical context of this book to broaden your understanding of who these women were and why they felt compelled to create cookbooks under bleak, cruel conditions. If you wish, reconstruct a story of this woman in her kitchen before the war.

INTRODUCTION

No matter how many times Anny told the story, its power to affect her and her listeners never diminished. She was not a person who cried easily; yet even before she began to speak, her lively brown eyes would be brimful of tears.

"I remember so well the day the call came," she would say as she brushed the dampness from her timeworn cheeks, "because it was my past at the other end of the line. 'Is this Anny Stern?' the woman on the phone asked me, and when I answered yes, she said, 'Then I have a package for you from your mother.'"

With those words, a quarter-century-long journey from the Czechoslovak ghetto/concentration camp of Terezín to an apartment building on Manhattan's East Side came to an end.[1]

Inside the package was a picture taken in 1939 of Anny's mother, Mina Pächter, and Anny's son, Peter (now called David). His arms are around her neck, her beautiful gray hair is swept back, and they are both smiling—but dark circles ring Mina's eyes. There were letters, too—"Every evening I kiss your picture...please, Petřičku, do not forget me," Mina had written to her grandson. But it was a fragile, hand-sewn copy book that made up the bulk of the package, its cracked and crumbling pages covered with recipes in a variety of faltering scripts.[2]

Born out of the abyss, it is a document that can be comprehended only at the farthest reaches of the mind. Did setting down recipes bring comfort amid chaos and brutality? Did it bring hope for a future in which someone might prepare a meal from them again? We cannot know. But certainly the creation of such a cookbook was an act of psychological resistance, forceful testimony to the power of food to sustain us, not just physically but spiritually.

Food is who we are in the deepest sense, and not because it is transformed into blood and bone. Our personal gastronomic traditions—what we eat, the foods and foodways we associate with the rituals of childhood, marriage, and parenthood, moments around the table, celebrations—are critical components of our identities. To recall them in desperate circumstances is to reinforce a sense of self and to assist us in our struggle to preserve it. "My mother was already in her seventies at this time," said Anny, "yet this book shows that even in adversity her spirit fought on." And so, too, did the spirits of her friends.

Among their weapons were *Heu und Stroh,* fried noodles topped with raisins, cinnamon, and vanilla cream; *Leberknödel,* liver dumplings with a touch of ginger; *Kletzenbrot,* a rich fruit bread; and *Zenichovy Dort,* or Groom's Cake. There were *Erdäpfel Dalken,* or potato doughnuts; and *Badener Caramell Bonbons,* caramels from Baden Baden—about eighty recipes in all. Some were hallmarks of Central European cookery. A few, like *Billige Echte Jüdische Bobe,* cheap real Jewish coffee cake, were specifically Jewish. And one, written down by Mina, is particularly poignant. For *Gefüllte Eier,* stuffed eggs with a variety of garnishes, the recipe instructs the cook to "Let fantasy run free."

"When first I opened the copybook and saw the handwriting of my mother, I had to close it," said Anny of the day she received the package. "I put it away and only much later did I have the courage to look. My husband and I, we were afraid of it. It was something holy. After all those years, it was like her hand was reaching out to me from long ago."

In a way, it was. Just before Mina died in Theresienstadt, she entrusted the package to a friend, Arthur Buxbaum, an antiques dealer, and asked him to get it to her daughter in Palestine. But because most of Anny's letters hadn't reached Mina during the war, she couldn't provide him with an address.

Unable to honor his friend's deathbed wish, Buxbaum simply kept the package. Then one day in 1960, a cousin told him she was leaving for Israel. Still mindful of his promise, he asked her to take the manuscript along, but by the time she got news of Anny and her husband, George Stern, they had moved to the United States to be near their son.

No one knows exactly what happened after that. A letter found in the package and written in 1960 indicates that just as it had been entrusted first to Buxbaum and then to his cousin, so it was entrusted to someone else to carry to New York. Yet according to Anny, it didn't arrive until almost a decade later.

It was then that a stranger from Ohio arrived at a Manhattan gathering of Czechs and asked if anyone there knew the Sterns. "Yes, I have heard of them," responded one woman. A moment later he had produced the parcel and she had become its final custodian. At last, Mina's deathbed gift to her daughter, her startling *kochbuch,* was to be delivered.

Its contents, written in the elliptical style characteristic of European cookery books, are evidence that the inmates of Terezín thought constantly about eating. "Food, memories of it, missing it, craving it, dreaming of it, in short, the obsession with food colours all the Theresienstadt memoirs," writes Ruth Schwertfeger in *Women of Theresienstadt, Voices from a Concentration Camp.*[3]

Bianca Steiner Brown, the translator of the recipes in this book and herself a former inmate of Terezín, explains it this way: "In order to survive, you had to have an imagination. Fantasies about food were like a fantasy that you have about how the outside is if you are inside. You imagine it not only the way it really is but much stronger than it really is. I was, for instance, a nurse, and I worked at night and I looked out at night—Terezín was a town surrounded by walls, a garrison town. So I looked out at all the beds where the children were, and out of that window I could look into freedom. And you were imagining things, like how it would be to run around in the meadow outside. You knew how it was, but you imagined it even better than it was, and that's how it was with food, also. Talking about it helped you."

Most of us can understand that. Far more disquieting is the idea that people who were undernourished, even starving, not only reminisced about favorite foods but also had discussions, even arguments, about the correct way to prepare dishes they might never be able to eat again.

In fact, such behavior was frequent. Brown remembers women sharing recipes in their bunks late at night. "They would say, 'Do you know such and such a cake?'" she recounts. "'I did it in such and such a way.'"

"The hunger was so enormous that one constantly 'cooked' something that was an unattainable ideal and maybe somehow it was a certain help to survive it all," wrote Jaroslav Budlovsky on a death march from Schwarzheide to Terezín in 1943.[4]

And Susan E. Cernyak-Spatz, professor emeritus at the University of North Carolina and a survivor of Terezín and Auschwitz, describes people in both places as speaking of food.

FRÜCHTE REIS

Koche in 1 Liter Milch den besten Reis vorsichtig, doss er sich nicht zerkocht; er muss weich und sehr fest sein. Jetzt gebe es in die Schüssel gebe dazu vorher aufgelöste Chelatine [sic], 50 Deca Zucker, Zitronenschale, 1 Glas Maraschino, ½ Liter geschlagene Schlagsahne, Vanille. Jetzt gebe dazu eingelegte Kirschen, Erdbeeren, wenn möglich Stückchen Ananas; gebe es in eine Gefrierform. Lasse es über Nacht am Eis stehen. Stürze es den nächsten Tag aus und gebe es mit Hohlhippen zur Tafel.

RICE WITH FRUITS

Cook the best rice carefully in 1 liter milk so that it doesn't overcook—until the rice is tender, but [still] very firm. Now put it into a bowl. Add previously dissolved gelatin, 50 decagrams sugar, lemon rind, 1 glass maraschino [liqueur], ½ liter whipped heavy cream, vanilla. Now add home-canned cherries, strawberries, if possible pineapple pieces. Put it into an ice cream mold. Keep it on ice overnight. Unmold it the next day and bring to the table with thin rolled wafers.

Endnotes

1 Terezín is also known as Theresienstadt, its German-Austrian name. Both names will be used interchangeably here.

2 The history of the Terezín cookbook, as recounted here, is in the form in which Anny Stern told it over the last dozen years of her life. There are several uncertainties in it, but too many people have died to permit resolving them.

3 New York: Berg, 1989, p. 38.

4 The Budlovsky manuscript is in the holdings of Beit Theresienstadt at Kibbutz Givat Chaim—Ichud, Israel.

Marguerite Gilbert McCarthy
The Cook Is in the Parlor,
Excerpt and Recipes

This book was written and published in the late 1940s. What about this excerpt tells the reader—and potential cook—something about the assumptions behind the purpose of this book? Think, for instance, about the title—and the word "parlor"—and about the other thoughts about how to entertain, who cooks, and the like.

Many of the articles in this book open up discussions about gender and food. *The Cook Is in the Parlor* implies attitudes about gender and food—and about class status. Analyzing both the recipes and the excerpt from the introduction, discuss the ways in which the author reveals these attitudes.

INTRODUCTION

This is my own personal cook book. It is not intended for those who need to learn how to cook, but it will, I believe, be helpful to those who can cook and who wish to serve more imaginative and delectable food. It grew out of my own experience in arranging menus, in supervising the preparation of food, and in cooking food. It has really been written for the many friends who have said they enjoyed the food which they have shared with me in my city home and at my ranch.

There is actually no such thing as a book of entirely new and original recipes, since cooking has been going on in the world since Eve presumably first found that the fat from a roasted calf improved the taste of edible roots and grains, and since Charles Lamb's hero discovered that crisped pig was delicious. The fact that earlier generations enjoyed certain combinations of food is no reason for scorning them, but certainly they often may be improved in flavor and in nutriment, or prepared more easily than formerly.

Some combinations of ingredients were contrived in the spirit of the moment, and although immediately jotted down, never seemed afterwards to produce quite the fine flavor of my initial attempt. The real reason for the deviation may be that we rarely have exactly the same leftovers in the refrigerator. I recall one dish, highly approved when I served it, compounded of leftover fried rice, turkey dressing and gravy, bits of the turkey meat, soup meat with the soup stock, and some creamed onions—all "odds and ends" I found in the refrigerator. Probably I added Worcestershire sauce, a little Tabasco, and one of the many herbs always to be found in my kitchen. This mixture was tucked in a casserole, covered, and left to simmer gently until someone suggested it was time to eat. One of my sons-in-law mixed a green salad, someone else toasted French bread, and that, with some fruit, was all. But you can realize the difficulty of giving a measured recipe that would insure the same flavor as the mixture we had that night.

There is, of course, one ingredient needed for all recipes that only the cook can give. That is her interest in preparing food that will add to the enjoyment of her family and friends. A real love for what one is doing underlies all successful achievement, and especially the creation of delectable food.

SUNDAY MORNING BREAKFAST

Sunday morning offers an opportunity to entertain economically and with very little effort. The unhurried feeling about this particular morning immediately brings forth a desire for relaxation.

You will probably decide to serve breakfast around noon, thus combining two meals in one. Your party may be large or small, elaborate or simple, but no matter which, it should be fun. Everything should be so well organized that neither you nor your guests are compelled to dash around at the last minute. Nor should you keep your guests waiting while you putter around trying to cook breakfast.

In everything there is a key to efficiency, a short cut to success. One of the secrets to a successful party is service, and to give good service in a servantless home requires a system. Trays have often solved this problem for me. By using trays the food may be served from the buffet or right from the kitchen stove with little effort and everyone receives his food while it is still hot. These trays should be of lightweight composition, arranged attractively, and need not involve any great expense.

Here is one place where you can add that original touch to make your party different. If your home calls for Early American, use red and white checked gingham for doilies and napkins, and fringe the edges. For china, buy reproductions of milk glass, which can be found in the five and ten cent store. Or you might use unbleached muslin, dye it with bright colors—the doilies and napkins contrasting—and use Mexican pottery and glassware.

The china I use at my ranch I bought in Honolulu at a Chinese grocery store. The plates are decorated with an orange and black rooster, looking very silly under a large green cabbage leaf. As no cups came with the set, I found some made of clay in a glorious warm yellow. With that as a start, I collected animal salts and peppers as well as sugars and creamers. You can imagine the chuckles of my guests as they examine their trays on Sunday morning and pour cream from the mouth of a fish and shake salt from the topknot of a bird.

If you prefer to seat your guests at one large table, you can still keep everything gay. Use plenty of color, if only in your decorations. Bowls of flowers may pick up the color of your tablecloth and carry it on to the water glasses and compotes filled with jelly. Or fill a decorative piece of pottery with a combination of fruit and green leaves to give your room that needed spot of gaiety.

Sunday morning is one time when you really have leisure to enjoy your garden, so what more attractive place could you find to serve breakfast? Here you may use trays so that each person may seek out the particular spot that appeals to him, or you may decide to use the table that you have thoughtfully arranged beneath a large shady tree.

If the weather is too chilly for the garden, why not gather in the living room in front of the fireplace?

As for the food that you serve for your breakfast, some people find they can entertain more easily if they perfect one or two menus and stick to them. There is nothing wrong with that idea as long as you add a touch of originality to the perfection of the cooking. Far better to offer your guests well-cooked ham and eggs, displayed on amusing china, than to attempt an elaborate menu too complicated to be served with ease and satisfaction.

Perhaps your husband is the type who likes to help with the cooking. If he makes waffles—most men seem to make them better than their wives—suggest that he serve "Mystery Syrup" with them; it will keep everyone guessing all during breakfast. If he makes hot cakes, little thin ones, fill them with creamed chicken or creamed chipped beef.

You might like to show your skill to your admiring guests. Then why not give a kitchen party? I find, regardless of age or wealth or dignity, there is something fascinating to everyone about being in someone else's kitchen. It is such a friendly place, that is if the hostess is fairly orderly and has made her plans beforehand. Men always drift back to our kitchen, in town or at the ranch. After all, the kitchen, where good food is prepared, is the foundation of life, good health, and happiness.

So, whether you serve breakfast from a tray or from a table, whether in the garden or in the kitchen, whether your husband or you are the chef, make breakfast on Sunday morning a festive occasion—something to look forward to during the week.

Menu

TROPICAL COCKTAIL

OMELET WITH MUSHROOMS

BAKED POTATO BALLS

DELICIOUS MUFFINS

FIG JAM WITH LEMON AND NUTS

Tropical Cocktail

Mix equal proportions of orange and pineapple juice.

Omelet with Mushrooms

Sauté ½ pound of chopped mushrooms in 3 tablespoons of butter until brown and cooked through. Keep hot while your omelet is cooking. Beat together, with a fork, 10 eggs and 3 tablespoons of cream. Pour this mixture through a sieve covered with a cloth. Rub the surface of an iron frying pan with salt until smooth. Rinse. Melt 3 tablespoons of butter in the pan and then pour in the beaten eggs. Have the fire hot and, as the eggs start to cook on the bottom, lift the edges with a spatula, allowing the uncooked portion to flow down into the pan. When cooked, put the mushrooms on one half and fold over the other half. Serve on a hot platter and sprinkle with chopped parsley. Serves 6.

Baked Potato Balls

Mash boiled white potatoes, season, add milk and butter, making a stiff mixture. Shape into balls and roll in melted butter, then in crushed corn flakes. These may be made the day before and stored in the refrigerator. About ½ hour before they are to be served, remove from the refrigerator, place in a buttered pan, and heat through in a moderate oven.

Delicious Muffins

Sift together 1 cup of flour, 2 teaspoons of baking powder, 2 tablespoons of sugar, and ¼ teaspoon of salt. Add 2 tablespoons of soft butter and mix well with the tips of your fingers. Then add ½ cup of cream and 1 beaten egg. Beat well together, put in greased muffin tins and bake in a moderate oven (350°) for about 25 minutes. Makes 8 to 12 muffins.

Fig Jam with Lemon and Nuts

Peel black figs and cut into pieces. Measure cup for cup of figs and sugar. For 1 quart of figs, add 2 lemons, sliced thin, leaving the skin on. Boil until the syrup drops in clots from the side of the spoon. Add 1 cup of chopped walnut meats. Seal in sterilized jars.

Anna Thomas
The Vegetarian Epicure, Excerpt and Recipe

Published in 1973, *The Vegetarian Epicure* purported to bring meat-free cooking to the masses, part of a burgeoning movement. This book was highly successful, but we might now question the assumptions the book makes about what is healthy and "light." Looking at the excerpt from the introduction and the recipe, how might our attitudes today regarding health be different than they were in 1973? Why?

In the "Introduction," the author writes, "In these strange 1970s, ominous and dramatic new reasons are compelling people to reexamine their eating habits. More and more foods are being 'processed,' becoming the products of factories rather than farms. Chemical nonfood 'additives' alter the look of foods and prevent visible spoilage."

To what extent has Anna Thomas's cautionary tale become true? Look elsewhere in *Food: A Reader for Writers*—and expand your search—to create a presentation in which you analyze the extent to which Thomas's caution has become realized.

In these strange 1970s, ominous and dramatic new reasons are compelling people to reexamine their eating habits. More and more foods are being "processed," becoming the products of factories rather than farms. Chemical nonfood "additives" alter the look of foods and prevent visible spoilage, but the nutritive value of treated foods is hugely diminished—and their cost to you increased. Cattle and poultry are treated with silbesterol (a sex hormone) to promote growth—and profit—resulting in unknown danger to human consumers, including the possibility of various types of cancer.

The concentration of the pesticide DDT, banned at last by the U.S. Government in 1970, is so high throughout the world that none of us can escape having some of it in our bodies. All plants are likely to contain at least traces, but DDT is cumulative, so the body of an animal will contain all the DDT of all the plants and other animals it has eaten.

Much fresh-water and sea life, including tuna, swordfish, and shellfish, has been found to contain dangerous levels of mercury. Like DDT, mercury is not easily eliminated from the body. It can cause irreversible brain damage and death.

But this is a book about joy, not pollution. I hope that even if you are still in the habit of eating meat and fish, you will try some of the different ways and means of cooking suggested here. You might find yourself gradually and happily seduced.

People have approached me, puzzled, and asked how vegetarians eat. Their puzzlement is genuine. They try to imagine their own meals without meat and shudder. But when I imagine their meals I shudder too, because the standard American diet is so appalling in its lack of imagination. Even in finer cooking, the variety is largely limited to the preparation of the main course, almost without exception meat or fish. The menu is thus rigidly standardized. There is one important item: the entrée. In a very secondary place, really playing the role of uninspired accompaniment to the meat, are such things as salad, vegetables, and bread. The standard menu is served with but little change from day to day or week to week, the "square" meal certainly is.

Where meals are served in courses, the parts are still fitted into a relentless, unchanging pattern: soup, main course, salad, dessert. The first thing to do in considering the vegetarian cuisine is to get free of these stereotyped ideas. Otherwise, you may find yourself falling into the trap of "substitutions." Many vegetarian cookbooks have done this, imposing the old structure onto the vegetarian diet and trying to find "meat substitutes." They make a fundamental mistake (to say nothing of the fact that the food is apt to be stodgy rather than fresh and light).

Vegetarian cookery is not a substitute for anything. It is a rich and various cuisine, full of many marvelous dishes with definite characteristics not in imitation of anything else—certainly not in imitation of meat. The vegetarian menu lends itself to many structures. It is not the slave of the "main course," even as it does not avoid that arrangement when it seems fitting and useful. But it can also consist of several equally important courses, or several dishes served at once.

These ideas are neither new nor bizarre. We are all familiar with the Swedish smorgasbord. Many Oriental menus consist of several harmonious dishes. In Thailand, all the courses of a meal are served at once, in a half-moon arrangement around the plate, and one eats in whatever order seems appealing.

I think the only rules about arranging meals which need to be taken seriously are the rudimentary ones of pleasing the palate and maintaining good health. Many people seem worried about providing sufficient protein in a vegetarian diet. I haven't found it difficult. Any dish consisting in large part of eggs, milk, cheese, or other milk products is high in protein. Lentils, soybeans, and wheat germ are three of the most concentrated protein foods known to us, bar none. Peas, almost all beans, and whole grains are also extremely good protein sources. Buckwheat groats are phenomenal! Nearly all nuts are rich in protein, as are many seeds.

In fact, it is the possibility of endless variety that helps create a whole new style of eating—a new set of nonconventions. In the section on menus I suggest a few of the many combinations and arrangements possible with just the recipes in this book. I hope it serves as a starting point, leading quickly to even better ideas of your own with which to titillate your appetite.

I love to eat well, and I find there is a special added joy for the vegetarian epicure: the satisfaction of feeling a peaceful unity with all life.

FROMAGE ROMANESQUE

16 oz cream cheese
¾ cup sour cream
3 tsp honey
Salt
3 eggs, separated

Beat together the cheese and the sour cream, then blend in the honey, salt, and egg yolks. I suggest that this be done in the blender, for this mixture should be completely smooth and cream cheese likes to lump a little. When it is well beaten, separately beat the egg whites until they are stiff and fold them into the other mixture. Pour it all into a buttered baking dish, preferably a rather shallow, round one, and bake at 350 degrees for ½ hour. Serve hot. With it I recommend a delicate Mornay sauce, made from Béchamel (see page 85).

This is a peculiar dish: light, but very filling—delicate, but with a very definite character. It may be served as a separate course, with Mornay or another mild sauce, or it may be accompanied by some appropriate garden-fresh vegetable and slices of rich, dark bread to make a complete, light meal. Try it with young asparagus spears—*there* is a perfect pair. On the other hand, with the addition of a little more honey, it becomes a hot dessert, which can be accompanied well by fruit and a custard sauce.

This recipe makes 5 to 6 servings.

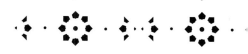

appendix B

Researching and Writing About Food
Barbara Rockenbach and Aaron Ritzenberg[1]

Research-based writing lies at the heart of the mission of higher education: to discover, transform, and share ideas. As a college student, it is through writing and research that you will become an active participant in an intellectual community. Doing research in college involves not only searching for information but also digesting, analyzing, and synthesizing what you find to create new knowledge. Your most successful efforts as a college writer will report on the latest and most important ideas in a field as well as make new arguments and offer fresh insights.

It may seem daunting to be asked to contribute new ideas to a field in which you are a novice. After all, creating new knowledge seems to be the realm of experts. In this guide, we offer strategies that demystify the research and writing process, breaking down some of the fundamental steps that scholars take when they do research and make arguments. You'll see that contributing to scholarship involves strategies that can be learned and practiced.

Throughout this guide we imagine doing research and writing as engaging in a scholarly conversation. When you read academic writing, you'll see

---

[1]Barbara Rockenbach, Director of Humanities & History Libraries, Columbia University. Aaron Ritzenberg, Associate Director of First-Year Writing, Columbia University.

that scholars reference the studies that came before them and allude to the studies that will grow out of their research. When you think of research as engaging in a conversation, you quickly realize that scholarship always has a social aspect. Even if you like to find books in the darkest corners of the library, even if you like to draft your essays in deep solitude, you will always be awake to the voices that helped you form your ideas and to the audience who will receive your ideas. As if in a conversation at a party, scholars mingle: they listen to others and share their most recent ideas, learning and teaching at the same time. Strong scholars, like good conversationalists, will listen and speak with an open mind, letting their own thoughts evolve as they encounter new ideas.

You may be wondering, "what does it mean to have an open mind when I'm doing research? After all, aren't I supposed to find evidence that supports my thesis?" We'll be returning to this question soon, but the quick answer is: To have an open mind when you're doing research means that you'll be involved in the research process well before you have a thesis. We realize this may be a big change from the way you think about research. The fact is, however, that scholars do research well before they know any of the arguments they'll be making in their papers. Indeed, scholars do research even before they know what specific topic they'll be addressing and what questions they'll be asking.

When scholars do research they may not know exactly what they are hunting for, but they have techniques that help them define projects, identify strong interlocutors, and ask important questions. This guide will help you move through the various kinds of research that you'll need at the different stages of your project. If writing a paper involves orchestrating a conversation within a scholarly community, there are a number of important questions you'll need to answer: How do I choose what to write about? How do I find a scholarly community? How do I orchestrate a conversation that involves this community? Whose voices should be most prominent? How do I enter the conversation? How do I use evidence to make a persuasive claim? How do I make sure that my claim is not just interesting but important?

GETTING STARTED

You have been asked to write a research paper. This may be your first research paper at the college level. Where do you start? The important thing when embarking on any kind of writing project that involves research is to find something that you are interested in learning more about. Writing and research is easier if you care about your topic. Your instructor may have given you a topic, but you can make that topic your own by finding something that appeals to you within the scope of the assignment.

Academic writing begins from a place of deep inquiry. When you are sincerely interested in a problem, researching can be a pleasure because it will satisfy your own intellectual curiosity. More important, the intellectual problems that seem most difficult—the questions that appear to resist obvious answers—are the very problems that will often yield the most surprising and most rewarding results.

Presearching to Generate Ideas

When faced with a research project, your first instinct might be to go to Google or Wikipedia or even to a social media site. This is not a bad instinct. In fact, Google, Wikipedia, and social media can be great places to start. Using Google, Wikipedia, and social media to help you discover a topic is what we call "presearch"—it is what you do to warm up before the more rigorous work of academic research. Academic research and writing will require you to go beyond these sites to find resources that will make the work of researching and writing both easier and more appropriate to an academic context.

Google Let's start with Google. You use Google because you know you are going to find a simple search interface and that your search will produce many results. These results may not be completely relevant to your topic, but Google helps in the discovery phase of your work. For instance, you are asked to write about food and culture.

This Google search (see Figure 1) will produce articles from many diverse sources—magazines, government sites, and corporate reports among them. It's not a bad start. Use these results to begin to hone in on a topic you are interested in pursuing. A quick look through your results may yield a more focused topic such as the impact of the fast food industry on diets in Asia.

Wikipedia A Wikipedia search on food and culture will lead you to several magazines and articles that address both concepts. The great thing about Wikipedia is that it is an easy way to gain access to a wealth of information about thousands of topics. However, it is crucial to realize that Wikipedia itself is not an authoritative source in a scholarly context.

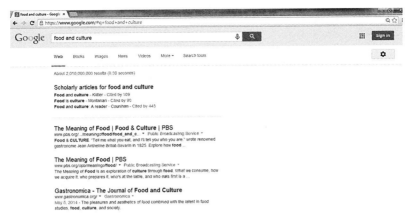

Figure 1 A Google search of "food and culture".

Although you may see Wikipedia cited in mainstream newspapers and popular magazines, academic researchers do not consider Wikipedia a reliable source and do not consult or cite it in their own research. Wikipedia itself says that "Wikipedia is not considered a credible source . . . This is especially true considering that anyone can edit the information given at any time." For research papers in college, you should use Wikipedia only to find basic information about your topic and to point you toward scholarly sources (see Figure 2). Wikipedia may be a great starting point for presearch, but it is not an adequate ending point for research. Use the references section at the bottom of the Wikipedia article to find other, more substantive and authoritative resources about your topic.

Using Social Media Social media such as Facebook and Twitter can be useful in the presearch phase of your project, but you must start thinking about these tools in new ways. You may have a Facebook or Twitter account and use it to keep in touch with friends, family, and colleagues. These social networks are valuable, and you may already use them to gather information to help you make decisions in your personal life and your workplace. Although social media is not generally useful to your academic research, both Facebook and Twitter have powerful search functions that can lead you to resources and help you refine your ideas.

After you log in to Facebook, use the "Search for people, places, and things" bar at the top of the page to begin. When you type search terms into this bar, Facebook will first search your own social network. To extend beyond your own network, try adding the word "research" after your search terms. For instance, a search on Facebook for "food and culture" may lead

Figure 2 Wikipedia entry for "Fast Food".

you to a Facebook page that is relevant to your work (see Figure 3). The posts on the page may link to current news stories on food, links to relevant research centers, and topics of interest in the field of food and culture. You can use these search results as a way to see part of the conversation about a particular topic. This is not necessarily the scholarly conversation we referred to at the start of this guide, but it is a social conversation that can still be useful in helping you determine what you want to focus on in the research process.

Figure 3 Facebook page for USDA.

Twitter is an information network where users can post short messages (or "tweets"). Although many people use Twitter simply to update their friends ("I'm going to the mall" or "Can't believe it's snowing!"), more and more individuals and organizations use Twitter to comment on noteworthy events or link to interesting articles. You can use Twitter as a presearch tool because it aggregates links to sites, people in a field of research, and noteworthy sources. Communities, sometimes even scholarly communities, form around topics on Twitter. Users group posts together using hashtags—words or phrases that follow the "#" sign. Users can respond to other users using the @ sign followed by a user's twitter name. When searching for specific individuals or organizations on Twitter, you search using their handle (such as @barackobama or @whitehouse). You will retrieve tweets that were created either by the person or by the organization or tweets that mention the person or organization. When searching for a topic to find discussions, you search using the hashtag symbol, #. For instance, a search on #foodpolitics will take you to tweets and threaded discussions on any number of ideas, some of them relevant, many of them not.

There are two ways to search Twitter. You can use the search book in the upper right-hand corner and enter either a @ or # search as described above. Once you retrieve results, you can search again by clicking on any of the words that are hyperlinked within your results such as #fooddeserts.

If you consider a hashtag (the # sign) as an entry point into a community, you will begin to discover a conversation around many topics. News agencies such as Reuters are also active in Twitter, so an article from a Reuters publication will be retrieved in a search. Evaluating information and sources found in social media is similar to how you evaluate any information you encounter during the research process. And, as with Wikipedia and Google searches, this is just a starting point to help you get a sense of the spectrum of topics. This is no substitute for using library resources. Do not cite Facebook, Twitter, or Wikipedia in a research paper; use them to find more credible, authoritative sources. We'll talk about evaluating sources in the sections that follow.

Create a Concept Map

Once you have settled on a topic that you find exciting and interesting, the next step is to generate search terms, or keywords, for effective searching. Keywords are the crucial terms or phrases that signal the content of any given source. Keywords are the building blocks of your search for information. We have already seen a few basic keywords such as "food" and "culture." One way to generate keywords is to tell a friend or classmate what you are interested in. What words are you using to describe your research project? You may not have a fully formed idea or claim, but you have a vague sense of your interest. A concept map exercise can help you generate more keywords and, in many cases, narrow your topic to make it more manageable.

A concept map is a way to visualize the relationship between concepts or ideas. You can create a concept map on paper, or there are many free programs online that can help you do this (see, for instance, http://vue .tufts.edu/, http://wisemapping.org, or http://freeplane.sourceforge.net). There are many concept mapping applications available for mobile devices; the concept map here was created using the app SimpleMind.

Here is how you use a concept map. First, begin with a term like "food." Put that term in the first box. Then think of synonyms or related words to describe food and culture, such as "food economy," "food culture," "localism," "worldwide sustainability," "food economy," and "food traditions." This brainstorming process will help you develop keywords for searching. Note that keywords can also be short phrases (see Figure 4).

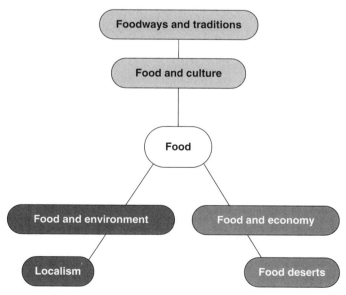

Figure 4 A concept map.

After some practice, you'll discover that some phrases make for excellent keywords and others make for less effective search tools. The best keywords are precise enough to narrow your topic so that all of your results are relevant, but not so specific that you might miss helpful results. Concept maps created using apps such as SimpleMind allow you to use templates, embed hyperlinks, and attach notes, among other useful functions.

Keyword Search

One of the hardest parts of writing is coming up with something to write about. Too often, we make the mistake of waiting until we have a fully formed idea before we start writing. The process of writing can actually help you discover what your idea is and, most important, what is interesting about your idea.

Keyword searches are most effective at the beginning stages of your research. They generally produce the most number of results and can help you determine how much has been written on your topic. You want to use keyword searches to help you achieve a manageable number of results. What is manageable? This is a key question when beginning research. Our keyword search in Google on food and culture produced millions of results. The same search in JSTOR.org produces thousands of results. Let's see how we can narrow our search.

Keyword searches, in library resources or on Google, are most effective if you employ a few search strategies that will focus your results.

1. Use AND when you are combining multiple keywords. We have used this search construction previously:

food AND culture

The AND ensures that all your results will contain both the term food and the term culture. Many search engines and databases will assume an AND search, meaning if you type

food culture

the search will automatically look for both terms. However, in some cases the AND will not be assumed and food culture will be treated as a phrase. This means that "food" will have to be next to the word "culture" to return results. Worse yet, sometimes the search automatically assumes an OR.

That would mean that all your results would come back with either food or culture. This will produce a large and mostly irrelevant set of results. Therefore, use AND whenever you want two or more words to appear in a result.

2. Using OR can be effective when you want to use several terms to describe a concept such as:

food OR eating OR consumption

A search on food and culture can be broadened. The following search casts a broader net because results will come back with food and either culture, ethnicity, or writing:

food AND (culture OR ethnicity OR writing)

Not all of these words will appear in each record. Note also that the parentheses set off the OR search indicating that food must appear in each record and then culture, ethnicity, or writing needs to appear along with food.

3. Use quotation marks when looking for a phrase. For instance, if you are looking for information on culture and food in corporations you can ensure that the search results will include all of these concepts and increase the relevance by using the following search construction:

Culture AND food AND "corporations"

This phrasing will return results that contain both the word food and the phrase "corporation."

4. Use NOT to exclude terms that will make your search less relevant. You may find that a term keeps appearing in your search that is not useful. Try this:

food NOT recipes

If you are interested in the linguistic side of this debate, getting a lot of results that discuss the politics of food may be distracting. By excluding the keyword politics, you will retrieve far fewer sources, and, perhaps, more relevant results.

Researchable Question

In a college research paper, it is important that you make an argument, not just offer a report. In high school you may have found some success by merely listing or cataloging the data and information you found; you might have offered a series of findings to show your teacher that you investigated your topic. In college, however, your readers will not be interested in data or information merely for its own sake; your readers will want to know what you make of this data and why they should care.

To satisfy the requirements of a college paper, you'll need to distinguish between a topic and a research question. You will likely begin with a topic, but it is only when you move from a topic to a question that your research will begin to feel motivated and purposeful. A topic refers only to the general subject area that you'll be investigating. A researchable question, on the other hand, points toward a specific problem in the subject area that you'll be attempting to answer by making a claim about the evidence you examine.

"Food and culture" is a topic, but not a researchable question. It is important that you ask yourself, "What aspect of the topic is most interesting to me?" It is even more important that you ask, "What aspect of the topic is it most important that I illuminate for my audience?" Ideally, your pre-search phase of the project will yield questions about food and culture that you'd like to investigate.

A strong, researchable question will not lead to an easy answer, but rather will lead you into a scholarly conversation in which there are many competing claims. For instance, the question, "what are the dietary staples of _____?" is not a strong research question because there may be only one correct answer and thus there is no scholarly debate surrounding the topic. It is an interesting question, but it will not lead you into a scholarly conversation.

When you are interested in finding a scholarly debate, try using the words "why" and "how" rather than "what." Instead of leading to a definitive answer, the words why and how will often lead to complex, nuanced answers for which you'll need to marshal evidence to be convincing. "How has the Irish potato famine affected contemporary Irish culture?" is a question that has a number of complex and competing answers that might draw from a number of different disciplines (political science, history, economics, linguistics, and geography, among others). If you can imagine scholars having an interesting debate about your researchable question, it is likely that you've picked a good one.

Once you have come up with an interesting researchable question, your first task as a researcher is to figure out how scholars are discussing your question. Many novice writers think that the first thing they should do when beginning a research project is to articulate an argument and then find sources that confirm their argument. This is not how experienced scholars work. Instead, strong writers know that they cannot possibly come up with a strong central argument until they have done sufficient research. So, instead of looking for sources that confirm a preliminary claim you might want to make, look for the scholarly conversation.

Looking at the scholarly conversation is a strong way to figure out if you've found a research question that is suitable in scope for the kind of paper you're writing. Put another way, reading the scholarly conversation can tell you if your research question is too broad or too narrow. Most novice writers begin with research questions that are overly broad. If your question is so broad that there are thousands of books and articles participating in the scholarly conversation, it's a good idea for you to focus your question so that you are asking something more specific. If, on the other hand, you are asking a research question that is so obscure that you cannot find a corresponding scholarly conversation, you will want to broaden the scope of your project by asking a slightly less specific question.

Keep in mind the metaphor of a conversation. If you walk into a room and people are talking about food and culture, it would be out of place for you to begin immediately by making a huge, vague claim, like, "gluten sensitivity is just a fad." It would be equally out of place for you to begin immediately by making an overly specific claim, like, "McDonalds is to blame for the obesity epidemic in the United States." Rather, you would gauge the scope of the conversation and figure out what seems like a reasonable contribution.

Your contribution to the conversation, at this point, will likely be a focused research question. This is the question you take with you to the library. In the next section, we'll discuss how best to make use of the library. Later, we'll explore how to turn your research question into an argument for your essay.

Your Campus Library

You have probably used libraries all your life, checking out books from your local public library and studying in your high school library. The difference between your previous library experiences and your college library experience is one of scale. Your college library has more stuff. It may be real stuff like books, journals, and videos, or it may be virtual stuff, like online articles, ebooks and streaming video. Your library pays a lot of money every year to buy or license content for you to use for your research. By extension, your tuition dollars are buying a lot of really good research material. Resorting to Google and Wikipedia means you are not getting out all you can out of your college experience.

Not only will your college library have a much larger collection, but also it will have a more up-to-date and relevant collection than your high school or community public library. Academic librarians spend considerable time acquiring research materials based on classes being taught at your institution. You may not know it, but librarians carefully monitor what courses are being taught each year and are constantly trying to find research materials appropriate to those courses and your professor's research interests. In many cases, you will find that the librarians will know about your assignment and will already have ideas about the types of sources that will make you most successful.

Get To Know Your Librarians! The most important thing to know during the research process is that there are people to help you. Although you may not yet be in the habit of going to the library, there are still many ways in which librarians and library staff can be helpful. Most libraries now have an e-mail or chat service set up so you can ask questions without even setting foot in a library. No question is too basic or too specific. It's a librarian's job to help you find answers, and all questions are welcome. The librarian can even help you discover the right question to ask given the task you are trying to complete.

Help can also come in the form of consultations. Librarians will often make appointments to meet one-on-one with you to offer in-depth help on a research paper or project. Chances are you will find a link on your library website for scheduling a consultation.

Among the many questions fielded by reference librarians, three stand out as the most often asked. Because librarians hear these questions with such regularity, we suggest that students ask these questions when they begin their research. You can go to the library and ask these questions in person, or you can ask vie e-mail or online chat.

1. How do I find a book relevant to my topic?

The answer to this question will vary from place to place, but the thing to remember is that finding a book can be either a physical process or a virtual process. Your library will have books on shelves somewhere, and the complexity of how those shelves are organized and accessed depends on factors of size, number of libraries, and the system of organization your library uses. You will find books using your library's online catalog and carefully noting the call number and location of a book.

Your library is also increasingly likely to offer electronic books or e-books. These books are discoverable in your library's online catalog as well. When looking at the location of a book you will frequently see a link for e-book versions. You will not find an e-book in every search, but when you do the advantage is that e-book content is searchable, making your job of finding relevant material in the book easier.

If you find one book on your topic, use it as a jumping off point for finding more books or articles on that topic. Most books will have bibliographies either at the end of each chapter or at the end of the book in which the author has compiled all the sources they used. Consult these bibliographies to find other materials on your topic that will help support your claim.

Another efficient way to find more sources once you've identified a particularly authoritative and credible book is to go back to the book's listing in your library's online catalog. Once you find the book, look carefully at the record for links to subjects. By clicking on a subject link you are finding other items in your library on the same subject. For instance, a search on

Food AND Culture

will take you to items with subjects such as

food habits

food—social aspects

food—history

2. What sources can I use as evidence in my paper?

There are many types of resources out there to use as you orchestrate a scholarly conversation and support your paper's argument. Books, which we discussed earlier, are great sources if you can find them on your topic, but often your research question will be something that is either too new or too specific for a book to cover. Books are very good for historical questions and overviews of large topics. For current topics, you will want to explore articles from magazines, journals, and newspapers.

Magazines or periodicals (you will hear these terms interchangeably) are published on a weekly or monthly schedule and contain articles of popular interest. These sources can cover broad topics like the news in magazines such as *Newsweek, Time,* and *U.S. News and World Report.* They can also be more focused for particular groups like farmers (*Dairy Farmer*) or photographers (*Creative Photography*). Articles in magazines or periodicals are by professional writers who may or may not be experts. Magazines typically are not considered scholarly and generally do not contain articles with bibliographies, endnotes, or footnotes. This does not mean they are not good sources for your research. In fact, there may be very good reasons to use a magazine article to help support your argument. Magazines capture the point of view of a particular group on a subject, like how farmers feel about increased globalization of food production. This point of view may offer support for your claim or an opposing viewpoint to counter. Additionally, magazines can also highlight aspects of a topic at a particular point in time. Comparing a *Newsweek* article from 1989 on GMOs and food production with an article on the same topic in 2009 allows you to draw conclusions about changing perspectives over 20 years.

Journals are intended for a scholarly audience of researchers, specialists, or students of a particular field. Journals such as *Globalization and Health, Gastrononica,* or *Food, Culture, and Society* are

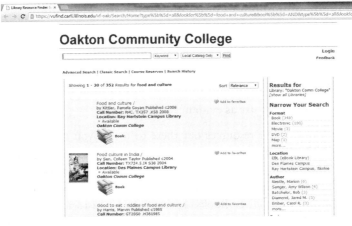

Figure 5 College library catalog search online.

all examples of scholarly journals focused on a particular field or research topic. You may hear the term "peer-reviewed" or "referred" in reference to scholarly journals. This means that the articles contained in a journal have been reviewed by a group of scholars in the same field before the article is published in the journal. This ensures that the research has been vetted by a group of peers before it is published. Articles from scholarly journals can help provide some authority to your argument. By citing experts in a field, you are bolstering your argument and entering into the scholarly conversation we talked about at the beginning of this guide.

Newspaper articles are found in newspapers that are generally published daily. There is a broad range of content in newspapers ranging from articles written by staff reporters, to editorials written by scholars, experts, and general readers, to reviews and commentary written by experts. Newspapers are published more frequently and locally than magazines or journals, making them excellent sources for very recent topics and events as well as those with regional significance. Newspaper articles can provide you with a point of view from a particular part of the country or world (how do Texans feel about GMOs vs New Yorkers) or a strong opinion on a topic from an expert (an economist writing an editorial on the effects of food deserts).

A good argument uses evidence from a variety of sources. Do not assume you have done a good job if your paper only cites newspaper articles. You need a broad range of sources to fill out your argument. Your instructor will provide you with guidelines about the number of sources you need, but it will be up to you to find a variety of sources. Finding two to three sources in each of the categories above will help you begin to build a strong argument.

3. Where should I look for articles on my topic?

The best way to locate journal, magazine, or newspaper articles is to use a database. A database is an online resource that organizes research material of a particular type or content area, For example, *PsycINFO* is a psychology database where you would look for journal articles (as well as other kinds of sources) in the discipline of psychology. Your library licenses or subscribes to databases on your behalf. Finding the right database for your topic will depend on what is available at your college or university because every institution has a different set of resources. Many libraries will provide subject or research guides that can help you determine what database would be best for your topic. Look for these guides on your library website. Your library's website will have a way to search databases. Look for a section of the library website on databases, and look for a search box in that section. For instance, if you type "food" in a database search box, you may find that your library licenses a database called *MLA International Bibliography* (Modern Language Association). A search for "history" in the database search box may yield *American History and Life* or *Historical Abstracts*. In most instances, your best bet is to ask a librarian which database or databases are most relevant to your research.

When using these databases that your library provides for you, you will know that you are starting to sufficiently narrow or broaden your topic when you begin to retrieve 30–50 sources during a search. This kind of narrow result field will rarely occur in Google, which is one of the reasons why using library databases is preferable to Google when doing academic research. Databases will help you determine when you have begun to ask a manageable question.

When you have gotten down to 30–50 sources in your result list, begin to look through those results to see what aspects of your topic are being written about. Are there lots of articles on food, GMOs, and the United States? If so, that might be a topic worth investigating because there is a lot of information for you to read. This is where you begin to discover where your voice might add to the ongoing conversation on the topic.

Using Evidence

The quality of evidence and how you deploy the evidence is ultimately what will make your claims persuasive. You may think of evidence as that which will help prove your claim. But if you look at any scholarly book or article, you'll see that evidence can be used in a number of different ways. Evidence can be used to provide readers with crucial background information. It can be used to tell readers what scholars have commonly thought about a topic (but which you may disagree with). It can offer a theory that you use as a lens. It can offer a methodology or an approach that you would like to use. And finally, evidence can be used to back up the claim that you'll be making in your paper.

Novice researchers begin with a thesis and try to find all the evidence that will prove that their claim is valid or true. What if you come across evidence that doesn't help with the validity of your claim? A novice researcher might decide not to take this complicating evidence into account. Indeed, when you come across complicating evidence, you might be tempted to pretend you never saw it! But rather than sweeping imperfect evidence under the rug, you should figure out how to use this evidence to complicate your own ideas.

The best scholarly conversations take into account a wide array of evidence, carefully considering all sides of a topic. As you probably know, often the most fruitful and productive conversations occur not just when you are talking to people who already agree with you, but when you are fully engaging with the people who might disagree with you.

Coming across unexpected, surprising, and contradictory evidence, then, is a good thing! It will force you to make a complex, nuanced argument and will ultimately allow you to write a more persuasive paper.

Other Forms of Evidence

We've talked about finding evidence in books, magazines, journals, and newspapers. Here are a few other kinds of evidence you may want to use.

Interviews Interviews can be a powerful form of evidence, especially if the person you are interviewing is an expert in the field that you're investigating. Interviewing can be intimidating, but it might help to know that many people (even experts!) will feel flattered when you ask them for an interview. Most scholars are deeply interested in spreading knowledge, so you should feel comfortable asking a scholar for his or her ideas. Even if the scholar doesn't know the specific answer to your question, he or she may be able to point you in the right direction.

Remember, of course, to be as courteous as possible when you are planning to interview someone. This means sending a polite e-mail that fully introduces yourself and your project before you begin asking questions. E-mail interviews may be convenient, but an in-person interview is best because it allows for you and the interviewee to engage in a conversation that may take surprising and helpful turns.

It's a good idea to write down a number of questions before the interview. Make sure not just to get facts (which you can likely get somewhere else). Ask the interviewee to speculate about your topic. Remember that "why" and "how" questions often yield more interesting answers than "what" questions.

If you do conduct an in-person interview, act professionally. Be on time, dress respectfully, and show sincere interest and gratitude. Bring something to record the interview. Many reporters still use pens and a pad because these feel unobtrusive and are very portable.

Write down the interviewee's name, the date, and the location of the interview, and have your list of questions ready. Don't be afraid, of course, to veer from your questions. The best questions might be the follow-up questions that couldn't have occurred to you before the conversation began. You're likely to get the interviewee to talk freely and openly if you show real intellectual curiosity. If you're not a fast writer, it's certainly OK to ask the interviewee to pause for a moment while you take notes. Some people like to record their interviews. Just make sure that you ask permission if you choose to do this. It's always nice to send a brief thank you note or e-mail after the interview. This would be a good time to ask any brief follow-up questions.

Images Because we live in a visual age, we tend to take images for granted. We see them in magazines, on TV, and on the Internet. We don't often think about them as critically as we think about words on a page. Yet, a critical look at an image can uncover helpful evidence for a claim. For example, if you are writing about the impact of food advertising on body image, you could introduce an image of a sign such as the one pictured below.

Search online for "McDonald's in China"—or choose the name of any multinational food corporation—and you likely will see images of the corporate logo. In the case of "McDonald's in China," although many of us might not be able to read the Chinese alphabet, the image itself is still recognizable. This image allows a discussion of visual elements (the distinctive logo, the brand colors, etc.) and how they can be read like a language—a language that is increasingly global. No matter where you are in the world, you can recognize the characteristic yellow arches of a McDonalds. Images can add depth and variety to your argument and they are generally easy to find on the Internet. Use Google Image search or flickr.com to find images using the same keywords you used to find books and articles. Ask your instructor for guidance on how to properly cite and acknowledge the source of any images you wish to use. If you want to present your research outside of a classroom project (for example, publish it on a blog or share it at a community event), ask a research librarian for guidance on avoiding any potential copyright violations.

Multimedia Like images, multimedia such as video, audio, and animations are increasingly easy to find on the Internet and can strengthen your claim. For instance, if you are working on food and culture, you will find audio or video news clips illustrating the effects of overfishing on local economies. There are several audio and video search engines available such as Vimeo (vimeo.com) or Blinkx (blinkx.com), a search engine featuring audio and video from the BBC, Reuters, and the Associated Press among others. As with images, ask your instructor for guidance on how to properly cite and acknowledge the source of any multimedia you wish to use. If you want to present your research outside of a classroom project (for example, publish it on a blog or share it at a community event), ask a research librarian for guidance on avoiding any potential copyright violations.

Evaluating Sources

A common problem in research isn't a lack of sources, but an overload of information. Information is more accessible than ever. How many times have you done an online search and asked yourself the question: "How do I know what is good information?" Librarians can help. Evaluating online sources is more challenging than traditional sources because it is harder to make distinctions between good and bad online information than with print sources. It is easy to tell that *Newsweek* magazine is not as scholarly as an academic journal, but online everything may look the same. There are markers of credibility and authoritativeness when it comes to online information, and you can start to recognize them. We'll provide a few tips here, but be sure to ask a librarian or your professor for more guidance whenever you're uncertain about the reliability of a source.

1. **Domain**—The "domain" of a site is the last part of its URL. The domain indicates the type of website. Noting the web address can tell you a lot. A .edu site indicates that an educational organization created that content. This is no guarantee that the information is accurate, but it does suggest less bias than a .com site, which will be commercial in nature with a motive to sell you something, including ideas.

2. **Date**—Most websites include a date somewhere on the page. This date may indicate a copyright date, the date something was posted, or the date the site was last updated. These dates tell you when the content on

the site was last changed or reviewed. Older sites might be outdated or contain information that is no longer relevant.

3. **Author or editor**—Does the online content indicate an author or editor? Like print materials, authority comes from the creator or the content. It is now easier than ever to investigate an author's credentials. A general Google search may lead you to a Wikipedia entry on the author, a Linked In page, or even an online resume. If an author is affiliated with an educational institution, try visiting the institution's website for more information.

Managing Sources

Now that you've found sources, you need to think about how you are going to keep track of the sources and prepare the bibliography that will accompany your paper. Managing your sources is called "bibliographic citation management," and you will sometimes see references to bibliographic citation management on your library's website. Don't let this complicated phrase deter you—managing your citations from the start of your research will make your life much easier during the research process and especially the night before your paper is due when you are compiling your bibliography.

EndNote and *RefWorks* Chances are your college library provides software, such as *EndNote* or *RefWorks*, to help you manage citations. These are two commercially available citation-management software packages that are not freely available to you unless your library has paid for a license. *EndNote* or *RefWorks* enable you to organize your sources in personal libraries. These libraries help you manage your sources and create bibliographies. Both *EndNote* and *RefWorks* also enable you to insert endnotes and footnotes directly into a Microsoft Word document.

Zotero If your library does not provide *EndNote* or *RefWorks*, a freely available software called *Zotero* (Zotero.org) will help you manage your sources. *Zotero* helps you collect, organize, cite, and share your sources and it lives right in your web browser where you do your research. As you are searching Google, your library catalog, or library database, *Zotero* enables you to add a book, article, or website to a personal library with one click. As you add items to your library, *Zotero* collects both the information you need for you bibliography and any full-text content. This means that the content of journal articles and e-books will be available to you right from your *Zotero* library.

To create a bibliography, simply select the items from your *Zotero* library you want to include, right click, and select "Create Bibliography from Selected Items...," and choose the citation style your instructor has asked you to use for the paper. To get started, go to *Zotero.org* and download *Zotero* for the browser of your choice.

Taking Notes It is crucial that you take good, careful notes while you are doing your research. Not only is careful note taking necessary to avoid plagiarism, but also careful note taking can help you think through your project while you are doing research.

Although many researchers used to take notes on index cards, most people now use computers. If you're using your computer, open a new document for each source that you're considering using. The first step in taking notes is to make sure that you gather all the information you might need in your bibliography or works cited. If you're taking notes from a book, for instance, you'll need the author, the title, the place of publication, the press, and the year. Be sure to check the style guide assigned by your instructor to make sure you're gathering all the necessary information.

After you've recorded the bibliographic information, add one or two keywords that can help you sort this source. Next, write a one- or two-sentence summary of the source. Finally, have a section on your document that is reserved for specific places in the text that you might want to work with. When you write down a quote, remember to be extra careful that you are capturing the quote exactly as it is written—and that you enclose the quote in quotation marks. Do not use abbreviations or change the punctuation. Remember, too, to write down the exact page numbers from the source you are quoting. Being careful with small details at the beginning of your project can save you a lot of time in the long run.

WRITING ABOUT YOUR TOPIC

In your writing, as in your conversations, you should always be thinking about your audience. Although your most obvious audience is the instructor, most college instructors will want you to write a paper that will be interesting and illuminating for other beginning scholars in the field. Many students are unsure of what kind of knowledge they can presume of their audience. A good rule of thumb is to write not only for your instructor but also for other students in your class and for other students in classes similar to yours. You can assume a reasonably informed audience that is curious but also skeptical.

Of course it is crucial that you keep your instructor in mind. After all, your instructor will be giving you feedback and evaluating your paper. The best way to keep your instructor in mind while you are writing is to periodically reread the assignment while you are writing. Are you answering the assignment's prompt? Are you adhering to the assignment's guidelines? Are you fulfilling the assignment's purpose? If your answer to any of these questions is uncertain, it's a good idea to ask the instructor.

From Research Question to Thesis Statement

Many students like to begin the writing process by writing an introduction. Novice writers often use an early draft of their introduction to guide the shape of their paper. Experienced scholars, however, continually return to their introduction, reshaping it and revising it as their thoughts evolve. After all, because writing is thinking, it is impossible to anticipate the full thoughts of your paper before you have written it. Many writers, in fact, only realize the actual argument they are making after they have written a draft or two of the paper. Make sure not to let your introduction trap your thinking. Think of your introduction as a guide that will help your readers down the path of discovery—a path you can only fully know after you have written your paper.

A strong introduction will welcome readers to the scholarly conversation. You'll introduce your central interlocutors and pose the question or problem that you are all interested in resolving. Most introductions contain a thesis statement, which is a sentence or two that clearly states the main argument. Some introductions, you'll notice, do not contain the argument, but merely contain the promise of a resolution to the intellectual problem.

Is Your Thesis an Argument?

So far, we've discussed a number of steps for you to take when you begin to write a research paper. We started by strategizing about ways to use pre-search to find a topic and ask a researchable question, and then we looked at ways to find a scholarly conversation using your library's resources. Now we'll discuss a crucial step in the writing process: coming up with a thesis.

Your thesis is the central claim of your paper—the main point that you'd like to argue. You may make a number of claims throughout the paper; when you make a claim, you are offering a small argument, usually about a piece of evidence that you've found. Your thesis is your governing claim, the central argument of the whole paper. Sometimes it is difficult to know if you have written a proper thesis. Ask yourself, "Can a reasonable person disagree with my thesis statement?" If the answer is no, then you likely have written an observation rather than an argument. For instance, the statement, "Hamburgers are often loaded with fat" is not a thesis because this is a true fact. A reasonable person cannot disagree with this fact, so it is not an argument. The statement, "Fast food became a dietary mainstay because of availability" is a thesis because it is a debatable point. Remember to keep returning to your thesis statement while you are writing. Not only will you be thus able to make sure that your writing remains on a clear path, but also you'll be able to keep refining your thesis so that it becomes clearer and more precise.

Make sure, too, that your thesis is a point of persuasion rather than one of belief or taste.

"Chinese food tastes delicious" is certainly an argument you could make to your friend, but it is not an adequate thesis for an academic paper because there is no evidence that you could provide that might persuade a reader who doesn't already agree with you.

Organization

For your paper to feel organized, readers should know where they are headed and have a reasonable idea of how they are going to get there. An introduction will offer a strong sense of organization if it:

- Introduces your central intellectual problem and explains why it is important;
- Suggests who will be involved in the scholarly conversation;
- Indicates what kind of evidence you'll be investigating; and
- Offers a precise central argument.

Some readers describe well-organized papers as having a sense of flow. When readers praise a sense of flow, they mean that the argument moves easily from one sentence to the next and from one paragraph to the next. This allows your reader to follow your thoughts easily. When you begin writing a sentence, try using an idea, keyword, or phrase from the end of the previous sentence. The next sentence, then, will appear to have emerged smoothly from the previous sentence. This tip is especially important when you move between paragraphs. The beginning of a paragraph should feel like it has a clear relationship to the end of the previous paragraph.

Keep in mind, too, a sense of wholeness. A strong paragraph has a sense of flow and a sense of wholeness: not only will you allow your reader to trace your thoughts smoothly, but also you will ensure that your reader understands how all your thoughts are connected to a large, central idea. Ask yourself as your write a paragraph: what does this paragraph have to do with the central intellectual problem that I am investigating? If the relationship isn't clear to you, then your readers will likely be confused.

Novice writers often use the form of a five-paragraph essay. In this form, each paragraph offers an example that proves the validity of the central claim. The five-paragraph essay may have worked in high school because it meets the minimum requirement for making an argument with evidence. You'll quickly note, however, that experienced writers do not use the five-paragraph essay. Indeed, your college instructors will expect you to move beyond the five-paragraph essay. This is because a five-paragraph essay relies on static examples rather than fully engaging new evidence. A strong essay will grow in complexity and nuance as the writer brings in new evidence. Rather than thinking of an essay as something that offers many examples to back up the same static idea, think of an essay as the evolution of an idea that grows ever more complex and rich as the writer engages with scholars who view the idea from various angles.

Integrating Your Research

As we have seen, doing research involves finding an intellectual community by looking for scholars who are thinking through similar problems and may be in conversation with one another. When you write your paper, you will not merely be reporting what you found; you will be orchestrating the conversation that your research has uncovered. To orchestrate a conversation involves asking a few key questions: Whose voices should be most prominent? What is the relationship between one scholar's ideas and another scholar's ideas? How do these ideas contribute to the argument that your own paper is making? Is it important that your readers hear the exact words of the conversation, or can you give them the main ideas and important points of the conversation in your own words? Your answers to these questions will determine how you go about integrating your research into your paper.

Using evidence is a way of gaining authority. Although you may not have known much about your topic before you started researching, the way you use evidence in your paper will allow you to establish a voice that is authoritative and trustworthy. You have three basic choices to decide how best you'd like to present the information from a source: summarize, paraphrase, or quote. Let's discuss each one briefly.

Summary You should summarize a source when the source provides helpful background information for your research. Summaries do not make strong evidence, but they can be helpful if you need to chart the intellectual terrain of your project. Summaries can be an efficient way of capturing the main ideas of a source. Remember when you are summarizing to be fully sympathetic to the writer's point of view. Put yourself in the scholar's shoes. If you later disagree with the scholar's methods or conclusions, your disagreement will be convincing because your reader will know that you have given the scholar a fair hearing. A summary that is clearly biased is not only inaccurate and ethically suspect, but also it will make your writing less convincing because readers will be suspicious of your rigor.

Let's say you come across the following quote that you'd like to summarize. Here's an excerpt from *The Language Wars: A History of Proper English*, by Henry Hitchings. Although you might wonder why we haven't shown you something obviously related to food, it's the principle we are trying to illustrate with the following:

> No language has spread as widely as English, and it continues to spread. Internationally the desire to learn it is insatiable. In the twenty-first century the world is becoming more urban and more middle class, and the adoption of English is a symptom of this, for increasingly English serves as the lingua franca of business and popular culture. It is dominant or at least very prominent in other areas such as shipping, diplomacy, computing, medicine and education. (300)

Consider this summary:

> In *The Language Wars*, Hitchings says that everyone wants to learn English because it is the best language in the world (300). I agree that English is the best.

If you compare this summary to what Hitchings actually said, you will see that this summary is a biased, distorted version of the actual quote.

Hitchings did not make a universal claim about whether English is better or worse than other languages. Rather, he made a claim about why English is becoming so widespread in an increasingly connected world.

Now let's look at another summary, taken from the sample paper at the end of this research guide:

> According to Hitchings, English has become the go-to choice for global communications and has spread quickly as the language of commerce and ideas. (300)

This is a much stronger summary than the previous example. The writer shortens Hitchings's original language, but she is fair to the writer's original meaning and intent.

Paraphrase Paraphrasing involves putting a source's ideas into your own words. It's a good idea to paraphrase if you think you can state the idea more clearly or more directly than the original source does. Remember that if you paraphrase, you need to put the entire idea into your own words. It is not enough for you to change one or two words. Indeed, if you only change a few words, you may put yourself at risk of plagiarizing.

Let's look at how we might paraphrase the Hitchings quote that we've been discussing. Consider this paraphrase:

> Internationally the desire to learn English is insatiable. In today's society, the world is becoming wealthier and more urban, and the use of English is a symptom of this. (Hitchings 300)

You will note that the writer simply replaced some of Hitchings's original language with synonyms. Even with the parenthetical citation, this is unacceptable paraphrasing. Indeed, this is a form of plagiarism because the writer suggests that the language is his or her own, when it is in fact an only slightly modified version of Hitchings's own phrasing.

Let's see how we might paraphrase Hitchings in an academically honest way.

> Because English is used so frequently in global communications, many people around the world want to learn English as they become members of the middle class. (Hitchings 300)

Here the writer has taken Hitchings's message, but has used his or her own language to describe what Hitchings originally wrote. The writer offers Hitchings's ideas with fresh syntax and new vocabulary, and the writer is sure to give Hitchings credit for the idea in a parenthetical citation.

Quotation The best way to show that you are in conversation with scholars is to quote them. Quoting involves capturing the exact wording and punctuation of a passage. Quotations make for powerful evidence, especially in humanities papers. If you come across evidence that you think will be helpful in your project, you should quote it. You may be tempted to quote only those passages that seem to agree with the claim you are working with. But remember to write down the quotes of scholars who may not seem to agree with you. These are precisely the thoughts that will help you build a powerful scholarly conversation. Working with fresh ideas that you may not agree with can help you revise your claim to make it even more persuasive because it will force you to take into account potential counterarguments. When your readers see that you are grappling with an intellectual problem from all sides and that you are giving all interlocutors a fair voice, they are more likely to be persuaded by your argument.

To make sure that you are properly integrating your sources into your paper, remember the acronym ICE. ICE stands for introduce, cite, and explain. Let's imagine that you've found an idea that you'd like to incorporate into your paper. We'll use a quote from David Harvey's *A Brief History of Neoliberalism* as an example. On page 7, you find the following quote that you'd like to use: "The assumption that individual freedoms are guaranteed by freedom of the market and of trade is a cardinal feature of neoliberal thinking, and it has long dominated the US stance towards the rest of the world."

1. The first thing you need to do is **introduce** the quote ("introduce" gives us the "I" in ICE). To introduce a quote, provide context so that your readers know where it is coming from, and you must integrate the quote into your own sentence. Here are some examples of how you might do this:

     In his book *A Brief History of Neoliberalism*, David Harvey writes . . .

     One expert on the relationship between economics and politics claims . . .

     Professor of Anthropology David Harvey explains that . . .

In a recent book by Harvey, he contends . . .

Note that each of these introduces the quote in such a way that readers are likely to recognize it as an authoritative source.

2. The next step is to **cite** the quote (the C in ICE). Here is where you indicate the origin of the quotation so that your readers can easily look up the original source. Citing is a two-step process that varies slightly depending on the citation style you're using. We'll offer an example using MLA style. The first step involves indicating the author and page number in the body of your essay. Here is an example of a parenthetical citation that gives the author and page number after the quote and before the period that ends the sentence:

> One expert on the relationship between economics and politics claims that neoliberal thinking has "long dominated the US stance towards the rest of the world" (Harvey 7).

Note that if it is already clear to readers which author you're quoting, you need only to give the page number:

> In *A Brief History of Neoliberalism*, David Harvey contends that neoliberal thinking has "long dominated the US stance towards the rest of the world" (7).

The second step of citing the quote is providing proper information in the works cited or bibliography of your paper. This list should include the complete bibliographical information of all the sources you have cited. An essay that includes the quote by David Harvey should also include the following entry in the Works Cited:

> Harvey, David. *A Brief History of Neoliberalism*. New York: Oxford UP, 2005. Print.

3. Finally, the most crucial part of integrating a quote is **explaining** it. The E in ICE is often overlooked, but a strong explanation is the most important step to involve yourself in the scholarly conversation. Here is where you will explain how you interpret the source you are citing,

what aspect of the quote is most important for your readers to understand, and how the source pertains to your own project. For example:

> David Harvey writes, "The assumption that individual freedoms are guaranteed by freedom of the market and of trade is a cardinal feature of neoliberal thinking, and it has long dominated the US stance towards the rest of the world" (7). As Harvey explains, neoliberalism suggests that free markets do not limit personal freedom but actually lead to free individuals.

or:

> David Harvey writes, "The assumption that individual freedoms are guaranteed by freedom of the market and of trade is a cardinal feature of neoliberal thinking, and it has long dominated the US stance towards the rest of the world" (7). For Harvey, before we understand the role of the United States in global politics, we must first understand the philosophy that binds personal freedom with market freedom.

Novice writers are sometimes tempted to end a paragraph with a quote that they feel is especially compelling or clear. But remember that you should never leave a quote to speak for itself (even if you love it!). After all, as the orchestrator of this scholarly conversation, you must make sure that readers are receiving exactly what you'd like them to receive from each quote. Note, in the above examples, that the first explanation suggests that the writer quoting Harvey is centrally concerned with neoliberal philosophy, whereas the second explanation suggests that the writer is centrally concerned with U.S. politics. Both of these will have to be related to a more central argument about food and culture—which, as this book shows, is often related to history and political worldviews. The explanation, in other words, is the crucial link between your source and the main idea of your paper.

Avoiding Plagiarism

Scholarly conversations are what drive knowledge in the world. Scholars using each other's ideas in open, honest ways form the bedrock of our intellectual communities and ensure that our contributions to the world of thought are important. It is crucial, then, that all writers do their part in maintaining the integrity and trustworthiness of scholarly conversations. It is crucial that you never claim someone else's ideas as your own and that you always are extra careful to give the proper credit to someone else's thoughts. This is what we call responsible scholarship.

The best way to avoid plagiarism is to plan ahead and keep track careful notes as you read your sources. Remember the advice (above) on *Zotero* and taking notes: find the way that works best for you to keep track of what ideas are your own and what ideas come directly from the sources you are reading. Most acts of plagiarism are accidental. It is easy when you are drafting a paper to lose track of where a quote or idea came from; plan ahead and this won't happen. Here are a few tips for making sure that confusion doesn't happen to you.

1. Know what needs to be cited. You do not need to cite what is considered common knowledge such as facts (the day Lincoln was born), concepts (the earth orbits the sun), or events (the day Martin Luther King was shot). You do need to cite the ideas and words of others from the sources you are using in your paper.
2. Be conservative. If you are not sure if you should cite something, either ask your instructor or a librarian or cite it. It is better to cite something you don't have to than not cite something you should.
3. Direct quotations from your sources must be cited as well as any time you paraphrase the ideas or words from your sources.
4. Finally, extensive citation not only helps you avoid plagiarism, but also boosts your credibility and enables your reader to trace your scholarship.

Citation Styles

It is crucial that you adhere to the standards of a single citation style when you write your paper. The most common styles are MLA (Modern Language Association, generally used in the humanities), APA (American Psychological Association, generally used in the social sciences), and Chicago (*Chicago Manual of Style*). If you're not sure which style you should use, you must ask your instructor. Each style has its own guidelines regarding the format of the paper. Although proper formatting within a given style may seem arbitrary, there are important reasons behind the guidelines of each style. For instance, whereas MLA citations tend to emphasize authors' names, APA citations tend to emphasize the date of publications. This distinction makes sense, especially given that MLA standards are usually followed by departments in the humanities and APA standards are usually followed by departments in the social sciences. Whereas papers in the humanities value original thinking about arguments and texts that are canonical and often old, papers in the social sciences tend to value arguments that take into account the most current thought and the latest research.

There are a number of helpful guidebooks that will tell you all the rules you need to know to follow the standards for various citation styles. If your instructor hasn't pointed you to a specific guidebook, try the following online resources:

Purdue Online Writing Lab: owl.english.purdue.edu/

Internet Public Library: www.ipl.org/div/farq/netciteFARQ.html

Modern Language Association (for MLA style): www.mla.org/style

American Psychological Association (for APA style): www.apastyle.org/

The Chicago Manual of Style Online: www.chicagomanualofstyle.org/tools_citationguide.html

Constance Calice

Professor Walsh

English 101

15 May 2014

Watch What You Eat: Reconfiguring "Diet"

While Americans are obsessed with weight, popular belief affirms that Americans are the fattest population in the world, followed by countries that have begun to adopt our ways of eating. And yet the United States is also home to the largest number of dieters in the world. Reflecting our obsession, the food market is full of products to help consumers lose weight. Almost any magazine, print or online, will have an article or advertisement on how to lose weight. How is it that a country so obsessed with weight and staying trim can be getting fatter? What benefits are we seeing to all of our calorie counting and "sacrifice?"

Perhaps dieting just isn't the answer. The problematic nature of dieting—and that it often simply doesn't work—has become common knowledge. Similarly, it has become known that fat does not necessarily lead to ill health; some people can be fat and just as healthy as their thin counterparts. But eating (and its presumptive consequence, dieting) is not just a scientific process of burning calories in order to ensure survival. Rather, eating is also personal, emotional, spiritual, cultural and aesthetic. Sharing foods and meals connects us—human to human. To ignore these complex, nuanced aspects of food and to strip them down to calories and nutrients leaves us with "empty food." That is, dieting encourages looking at foods as quantities of protein, fat, and carbohydrates that need to be controlled, rather than as whole foods and meals that bring joy. Dieting asks us to look at our bodies, find what is imperfect, and "watch what we eat" to improve, or perhaps eliminate, our imperfections.

Diet, as I will use it in this analysis, refers to the selection of foods that a person or group of people eats. Dieting, on the other hand, refers to the specific practice of altering (and often limiting) one's food selections for the purpose of weight loss or body modification. Historically, dieting has been a practice more often associated with women, particularly in the media and advertisements. But today, dieting is less and less a strictly gendered practice as many men also feel considerable pressure to change their eating habits for the purpose of body modification. Indeed, dieting is moving toward being a universal issue of the industrialized world. Men and women alike are becoming obsessed with eating "right," but perhaps the question is this: are we eating *well*?

To address this larger "whole"—that food is personal, emotional, spiritual, cultural, and aesthetic—the entire rhetorical context for food must contrast with the limited and limiting rhetoric of dieting, I will examine the rhetoric of what is commonly known as the Local Foods Movement. While I do not see the Local Foods Movement as a neat solution to the issues I raise above, I do see it as a way to identify those problems. To do this I will set up a backdrop of aspects of current discourse on food using Michael Pollan's notion of the Western diet and "nutritionism."

Eating by the Book

Within the past five years *New York Times* contributor and best selling author, Michael Pollan, has captured America's attention with his investigation of food production and consumption in his books *The Omnivore's Dilemma* (2006) and *In Defense of Food: An Eater's Manifesto* (2009). *In Defense of Food* examines what Pollan calls the Western diet[1], the problematic nature of this diet, and how to reverse these negative effects through our own food choices. One of the key aspects of the Western diet is what Pollan calls nutritionism; he identifies nutritionism as the scientifically driven ideological paradigm of understanding food as a set of nutrients rather than "whole" foods. Within this context whole foods are understood as food items that exist naturally without any other ingredients, such as carrots, oats, milk, etc. Nutritionism supports the idea that a food's value is determined by the sum of its scientifically identified nutrients. While the concept of nutrients—proteins, carbohydrates and fats (known to us today as micronutrients)—has been around since the early 19th century, the term nutritionism was only recently coined in 2002 by Australian sociologist Gyorgy Scrinis (Pollan, *In Defense of Food* 27). As Pollan points out, since nutrients are impossible to identify without some scientific knowledge, nutritionism requires a scientist to identify "good" and "bad" foods for us. Paired with scientific evidence, food companies and their marketing experts often offer us not so subtle suggestions of what to eat. This nutritionist model of eating takes foods that we once understood as simply a part of living, and turns them into mysterious items that need to be de-coded by authoritative figures that control our food supply.

Michael Pollan has built up his fan base with books critiquing the industrial food system and the lack of intuitive understanding of food on behalf of the general consumer. He seems to argue against all the media hype on what to eat and marketing of "good" foods. Yet his most recent book, *Food Rules* (2009), is an entire book of rules for what to eat, what not to eat and how to eat. Why, all of a sudden, do we need so much help figuring out what is good to eat? Pollan raises this question in his previous book, *In Defense of Food.*

I must clarify here that I do not think Pollan's rules are bad; in fact, I think they are a great guide to understanding the industrial food system and eating "around" it. In fact, one of the rules in *Food Rules* is to not always follow the rules. Clearly, Pollan himself sees the problematic nature of making a Food Rule Book that condenses everything down and fits it into a convenient pocket book.

Low-Cal Living

Dieting is the practice ultimately produced by nutritionism and the ideology of the modern era. In the language of Susan Bordo in her work *Unbearable Weight: Feminism, Western Culture, and the Body*, dieting is the crystallization of the ideology of our culture. Dieting affects both men and women and people of every age—even young children (Butryn and Wadden; Claus, Braet and Decaluwé; Yanovski). In 2004, forty-six billion dollars was spent on weight loss products and programs, not including weight loss surgery (Gibbs, quoted in Lyons 77). And of course the diet industry cannot actually be invested in helping consumers lose weight when their pursuit of weight loss is what is making these huge profits. Pat Lyons critiques the diet industry saying, "Enormous corporate profits are at stake, and maintaining public distress and biased attitudes about weight ensures the continued production of those profits" (76).

The rhetoric of dieting that we have become so accustomed to has not always existed. Throughout history it has been fashionable to be plump—excess weight was a sign of prosperity, aristocracy, and leisure. Artists have long portrayed women with ample curves and jolly old men with large round bellies. Fat was seen more as something that came with age to those with enough wealth to eat heartily. But in the 19th century industrialization brought about great changes in the Western world, particularly in the United States. For the first time food was being produced on an industrial scale and more and more people were able to eat, while less and less were required to produce it. Those who had once worked the land moved into the city to work in factories and service jobs. Additionally, there was a huge influx of immigrants, many genetically shorter and rounder than the earlier American settlers. Laura Fraser writes, "people who once had too little to eat now had plenty, and those who had a tendency to put on weight began to do so. When it became possible for people of modest means to become plump, being fat no longer was a sign of prestige" (Fraser 12). These changes were occurring among many in American life, including changes in the world of fashion and an increased understanding of reliance upon scientific knowledge. Some, including Woods Hutchinson—a medical professor and one-time president of the American Academy of Medicine—were wary of the turn towards thinness. In a 1926 issue of the *Saturday Evening Post* he wrote,

In this present onslaught upon one of the most peaceable, useful and law-abiding of our tissues, fashion has apparently the backing of grave physicians, of food reformers and physical trainers, and even of great insurance companies, all changing in unison the new commandment of fashion: 'Thou shalt be thin!' (quoted in Fraser 11).

For the first time in history, multiple powerful social forces deemed fat unseemly and being thin fashionable, high class and healthy. Suddenly, the foods of the past—of the farm and the "motherland"—became unhealthy and the grocery store became the safe place to buy modern, healthy, scientifically-proven products. At the same time, magazines began advertising recipes for meals made entirely from grocery store bought ingredients, with an emphasis on fat content or health benefits. Together, the fashion industry, food reformers and many powerful companies—all fueled by industrialization—were able to shift the national discourse on fat and food away from farms and feeding to products and weight loss.

Weight loss products have only been created and promoted to consumers since the 19th century. In the 1950's and 60's weight loss programs and products gained the attention—and money—of millions of Americans, particularly women (Lyons 76). It was during this time that amphetamines, diuretics, and "low-cal" products began being sold for the purpose of weight loss. During this time what increased along with the introduction of weight loss programs and products was a bias against the fat and obese—a bias that has only gained strength recently in the age of the "Obesity Epidemic." Many studies prove that dieting simply does not work: Many end up lowering their self-esteem, becoming less motivated, and more unhealthy than when they started because they plunge back into the eating patterns that made them overweight in the first place. Despite this, we continue to wage war on our fat along with the help of myriad drugs and diet programs. Researchers are beginning to give attention to the act of over dieting and the due health consequences. While it is not yet recognized by the *Diagnostic and Statistical Manual of Mental Disorders,* there is burgeoning academic research underway to investigate orthorexia nervosa[2]—the act of dieting obsessively to the point of detriment to one's mental or physical health.

Inviting Foucault to the Table

The popularity of Michael Pollan's books has drawn a great deal of mainstream attention to food discourse. Pollan and, in its own right, the rise in popularity of the local foods movement has made clear that there is a great deal of power at stake in who controls our food. Michel Foucault has written extensively on power and how it has been used throughout history. In his work *Discipline & Punish,* Michel Foucault suggests that throughout history power and the way it is exerted has evolved. Foucault specifically traces a genealogical path of power from the seventeenth century to the nineteenth century and the birth of modern power.

He identifies the mode of power in the seventeenth century as Sovereign, and that of modern power as Discipline. Within each time period the given mode of power is acted out by particular entities that hold power. In the seventeenth century the King held the sovereign power, but in the nineteenth century discipline is enacted by "the expert." This expert is one who holds and produces knowledge that is valued by the dominant group of society.

How does discipline actually work? To explain this Foucault gives us the example of the "Panopticon." The panopticon was an architectural design for a prison designed by Jeremy Bentham in 1785. The concept of the panopticon was for the prison guard to be able to monitor all of the prisoners without them being able to know when he is watching. In the design the building has a center chamber for the guard and in a circle around him are individual cells. Each cell is lit in such a way that the prisoner can never see the guard in the central tower. Because the prisoners never know exactly when they are being watched, they must behave as though they are being watched all the time. Foucault was interested in this architectural concept as a model for the type of control exerted in a disciplinary society. But the image of the panopticon can be extended out even to our everyday lives. Out in public, one never know who is truly watching, who is the one that will notice a discretion, and so one must act as though someone is watching all the time. This behavior is internalized and the subject develops a sense that someone is watching all the time, but really it is only the person watching himself. While Foucault was primarily studying sexuality in his exploration of this technology of power, it can easily be applied to many more facets of Western culture in the twentieth and twenty-first centuries, including the rules that dictate how we eat (Nealon 47).

Naturalizing Nutritionism

This stage of power and discourse is quite evident in food as it is in other large social systems. Following Foucault's argument, the processes of power during the nineteenth century made us docile bodies in how we eat by establishing the necessity for experts to help us to understand what to eat. Within the world of food the "experts" are the nutritionists and bariatric doctors—diet doctors and weight loss surgeons—that study what is "good" for us. The nutritionist, with his advanced degrees and association with the field of science, quickly gained more power than those who had informed us about food for thousands of years—farmers and families. The nutritionist, the journalist, the celebrity chef—these roles became the privileged ones and it is their understanding of food that created the dominant discourse that shapes our diet today. While members of society do not have an individual connection to "the experts," we receive information from them through the media we interface with in our daily lives.

For instance, in the February 2011 issue of *Fitness* magazine an advertisement for Eggland's Best eggs is placed within the section of *Fitness* magazine titled "Eat Right." Within this twenty-four-page section there are eleven full-page advertisements advertising nine different products or companies. Of these nine products and companies six are food products and two are weight loss supplements. The ad reads, "The *best* nutrition just got better" and has a picture of two Eggland's Best eggs surrounded by nutritional facts. The advertisement claims that compared to ordinary eggs, Eggland's Best eggs are "high in vitamin E, have twenty-five percent less saturated fat, four times more vitamin D, over three times more omega 3, forty-six percent more lutein, nineteen percent less cholesterol and a good source of vitamins A and B." The advertisement offers no explanation how Eggland's Best eggs could possibly have more vitamins and less fat and cholesterol that any other brand of egg.

This advertisement is a clear example of nutritionism hard at work. Here, eggs are illustrated as being valuable because of the combined value of their nutritional components, rather than because of their place within a complete diet. In this ad emphasis is placed on the amount of vitamins and the fat content of the eggs, but the critical reader asks, how on earth do they make an egg more nutritious and less fattening than any other egg? This question should point us, rather, in the direction of the egg production. What are the chickens eating who are laying these eggs? Is it their natural diet or a synthetic additive? This advertisement also appeals to the notion that one cannot select a food without knowing its nutritional composition and therefore without an expert's help to point out such helpful statistics such as vitamin and fat content. The impression we get from this gleaming white ad is that these eggs are not being sold by a farmer, but rather a scientist, one who has perfected that which nature seemed to have missed.

A Diet of Consciousness and Complexity

If nutritionism is so ingrained in our society today and is a part of a seemingly untouchable power structure, how can our discourse on food ever change? My own shift in food thinking has revolved around the "Local Food Movement"— a popular movement, with little specific organization or management, to buy foods produced within geographic proximity to one's own home. The local food movement and the related slow food movement[3] call for a way of eating that contrasts with the industrialized and fast food systems that became so predominant in the twentieth century. These movements call upon us to look at foods as food—within a geographic, communal and culinary context—rather than as calories, nutrients, fats or proteins.

One way of joining the local food movement and integrating local foods into the diet is to join a Community Supported Agriculture group. Community Supported Agriculture (CSA) is a system of farming wherein a farmer sells "shares" to the public, and in exchange these public "members" receive produce throughout the season from the farm. Most CSA farms give each member a box of produce each week with a mix of everything they have available that week. Some farms also include dairy, grain, honey, fruit preserves and other items produced on the farm. The beauty of the Community Supported Agriculture model is that farmers have the capital they need to get the farm going ahead of time when they need it most. It also causes consumers to have a stake in the harvest and does not leave the farmer holding the entire burden of loss if a given crop does not do well.

CSA members experience the difference eating local food makes and many have shared their experiences in various media, including online blogs. As one CSA member, CV Harquail writes for the blog, Authentic Food Organizations, "for me, being a CSA member clicks me into a different perspective, so that I'm aware of a whole new meaning of being part of this community. Being part of a community and having a way to create meaning together can really make a person feel good." Gary Hansen writes at fannetasticfood.com, "I love the community that we get from our CSA. There's a connection that we have with others as we run into each other at the pick-up site. Our food comes from the same soil. We all have a personal connection with the people who plant and harvest what we eat." These testimonials illustrate the way in which eating local connects us to both our food and other eaters. The rhetoric created by this emphasis on community is one of people, rather than calories. Dieting, on the other hand, is an isolated(-ing) activity that causes dieters to make up a personal diet that is different from those around them and to then shop for, prepare and eat that meal which may be completely different from family or friends around you. The local food movement is more concerned with who grew the food, where it came from and how people enjoy it, than with scientifically identifying health factors. It is a rhetoric of experience—of positive human experience. This illustrates that there is something in our food beyond the "food" part, something *in* the experience of eating that affects us.

This positive human experience, this relationship—one between consumers and farmers, among those who purchase and consume this food, and the like—is one that removes discipline from the equation. Studies have shown that the very act of dieting actually worsens the health of some by adding to their lack of self-esteem while they continue to struggle to lose any weight (Lyons 82). The local food movement, in contrast, offers a way of eating that is potentially free of the shame that can come with self-discipline. Unlike dieting, then, the local food movement breaks down the prison cell and prison guard mentality of eating based around monitoring the self and caloric intake. Eating local has no scientific system of monitoring one's eating; there are no rules about how much to eat or what types of food to eat.

I do not wish to imply that the local foods movement is the perfect solution to problematic discourses surrounding food, but rather that it is a step in a good direction. The rhetoric of the local food movement—seasonality, community building, fresh, ethically grown, sustainable, often heirloom produce—is certainly more conscious of ethical issues in the production of food than that which comes from dieting and nutritionism. (But there is often a gap between the rhetoric and actual practice of those who identify themselves with the local food movement. When it comes down to it, it is often a movement of a bunch of well-off, white people enjoying heirloom tomatoes and artisanal cheese, but not truly engaging in a true political shift that would allow everyone access to these foods.) However, the local food movement is just one site of resistance to the dominating, disciplinary food rhetoric among many. While Foucault talks about power, he also suggests that resistance to that power works in a mirrored way—resistance must become its own kind of power. The local food movement must produce its own powerful discourses.

Where Do We Go from Here?

I believe the answer lies not in extremes—of counting calories, or eating only foods grown in your back yard—but in a more complicated food discourse that empowers eaters and acknowledges the social disparities that greatly affect who can eat what in our country. I came to this issue as one of those people who was very influenced by the food pyramid in my youth (MyPyramid). I have come to realize that there is more to food than the metrics of nutrition. There is a space in food that holds spirit, love, family, heritage, identity, and we commune with it every day. Through a more nuanced understanding of why, how, and what we eat, we can change the rhetoric and language of eating from one of struggle to one that embraces possibility rather than restriction.

Endnotes

1. Throughout his work Pollan refers to the Western diet; this is a term I will also be using to discuss the current state of food politics. The term Western diet refers to the food system that has come into being particularly in the United States and Western Europe through industrialization. Namely, it is a diet high in processed foods, refined grains, sugars and fats; there is use of chemicals and industrial systems to raise plants and animals in large monocultures; and it represents a narrowing of the biological diversity of the human diet (Pollan, *In Defense*

of Food 10). While the Western diet is most closely associated with the United States, these food practices are rapidly spreading across the globe, giving the term more ideological rather than merely geographical significance.

2. The term orthorexia, closely related to the well-researched eating disorder anorexia nervosa, was first proposed by American physician Steven Bratman in 1996. (Pollan, *In Defense of Food* 9.)

3. The slow food movement is spearheaded by the non-profit, grass-roots organization Slow Food International®. Slow Food is supported by its 100,000 members in 150 countries around the world. According to its official website the organization was founded in 1989 to "counter the rise of fast food and fast life, the disappearance of local food traditions and people's dwindling interest in the food they eat, where it comes from, how it tastes and how our food choices affect the rest of the world" through the practice of small-scale and sustainable production of quality foods (About Us).

Works Cited

"About Us." *Slow Food International—Good, Clean and Fair Food.* Web. 27 Feb. 2011.

Bordo, Susan R. *Unbearable Weight.* Berkeley, CA: University of California, 2003. Print.

Butryn, Meghan L., and Thomas A. Wadden. "Treatment of Overweight in Children and Adolescents: Does Dieting Increase the Risk of Eating Disorders?" *International Journal of Eating Disorders* 37.4 (2005): 285–93. *Academic Search Premier.* Web. 27 Feb. 2011.

Claus, Line, Caroline Braet, and Veerle Decaluwé. "Dieting History in Obese Youngsters with and without Disordered Eating." *International Journal of Eating*

Disorders 39.8 (2006): 721–28. *Academic Search Premier*. Web. 27 Feb. 2011.

"Community Supported Agriculture—Local Harvest." *Local Harvest/Farmers Markets/Family Farms/CSA/ Organic Food*. 2010. Web. 24 Feb. 2011. <http:// www.localharvest.org/csa/>.

Eggland's Best. Advertisement. *Fitness* (Feb. 2011): 124. Print.

Foucault, Michel. *Discipline and Punish: the Birth of the Prison*. New York: Vintage, 1995. Print.

Fraser, Laura. "The Inner Corset: A Brief History of Fat in the United States." Rothblum 11–14.

Gibbs, W. "Obesity: An Overblown Epidemic?" *Scientific American* 292.6 (2005): 70–77. Web.

Hansen, Gary. "Guest Post: Why I Love My Community Supported Agriculture (CSA)." *FANNEtastic Food*. 24 Nov. 2010. Web. 27 Feb. 2011. <http://www. fannetasticfood.com/2010/11/24/guest-post-why-i- love-my-community-supported-agriculture-csa/>.

Harquail, CV. "Authentic Food Organizations: Why I Love My CSA." *Authentic Organizations—Aligning Identity, Action and Purpose*. 29 May 2008. Web. 27 Feb. 2011. <http://authenticorganizations.com/har- quail/2008/05/29/authentic-food-organizations-why-i- love-my-csa/>.

Lyons, Pat. "Prescription for Harm: Diet Industry Influence, Public Health Policy, and the 'Obesity Epidemic.'" *The Fat Studies Reader*. Rothblum 75–87.

MyPyramid.gov—United States Department of Agriculture—Home. 10 Feb. 2011. Web. 20 Feb. 2011. <http://www.mypyramid.gov/>.

Nealon, Jeffrey T. *Foucault beyond Foucault: Power and Its Intensifications since 1984*. Stanford, CA: Stanford UP, 2008. Print.

Pollan, Michael. *Food Rules: an Eater's Manual*. New York: Penguin, 2009. Print.

Pollan, Michael. *In Defense of Food: an Eater's Manifesto*. New York: Penguin, 2008. Print.

Pollan, Michael. *The Omnivore's Dilemma*. New York: Penguin, 2006. Print.

Scrinis, Gyorgy. "Sorry, Marge." *Meanjin* 61.4 (2002): 108–16. Print.

Yanovski, Jack A. "The Perceived Onset of Dieting and Loss of Control Eating Behaviors in Overweight Children." *International Journal of Eating Disorders* 38.2 (2005): 112–22. *Academic Search Premier*. Web. 27 Feb. 2011.

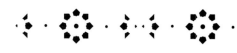

credits

Chapter 1: Food as Memory and Identity

Page 2 Fisher, M. F. K. "The Measure of My Powers" and "A Thing Shared." Reprinted with the permission of Scribner Publishing Group from *The Gastronomical Me* by M. F. K. Fisher. Copyright © 1943, 1954 by M. F. K. Fisher. All rights reserved.

Page 6 Squillante, Sheila. "Four Menus," published in *Brevity* (25), an online journal of creative nonfiction. Reprinted by permission of the author.

Page 9 Bauer, Douglas. "What Was Served," © Douglas Bauer, published in *Fried Walleye and Cherry Pie: Midwestern Writers on Food*, edited by Peggy Wolff. Reprinted by permission of the author.

Page 17 Narayan, Shoba. "The God of Small Feasts," originally published in *Gourmet* magazine, January 2000. Reprinted by permission of the author.

Page 22 Ahn, Roy. "Home Run: My Journey Back to Korean Food," by Roy Ahn, from *Gastronomica,* Fall 2009, 9(4): 12–15. Copyright © 2009, The Regents of the University of California. Used by permission.

Page 30 Sedaris, David. "Tasteless," first published in *The New Yorker* and reprinted by permission of Don Congdon Associates, Inc. Copyright © 2007 by David Sedaris.

Chapter 2: Food and Environment

Page 36 Berry, Wendell. "The Pleasures of Eating," from *What Are People For? Essays*, by Wendell Berry. Copyright © 1990, 2010 by Wendell Berry. Reprinted by permission of Counterpoint.

Page 43 Meehan, Peter. "Seafarming at the End of the World," by Peter Meehan from *Lucky Peach*, issue 6, Winter 2013. Reprinted by permission of the author.

Page 51 Frisch, Tracy. "Sowing Dissent," by Tracy Frisch from *The Sun Magazine*, October 2012. Republished by permission of the author.

Page 63 Kliman, Todd. "The Meaning of Local," published in *The Washingtonian*, May 6, 2013. Reproduced with permission by Washingtonian Magazine.

Page 82 Entine, Jon. "2000+ Reasons Why GMOs Are Safe to Eat and Environmentally Sustainable," by Jon Entine and JoAnna Wendel, from *Forbes,* 10/14/13, © 2013 Forbes. All rights reserved. Used by permission and protected by the Copyright Laws of the United States. The printing, copying, redistribution, or retransmission of this Content without express written permission is prohibited.

Page 86 Mather, Robin. "The Threats from Genetically Modified Foods," by Robin Mather, from *Mother Earth News*, Apr/May 2012. Used by permission.

Page 100 Shaw, Hank. "On Killing," originally published on website *Hunter, Angler, Gardener, Cook* located at http://honest-food.net. Reprinted by permission of Paradigm Agency on behalf of Hank Shaw.

Chapter 3: The Politics of Food

Page 108 Wallace, David Foster. "Consider the Lobster," from *Consider the Lobster and Other Essays* by David Foster Wallace. Copyright © 2005 by David Foster Wallace. By permission of Little, Brown and Company. All rights reserved.

Page 127 Guthman, Julie. "Can't Stomach It: How Michael Pollan et al. Made Me Want to Eat Cheetos," by Julie Guthman, from *Gastronomica,* Summer 2007, 7(3): 75–79. Copyright © 2007, The Regents of the University of California. Used by permission.

Page 136 Williams-Forson, Psyche. "Suckin' the Chicken Bone Dry: African American Women, History, and Food Culture," by Psyche Williams-Forson, from *Cooking Lessons: The Politics of Gender and Food*, edited by Sherrie A. Inness. Reprinted by permission of Rowman & Littlefield Publishing Group.

Page 160 Roseberry, William. "The Rise of Yuppie Coffees and the Reimagination of Class in the United States," by William Roseberry. Copyright © 1996, American Anthropological Association. Reproduced by permission of the American Anthropological Association from *American Anthropologist*, Volume 98, Issue 4, pages 762–777, December 1996. Not for sale or further reproduction.

Page 190 Shah, Riddhi. "Men Eat Meat, Women Eat Chocolate: How Food Gets Gendered," by Riddhi Shah. This article first appeared in *Salon.com*, at http://www.Salon.com. An online version remains in the Salon archives. Reprinted with permission.

Page 194 Meyers, B. R. "The Moral Crusade against Foodies," by B. R. Meyers. © 2011 The Atlantic Media Co., as first published in *The Atlantic Magazine*. All rights reserved. Distributed by Tribune Content Agency, LLC, and reprinted by permission.

Chapter 4: Food and Health

Page 206 Zinczenko, David. "Don't Blame the Eater," by David Zinczenko, originally published in *The New York Times*, Nov. 23, 2002, is reprinted by permission of William Morris Endeavor Entertainment.

Page 209 Pollan, Michael. "Our National Eating Disorder," by Michael Pollan, from *The New York Times Magazine*, Oct. 17, 2004. © 2004 by Michael Pollan. Used by permission. All rights reserved.

Page 215 Wehunt, Jennifer. "The Food Desert," by Jennifer Wehunt, published in *Chicago Magazine*, Aug. 11, 2009. Reprinted by permission of Wright's Media on behalf of Chicago Magazine.

Page 223 Allen, Patricia. "The Disappearance of Hunger in America," by Patricia Allen, from *Gastronomica*, Summer 2007, 7(3): 19, 21–23. Copyright © 2007, The Regents of the University of California. Used by permission.

Chapter 5: Food and American Culture

Chapter 6: Food Travel and Worldviews

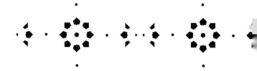

index